PAYING FOR THE PARTY

Paying for the Party

How College Maintains Inequality

Elizabeth A. Armstrong

Laura T. Hamilton

HARVARD UNIVERSITY PRESS
Cambridge, Massachusetts, and London, England   2013

Library of Congress Cataloging-in-Publication Data

Armstrong, Elizabeth A.
  Paying for the party : how college maintains inequality / Elizabeth A. Armstrong, Laura T. Hamilton.
      p. cm.
    Includes bibliographical references and index.
    ISBN 978-0-674-04957-4 (alk. paper)
   1. Women college students—United States—Social conditions.   2. Educational sociology—United States.   3. Public universities and colleges—United States.   I. Hamilton, Laura T. (Laura Teresa)   II. Title.
    LC1756.A76 2013
    378.19822—dc23   2012036068

To the women who shared their college experiences with us

Contents

Figures and Tables

Preface

In the fall of 2004, we settled into a room in a coeducational residence hall at a large public research university in the Midwest.[1] The authors, along with four graduate students and three undergraduates, spent a year observing and interacting with the women who lived on this floor.[2] Elizabeth's observations on a Friday evening in late August, two days after the fifty-three young women we studied moved in and before classes had even begun, capture the flavor of life on the floor:

> By 11:30, the floor was totally dead. All the doors were shut. An hour earlier the dorm was full of life and energy and cheerful sounds of partying, hair dryers, preparations. By 11:30 it seemed that virtually everyone was gone. Occasionally one could hear a door open or close or someone in the bathroom, providing evidence that at least a few souls were around. I . . . eventually spotted two women. [One was that] woman who just is not up to the high appearance standards of the hall. I just can't imagine how awful it would be to live in this residence hall if not a partier. I overhead one of them asking the other if she wanted to accompany her to [a university-sponsored midnight trip to Wal-Mart] (clearly the loser activity of the night), and the other one declined. . . . It would be interesting to delicately find out from the ones who stay behind if they . . . simply weren't invited by anyone (lack of network ties), or just do not enjoy partying. It would also be interesting to find out if it feels as terrible as it seems like it must. (Field Notes 8/27/2004)

We did not realize it at the time, but we were observing a new cohort of students being swept up onto the party pathway that defines a swath of undergraduate social life at this university and others. The two women stranded after the others had gone out for the night gave us our first glimpse of the status competition at the heart of mainstream American college life. We too would soon be ranked according to the principles of undergraduate peer cultures—and would be found lacking. In terms of social class and femininity, many of the women made us aware that we were "studying up" to a more elite population.[3] The effects on the researchers were palpable: Elizabeth, for example, found herself fussing over her wardrobe—even stopping at the mall on the way to the field site in a desperate search for something to wear.

Over the course of five waves of interviews, we would come to learn that these painful popularity contests and the stratification processes that concern economists and sociologists of education are linked. That is, those who most handily won—and for whom the whole competition seemed designed— were also far more likely to translate their MU experience into success. Although it is tempting to chalk this up to the effects of social background, we gradually realized that the university was implicated as well—the social and academic infrastructure of the university seemed tailor-made for a particular type of affluent, socially oriented student. The party pathway at MU was impossible to avoid—even by those who wished to. For students who could not afford or did not wish to join in on the revelry, it served as a constant reminder of their place in the university.

This finding emerged somewhat unexpectedly. At the start, the study was focused on college as a site for learning about sexuality. Sexuality and romance never dropped out of the story. As it turned out, we found that these were central mechanisms through which the college experience reinforced preexisting class differences. After all, whether, when, and who people marry are key determinants of adult life circumstances. Although few marry right out of college anymore, dating in college and after graduation sets the stage for marriage.

Near the completion of the book, we shared a laugh about a comment written in 2005 after a second-year interview. It read, "Note: I don't know how this project has become so much about class." Indeed, there was no escaping this fact as the study proceeded. We were greatly disappointed to find that the young women, similar except for class background, left college with vastly different life prospects. Few women from less privileged backgrounds would realize their dreams of upward mobility, whereas most from privileged backgrounds were poised to reproduce their parents' affluence.

We were initially puzzled by the extent to which the university's organizational arrangements disadvantaged all but the most affluent. After all, public universities were founded with the explicit intent of sponsoring mobility among disadvantaged groups. Through a deeper consideration of the history of American higher education, we learned that elite private education was founded to serve the affluent and that the consolidation of local elites has also been one of the missions of public universities. More recently, the tilt to the affluent has intensified, as declines in state funding have chipped away at the mission of public universities. Tuition increases and intensified pursuit of those who pay full tuition ensure that public universities cater to the often less studious segment of the affluent that they can successfully attract. As a result, we see a large and growing mismatch between what many four-year institutions provide and what most Americans seeking higher education need.

The title of the book reflects the cost of this mismatch. When universities direct resources to attracting and serving affluent, socially oriented students—"paying for the party," if you will—other students and families bear the cost. They place their faith in a system that does not serve them well, and pay the price with a lower-quality education and limited career options. American society also loses, as the potential of students from ordinary means remains unrealized.

This book would not exist without the generosity and openness of the women who shared five-plus years of their lives with us. It is for this reason that we dedicate the book to them. We did not initially intend this study to be longitudinal. We kept following them not only because we were curious about how their lives would turn out but also because we cared. We grew to see them as complex individuals, often entertaining, sometimes maddening, but all with something unique to offer. For example, although wealthy Hannah refused to recognize her class privilege, she was perhaps the most kindhearted woman on the floor. Similarly, we initially found it hard to deal with Whitney, who played the role of floor "mean girl," but we grew to enjoy her sharp intellect and wit. We could even explain her snubbing of some floormates as the anxieties of a middle-class woman seeking status in a stratified social world. Neither did it work to see the less privileged women as innocent, given the homophobia and anti-Semitism that some of them expressed. In short, we realized that there were no villains and no heroes. Our arguments sometimes require us to portray the women in unflattering ways. However, our loyalties fundamentally lie with them, and we were angry on behalf of many that they did not get more out of college.

This book is a product of our combined efforts. We have a working relationship that is—to our knowledge—fairly rare. It allowed us to create something that, alone, neither could have created. As such, we share authorship equally.

The nature of the collaboration evolved over time. When Elizabeth conceptualized the project, Laura started as a graduate assistant. Over the years she moved into the position of codirector. Laura did the majority of data collection—producing over half of the ethnographic field notes and conducting approximately 85% of the interviews. She was aided by biographical similarities. Laura is a white woman whose class background and family structure in some ways mirrored that of affluent women on the floor. When the study started, Laura was in her mid-twenties. Her youthful appearance, style of dress, and status as student registered her as not-quite-adult. The women were able to relate to her as an older sister or friend. Yet even with these similarities, rapport was not easy or automatic. Laura wore her hair very short at the outset of the ethnography. Some women were suspicious of this departure from the femininity valued on the floor, which—for a time—motivated Laura to grow out her hair.

Establishing connections was harder for Elizabeth, also a white Midwestern woman, who was an assistant professor in her late thirties in 2004—making her almost as old as some of the women's parents. In the first few days of the study, Elizabeth registered with horror that both the students and the parents assumed she was moving a child into the residence hall. A few days later, male students visiting women on the floor walked by our room and loudly exclaimed (as if to warn others) that there were "real adults on the floor" (Field Notes 8/27/04). Elizabeth's inability to converse about fashion, makeup, and other "girly" topics that served as cultural currency posed an additional barrier. As a consequence, Elizabeth reduced the time she spent on the floor and grew to rely heavily on Laura's relationships with the women.

The arguments of this book are the result of a constant, eight-year-long dialogue between us. At one point, the sheer amount of back-and-forth necessitated that we each get an e-mail account to use exclusively for our work together. During this time, we also worked on "Gendered Sexuality in Young Adulthood," in which we developed an understanding of how social class shapes college women's approaches to partying, sex, and romance.[4] This was a manageable way to ease into the larger arguments of the book.

In writing the book, each of us took the lead on different chapters, at which point we would trade and rewrite those drafts, in consultation with the other. If something was not working, we often jointly figured it out. In other cases, when one of us was stumped on how to tackle an issue, the other had a solution. By the end of this process, each of us had our hand in every word in this book. It is virtually impossible to say who developed specific chapters or pieces of the argument.

PAYING FOR THE PARTY

Introduction

Taylor and Emma started college at Midwest University during the fall of 2004.[1] They had a lot in common. They lived on the same residence hall floor and planned to pursue careers in dentistry.[2] Like virtually all of their floormates, they were white, American-born, heterosexual, unmarried with no children, and roughly eighteen years old.[3] Both had strong high school records: Emma had earned "straight A's and was in all of the advanced placement classes" (Y1).[4] Taylor reported a 3.78 high school grade point average (GPA). Although Taylor's family was more affluent than Emma's, both were from middle- or upper-middle-class families. The two women majored in biology and took advantage of opportunities to further their career goals.

Their circumstances one year after graduation differed dramatically. Taylor left with a 3.6 GPA and was enrolled in dental school. She was thrilled:

I decided on [Top 15 Dental School], and I'm really happy. I like it here. . . . Everyone I've talked to who's graduated has had [job] offers. . . . Starting salary's like $90,000, and then I think it can go pretty high from there. (Y5)

Emma graduated with a 3.0 GPA and was working as a dental assistant— making $11 an hour in a job that did not require a bachelor's degree. She, not surprisingly, was disappointed:

When I first started working, I felt ridiculous. I felt like I was wasting all of my schooling and I just felt that I didn't belong there with those people because I should be doing something else with people who have college degrees. (Y5)

Disparity in career prospects does not fully capture differences in their class trajectories at college exit. Emma was forced to return home and live with her parents in a small Rust Belt city, further constraining her job opportunities. Her $10,000 student loan bill, though small compared with those of others, loomed large given her income. Graduate school was not possible as she was in competition with science majors who did not get into medical school. Emma explained:

> I applied to a clinical laboratory scientist program. I didn't get in. . . . They only pick four students a year. A lot of kids . . . if they don't get into medical school then they apply to this program. . . . It was based off your GPA and a lot of these kids were coming in with extremely, extremely, high GPAs. (Y5)

Emma's lack of direction tied her closer to her boyfriend, Joe, a working-class man. She noted:

> The other option if I didn't get into the program was to move . . . and be with Joe. So this August, I will be moving. . . . Right now, it's like I have no choice. . . . It doesn't make any sense for me to stay in [my hometown] and do a job that I don't really like and I can't progress in. (Y5)

As Joe was in the military, the move would take her far from her family, to somewhere where she had no social ties. Living on base required being married and living off was more expensive, putting pressure on Emma to marry young. Joe's position offered health and educational benefits she could access as his wife, but his entry-level military pay was low.

In contrast, Taylor, in dental school, was enmeshed in a vibrant campus community. Generous parental support had allowed her to graduate with no debt, despite having to pay out-of-state tuition. Her parents were prepared to continue to cushion her transition to adulthood with substantial subsidies—although this would probably be unnecessary. Taylor was single and meeting fellow dental students but was in no rush to marry. Because she could support herself she did not need to settle. As Taylor told us, "I just want the perfect man" (Y5).

Taking into account past and future parental support and marital as well as career prospects, Taylor appeared on track to reproduce her upper-middle-class origins. Emma, conversely, left college at risk of downward mobility. It might be tempting to view these outcomes as meritocracy at work. Such an explanation is unconvincing, though, as Emma and Taylor were similarly well prepared and motivated at the outset of college. As we detail in Chapter 7, their fates diverged upon entering the organizational infrastructure of Midwest University. Here, relatively small class differences were magnified, sending them in different directions.

Inside the Black Box of Higher Education

In this book we argue that student experiences during college, and class trajectories at exit, are fundamentally shaped by the structure of academic and social life on campus. That is, in different institutional contexts, we might expect the same student to leave with better—or worse—chances for class reproduction or mobility. We argue that how Midwest University and many other large state schools currently organize the college experience systematically disadvantages all but the most affluent—and even some of these students.

Practically speaking, as college tuition has skyrocketed, students, parents, scholars, administrators, and policy makers have become worried about what students are getting out of college. The shelves of bookstores are lined with overwrought accounts of the decline of higher education, with titles such as *Higher Education? How Colleges Are Wasting Our Money and Failing Our Kids—and What We Can Do about It*.[5] As the example of Emma suggests, such concerns are well founded, although there is currently little consensus about what exactly the problems are and what to do.

Economists and sociologists of stratification have informed the discussion by offering sophisticated analysis of the returns to college.[6] As a result, we know that college graduates have higher incomes, employment rates, and chances of getting married than those who do not graduate from college.[7] There is strong evidence that parental resources (for example, money, social connections, cultural understandings, and educational aspirations) advantage affluent students in college access, admission, performance, and graduation.[8] We are learning more about who can expect the greatest returns from college—that is, science, math, and engineering majors—and there is an ongoing debate about whether those who are least or most likely to obtain a college education have the most to gain by attending.[9]

Based on large data sets and complex statistical models, this research tradition does not delve inside the university. This is a limitation, because without going inside the "black box" of higher education, scholars cannot understand how schooling produces expected results—much less unexpected results. Stratification scholars are aware that the types of data and methods used typically do not lend themselves to identifying mechanisms that generate outcomes of interest.[10] Some even call for more qualitative research on these processes.[11]

This study bridges scholarship on educational stratification and college cultures—research traditions that have remained largely separate.[12] We

use an ethnographic and longitudinal approach to develop a rich understanding of students' college experiences in a tiny slice of university life and
situate this slice in the context of Midwest University's campus, MU's campus
within the larger postsecondary system, and the system as it is today within
history. By adopting a qualitative approach to the study of class and stratification, we build on the work of a small but growing group of scholars.[13] Moving between the micro and macro allows us to see the ways in which our
participants' experiences were shaped by structures internal to the university, and to identify organizational processes that exacerbate or ameliorate
class differences. We are influenced by Michael Burawoy's extended case
method, in which particularity can be used to offer analytical leverage.[14]

Our project is part of a growing body of research on the "experiential
core of college life"—the time between college entry and exit.[15] Work in
this vein includes *Academically Adrift: Limited Learning on College Campuses*, in
which Richard Arum and Josipa Roksa measure college learning.[16] This
scholarship is part of a general move in the sociology of education to place
quantitative stratification research in dialogue with organizational, historical, political, and cultural scholarship.[17] These approaches promise to shed
light on the causes and consequences of the dramatic changes currently
under way in the American postsecondary sector.

The Study

This is a case study of a flagship public research university in the Midwest
ranked in the top 100 schools in the nation. Most in-depth scrutiny received
by higher education has focused on the very top of the system—particularly
Harvard, Yale, and Princeton—even though these schools educate a tiny
fraction of the population.[18] At the other end of the spectrum, community
colleges, which educate roughly half of today's students, are marginalized
in both the American cultural ideal of college and research on college student experiences.[19]

The role of public research universities—particularly state flagships—in
educating our population is critical to understand because of the pivotal
place they hold in the ecology of American higher education. These schools
bridge the elite and mass sectors of higher education. This bridge is ever
more important to understand—and arguably to protect—as elite schools
become more distant from the rest. In a recent essay, higher education
scholar Steven Brint refers to Ivy Leagues schools as "Ivy Islands," noting

that "As the Ivy Islands drift further from the mainland, we need to turn our sights more intensely on public universities; what happens in them will become more central to the future of American society."[20]

A third of American high school graduates matriculate at four-year public universities, founded with the intent of helping those who aspire to improve their circumstances.[21] Historically, taxpayers have funded these schools with the understanding that they serve the public, and public institutions have offered stepping-stones for many low-income, immigrant, and minority individuals.[22] It is an open question at this historical moment whether they are still serving this function or will continue to do so in the future.[23]

Public research universities are complex organizations. It is not easy to discern what they are doing, how well they are doing it, or for whom. Clark Kerr, former chancellor of the University of California at Berkeley, described post–World War II American universities as "multiversities," as these organizations attempt to satisfy a broad range of constituencies.[24] Trustees and legislatures want public universities to provide measurably high-quality education at low cost while at the same time generating world-class research. Faculty at state flagships—even middle-tier flagships—generally hail from elite doctoral programs. They seek resources to facilitate their research, including a light teaching load and minimal expectations of interaction with undergraduates.

Undergraduates arrive with a wide range of orientations and levels of preparation. More selective schools recruit many of the most accomplished students from privileged families. A far greater number of the brightest and most ambitious from less privileged families land at four-year public universities in their state, given class differences in willingness to move far from home.[25] Average (or less than average) students from affluent families flock to schools like MU, both in and out of state. Similar students from lower-income families are more likely to be absorbed by community colleges, regional commuter colleges, and for-profit schools, although some find their way to four-year, residential public universities—at least for a time.

Our arguments are based on a five-year ethnographic and interview study of a cohort of women who lived on the same residence hall floor on MU's campus during the 2004–2005 academic year. Our research team occupied a room on the floor the initial year of the study.[26] We met the women as they moved onto campus and, over the course of the year, observed life on the floor. We interacted with them as they did with each other—hanging out, watching television, eating pizza, studying, and providing company as they got dressed for parties or other social events. We also conducted a series of five annual interviews, following their lives as they moved through the university and into the work force.

Ninety-percent of the fifty-three women floor participated in at least one interview, and only two women opted not to participate in follow-up interviews. All women are included in ethnographic analyses, and forty-seven are at the center of the pathway analyses in Chapters 5–8.[27] All together, the data set consists of 202 interviews conducted over five years and over 2,000 pages of field notes.

The analytical power of our study derives not from the size of the sample but from the depth of the observations.[28] Because we got to know the women in an informal context and built our relationships over time, we heard accounts of college life not often captured by education researchers. We made no a priori assumptions about the centrality of academics to their lives. We listened and probed, trying to understand their experiences from their point of view. Our in-depth longitudinal approach, following women as they moved through college, is rare.[29] It allowed us to develop theories in one set of interviews that we could investigate in the next—to shift between inductive and deductive modes of research and analysis. We were able to move deeper into our investigation of campus life, arriving at an understanding of the university's role in shaping different women's trajectories.

We deliberately situated ourselves in the midst of the most visible and dominant aspect of MU undergraduate culture. MU is frequently ranked highly in various annual lists of American "party schools," and online Web sites invariably refer to its vibrant social life as a defining characteristic.[30] More than a dozen pilot group interviews conducted with a variety of student groups indicated that that each group defined itself in relation to MU's party scene. Thus, we chose to locate ourselves in a residence hall with a reputation as a "party dorm."[31] Party dorms housed about a third of the freshman class, making it a common way to start college at MU. Though the designation suggests the residence hall was the site of revelry, we observed little public drinking, as the dorm was heavily policed. The reputation came from the social orientation of many students, who partied off-site, typically at fraternity parties, returning late at night to continue their loud revels into the wee hours.

Although located in a party dorm, we were aware that many students at MU did not participate in this world. We quickly discovered that not even all the residents of the floor we studied partied. As we will show, the experiences of the women on our floor who did not do so were still shaped by the dominant culture of the floor. The experiences of other students on campus are similarly influenced by the large, visible party pathway—although how much depends largely on their distance from it socially, spatially, and academically. Alternative subcultures—such as lesbian and gay students, students of color, international students, or those devoted to the arts, music, sports, religion, or academics—survived through what we came to refer to as "protective segregation."

This is a study of college women. Women's experiences in higher education are paradoxical and thus worthy of close scrutiny. On the one hand, women today attend college in greater numbers than men, even leading some to consider "affirmative action for boys."[32] Women achieve higher GPAs and are more likely than men to graduate.[33] They also receive more parental aid for higher education.[34] On the other hand, women still shy away from math and science and experience high rates of sexual violence and other forms of sexual disrespect.[35] These contradictory experiences are, as we will argue, in part organizationally produced. Women are also interesting because their sexual and romantic strategies vary by social class and have consequences for future class position.

We use the word "trajectory" instead of "outcome" to assess women's circumstances at the end of college because the women were still quite young when we left them. Trajectories are also more encompassing than discrete outcomes—incorporating a number of dimensions. We anticipate adult class location on the basis of the last interview but do not foreclose the possibility of change in direction.

Overview of the Argument

Our rich data allowed us to develop a theoretical model explaining why some students, in certain higher education contexts, may fare better than others. Below we discuss this model in general terms, and throughout the book illustrate it with our data. However, as we have only one case, there are limits, and the model is indelibly imprinted by where in the sector we were located. We offer concepts to think with and invite others to extend and revise our model through application to different institutional environments and other types of students.

We argue that college experiences and class trajectories out of college are shaped by the fit between individual characteristics (resources associated with class background and orientations to college) and organizational characteristics—namely, the college pathways provided by a student's university. The pathways provided by the university are shaped by the collective class projects of constituencies attempting to achieve their own ends and the university's attempts to solve its organizational problems. Figure I.1 offers a visual representation of the general theoretical model.

Using more concrete terms, this model helps make sense of why, in the context of MU, the seemingly minor differences in class resources between Emma and Taylor mattered so much. Emma's failure to persist in her pursuit of a dental career had everything to do with the structure of the pathways available to her. As we will see in Chapter 7, without highly educated and well-informed parents like Taylor's, it was hard for Emma to entirely avoid the lure of the robust party pathway at MU. That this pathway reigned supreme was in part a consequence of MU's pursuit of solvency in the face of declining state support and the solution it found in supporting the class project of affluent, socially oriented students.

In Table I.1 we provide a concrete summary of the ways in which class projects, college pathways, and organizational imperatives intersect to shape the flow of students through the university. Along with Figure I.1, this table should help the reader follow the discussion below. As class projects form an important link between the interests of individuals and the structure of postsecondary organizations, we start there. We then look at the university

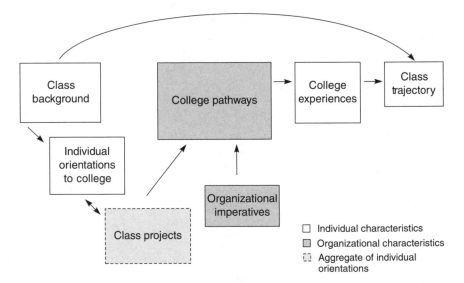

Figure I.1. Accounting for college experiences and class trajectories

Table I.1. Class projects, college pathways, organizational imperatives, and the flow of students through the university

Class projects	College pathways	Organizational imperatives	Class background	Orientations to college	College experiences	Class trajectory
Reproduction via social closure	Party	Solvency	Upper Upper-middle	Primed to party	Socialite (Wannabe)	Reproduction (Downward)
Mobility	Mobility	Legitimacy	Lower-middle Working class	Motivated for mobility	Striver	Upward or mobility at risk
Reproduction via achievement	Professional	Prestige maximization	Highly educated upper classes	Cultivated for success	Achiever (Underachiever)	Reproduction (Downward)

as an organization, examining three main pathways and the organizational imperatives that influence how these pathways are provisioned. Finally, we focus on the implications of different pathways for students with varied class resources and orientations to college. Although abstract, this general discussion provides insight into the ways in which class interests are built into the architecture of the university and why it serves some students better than others.

Class Projects

Social class shapes what families want and need from universities to improve (or at least reproduce) their life circumstances. Students from similar class backgrounds share financial, cultural, and social resources, as well as lived experiences, that shape their orientations to college and the agendas they can reasonably pursue. Although they mostly act independently, a large number of students who share agendas become a constituency to be reckoned with—even without recognizing, or wanting to recognize, that they have become a group.[36] The aggregate of individual, class-based orientations and agendas are what we refer to as "class projects."

As class relies on positioning in labor and marital markets, and higher education prepares students to enter both, class projects necessarily involve approaches to romance as well as to academics. We describe three distinct class projects. Each assumes a different model of career and family formation, in which assumptions about men's and women's roles are embedded. Individuals seek out higher education contexts where they can cultivate the skills, interests, tastes, appearances, and interactional styles deemed essential for women (or men) of their social class to achieve economic security. In this sense, class projects are also deeply gendered.

Class Reproduction through Social Closure

Partying appears to be among the most democratic of activities, and many college students party heavily at one time or another. Yet, for a fraction of the upper classes, socializing is the central point of college. These students associate with similarly privileged others, in exclusive contexts, and in ways that allow them to expand their circle of similarly privileged acquaintances. They accomplish "social closure" in the classic Weberian sense of the term by monopolizing access to valuable ties and the experiences that constitute them as of a certain class. Classes, grades, and professors factor in out of necessity but are relegated to the background.[37]

Key to this form of social reproduction is isolation from less privileged others during years in which cultural tastes, social styles, friendships, and marital relationships are formed and solidified. This is ensured in part by the sheer expense of the college social whirl—as it involves sorority and fraternity fees, late-model cars, booze, dining at restaurants, spring break vacations, study abroad, fashionable clothing and accessories, and the grooming necessary to achieve the right personal style. High levels of parental funding are required, as full immersion allows little time for paid employment.[38]

This orientation to college is not new. In fact, it originated with wealthy young men who relied on family background, social connections, and personal charisma to build careers in business and politics after college.[39] Elite institutions played a central role in this process. As Jerome Karabel detailed in *The Chosen: The Hidden History of Admission and Exclusion at Harvard, Yale, and Princeton*, the president of Princeton in the early twentieth century described the university as "the finest country club in America" and admonished the faculty as follows: "Gentlemen, whether we like it or not, we shall have to recognize that Princeton is a rich man's college and that rich men do not frequently come to college to study."[40]

Much has changed since this time. Yet even today's graduates are not equally dependent on academic achievement for their life chances. Some come from such affluence that they will be wealthy irrespective of how they spend their time in college. Others may seek to capitalize on social skills, connections, and looks—which matter more in some arenas than others. These students can take familial support after college graduation for granted, considerably reducing the stakes of academic performance.

If these individuals do not apply themselves in college, why do they bother to attend? College provides a necessary labor market credential and is also the only place to engage in four years of intensive interaction with similar peers.[41] Friendships that link people to job opportunities and potential mates are generated. Young men and women are able to refine classed, raced, and (hetero)sexualized forms of masculinity and femininity, allowing them to fit smoothly into elite social and professional contexts—without appearing to work too hard at it.[42]

Women with this orientation to college take a gender complementary approach to economic security. Implicit is the assumption that being really good at being a "girl" has social value and can be exchanged for certain types of career success and—most importantly—a well-heeled male breadwinner. In the past, many affluent women went to college to acquire the so-called MRS degree. Today, they may still meet their mates in college, but most wait until the earning potential of a future mate is certain before committing.[43] Eventual marriage within social class is thus pivotal to this approach.

Class Mobility

Many members of the working and middle classes view higher education as a primary avenue to social mobility. This view has its roots in the American Dream, according to which anyone can make it to the top—if they just work hard enough to get on and stay on what essayist Calvin Trillin described as a "special, reservations-only escalator to success."[44]

The educational investments of this group come at a great cost—they dig deep into sparse family resources, take out loans, and work long hours to make college a possibility.[45] Pragmatic and vocationally oriented, these students seek practical majors and prioritize securing a credential leading to gainful employment. Their approach is defined by hard work and dedication to studies. Motivation, lack of time, and limited funds help them to ignore the siren song of the party scene. Even if inclined to participate, they are often excluded.

Individuals seeking to improve their lot in life have long been present on campus and are captured in the popular image of the "nerd" or the "grind."[46] This is particularly true at public universities, where social origins have played a far less important role in admissions than at elite, private schools. The composition of this group has shifted over time, at various points including children of immigrants (first Eastern European, later Asian, and then Central American), sons and daughters of rural farmers, blacks, Jews, and women of all classes.[47]

Today, less privileged women are more likely than their male counterparts to look to higher education as a route to mobility. They seek access to jobs that pay more and offer greater security than the childcare, cashiering, or waitressing jobs that would otherwise be their lot.[48] These women are often tough and self-reliant, with insufficient time or money to cultivate the femininity characteristic of affluent partiers. However, in other ways, they are gender traditional. Most are unlikely to leave behind realms of work coded as feminine, turning to pink-collar vocational majors that promise

an immediate "step up."[49] They also see benefits in a relatively early marriage. For those without parental assistance, there are "economies of scale"
in combining resources and efforts, rather than maintaining an independent
household.[50]

The problem these women face is access to potential mates that can
contribute to, rather than drain, the resources of the couple. It can be a challenge to locate them—few men who share their social origins (and a more
rapid timeline for marriage) can be found at college.[51] Research has illustrated that the marital benefits of college—a higher likelihood of marrying
and of marrying well to a similarly educated individual—do not extend to
the least advantaged of college-goers.[52] The fate of these women's mobility
projects oftentimes rests on their ability to avoid or end relationships with
less ambitious men.

Class Reproduction through Achievement

Students from a range of class backgrounds arrive on campus intending to
embark upon well-compensated and high-status professional careers. Those
who win might be referred to as "the elite"—or perhaps "Super People," as
the *New York Times* dubbed them.[53] They are the accomplished young, with
stellar SAT scores, near-perfect high school GPAs, and Advanced Placement
(AP) credits. The educational and economic resources required to produce
individuals with such outstanding profiles sharply restricts access to these
positions.[54] In this "inherited meritocracy," the means to do well are typically
handed down from one generation to the next.[55]

Evidence suggests that these families are engaged in a parenting arms
race—spending more time and money longer into the life course to guarantee their children's success.[56] Admission to the "right" college is a defining
moment. However, privileged parents also pay careful attention to their
children during college, monitoring choice of majors, class selection, the
quality of advice given by advisors, choice of romantic partners, and time
spent socializing. They help their offspring craft the most appealing array
of extracurricular activities and scout for beneficial internships.[57] For these
parents, the nest is not empty; it has just been relocated.

Changes in the organization of higher education have increased the cost
and likelihood of mistakes. Skyrocketing tuition has intensified parental
attention to the quality and payoff of their investments.[58] There has been an
explosion of different types of postsecondary organizations and curricular

options, which range wildly in quality and marketability.[59] Universities have also stepped out of a paternalistic role with regard to curricular plans and social life on campus (with the decline of *in loco parentis*).[60] However, college students of today are no more adult than in the past, and arguably less so, given the lengthening transition to adulthood.[61] University abdication of a supervisory role shifts the burden back to parents.[62]

Women are well represented among those oriented to achievement. Along with better performance in college, they enter into graduate school at higher rates and hold the majority of management and professional jobs.[63] The decline in young men's earning power since the 1960s, the women's movement, the advent of reliable contraception, and liberalization of sexual attitudes together have made economic dependence on men less desirable.[64] Now it is acceptable for women to delay marriage and childbirth in pursuit of high-powered careers.[65]

As daughters of professional women and products of liberal feminism, these are not the low-achieving girly girls of the party pathway, though they also aspire to beauty, fitness, and femininity.[66] As a 2003 report on the status of women at Duke University described, these women strive for "effortless perfection":

> [The] expectation that [they] should excel in everything. They should be great students, with exciting summer jobs and internship opportunities; they should join high-status sororities and be popular with their peers; they should be campus leaders; and they should have physically fit bodies and high-fashion wardrobes. . . . They ha[ve] to act as if doing so [is] easy and require[s] no effort whatsoever.[67]

Men's monetary and career success may bleed over to some extent into romantic and social success, but for women these realms have traditionally been in competition. Succeeding in all arenas at the same time is a challenging and exhausting project.

High-achieving women, like many of their male counterparts, shore up privilege by maximizing the odds of success in both elite labor and marital markets. They set aside an extended period of time for heavy academic and career development, so that financial independence is reached well before marriage and childbearing. This is a relatively new strategy for class reproduction—the consolidation of privilege. Here both women and men secure a spot in the privileged classes by maximizing their own earning power and that of their partner. This approach is fairly gender-neutral—being dependent on the combination of two successful individuals.[68]

College Pathways

When the university structures the interests of a constituency into its organizational edifice, we say that it has created a "pathway." Pathways are simultaneously social and academic and coordinate all aspects of the university experience.[69] Just as roads are built for types of vehicles, pathways are built for types of students. The party pathway is provisioned to support the affluent and socially oriented; the mobility pathway is designed for the pragmatic and vocationally oriented; and the professional pathway fits ambitious students from privileged families.

The Party Pathway

The party pathway is built around an implicit agreement between the university and students to demand little of each other.[70] Extremely affluent students with middling academic credentials are the ideal candidates. They cost the university the least, as they are not eligible for need-based aid, are less competitive for merit scholarships, do not demand much time with faculty, and do not require remedial assistance. Legacy policies (sometimes referred to as "affirmative action for the rich") and comparatively low academic standards make it easier for universities to admit more of these students.[71]

Murray Sperber, in his 2000 book, *Beer and Circus: How Big-Time College Sports Is Crippling Undergraduate Education*, suggests that students are, in essence, bribed with "beer and circus" in exchange for minimal contact with faculty and low academic demands.[72] Yet, "beer and circus" is exactly what some affluent students seek. Building the social side of the party pathway involves creating big-time sports teams and facilities, as well as other "recreational" aspects of student life (for example, fitness and student centers).[73] It means establishing ways of policing student revelry that protect life, property, and reputation without putting too much of a damper on student socializing. Most centrally, it requires solving the puzzle of how to systematically, and in large-scale fashion, generate "fun."

Sororities and fraternities are often part of the solution: umbrella organizations at both local and national levels ease the planning of campus-wide social events. Universities can further support these organizations by allowing them to operate on campus, facilitating purchase of property on university grounds, and exempting them from rigorous policing. In doing so, schools provide a way for affluent, white, socially oriented students to isolate themselves from their less privileged peers.[74] They also ensure that such students have the organizational infrastructure necessary for their sexual and romantic projects—fraternities sponsor an erotic marketplace in which students gain status and make connections through "hooking up."[75] By pairing opposite-sex houses for events, Greek organizations engineer this process, effectively creating what demographers call "endogamy" or "homogamy"—pairing like with like or, in this case, affluent white women with affluent white men.[76]

Regardless of how much students value fun and socializing, few of their parents would pay tuition without at least the promise of some academic edification. Classes and grades legitimate the college experience. Yet serious scholarship is time-consuming. This produces a conundrum: How can students have a primarily social experience without failing academically? Universities have solved the problem by allowing easy majors to develop.

In his contribution to *The Future of the City of Intellect: The Changing American University*, Steven Brint refers to these majors as "the practical arts" or "occupational and professional programs often housed in their own schools and colleges."[77] They include business, public administration, communications, tourism, recreation studies, education, human development, fitness, and fashion, among others. Easy majors contrast with the more challenging sciences and humanities that are generally part of colleges of arts and sciences. They are associated with higher overall GPAs and less measurable learning.[78] In many—although not all—easy majors, career success depends on personal characteristics developed outside of the classroom, even prior to college. For example, appearance, personality, and social ties matter at least as much—if not more—than GPA for media, sports, or fashion careers.

A developed party pathway requires that easy majors be richly variegated, with many possible sub-subspecialties, ways to opt out of challenging requirements (for example, language, science, and math classes), and schedules compatible with partying (that is, no Friday classes). When a party pathway is robust, these majors are well advertised, recommended by advisors, and generally supported by the school.

The Mobility Pathway

The mobility pathway provides vocational training to anyone who is willing to work hard to acquire it. It is explicitly inclusive and pragmatic in nature.

A central feature of the mobility pathway is the leveling of the playing field for those who do not have the advantages necessary to sail through college on their own.

Compensation starts with access. Less privileged students benefit when tuition costs are low, financial aid is adequate, and it takes the form of grants rather than loans; thus, these students are vulnerable to downturns in federal and state financing for higher education. Institutions can offer a buffer via need-based aid or sliding-scale tuition.[79] Many students from disadvantaged backgrounds also fail to meet admission guidelines, due to poor academic preparation.[80] Class-based affirmative action is one remedy; however, affirmative action policies, to the extent that they exist, have been mainly based on race. Research indicates that programs admitting all students above a certain high school class rank (regardless of GPA or test scores) are also not sufficient.[81]

Mobility and professional pathways overlap. However, the mobility pathway is built primarily around majors that do not require family intervention for eventual success. There is no question as to what jobs they feed directly into, and students are trained for a particular profession (for example, nursing, accounting, or teaching). Classes need to be as substantive as possible—not an aid for heavy socializing—as students on this pathway will rely on what they learn in the classroom, rather than family ties or money, to get them a job. Opportunity for late entry to programs with more challenging requirements is necessary, so that students who arrive with less than stellar records or take a while to get adjusted to college are not left behind.

The mobility pathway builds academic and social guidance and financial support into the function of the university—rather than outsourcing it to individuals and their families.[82] To determine exactly what is needed, programs must assess the whole student—his or her class background, prior academic record, work and family obligations, and educational and career aspirations. The burden of locating help cannot be placed on students themselves, as many are ill-equipped to find it and unaware they need it. Special programming works best when offered to all first-generation and less privileged students or is made mandatory.[83] Active advising, to the point of being intrusive, must accompany all interventions so that students are aware of where they stand, what services are available to them, what they need to do, and how they might change course.[84] Ideally, students see the same primary advisor from the time they step foot on campus until graduation.

Social integration is also key for the educational performance and persistence of less privileged students.[85] Integration is often treated as assimilation into the dominant current of (privileged) student life. However, on many campuses this would require pulling less privileged students off the mobility pathway and onto the party pathway—defeating the whole purpose. A better solution is to increase the proportion of less privileged, nontraditional, and first-generation students already on campus, so that newcomers will more easily find a place. "Protective segregation," or social spaces where students can avoid the party scene, may serve as a stopgap measure—assuming all students who need such protection can find it.

The Professional Pathway

At the heart of the professional pathway is competition—for admission, merit-based financial awards, entry to top programs, internships, and attention from professors. Class resources (for example, private SAT preparation, tutors and coaches, freedom from paid employment, attendance at top high schools, and parental connections) give some students an edge in these contests. The professional pathway facilitates the conversion of class advantage into academic merit—a process Mitchell Stevens refers to as "laundering privilege" in *Creating a Class: College Admissions and the Education of Elites*.[86] For example, SAT scores play an important role in admissions, even though they are poor predictors of college performance.[87] This benefits affluent students, who are far more likely to enroll in private test preparation and take the test multiple times to boost scores.[88]

Unforgiving tracking systems, early high-stakes sorting, and no tolerance for educational deficits ensure that access to the best training and opportunities are restricted to a small group of well-prepared students. For instance, students with AP credits leapfrog over much basic college coursework, moving rapidly into small, intensive seminars taught by committed faculty. Heavy math, science, and language requirements "weed out" all but the most select students from the most lucrative professional tracks.

Chances to demonstrate excellence extend beyond the classroom. A variety of student organizations, leadership positions, and philanthropic opportunities are available, and policies are in place that allow for the proliferation of more. Here the professional and party pathways share some organizational infrastructure. Participation in Greek organizations and other elite social clubs can offer (measured) release from the grind of academic work and provide access to valuable student and alumni networks.

The professional pathway does not compensate for individual or family "deficits" in navigating the academic and social challenges of college. Instead, it explicitly employs parents in the task of creating successful graduates. Universities handle parents carefully, arranging special parental orientations and establishing channels for parents to have contact with residence life staff and other administrators.[89] Their children are, after all, desirable admits precisely because of heavily invested parents. Schools need parents to keep up the good work—and to keep their pocketbooks open. Students on the professional pathway are heavily subsidized by parental funds—for tuition, living expenses, study abroad, and unpaid summer internships—reducing the financial contributions needed from the university.

Organizational Imperatives

Pathways require considerable university resources (time, energy, and funds) to create and maintain. Supporting one pathway often comes at the cost of another, and some do not easily coexist. Universities have their own interests that guide investment in the infrastructure necessary for pathways. These interests vary across time, among schools, and even internally. Which constituencies are best served depends on how university administrators define the current goals of the organization.

In order to survive and situate themselves in relationship to other postsecondary organizations, universities must balance three competing imperatives. The first is solvency. As economist Gordon C. Winston observes, if universities—even nonprofit schools—do not take in as much as they spend, they, like other organizations, face potential extinction.[90] University revenues come from two sources: tuition and "charitable donations," which include legislative appropriations, gifts, and asset earnings. Charitable donations heavily subsidize students' educations so that most do not pay the full cost. When charitable donations fall—for example, when legislatures withdraw support from public universities—the result is hikes in tuition and increased pursuit of students who do not need financial aid.[91]

"Equity" is also valued across the American higher education sector but is especially central to the missions of public research universities. As John A. Douglass explains in *The Conditions for Admission: Access, Equity, and the Social Contract of Public Universities*, public universities "were conceived, funded, and developed as tools of socioeconomic engineering . . . open . . . to the farmer and the laborer as well as the more well to do—to all that demonstrated academic and civic talent."[92] It is important for universities to signal their commitment to meritocracy and mobility—even if this is more a matter of perception than reality. Failing to do so may not jeopardize survival as quickly as an immediate lack of revenue; however, it will damage the legitimacy of an institution and the likelihood of securing donations.

At the same time, universities engage in "prestige maximization."[93] Status is, by definition, relative. Colleges and universities jockey with each other for position. They compete, for instance, over the perceived quality of undergraduate education, generally measured through the percentage of applicants turned away and the quality of those accepted. Yet undergraduate education is only one of many dimensions on which universities are ranked, and it is typically not the most central one. Universities can—and do—redirect revenues from low-status to high-status activities, say from undergraduate tuition to graduate education or faculty research. Sources of prestige are also historically variable. For example, Karabel and Stevens, read together, describe how student body diversity moved from a threat to university prestige to a source of it.[94]

Just as individuals look to schools to improve their life chances, universities look to students to help solve universities' problems. The ideal solution is to matriculate students who simultaneously solve multiple organizational problems. Admissions committees love students who can pay full tuition but also have high SAT scores, perfect high school grades, and other accomplishments that bring status to the university. Even better are students who also add to diversity, contributing to the perception of the university as inclusive and meritocratic. Admissions committees at elite colleges flag these applications. Stevens even quotes an admissions officer justifying an admit decision on the grounds that "He helps us in every way that's quantifiable."[95]

Happily for admissions committees, many students who bring the most to the table in terms of status can also pay full tuition. In this way, the affluent professional class and elite schools bless each other—these families deliver precisely the students schools need, and in exchange, schools provide the admission, education, and credentials such families seek. That schools offer a professional pathway to service well-paying, high-achieving students is obvious. However, these students are in limited supply. In *Creating a Class*, Stevens chronicles the anxieties of admissions officers at a selective liberal arts college, whose job it is to identify and matriculate this small, valuable constituency.[96] Most public universities cannot compete for these students.

Admitting and educating talented low-income students fulfills the university's commitment to equity. Educating such students is, however, costly, as they can afford little in the way of tuition. In the mid-twentieth century, generous state support of higher education and federal programs such as the GI Bill, Pell Grants, and work–study allowed for the education of low-income students to be heavily subsidized.[97] As these sources of revenue have diminished—and public commitment to equity has waned—universities are sometimes forced to choose between admitting qualified students who cannot pay and less qualified students who can.

For many public universities, the "typical student" who provides the "sustenance that the College relie[s] upon most heavily to maintain its financial prosperity" is affluent, socially oriented, and academically unexceptional.[98] Most are unremarkable except in their family's ability to pay. These schools profit from local elites' reliance on college life at big state schools to solidify political and economic networks.[99] For example, The *New York Times* profiled one of the University of Mississippi's weekend-long football tailgating parties. The paper quoted Doug Hederman, "whose family not only owns a commercial printing company but also dominated newspaper publishing in the state for over 50 years," about the tradition:

> It is a tremendous network, that works. What you'll find here on a regular basis is presidents, C.E.O.'s of Fortune 500 companies. It's a great opportunity to meet somebody you're not doing business with. Plus you start thinking of the political influence here. Homecoming of last year, Senators Lott and Cochran were both here, and Governor Barbour. It's pretty powerful.[100]

In recent years, children of affluent urban and coastal families have also landed at public universities as these schools have intensified their efforts to recruit and competition for the small number of slots at elite colleges has increased.[101]

In the context of most big state universities—particularly outside of the most elite—the party pathway is a main artery through the university, much like a well-paved, eight-lane highway directing traffic into a major city: on-ramps are numerous and well marked, and avoiding it completely requires intent, effort, and intricate knowledge of alternative routes. Providing this pathway attracts those whose dollars fuel the university. The professional pathway—catering as it does to another wealthy (but difficult to secure) set of clientele—still exists, but it is narrow, harder to spot, and fast moving—like an express lane where cars continually pick up speed. Those who got on the highway early are heavily advantaged, although they may just be going with the flow. The later that one tries to enter, the more difficult the task of merging into fast traffic. The mobility pathway suffers the most; over time, neglect and lack of support stymie development and lead to disrepair. This pathway is like a side road riddled with potholes and major obstacles; often it simply goes nowhere.

The Flow of Students through the University

For decades scholars have studied how primary and secondary school students are "tracked" into different courses of study.[102] Yet there has been little formal research on how students are channeled within four-year residential colleges.[103] The absence of such research is likely due to an intertwined set of assumptions: Students freely choose their paths through college; the diversity of majors, extracurricular activities, and available social worlds thwart the possibility of hierarchies; and the variety of paths through higher education are so numerous as to make the finding of general patterns impossible. This assumption is not true, as at most schools there is an elaborate process of sorting that moves people onto distinct pathways.

Self-selection is one sorting mechanism. At the aggregate level, class background and orientations to college are sufficiently linked so that universities can take into account class projects in constructing organizational arrangements. At the individual level, however, the relationship between class background and orientation to college is messy. Students sometimes develop educational expectations and goals inconsistent with the class resources available to them.

A common misfit occurs when students who cannot afford a primarily social college experience still aspire to it. The idea that college is about having "the best time of one's life" has diffused far beyond its historical origins in the upper class. Not a hard sell, this notion is celebrated in popular culture and actively promoted by the leisure and alcohol industries. A number of observers have suggested that a social orientation is now the mainstream American approach to college—crossing all classes and social groups.[104]

Self-selection is only half the story, though. Both the university infrastructure and student peer cultures play a role in sorting students. Students who arrive at college with vague or contradictory agendas are most affected by the configuration of pathways at a particular university and tend to gravitate toward the most visible and accessible option. Some sorting is dependent on chance (for example, unexpected success in sorority recruitment or an early connection with an invested professor) and where in the university students land. For instance, although some of the women we studied knowingly requested assignment to a party dorm, others arrived there unwittingly. These individuals were, in effect, dumped onto the party pathway on-ramp, irrespective of whether they had the resources to succeed on it.

How students were sorted onto pathways matters, as students have better experiences when they land on a pathway for which they have appropriate resources—that is, when there is a good fit between the individual and the pathway. We classify women in our study by pathway and fit.[105]

Women whose primary—although not necessarily exclusive—approach to college was social are *socialites* or *wannabes*.[106] Thirty-four percent of women interviewed fell into one of these groups, including those who started college "primed to party" and those who were swept up into this world. Socialites had the necessary resources for full participation in the party pathway, whereas wannabes participated even though they did not. Wannabes exemplify the consequences of misfit between an individual and a pathway. Without parental resources to compensate for poor achievement and limited skill acquisition, a number left college at risk of downward mobility. In contrast, socialites suffered few or no negative consequences as they moved into life after college.

We call those in search of the mobility pathway *strivers*.[107] Many (although not all) arrived "motivated for mobility." They worked long hours to support themselves in the hope of completing a degree that would translate into secure employment. Twenty-eight percent—the most economically disadvantaged women—fell into this group. One was pulled into a tiny program designed to cultivate the brightest of the less privileged. Everyone else encountered a mobility pathway in disrepair. Around half transferred, typically to regional four-year campuses, where they had greater success. Compared with their peers in the small towns they came from, most of those who left MU were upwardly mobile. Those who stayed at MU, however, tended to face grimmer prospects.

We refer to the 38% of women who pursued the professional pathway (with varying degrees of intent and success) as *achievers* and *underachievers*. None of these women were entirely consumed by the party scene or came from extremely difficult economic circumstances. Roughly 40% of women on the professional pathway resembled Taylor: they graduated with a solid major and GPA, moved into good entry-level employment or admission to graduate school, and were well positioned to meet and marry a similarly successful spouse. In contrast, 60% of those on the professional pathway were underachievers, like Emma. These women left with GPAs too low to get into graduate school, were often unemployed or working in positions that did not require a college degree, and had more constrained marital options. We explain these disparities with a careful look at what it takes to successfully navigate the narrow, high-stakes, and time-sensitive professional pathway. Only achievers, most of whom arrived "cultivated for success," aligned on all criteria.

Women's experiences on college pathways produced distinctive combinations of major, GPA, extracurricular activities, and network ties that, depending on their class background, were more or less transferable into economic security. As the vignettes at the start of the chapter suggest, class trajectories were shaped not only by income and occupation but also by the amount of debt women carried, how much financial assistance they could expect from their parents, their social networks, and their romantic prospects. These aspects of their lives were interconnected and packaged in particular ways so that some combinations were common, whereas others did not exist.

Structure of the Book

Chapter 1 introduces the women who lived on the floor, describing their class backgrounds and individual orientations to college. Chapter 2 focuses on the organizational infrastructure of "the party pathway"—the most accessible, visible, and organizationally resourced pathway available at MU and many other schools. In Chapter 3, "Rush and the Party Scene," we examine the hierarchical peer cultures created by the intersection of socially oriented students and a resource rich party pathway. In Chapter 4, "The Floor," we use our year of ethnographic observation to describe how a minority of affluent partiers came to dominate the floor and examine the long-term consequences of social isolation for those who were not included.

Chapters 5 through 7 focus on the experiences of women on each of the three pathways available at MU. In Chapter 5, "Socialites, Wannabes, and Fit with the Party Pathway," we contrast the experiences of socialites and wannabes, given their different levels of fit and misfit with the party pathway. Chapter 6, "Strivers, Creaming, and the Blocked Mobility Pathway," follows working-class and lower-middle-class women who struggled to find a mobility pathway at MU. In Chapter 7, "Achievers, Underachievers, and the Professional Pathway," we explain how downward mobility—even among less social but relatively privileged youth—may occur.

In the final two chapters, we survey our empirical findings and discuss their implications. Chapter 8, "College Pathways and Post-College Prospects," concludes that college did not close the gap between more and less privileged women in our study. We examine the role that the organizational environment at MU plays in contributing to class and gender inequities. In Chapter 9, "Politics and Pathways," we argue that schools like MU need to be reengineered with attention to the needs of most students, identify changes that move in this direction, and highlight potential obstacles.

CHAPTER 1

The Women

Hannah, an East Coast student who lived on our floor, described her grandparents as "rich beyond the money world" (Y1). Her grandparents paid for all nine grandchildren's college expenses even though Hannah's father was the chief financial officer of a Fortune 500 company. Hannah matriculated at MU after an extensive college search. She initially focused on Penn State, UConn, Rhode Island, and Delaware, but her high school advisor suggested that she look at "[Big State U] and MU because they are [in the same football conference] and [have] the huge big feeling of spirit" (Y1). She visited both, and although she thought that Big State U had a gorgeous campus, she found the city too gritty. She told us, "Then I came here to Fairview and I was like, Oh my God, the campus was gorgeous. It's a college town, everything is about college life. I loved it" (Y1). With its beautiful buildings and small-town location, MU appealed to her. (The university is well aware of its charm, advertising its campus on its Web site as "one of the most beautiful in the world.") Hannah was one of many affluent out-of-state students on our floor lured by the campus and the promise of "college life."

Not all of the students we studied were affluent, though. Hannah's roommate, Alyssa, was decidedly not rich. Her father was a mechanic. At one point in college, her parents were so in debt that their credit cards were canceled, and Alyssa, who worked full-time while in school, started covering basic household living expenses for them. As she explained:

> I'll make . . . one of their [car] payments, and they need toilet paper, I'll go pick up some toilet paper. Just things that I noticed that they may not have at that time, that I try to help them with. It may not be $500 a week or something like that, but it's just something . . . that I can try to contribute. (Y5)

Although Hannah and Alyssa managed to avoid overt conflict, they did not become friends. Hannah, who was very gregarious, tried to connect with Alyssa, asking "her to go out to parties, dinners, and just to hang out and watch movies," but Alyssa never accepted. More frustrating to Hannah were Alyssa's complaints about "not being networked in the hall and not having many friends here" when, in Hannah's view, the women were willing to include her (Field Notes 10/2/04). Hannah attributed Alyssa's reticence to her relationship with a boyfriend back home, as she had walked in on Alyssa crying while talking with him over the phone. Although Hannah was willing to be supportive, Alyssa refused to talk about the relationship. After the first semester, Hannah moved into a room down the hall with a more affluent woman. Interviewed in her second year, she told Laura that "if I ever had to do the first few months again with that girl Alyssa . . . like I would never want to do that ever again" (Y2).

Hannah never understood that a class chasm divided them, in part because Alyssa rarely spoke about her background. Alyssa explained, "I didn't ever bring it to their attention. I'm pretty sure they probably knew [that] I wouldn't just go shopping and spend money. . . . I would just kind of seclude myself to where, you know, they wouldn't even ask me to go" (Y4). Laura tried to get Hannah to talk about the class difference, asking her whether she thought it might have been "hard for Alyssa, like realizing that a lot of people probably have more money than her?"(Y1). Hannah did not register the question, instead describing how wealthy all of her friends and family were. The closest Hannah came to acknowledging the existence of less affluent students was in her discovery that some people pay for college themselves. She arrived at this insight at a basketball game, where she and a friend charged all of their expenses to the bursar. An acquaintance they were with asked, "What's the bursar?" Hannah told them, "It's the thing your parents pay for." The acquaintance responded, "My parents don't pay for it. I pay for everything." Dumbfounded, Hannah replied, "What? I can't imagine paying for everything!"(Y1).

In contrast, Alyssa quickly became aware of how little she had in common with Hannah—as well as other affluent students at MU. As she described years later:

Coming from where I come from, and not really being able to relate to some of the girls that were there, really kinda made it hard. I'm from a small town, have to make do with what I have. Whereas, living where I was at, girls were just given—they pretty much can do whatever they want. I feel like it came a lot easier for them than it did for me. It took a lot of studying and sacrifices for me to pull off my grades and to do well, and I just wasn't the same as them. They could go and do whatever they wanted, and I was kind of limited on money. (Y4)

Although they were roommates, Hannah and Alyssa did not start college on an equal footing. They had at their disposal quite different financial, but also social and cultural, resources. Their stories suggest the striking class differences that exist among students who cross paths at large public schools like MU.

Who Attends Midwest University?

Hannah and Alyssa were among 1.28 million[1] other students—48.1% of their high school graduating class[2]—starting college at a four-year institution in 2004. More than 850,000 fellow graduates, almost a third of their cohort (and a full two-thirds of all four-year college-goers), attended a public institution. As MU is only "moderately selective," the 16% of their graduating class who enrolled in "highly selective" four-year institutions outstripped Hannah and Alyssa in terms of educational accomplishment. Yet by making it to MU, Hannah and Alyssa placed in the top 38% of their cohort. Nearly 600,000 students, 22.5% of the cohort (and almost half of those attending a four-year college)—found themselves at a "moderately selective" public four-year institution.[3]

Women were overrepresented among those starting college in 2004. The widening gender gap in college attendance and completion is striking and the subject of a growing body of research.[4] Overall, 41% of women in the 2004 graduating class enrolled in "highly" or "moderately" selective four-year schools, as compared with 36% of their male peers. This pattern reflects a rapid reversal in the educational fates of young women and men: in 1960, men received 65% of all bachelor's degrees, but by 2004 women had taken the lead, receiving 58% of all degrees.[5] In studying college women, we are thus capturing today's modal college student. The feminization of higher education is particularly stark among lower-income students; this pattern shaped the lives of our working-class participants, who—by going to college—left the men in their hometown communities behind.[6]

Public universities have dealt with the higher education gender gap in different ways. Many have experienced, or continue to experience, highly skewed gender ratios on campus. The *New York Times*, for example, recently profiled the University of North Carolina at Chapel Hill as having nearly a 60–40 split in favor of women.[7] When our participants arrived at MU in 2004, the split was much less severe, as 52% of students were female. By 2010, women even comprised slightly less than 50% of the study body. MU is not alone in gradually shrinking the gender gap on campus, despite the fact that female college applicants increasingly outshine males.[8]

Hannah and Alyssa, along with all the other women on our floor, were white. Students of color are underrepresented in higher education in general and at Midwest University in particular. Low college enrollment rates among blacks can be attributed to disparities in socioeconomic status and academic performance—and reflect the intransigent racial achievement gap in K–12 education.[9] Only 23% of black high school graduates enrolled in "highly" or "moderately" selective four-year schools, compared with 45% of whites.[10]

There is intense competition among colleges for minorities eligible for admission to these schools.[11] With deep pockets, status, and the ability to recruit nationally and internationally, most elite private schools are more diverse than many middle-tier public schools. Institutions located in predominantly white states like that of MU, which was above 80% white in 2010, find it challenging to recruit minority students. State laws preventing affirmative action also hinder public universities, whereas private schools are not subject to the same restrictions.[12] Consequently, only 4% of the student body at MU in 2004 was composed of blacks. A similar number of Asians, far fewer Latinos, and very few Native Americans were part of the student population.

Class background is strongly associated with attending a four-year university and particularly with attending a "highly selective" university. In 2004, 50% of children with at least one college-educated parent and 72% of those with a parent who achieved a graduate or professional degree attended a "highly" or "moderately" selective four-year postsecondary school.[13] Thus, Hannah's attendance at MU is not surprising. Relative to others with a similar background, she was not an academic star—even in her own family. As she describes:

My cousin just graduated from Georgetown this year. And my other cousin is at NYU. Patricia [is] gonna be the smartest out [of] all of them, by far. She's a genius. She got higher than me on SATs in the 7th grade. Me, Emily, and Jason are like really dumb. My other two cousins, they both go to Georgetown too. (Y2)

When asked if she applied to Georgetown, Hannah replied:

> No. Absolutely not. I would have never ever gotten in there, but [my cousin is] a genius. He comes to sit and eat dinner with us, brings his book, he's reading, very studious guy. (Y1)

Hannah's placement of herself in the bottom third among her cousins may not be far from her position among equally privileged peers. In contrast, relative to others with similar family backgrounds, simply enrolling at MU placed Alyssa at the high end of educational achievement. Less than 20% of students whose parents had a high school education or less and 30% of those with a parent who attended some college enrolled in "highly" or "moderately" selective four-year schools.[14]

The percentage of students from out of state has increased in recent years at MU. In 2010, 40% of all students (and 36% of undergraduates) were from out of state. These numbers represent 20% and 16% increases, respectively, for the years during which our participants moved through college. When they attended MU, tuition, fees, and room and board came to more than $23,000 for out-of-state students. For in-state students, the total was $12,000. The disparity between these amounts continues to grow, reflecting increasing reliance on out-of-state tuition dollars among public universities nationwide.

In- and out-of-state students differ economically, educationally, and culturally and can be seen as quite distinct flows of students moving into the university. Out-of-state students, hailing as they do from the best school districts in the country, tend to be academically well prepared. Even those with primarily social ambitions arrive without the need for remedial courses. With good grades and strong SAT scores, recruiting these students not only increases revenue, but also the status of the university. Attracting this constituency is thus a win for universities.

In the years immediately after the cohort we studied matriculated, MU grew more selective, likely in part through successful recruitment of out-of-state students. The profile of the university changed rapidly between 2004 and 2009. For example, the applicant pool grew from 21,000 to 33,000, the average SAT score crossed the 1200 mark for the first time ever (after making a 90-point jump), and the average GPA went from 3.4 to 3.7. Between 2006 and 2010, the acceptance rate at MU also went from 83% to 69%. The composition of the student body now is academically stronger than it was during our study.

Table 1.1. MU undergraduates, 2004–2005, versus floor residents

Characteristic	MU	Floor
White	88%	100%
Female	55%	100%
Working class	20%–25%	13%
Out of state	38%	45%
Greek affiliated	17%	43%
Jewish	14%	28%

There are reasons to believe, however, that this trend cannot continue. All large public universities are trying to recruit from the same small pool of students: Only 20% of college-goers attend college out of state, and more than half of these students attend private colleges.[15] At some point in the near future, MU—like other universities—will exhaust the share of the out-of-state students for which it can compete. In fact, the finite nature of the domestic market has led to increasing efforts to secure international tuition dollars.[16]

The study participants were a function not only of MU's position in the higher education system and the time during which these women were enrolled, but also of the particular residential floor that we studied. In the Introduction we noted that this floor was in a "party dorm." As we will see in more detail in Chapter 2, the existence of well-known dorm reputations, a residence hall assignment procedure that allowed students to request residential neighborhoods, and a strong preference among affluent, out-of-state students for "party dorms" shaped our sample. The floor that we studied was composed of more white, affluent, out-of-state, and Greek-oriented students than the MU undergraduate population as a whole (see Table 1.1).

Class Background of Study Participants

We identified five distinct class groupings based on parental education, occupation, and family economic resources—upper class, upper-middle class, middle class, lower-middle class, and working class.[17] Table 1.2 identifies the typical characteristics of each group and the number and percentage of women in the study that fell into each group.[18]

Table 1.2. Class background of study participants

Class	Mother education	Father education	Mother occupation	Father occupation	Employed during school	Loans	Family structure	Residency	n
Upper	College degree	≥ College degree	Homemaker	CEO/CFO	None	None	Intact	Out of state	9 (19%)
Upper-middle	≥ College degree	≥ College degree	Teacher, social services	Professional	Few	None	Intact	Mixed	17 (36%)
Middle	College degree	College degree	Teacher, management	Sales mgmt.	Few	Some	Mostly intact	Mostly in-state	6 (13%)
Lower-middle	≤ Some college	Some college	Secretarial or sales positions	Sales mgmt.	All	Most	Mixed	In-state	9 (19%)
Working	≤ Some college	≤ Some college	Low-paying service work	Manual labor	All	All	Mixed	In-state	6 (13%)
Total									47 (100%)

Upper Class. The fathers of the nine participants (19%) from upper-class families were either chief executive or chief financial officers of companies, entrepreneurs who owned highly successful businesses, or professionals in the finance industry (for example, wealth management, commodities trading). Their mothers did not work outside of the home. All but one was from an intact family. Upper-class women grew up surrounded by wealth: Brenda traveled on her father's private jet, and Hannah brought friends with her on lavish, international family vacations. They experienced no financial constraints—paying for an out-of-state public university education was not a burden for their parents, nor did their parents balk at their daughters' expensive tastes in clothes and leisure. Upper-class women expected that their families would continue to provide for them at the same high level after college, at least until they married.

Upper-Middle Class. The largest group of participants (17 women, 36%), came from upper-middle-class families. In these families, both parents had college degrees, and at least one parent worked in a well-compensated professional field. For example, Bailey's father was a doctor, while both Lydia's and Taylor's fathers were accountants. Taylor's mother was a professor. All but one of these families was intact. Upper-middle-class families typically did not take out loans or expect their daughters to work during the academic year. Yet the way that most of these women talked about money differed from the upper-class women, in that there was a sense of money as finite—money devoted to one expense was money forgone from another.

However, in this group more than others, there was variation. Some families were securely upper-middle class—almost on the cusp of the upper class. Others were more tenuously so, to the point of being one job loss or financial catastrophe away from the middle class. Whether a woman's family was on the secure versus tenuous end of the upper-middle class was more consequential for out-of-state students, given the heavy financial burden of attending college from out of state. The families of in-staters and financially comfortable out-of-staters had more resources left to assist after college.

Middle Class. Relatively few women in the study (6 women, 13%) came from middle-class families. We suspect that this may reflect the increasing class polarization of American society, but our data provide no insight into the puzzle of the absent middle class. Although both parents had college degrees, these families lacked the economic resources of upper-middle-class families. In one case, serious illness bankrupted a father's business. Divorce reduced resources for other families. Often neither parent was employed in a lucrative field. Some women in this group worked for pay during the school year or took out loans. A couple understood themselves to be at the top of the economic ladder of their small in-state towns, but their resources were constrained relative to individuals they encountered at MU. Any financial reserves these families had earmarked for launching their daughters into adulthood were drained by the end of college.

Lower-Middle Class. The nine participants (19%) from lower-middle-class backgrounds had parents with some experience in college, although none had two parents with college degrees. Their parents typically worked in sales or as secretaries; however, at least one parent (often the father) had a managerial position in which other workers reported to them. Thus, while Valerie's mother worked in retail, her father was a midlevel manager in a hotel. Economic constraint was a constant in the lives of these women. Attending college out of state was not possible, and work for pay during the school year was necessary, as were loans. Most of these families had experienced divorce or parental death, which contributed to financial constraint. For example, although Becky's mom did not have a college degree, she made a good living in her sales position. Combined with another income, her position would have been solidly middle class. As a single mother, her resources—both in terms of time and money—were limited.

Working Class. Six participants (13%) were from working-class families. The parents of these women did not have college degrees, and in most cases neither parent had any college experience. Their mothers tended to work in low-paying service jobs, while their fathers did some form of manual labor. For instance, Megan's mother worked as a day care worker, while her father worked in highway construction. Several of their families had dealt with death or divorce. Working-class women received the least amount of financial support from their families. Consequently, these young women took out loans, worked for pay, and sometimes even assisted their families in making ends meet. All were from in state, most from rural areas, and—unlike lower-middle-class women from urban high schools—most knew virtually no one on campus. Getting to the flagship was such a reach from where they came from that they had left their peers behind.

Throughout the book we sometimes refer to upper- and upper-middle-class women as "more privileged" or "affluent" and to those from middle-, lower-middle-, and working-class backgrounds as "less privileged" or "disadvantaged." We group middle-class women with the "less privileged" because the most meaningful dividing line at MU was between upper- and upper-middle-class women, who could fully participate in the social life of the university, and everyone else—whose college experience was defined by a sense of financial constraint. Fifty-five percent of student participants (and women on the floor more generally) were from more privileged backgrounds, while the remaining 45% were from less privileged backgrounds.

Class Culture and Class-Based Resources

Background characteristics such as parental education, occupation, and economic resources are associated with a variety of other differences. To look at Amy—a working-class woman—is to see how social class permeates all aspects of experience and presentation.[19]

Amy grew up on a farm outside of an in-state town so small that she was excited when a member of the research team—a lifelong resident of the state—had actually heard of it. She explained that "everybody knows everybody's business. At home, I go to the gas station and know everyone who works there, and pretty much everyone I see along the way." She knew exactly three people from high school who attended MU: one close friend, one older student, and a guy she described as a "dirty boy." It is not clear what she meant by this. She did communicate, though, that she did not view him as a possible source of social support. She relied heavily on her friend from home who lived downstairs in the same dorm. She looked forward to eating with her on Monday, Wednesday, and Friday. The rest of the time she "grabbed something" from the food court, as she had no one to eat with and was unwilling to eat alone. In contrast, affluent women tended to arrive knowing a lot of people on campus and thus had many possible dinner partners.

Amy was very lonely and nearly broke down in tears during one of our first conversations. She found just about everything about the university and Fairview overwhelming and scary. Making matters worse was the fact that her assigned roommate didn't show up, leaving her alone in her room during the first crucial weeks of the year. She felt so isolated that she slept with the door open and the TV on the first few nights. She told us that she couldn't go anywhere alone—not to meals, not to class, not anywhere. We asked her why, to which she responded that she was not used to the "city." She told us that she was "afraid someone is going to reach out and grab me." She laughed as she said this, but she seemed seriously afraid. Unlike students from New York and Chicago, who found Fairview quaint, she found it terrifying. She lacked life experiences that would have made adjusting to college easier. Although she was wickedly funny, she didn't have the right set of social expectations or social skills for this context. As Jenny Stuber argues in her book, *Inside the College Gates: How Class and Culture Matter in Higher Education,* more affluent students approach college primed to "meet people" and see the expansion of social networks as a central part of college.[20]

Making matters still worse for Amy was the fact that Residential Life did not allow students to occupy a double room alone unless they paid more. As this was out of the question, she spent her first month on campus uncertain about her living situation. She was going to have to move to a different room or get a roommate but did not know which would happen. Amy was scared of moving because she was worried about how she would transport her stuff even though—compared with others on the floor—she had only a few, comparatively cheap, belongings. When asked whether her dad might come back to help, she seemed to think that was ridiculous. In contrast, most of the upper-middle-class women took parental rescues for granted. For example, when Julie's roommate moved out, her upper-middle-class parents drove several hours to move Julie's best friend, Angela, into the room. Not only did they move Angela's stuff, but they bought a new carpet for the room, cut and fit it, and rearranged the furniture—including bunking the beds (a task requiring a nontrivial amount of labor, frustration, and a specific tool only available from residence hall staff).

Amy seemed to view college as something to endure. She seemed to have missed the pep talk on college as the "best time of your life." While her initial experiences did not provide any reason to believe that college was fun, affluent women who had a rough start were more likely to have an optimistic (and somewhat self-fulfilling) belief that that the fun was about to begin. More privileged women approached college with the expectation that attendance and graduation were inevitable. As upper-class Abby told us, "I don't really know anyone who didn't go to college. By me, everyone goes to college and everyone's parents have gone to college. I never thought of another option. I thought it would be real fun" (Y4). In contrast, Amy's dad would have preferred her to join the military.[21]

Amy's challenges extended beyond the social. She was overwhelmed by her classes almost as soon as the semester started, although her schedule was composed of basic algebra (a remedial non-credit math course), criminal justice, karate, and a remedial English class. Her remedial classes hint at the quality of the high school she attended and her low level of academic preparation. At this pace, it would take semesters to simply catch up, before enrollment in all credit-earning classes was possible. Amy also faced technical barriers that made completing her schoolwork difficult; for example, she could not get her computer to work. She took it to university services to get it fixed, but they broke it further, which left her stumped. Whereas the parents of more affluent students had resources to buy a new computer, or find an expert in town to fix it immediately, Amy was left with a nonfunctional machine.

Like Amy, other less privileged women started college short not only on funds but on other class-based resources. Table 1.3 details some of the most crucial of these resources that divided affluent and disadvantaged women from the moment they set foot on campus. Throughout the book we will see the myriad ways these class-based resources mattered.

Table 1.3. Class-based resources

- How many people women knew on campus, who they knew, who parents knew ("social capital")
- Expectation of college attendance and graduation
- Extensiveness of college search and selection process
- Expectation that college will be fun, orientation to "meeting people"
- Experience with cities, racial and religious diversity, cosmopolitanism
- Experience living away from home or traveling with peers (summer camps, sports)
- Academic preparation
- Expense and number of material possessions (e.g., cars, comforters, electronics)
- Self-presentation—orthodontia, fashion, makeup, grooming (hair care, tanning, etc.)
- Quality of parental academic advising
- Availability of parents for "rescues"
- Parental support of tuition, fees, books, living expenses, study abroad, unpaid internships, etc.

Social Class, Gender Style, and Orientations to College

Women also differed with respect to why they chose MU and what they expected from college (see Appendix A for women's initial orientations). The relationship between class background and orientation to college is complex. Just over half (25 women, 53%) could be classified as direct recruits, in that they came to college with the intent to embark on one of the three pathways described in the Introduction. These women had distinct sets of resources, gender styles, and ideas about what college should be about; as a result, they were *primed to party, cultivated for success,* or *motivated for mobility* before they even encountered the institutional environment at MU. Direct recruits were more likely than others to stay on track; however, those not looking for the party pathway still had to contend with the temptations and obstacles that it presented.

The second group (22 women, 47%) included those for whom it was much less clear which pathway they would take. Most were at MU by default—from feeder high schools or because other options fell through. Their profiles were marked by greater ambiguity and indecision and did not neatly coalesce into one of the three types listed above. As a result, no single pathway was, at least initially, an obvious fit. Coming in the most malleable, these women were most shaped by the organizational arrangements they encountered.

Primed to Party

Students from out of state had to make an intentional decision to cross state boundaries to attend college. Most visited or considered at least half a dozen schools. For ten affluent, out-of-state women (21%, or 48% of those from out of state) MU's reputation as a "party school" with big-time sports and "spirit" was the primary draw.[22] Socialites Tara and Naomi, profiled in Chapter 5, exemplify women who were primed to party and, as such, were direct recruits to the party pathway. As Tara described, she wanted "a college town and a big school [and] sports and everything. I looked at three other schools but I really liked it here and knew people that went here. . . . I think it's really pretty" (Y1).

Although other students appreciated these same features, these women were unique in the weight they gave to social concerns. Naomi's parents, for example, initially wanted her to stay in state and attend a roughly comparable school. But Naomi worried that she would "hang out with the same people from high school" as "it's mainly [in-state] people. It doesn't really bring in a lot of outside [people]" (Y1). MU was a place where she knew some people already but where she would be able to expand her networks and "meet new people." In addition, Naomi had set her sights on the MU pom team. She noted, "I was looking for a dance team. That was my top thing" (Y1). She was able to convince her skeptical parents to shell out considerably more money for MU on the basis of social rather than academic reasons.

In selecting MU for its social appeal, women like Tara and Naomi were expressing their identities. Most had been in the thick of social life in their high schools—involved in cheer or dance teams, student government, the yearbook, and other highly visible activities. For example, Tara explained: "I've always been involved, so I wanted to be in an organization. . . . I wanted to meet new people. I grew up with activities and parties. I like dances and stuff like that" (Y1). They were overtly feminine and identified as "girly." When asked what she liked to do with her friends, Tara listed shopping, "talk[ing] about boys, read[ing] magazines. I love doing all the girly stuff with girlfriends" (Y1). Most had interest in expensive things and looking good. As Naomi proclaimed, "I'm high maintenance. . . . I like nice things [laughs]. I guess in a sense, I like things brand name" (Y1).

At the same time, most of these women did not view themselves as academically talented. Tara, when asked to describe herself, told Laura that "I'm athletic and I'm not that smart but I have common sense, like I've never been book smart" (Y1). Academic motivation was also an issue. For example, Naomi was from a state with a top flagship institution. Her siblings had both gone to this school, but she did not want to go there because she "thought it would be too hard so I just didn't even want to try it" (Y1). She was interested in MU because she perceived the academics to be less rigorous than at a more elite public school.

Attractive, social, and conventionally feminine women like Tara and Naomi expected college to provide opportunities to build on the successes that had defined their lives in high school. They correctly understood that participation in the Greek system was the way to do this. They anticipated sorority life well in advance of arrival on campus and were impatient for it to begin. Naomi, among others, felt that school "sucked the first month 'cause rush usually begins in September in most schools and in this case it didn't start until January" (Y1).

This approach to college is not possible without high levels of parental financial support. The costs of supporting socially oriented children during college were vast. For instance, beyond out-of-state tuition, fees, and room and board, Naomi's additional monthly upkeep her first year was (conservatively) around $600: $250 for clothes, $150 for dinners, $100 toward appearance (for example, makeup, hair, nails), $50 in alcohol, and $50 for taxis. These women would also require considerable support after college to maintain their lifestyles. Some, in crossing state lines for the perfect party experience, would actually exceed their parents' (considerable) means. The costs of this decision would become clear only after graduation.

Most did not imagine themselves as heading toward graduate or professional school. To the extent that they envisioned careers, they imagined working in fashion or the media—something "stylish." As Tara told us, "I just want to work in the media, whether it's TV or radio or movies or music. I like entertainment, sports, fashion" (Y3). Their plans with respect to marriage and children were often more defined than their career goals. In her first interview, Tara stated that she was "definitely wife material. I'm gonna be such an amazing wife" (Y1). At eighteen, Naomi had even decided the gender and order of her future children—"girl boy girl that's how my family is . . . or my mom's family was. I just like it like that" (Y1).

For Tara, like many others, it was a given that her husband would be successful. None of the women were so crass as to explicitly say that they would only marry someone who made a lot of money. However, they recognized the basic sociological fact that people tend to associate with others like themselves.[23] Thus, Tara was not worried about finding the right man. As she explained:

> I'm honestly just attracted to someone that's ambitious and driven. That's what I am attracted to so I don't really worry that the person I fall for will be like that. I feel like social classes fit together. The people I run around with come from money and they're all on the right path to finding good careers. . . . I don't feel like it's I would have to go and search for [them]. It's [who] I hang out with. (Y5)

In previous generations, women like Tara might have sought a husband in college. However, none of these women expected to be engaged by graduation, and most were aiming for marriage closer to thirty than twenty.

Women who were primed to party would enter into the most accessible and developed pathway on campus. However, not all of these women had equal resources. As we will see in Chapter 5, variations in resources shaped their experiences both in college and in the transition out.

Cultivated for Success

Seven affluent out-of-state students (15%, or 33% of those from out of state) chose MU for academic reasons. Women like Erica and Taylor, achievers profiled in Chapter 7, had been cultivated for success and were thus direct recruits to the professional pathway. The parents of these women took an active role in the college selection process, researching MU's academic programs with their children. "Fit" with women's interests and abilities—along with the quality of selected programs—trumped price in the decision-making calculus.

The involvement of parents is woven through the narratives of these women (and strikingly absent from those of other groups). Statements like "Dad made me look here my junior year" (Brenda, Y1) and "I didn't even really want to visit. But my dad knew the business school was really good" (Lydia, Y1) made it evident that their selection of MU was heavily guided. Erica's story is typical. Her parents not only helped her identify a school and a major, but they also set clear expectations for academic performance. They let her know that they were sending her out of state to MU for the business school and only the business school: "My mom told me, 'If you're not gonna get into business school, then you're gonna transfer.' So I made it a serious goal to get in" (Y2).

These women benefited heavily from their parents' intimate knowledge of higher education. Upon arrival at MU, they had absorbed the importance of obtaining an education, developed confidence in their ability to do so, and internalized a work ethic that would guide them through. For example, Taylor credits her parents—a professor and CPA—with far more than helping her get into MU:

> My parents have always really valued education. I think they pretty much told my sister and I we can do whatever we want, [and] they really meant it. I just don't think a lot of people are even offered like, "Oh, maybe you can be a doctor." They said, "If you want to do it, you can do it." Not "Oh, you're not smart enough," or "That's not for you." I just think they really

encouraged us. They were both very successful and they both worked hard for what they did. So they're a role model, and I just always felt like they were supporting me whatever I decided. (Y5)

In Chapter 7, we will see that high levels of parental involvement defined the college careers of the most academically successful group of women.

Women who were cultivated for success rejected the extreme "girliness" of those who arrived primed to party. Still conventionally feminine, they devoted significantly less time to personal appearance. As a sophomore, Erica ranted about what she referred to as "dumb girls":

No one wants to be friends with a dumb girl. . . . So many girls . . . care too much about unimportant things. . . . [A dumb girl] just cares so much about boys, cares so much about her weight, cares so much about what other people think about her. (Y2)

They also had more defined career goals and prioritized these highly. As Erica told Elizabeth:

Whether that's based on what my parents have instilled in me or what. . . . I've always been someone who wants to have my own money, have my own career. . . . I just don't see myself being someone who marries young and lives off of some boy's money. (Y4)

Taylor expressed a similar sentiment:

A lot of these girls are like, "I'm just going to marry a rich man." . . . I just think there's a more important idea than I'm going to be tanned and cute to find a guy. . . . It's just weird to me. . . . I think some of the sororities were called the "perfect wife" sorority. That was their reputation. (Y5)

By rejecting dependence on a man (as well as a heavily feminine interactional style), these women defined themselves as "professionals" who would be able to support themselves.

Yet they were not wallflowers. They saw MU's social opportunities as a plus. Erica and Taylor were roommates and were interviewed together their first year. Both admitted that the strong Greek system was a big factor in their decisions to attend MU. Taylor was entranced by the scale of MU's Greek system: "I just love the houses here, they're like mansions." They both mentioned that they had heard that MU was a party school, and they liked this idea because to them it meant that "there's always something to do, like always an event to go to," not "like a small school where sometimes there's like absolutely nothing to do." Erica and Taylor were also excited by sororities as a "way to meet people and make friends" (Y1).

That Erica and Taylor, who were carefully groomed by their parents to pursue academic success, were so enamored of the social world of MU suggests the widespread appeal of the party pathway. In Chapter 7, we will learn more about how direct recruits to the professional pathway responded to the seductions of the party scene.

Motivated for Mobility

At the other end of the class spectrum were women whose very different circumstances led them to seek out an MU education. This group included six women who hailed from working-class communities, as well as two lower-middle-class women who were from similar hometowns (17%, or 31% of those from in state). Attending MU marked women like Megan, Heather, and Stacey (strivers profiled in Chapter 6) as the most ambitious of their peers, with potential for upward mobility. A few would come to view their hometowns in a positive light and identify with their working-class roots. However, they were initially motivated by dreams of escape.

Some of these women were from small, rural towns in which cornfields stretched as far as the eye could see. As Megan described of her hometown:

> It's a really, really, little town. I live in the country. . . . If you drive around there is like one house on a road. . . . We tore down our barn a long time ago, because it was really old and it was like falling down and stuff. In the summer we're going to build a new barn because my grandpa is running out of room because he has like four horses. (Y5)

Others came from small, predominantly working-class agricultural cities that, like Megan's little town, had a median family income well below the state average and lower high school graduation rates. Such areas were also characterized by cultural homogeneity. As Heather and her roommate, Stacey, who often finished each other's sentences, noted:

Heather: Everybody's a farmer, everybody's the same, there's like—
Stacey: No Jews, not many blacks, lotta Mexicans . . . hardly gays or anything. (Y1)

A lack of exposure to diversity sometimes translated into attitudes about race, sexuality, and religion at odds with those they encountered on campus.

These women were unique in that they actually left these communities. They described the bleak realities of those who stayed behind. Heather told us, "A lot of our friends that we used to hang out with all the time—the ones that have stayed there—are just worthless. They're not doing anything with their lives. It's not what I want for myself" (Y1). They watched as friends and relatives with little economic prospects fell into drug and alcohol abuse—in one case even dying from an overdose. They listened when their parents told them that they "can't even get more than $13 an hour without a degree" and looked on as "seventeen- to twenty-year-old girls" in their hometowns had babies (Amanda Y4, Y3).

These women told narratives of escape, in which attending a large state school played a central role. As one explained:

> My cousins, my best friends, they're gonna live in [my hometown] forever, in that same house and work for their dad. . . . They didn't want to go to college. They didn't want to travel. They didn't want to do different things all the time and see different places. They want to stay in their comfort zone and do that. And so, I can respect that that's what they wanna do. *It's just somehow I wiggled through.* (Alana Y1, emphasis added)

Heather, like others, indicated that these escapes were narrowly achieved and highly precarious:

> The thing with that town . . . It's like a black hole. It really is. It's . . . that town just sucks. Like, you get sucked in and if you don't get out, you never will. . . . I really don't ever wanna go back there. (Y4)

As she realized, the problem with a black hole is that it continues to exert gravitational pull. She continued, "a lot of people try to go away and they always end up back there" (Y4). Escape thus required constant vigilance and sustained effort.

As much as they wanted to escape, these women's identities were tightly linked to home.[24] As Megan noted, home was a place where "home town people, who . . . like me, live out in the country and are laid back" were located (Y2). They were also embedded in dense webs of connection and support. Megan's best friends whom she had known since grade school were all still back home, as was her boyfriend, both of her (divorced) parents, her much younger brother, her older brother (who never finished high school), her grandparents, and the family farm. When she was living at home, she contributed by doing chores, babysitting her younger brother, and offering some of her funds from outside work to the family. Whereas affluent youth were expected, as a rite of passage, to leave home, these women were integral parts of local emotional and labor ecosystems. Leaving meant potentially severing deep and meaningful ties to their communities.

Most were highly pragmatic in their approach to college. For example, Stacey was aware of the need to make her education translate directly into employment. As she described:

> I just want my major to be something I'm gonna use. There's so many people who are like, I'm gonna do this. Well, what are you gonna do with that? Like are there jobs out there when you're out of college? . . . So I don't want to be like that. I want to know that when I get out of college there's gonna be a job for me. (Y1)

They tended to believe that if they worked hard, then they would realize the promise of a college education. As Megan noted, "I take [school] very, very seriously. . . . I feel like I have to get A's or I just didn't do good enough, like I didn't try hard enough" (Y2).

This population needed college to provide the credentials, skills, training, and knowledge necessary for upward mobility. All of these women had to take on substantial debt to attend MU and had to work long hours as well. As MU was substantially more expensive than the regional campuses and community colleges closer to home, the decision to attend was a bold and difficult investment in the future. As Megan told us, "I choose the hardest way to do it, I chose the hardest way. . . . It would be much simpler just to live at home and to drive to [closer college] and then save like $6,000" (Y1). Yet women like Megan overcame these barriers to attending MU because, as another put it, "[MU] was my dream college and my dream place, and I just wanted to go for at least one year" (Alyssa Y5).

As Amy's story suggested, these women lacked the time or the money to pull off the polished femininity of the socialites. For Megan, socialite attention to appearance was yet another off-putting difference: "People at MU are like, they have to do their hair before class. They have to look a certain way. . . . I don't care, I pull my hair up in a ponytail and go. I don't have time to do my hair. . . . I couldn't relate to them in any way" (Y2). Others, like Heather and Stacey, displayed a louder femininity that clashed with the gender styles of their affluent floormates.

Virtually all of these women arrived in a relationship with a man who was not attending college. Such a pairing was almost nonexistent among the affluent women but typical for those motivated by mobility. For example, when I asked Megan whether her boyfriend (and future husband) had gone to college, she exclaimed, "No. Oh my gosh, he barely made it through high school! Some people just don't take to school" (Y3). Given the gender gap in college attendance among the less affluent, this is not surprising. Knowing that their mates' economic prospects were limited, these women never entertained the possibility of dependence on a man. Their success or failure rested not only on navigating higher education but also on cultivating relationships with men who were supportive of their career goals.

These women were extraordinary young people from ordinary places, as opposed to the somewhat ordinary women from extraordinary privilege. With little or no support from their parents—no college tours, consultations about majors or requirements, and little help in footing the bill—attending college was far from inevitable. Our interactions with these women over five years led us to believe that a number of the brightest of the women were in this group, although we did not measure this with any objective indicators. Their drive also distinguished them from most of the more privileged women, for whom college was an entitlement—not a hard-earned dream.

These women would run up against frustrating and relentless obstacles, many of which were posed by the dominance of the party pathway at MU. Like others, some were tempted to participate in the party scene—although their limited resources would doom such attempts to failure. In Chapter 6 we detail the ways that the social environment and academic infrastructure tailored to socialite interests posed unique challenges for those seeking mobility.

MU by Default

Women in this group did not come to MU with a singular focus on the party scene. Although some were oriented toward achievement, none had been carefully cultivated for success. From predominately middle-class hometowns and better schools, they did not display a driving determination to escape their circumstances. Instead, these 22 women (47%, or 69% of those from in state and 19% of those from out of state) landed at MU seemingly by default. Unlike other groups, these women represented a range of class backgrounds, from upper class to lower-middle class.

Upper-middle-class roommates Morgan and Natasha arrived at MU the way most in-state women did—from an in-state feeder high school. As they explained:

Morgan: There's probably like . . . 250 people from [capital city suburb] that go here.
Brian: And how many high schools does [your hometown] have?[25]
Morgan: Just one. We had a class of like 880.
Brian: So at any given time, like right now, you're saying that there are 250 [suburb] kids [entering MU]?
Natasha: That graduated with us.
Brian: Who all came here?
Natasha: Yeah.
Brian: So it's maybe like one-fourth of your class came here?
Morgan: Yeah. [And] like one-fourth went to Rival U, one-fourth didn't go anywhere, and [one-fourth went to]—
Natasha: Midwest State.
Morgan: Yeah, and everywhere else.

For those coming from high schools where the majority of the graduating class moved on to an in-state university, attending MU was simply what you did next. It was not a process that necessarily involved much thought. Natasha, for example, "applied here, Rival U, and Private U at my mom's request. And I was kind of deciding between Rival U and MU, and I don't know, I just decided to go here. *No particular reason*" (Y1, emphasis added). Similarly, Morgan told us, "You just go to MU or Rival U." Having decided that Rival U's campus was "really ugly," she simply came here (Y1).

Neither Morgan nor Natasha was particularly academically inclined. There was even some question about whether Morgan would get in to MU with her high school grades. Nor were they socially oriented. In fact, they claimed not to be friends with any of the 250 high school peers that accompanied them to college. Although this duo was unusually passive, vague expectations defined all of the women in this group.

Take middle-class Blair: Like many others, her selection of MU over other in-state schools was based in part on family loyalties to the university. Her mother had spent a few years at MU, and her older brother was also enrolled there at the time she entered. Blair first claimed that she "thought I'd get a better education here than Midwest State. So that's basically why I came." Within the span of a minute she also admitted, "I was just excited 'cause it belonged to a major football conference school [laughs]. You know it's gonna be fun" (Y1). Blair was hardly unusual. Many students in this group came with an inchoate idea of college as about both hitting the books and partying hard, but mostly without well-developed plans of how to do either of these things well.

In the case of less privileged women, limited family resources contributed to a lack of clarity. Lower-middle-class Carrie, for instance, had five siblings. During her high school years, a messy divorce demanded most of her parents' attention and decimated their already limited finances. Carrie was "really shy in [high] school" and had only a few friends—one of them being Blair, whom she followed to MU (Y1). Carrie's older sisters, graduating in better times for the family, had left high school with strong academic records, and her mother—an educator—had helped them to apply for merit-based scholarships. Carrie herself had slipped through the cracks with solid but not stellar grades and did not describe herself as academically talented like her sisters. When we first met her, Carrie seemed lost. She was unsure about what she wanted to study, ultimately changing majors several times.

For some of these women, MU was also far from a first choice. For example, in high school, upper-middle-class Bailey had planned on playing volleyball at an out-of-state college of her choice. Stress fractures in her shins her senior year foreclosed that possibility. Without volleyball, it was MU or Rival U, and Rival U was just too close to home. A few affluent out-of-state women also arrived at MU following disappointing rejections from top flagship schools. They were anything but thrilled with the prospects of landing at MU. As one noted, "I really didn't like this school. I thought it was depressing" (Abby Y1).

Two outliers in this group were Whitney and Alicia, who had equally developed social and academic plans. For example, Whitney "just couldn't imagine doing anything else" other than joining a sorority. She had even tried to get an early edge on the college social scene: "I was [at MU] almost every weekend last year, so I got out into the party scene, and I totally understood everything." At the same time, Whitney had been at the top of her high school class, initially planned to go into the competitive business school, and anticipated a career "in executive management. An upper position, for sure" (Y1). Straddling two clashing orientations, however, made her vulnerable to being pushed in one direction or another.

Women who arrived at MU by default highlight the importance of institutional context. From where they started college (in a "party dorm" at a middle-tier state school), the party pathway was an unavoidable feature of the environment—one to which they were neither entirely inclined nor disinclined from the start. The directions they took were not determined by who they were or what they wanted at the start of college, but were instead a result of interaction with the organizational features of MU. For these women, being at another type of university, or possibly just a different dormitory, might have set them on a different pathway.

CHAPTER 2

The Party Pathway

Web sites designed to match students to colleges consistently refer those looking for the "party scene" and "Greek life" to Midwest U. On one, an insider asked to provide the stereotype of students at MU noted that the university is full of kids who came to party and that academics suffer as a result. Some commenters sought to debunk the assumption that this applies to all MU students. For example, one even reassured future non-Greeks that they would be part of the majority. However, no one pretended that it was easy to ignore the Greek system. Another insider warned prospective students that they might find themselves overwhelmed and "disgusted" by the Greek lifestyle.

In labeling MU as a party school, observers refer not only to the predilections of a highly visible minority, but also to aspects of the university infrastructure. Supports for a social approach to college are built into the university, enabling MU to offer students a robust party pathway. Given the ubiquity and breadth of the party pathway, we devote a chapter to describing it. We show that university-controlled resources are unevenly distributed in favor of the Greek system—the organizational heart of MU's party scene. We discuss ways that Greek life is "greedy," making it hard for members to focus on studies or employment or to form ties with non-Greeks. We describe the organization of the residence hall system, which funnels socially oriented freshmen into sororities and fraternities. In terms of academics, we show that the university enables student social lives through the provision of "easy" majors.

Greek Life

MU's campus is dotted with over forty large, stately mansions housing Greek organizations. White columns, massive wooden doors, large porches, and meticulously groomed grounds make them one of the more picturesque features of the campus. These houses are mostly located in two places. The first Greek area runs down Main Street and, perhaps symbolically, through an academic center of campus. Here, Greek houses directly face classroom buildings and libraries. On balmy spring and summer days, students taking a test in one building can hear the party across the street. If they look out the window they may see sorority women sunning on front lawns or splashing in baby pools, groups of boisterous beer holding students, or perhaps a game of golf winding its way over academic grounds. The second area is a long street dominated entirely by fraternity and sorority houses. It stretches from the recreation center and sweeps around the grounds of the football stadium, curving toward the basketball arena. On game days, the street comes alive as Greek students head out in force to tailgate: drinking, partying, and otherwise creating MU school spirit.

Thursday through Saturday nights in the fall and late spring, throngs of scantily clad women—dressed in their party best and stumbling drunkenly in high heels—can be seen making their way across fraternity lawns. Often a pattern becomes apparent. Lingerie suggests a "Victoria's Secret" party; low-cut and undersized golf wear points to the "Golf Pro/Ho" theme; and groups of underdressed schoolgirls to a "School Teacher/Sexy Student" night. Loud music throbs and a sense of excitement pervades. If you get close enough, the smell of stale beer seeps out of the houses.

University Resources and Support for Greek Life

Only 17% of MU's undergraduate population is Greek. Seemingly, Greek houses should have only a bit part to play in defining life at Midwest University. However, the nature and extent of socializing here—as at many large state universities—is strongly influenced by the social mission of the Greek system. Other vibrant social scenes exist, but Greeks are considerably more visible and powerful on campus than their numbers suggest. This is a result of explicit university support and Greek monopoly over crucial resources.

The buildings housing fraternities or sororities are generally owned either by the national organization or the local chapter—not by the university. MU's predominantly white Greek chapters own valuable property on and near campus, which affords these organizations a measure of power unlike any other student organization. Even if the university banned all Greek chapters from campus, it would be unable to touch the property. This ties the hands of university officials—turning Greek row into a ghost town would not only hurt the marketable charm of MU but reduce student housing near campus.

Fraternities and sororities are subject to the same rules as other student organizations, and MU has responded to alcohol and hazing infractions by expelling chapters from campus. However, this is a lengthy and complicated process. The recent expulsion of a fraternity chapter at MU was a multiyear process accomplished only after repeated infractions. Reports of hazing and alcohol violations had placed this fraternity on MU's radar for years. The organization was given a "deferred suspension" and required to avoid further incidents in order to remain in good standing. Parents subsequently contacted the university to complain that their children—pledges in the fraternity—had been deprived of sleep, yelled at and intimidated, dropped off in the country, and forced to find their way home. The Student Organization Ethics Board conducted an investigation and, bolstered by a former member's confirmation of hazing, found the fraternity in violation of the Student Organization Code. They recommended a two-year expulsion, which was instituted three years after the initial complaints. The MU chapter was reinstituted in 2010, after being "recolonized" with new members.

In part because the process of expelling a house is so complicated, these events usually only occur every few years. They tend to be cyclical, with expulsions involving the same "problem" houses over time.[1] There are few lasting consequences for the system itself. Making an example of a particular house and its members reduces university liability, but the Greek system continues to thrive.

The alcohol-fueled underage party scene on campus is mostly located in fraternities. This is due in part to the university's uneven enforcement of state drinking laws, which have the effect of pushing partying out of residence halls and into fraternities. Enforcement is most rigorous in the residence halls. During the time of our study, resident assistants, police officers, and gun-carrying peer police patrolled the halls enforcing a zero-tolerance policy for drugs or alcohol. Several women on our floor were documented for infractions—such as simply having alcohol in their rooms—that they felt were minor. These infractions came with steep consequences: a $300 fine, mandatory attendance at an eight-hour alcohol class, and a year's probation.

In contrast, massive quantities of alcohol are readily available at fraternity parties. The Interfraternity Council (IFC), which oversees the fraternities, intervenes when parties become particularly loud or boisterous. After the IFC issues advance warning of entry, the party goes into lockdown. During lockdown fraternity members call for all underage drinkers to vacate the main rooms of the house—sometimes literally shoving them into rooms and stairwells and locking the doors. As one woman described:

> They go into lockdown a lot here. . . . Everyone has to go into a room and the doors are closed, it's just really dumb. . . . Literally a red light goes on. I thought it was a joke at first but there's a red light. The last time I went . . . I was just like "alright this is ridiculous." (Leah Y1)

Lockdown sometimes endangered women's safety. For example, Alicia's arm was injured during a raid, requiring a hospital visit. Being trapped in stairwells and private rooms with drunk men also restricted women's ability to leave uncomfortable or threatening situations.

IFC intervention, however, effectively serves as a "cop prevention system." Typically, by the time IFC officers enter, the party has quieted down and evidence of underage drinking has been hidden. MU police tend to intervene only when Fairview residents complain or if IFC reports an out-of-control party. Perhaps the biggest legal threat for students associated with attending a fraternity party comes when trying to leave—we found that MU police tested, cited, and sometimes arrested drunk students as they walked home.[2]

MU's fraternity houses thus control some of the most valuable resources on campus: space to congregate socially, a large supply of alcohol, and the promise of legal impunity. Insufficient financial resources prevent black and multicultural Greek organizations from owning chapter houses in which to host large parties.[3] They can organize off-campus parties in houses or apartments, without the benefit of IFC or university protection. The national chapters of most sororities restrict them from hosting parties. Sororities sometimes organize sober transportation to lessen the threat of legal sanction while walking home or of sexual assault in staying overnight with men they do not trust. Other women have to rely on cabs or the campus "drunk bus"—neither of which are reliable given the high demand.

Even if women are willing to socialize without alcohol, the university offers comparatively few opportunities. As described later, sterile dormitories are structured in ways that reduce coed group interaction. University dinners and movies occur long before most parties begin, and the few university-sponsored nighttime activities, like the midnight run to Wal-Mart, are seen as uncool. The women on our floor, who loved to dance, often complained that there was nowhere to do this other than fraternities.

House parties and bars offer social alternatives for upperclassmen, who are allowed to live off of campus and are often of legal drinking age, but freshmen have no such outlets. This has consequences for the distribution of power on campus. Fraternity men choose party themes, distribute alcohol to engineer social interactions in their favor, decide who can enter and who can leave parties, and generally dictate the social lives of the campus's youngest and most vulnerable residents.[4]

Greek chapters—and particularly fraternities—at MU also have strong ties to the administration. One of the Greek system's staunchest supporters during our study was the dean of students. The dean of students had himself been a member of a fraternity and the recipient of Greek-related awards. His view of Greek life was positive. For example, in an interview with a national sorority, he explained his views on Greek life:

> Host institutions haven't always moved into that positive arena where they can see the advantage of partnerships with fraternities and sororities. Institutions have, in the past, tended to have a supervisory mentality about fraternal organizations. Today I think they are moving away from that and toward a partner mentality.[5]

Most notable here is the language of "partnership." Rather than subjugating the Greek system to the authority of the university, the two are described as equals. In this model, the university affords these organizations special respect and treatment. The university's partnership with the Greek system is institutionalized, most notably in an advisory board that provides direct access to the dean. Having the ear of university leadership represents a powerful advantage for Greeks on campus—one not available to most students.

Greek Bureaucracy and the Social Calendar

Greek chapters are part of (and are themselves) highly structured, hierarchical, and bureaucratic organizations. For example, at the national level, the North-American Interfraternity Conference oversees fraternities, while the National Panhellenic Conference oversees sororities. Each chapter is also part of a national organization that represents the particular sorority or fraternity across the country. Along with the campus-level IFC there is a campus-level "Panhell," and both answer to their parallel national organizations. These organizations help to create a unified Greek front and facilitate cooperation among houses. Greek students thus become a powerful constituency, with shared leadership, interests, and goals. Other groups and organizations are rarely able to combine forces under a single focus or access such a large block of similar students.

Within each house there is another layer of bureaucracy. At the top is an executive committee, typically composed of the president, vice president, and a series of "chairs"—for example, for finance, risk management, social events, and recruitment. Training for these positions can be intense. As one woman, who eventually became a chair of recruitment, reported:

> Second semester sophomore year [and] . . . first semester junior year I was a recruitment assistant. And then second semester junior year, first semester senior year, I'm the actual chair. 'Cause you train for a year. . . . It's a lot of work. . . . We're supposed to have four different recruitment retreats to get ready for recruitment. (Sydney Y4)

Specific social events, such as a big formal, also involve their own committees, with individuals in charge of specific tasks like securing a location or decorating. No task is left undelegated, and no social event goes unstaffed or unmanaged.

Having this structure in place allows Greeks to dominate the public social life of the campus. They execute large-scale social events in roughly the same fashion year after year. This regularity and predictability makes Greek-sponsored events the most well known. Over the years, this has had the effect of instituting a regular social calendar, around which much—but not all—of MU social life revolves (see Table 2.1).

Table 2.1. The social calendar

- Fraternity rush
- Homecoming
- Sorority rush
- Pledging and initiation
- MU Talent
- Spring break
- MU Game Week

The social year kicks off with fraternity rush in mid-September—just a few weeks after students arrive. This process, along with sorority rush, involves a series of social events that incorporate far greater numbers of students than actually join Greek houses. Preceding and during rush, fraternities throw massive parties to demonstrate their status (and lure potential members with the promise of beer and women). They quickly acquire pledges, who are assigned the grunt work of the party scene for the fall semester, before being initiated in the spring. Pledges, for example, were often the ones picking up women in front of their dormitories on weekend evenings for transportation to parties.

Sorority rush at MU is delayed, meaning it does not start until later in the fall semester and ends in January.[6] However, an informal social process begins almost immediately, with dinners and other mingling events. Many women on our floor, even those who did not end up in sororities, attended informal social events that enabled potential new recruits to meet sorority members. Even those who had no interest in Greek life were aware that such events were taking place. Two women, for instance, felt it necessary to post the following message on their door to head off questions about whether they were rushing: "Yes, that's right. We quit. The two females who live in this room have been officially disqualified [by choice] from the rush process" (Field Notes 10/22/04). Weeks before the semester break, houses around campus could be heard practicing their rush "chants" (that is, loud songs screamed into the night) to welcome potential recruits. After rush, the massive, colorful banners adorning the sorority houses, the announcements in the college paper, and the sudden explosion of Greek attire on campus alert all but the most oblivious students to what has just transpired.

Even the academic functions of the university are interrupted by rush. Women are required to attend parties at all houses on campus during a specified time window. Our year, missing any party without an excused absence from Panhell was grounds for elimination. However, about half a dozen of the women on our floor had a math test scheduled for the morning of the first day of parties. No doubt a similar scenario was occurring on most floors, as the large math class in which they were enrolled was a basic requirement. Rather than counting this test as an excused rush absence, the test itself was rescheduled. As we wrote at the time:

> It seemed that Panhell took the issue of the women's need to take the math
> test seriously, but they took the notion of women missing any one of the

parties even more seriously. The Rho Gamma [rush counselor] was working with the women to make sure that it was all set up for the women to do
both. It is unclear whether Panhell intervened on behalf of the rushees
with the math instructor/math department, or whether the women worked
it out on their own. In any case, several things were clear: Panhell and the
women assumed that rush trumped the math test, and that the math test
must be moved. (Field Notes 10/22/04)

In this case, academic requirements were arranged around the Greek social calendar, rather than the other way around.

Many additional events on the social calendar are not technically Greek-
only and are officially sponsored by the Midwest University Student Foundation or other campus-wide organizations. Yet a quick glance at who is
involved reveals that Greek organizations are the driving force. For example,
MU Talent was a large-scale variety show that sororities and fraternities
participated in each year, possible in part because houses demanded that
the newest members put in hours of practice each week. Indeed, as we discuss below, the time required of the Greek women on the floor was extensive, bordering on hazing.[7]

Similarly, MU Game Week centers around a sporting event open to any
all-female or all-male teams. Some dormitories field teams, and there is
always a highly competitive team drawing from the whole student body.
However, the event is mostly populated with Greeks. Many houses own
sporting gear, facilitating the training and enrollment of at least one team
each year. The partying that ensues during MU Game Week is certainly as
integral to the tradition as the sporting event itself and is most centrally
located in the fraternities—although Greeks and non-Greeks alike (especially women) are welcome to attend.

Other events, like Homecoming or big game days, are standard college
social fare. Yet the scale and nature of these occasions at MU bears a Greek
imprint. Homecoming, for instance, has in recent years been kicked off by
"Big Man on Campus," a Greek-organized charity fundraiser, where Greek
men compete for the title in a bawdy pageant.[8] Greeks are also an integral
part of the homecoming parade, turn out en masse for the game, and form
a critical component of spirited activities like the "Nearly Naked Mile Run."
On game days, groups of students in Greek gear are highly visible on the
tailgating area surrounding the football stadium.

Much off-campus partying surrounding social events is also linked to the
Greek system. Although off-campus houses and apartments offer non-Greek

upperclassmen a social refuge, Greek members in organizations that allow senior-year "living out" snatch up some of the choicest properties near campus. They can easily fill multiroom houses or blocks of apartments that serve as additional party spaces. Many campus bars are also dominated by Greeks. By junior year most sorority women had stopped regularly attending fraternity parties and shifted their attentions to the bar scene. As one sorority member noted, "Connelly's is the Greek bar. You know everyone in there" (Whitney Y4). Greek bar crawls, identifiable by matching T-shirts and boisterous crowds, claim other bars as temporarily Greek. Students who want to frequent a bar without encountering Greeks can do so but only if willing to stray further from campus or to bars with more niche reputations.

During spring break, the party spills out to tropical locations. Even here, Greek organizations are major players. It is not uncommon for travel companies to offer sorority and fraternity discounts, given that they facilitate the travel of large, well-to-do, party-centered groups. As one sorority member with a typical set of plans noted:

> We're planning to go on a cruise in the western Caribbean. It's Honduras, Belize, somewhere in Mexico. . . . There are about twelve of us. . . . We were trying to get everyone organized and we found out three extra people were gonna come last night. (Sydney Y4)

Clearly other students travel for spring break, but these massive groups—sometimes nearly whole fraternities or sororities—are a boon.

"Greedy" Greek Organizations

Another feature of Greek life keeps students on the party pathway: the Greek system is notoriously "greedy" of its members.[9] Particularly in top houses, the demands on students' time, commitment, and efforts limit their abilities to study, work, sustain romantic relationships, or form friendships outside of the Greek system.[10]

Just how consuming it was to be Greek was apparent when looking at our field notes from the weeks preceding MU Talent. One typical day Laura was hanging out with two roommates, Sydney and Hannah. As her notes recount:

> [Sydney] ran off and told Hannah she wouldn't be home too late (around 2 a.m.) since she had to get up early (around 7) the next morning for class.

After she left I told Hannah that 2 didn't seem early and that I didn't know how she was planning to get out of bed tomorrow. Hannah said that she really didn't have a choice since her sorority was MAKING them all go to an event tonight. She said that Sydney tried to get out of it because of her early class, but she was told that she had to go anyway (this after they had all been doing MU Talent every night). Sydney seemed tired, exhausted, and very hurried when she was there. (Field Notes 1/27/05)

Things did not necessarily get much better once women moved into their new houses the following year. As Hannah told us:

Inside of the house, there's so much stuff going on like every. . . . There's meetings we have to go to if we wanna be the special chair or something . . .'cause our whole house works on a point system. And to get the points, it's do the stuff. . . . Whoever gets the most points gets the first parking spot, gets the first room pick. . . . I'm just trying to rack enough points and do stuff and it's just so hard and . . . everything's so busy and last week with my four tests. . . . Ugh. (Hannah Y2)

Greek houses were also greedy with respect to academics. A 2.5 GPA was required to rush—and members had to meet minimum standards in order to avoid academic probation. Beyond this, skimping on studying was often critical for keeping up with the heavy demands of Greek life. This was evident in Sydney's and Hannah's experiences above, as it was for virtually all of our sorority women. For example, Whitney complained:

In the evenings, it's always something. A dinner, a meeting, stupid this, or . . . It's totally overwhelming right now. . . . I'm like, God! I don't want to do this. Just having to be somewhere at nine, right in the middle of studying in the evening. . . . Nine is a really inconvenient time. And people at the library have to come home, and then go back. It's really obnoxious. (Whitney Y2)

Staying in good standing in the sorority and with Greek peers was incompatible with doing more than the minimum necessary academically. Thus, all achiever women (discussed in Chapter 7) moved out of the sorority to finish up their degree. One explained:

I'm not there anymore. I'm done with the sorority stuff. . . . I'm not saying that people in my sorority don't [study], but they don't seem like they do. . . . It's just a crazier life . . . a lot more social functions. I love that about it, but I could never go back and do that. Going out three days, no, no, absolutely not. I can go out like once a week right now, if that. (Brenda Y5)

If keeping up with school work while being in a sorority was a challenge, working for money during the school year was virtually impossible. Not a single one of the sorority women whom we studied held a paid job while school was in session. This was in direct contrast to the striver women we discuss in Chapter 6, for whom college was as much about earning income as it was about attending classes. As one sorority woman—whose single mother was considerably less wealthy than the parents of her peers— told us:

[My mom] wanted me to do a work-study type program, and honestly I just didn't take the initiative to look into it. . . . Which is probably my fault. But I just didn't really want to do that. I just kind of felt like if it was prob- lematic for me to go here, then I shouldn't be here. And, you know, none of my friends really work. . . . [My mom] never, she would never . . . like she wants me to live up college as much as I want to do. (Mara Y4)

This quote highlights the tension between working and being fully present for the college experience available through the Greek system. For Mara, it simply was not worth it to be at MU unless she could "live up college" in a fashion similar to her friends. Despite evidence to the contrary, she ratio- nalized that her mother—if she were to fully understand the irreconcil- ability of working and being social during college—would not want her to work.

The demands of Greek life also posed problems for romantic relation- ships. Several women noted that it was difficult to find the time for a boy- friend. As Whitney—who had, in anticipation, ended a relationship before starting college—noted:

One of my friends in my house is starting to date someone, and we had so much stuff to do last night 'cause she had a paper. We had recruitment and school, a meeting, we had so much stuff to do. And then she's like, and now I have to go see him. She wants to, but now it's like an obligation. . . . It's hard. We're really busy right now, especially with recruitment. We have meetings all the time. It's just hard to manage time right now. (Whitney Y2)

Others who were interested in boyfriends during college reconsidered because of their schedules. As one explained:

I wouldn't mind having a boyfriend again, but it's a lot of work. . . . I was thinking even if I was still dating [my ex], I wouldn't have time even to see him. . . . I know girls in my [nursing] program do it. They have a boyfriend and they do nursing, but the people who do aren't really in sororities. . . . That's pretty much all they have going on. . . . Even tonight, there's phi-lanthropy and just little stuff with the house. . . . If I was doing nursing and I had a boyfriend and tried to be friends with people, it would be . . . really hard. (Brenda Y4)[11]

Here she suggests that having a boyfriend would require relinquishing the intense friendships required of sorority members—something that she was not willing to do at that point in college.

Sororities also made it hard to form and maintain friendships with non-affiliated students. Social ties with people outside of the Greek system tended to fall by the wayside quickly—even freshman year before people moved into their houses. Our resident assistant (RA), who saw this process play out repeatedly, described what it was like to be left behind:

I think the hardest part is seeing other people with their sorority stuff. They're only doing stuff with their sorority. I think that's the hardest part for them especially when they have really good friends on the floor. . . . [who] did get into the sorority and they didn't. And now [their old friends] don't have time for them anymore. . . . They're like, we were all tight. We used to hang out all the time and now you have your sorority you don't hang out with me anymore.

Despite living in close quarters with a number of non-Greek women their first year, most sorority women became close friends only with women from their house and relatively few got to know anyone outside the Greek system very well.

Indeed, although Greeks were a minority of students, they labeled every-one else as "GDIs" or "God Damn Independents." As a non-Greek woman told us:

You can tell that you get certain judgment from people . . . when you're out, and they're like—when you're first meeting someone—"oh you're in a house?" and I'm like "no." And then you can always see some sort of reaction. . . . Normally you get some kind of comment like oh GDI or some-thing like that. [Laura: What is that?] I think it stands for God Damn In-dependent. (Tracy Y4)

Greek networks were so tight that sorority members sometimes puzzled over where the rest of the campus was. As Whitney noted toward the end of her time at MU:

> It's really weird to think, where do the thirty-some thousand students live? It baffles me just 'cause I'm on [Greek row] and all I see is frats and sororities. And wherever I go, it's just, going up to meet with all of them—like the sororities and frats we hang out with. (Whitney Y4)

This had the effect of keeping Greek social worlds homogenous and closing off other options. Sorority women were unlikely to abandon a party pathway because they often had few acquaintances outside of this world.

Residence Life

In the contemporary imagination—and in carefully crafted public relations materials—college is a place where people encounter those different from themselves. In contrast, MU's residence halls were noticeably segregated. Just as academic disciplines are located in different buildings, so were various types of students. In MU residence halls, students were segregated not only by age, year in school, marital status, gender, and family situation, but also—to a large extent—by class, race/ethnicity, nationality, sexual orientation, religion, political views, fields of academic interest, and lifestyles.

Wealthy, white, out-of-state, social, Greek-oriented, and Jewish students were densely congregated in a few large residence halls (the so-called party dorms) in the "social" neighborhood. The "alternative dorm" was its own world, housing political, feminist, queer, nerdy, vegan, and intellectual students. In contrast, the modal resident of the "normal" neighborhood was less social and less affluent than those residing in the social neighborhood. Most international students lived there, as did a majority of graduate students residing on campus. Finally, the "artsy" neighborhood drew music and honors students and included a Living Learning Community (LLC) dedicated to the study of African American history and culture. This neighborhood was where many students of color lived.

The homogeneity that we observed at the first floor meeting was thus not a coincidence but a consequence of systematic sorting processes. A combination of university procedures and student preferences pooled "partiers"—

affluent white women who approached college with a social orientation—in dorms like the one that we studied. Party dorms served as on-ramps for the party pathway, feeding directly into the party scene and the Greek system.

Sorting into Residential Communities

Entering freshmen at MU are required to live on campus in university-run residence halls. This rule is based on evidence that students living on campus do better academically, are more involved on campus, and are more likely to graduate.[12] The policy works against segregation, as all students are presumably in the same boat, but there are exceptions to this rule. Married students, parents, transfer students, part-time students, those older than twenty-one, those with parents residing locally, and students pledging a fraternity in which they plan to live are permitted to live off campus.

As residence halls are designed to meet the needs of the majority of students who are single, childless, and of traditional college age, most of these exemptions are logical. These exemptions do, however, reduce diversity among students in university housing. As only freshmen are required to live on campus, most students living in the residence halls are eighteen or nineteen years old.[13] Because students who are local, have transferred, or are attending part-time are more likely to be from lower-income families, class diversity is also reduced. At the other extreme, only the most privileged of students are allowed to opt out of the first-year requirement for personal reasons rather than more practical concerns: the fraternity pledge exception—although rarely used—is available only to affluent white men, as only predominantly white fraternities have houses, and typically more affluent students join fraternities.[14]

Even with these exceptions, the fact that the majority of freshmen are required to live in the dormitories should produce heterogeneity in the residence halls. The fact that it does not is due to the overall homogeneity of the student body and the type and configuration of housing options offered by Housing Programs and Services (HPS). For example, as is the case at all but a few universities, MU's HPS places restrictions on coed living. Although both men and women are housed in the same residence halls, most floors are composed of all men or all women.

The limited number of coed floors is related to the structure of existing dormitories and administrators' notions of what is needed for such a living situation. MU trustees require different bathrooms for men and women and some kind of physical division between men's and women's sections of the floor. Thus, not all dormitories are even potential candidates for coed floors. As we detail below, single-sex floors remained even more gender-segregated because of rules limiting opposite-sex visitors—making the party scene, where women and men mingle freely, even more compelling.

Another way that the university produces housing segregation is by sponsoring an array of Living Learning Communities (LLCs) that appeal to certain types of students. Learning Communities pool those with similar backgrounds and interests on the same floor. Although these communities provide enriching experiences for those who participate, they also reduce the chances that other students on campus will have opportunities to interact with these students. For example, if fifty first-year African American students move into the LLC focused on African American history and culture, roughly 13% of the approximately 380 African American students in an entering class of about 7,300 live together on one floor. This LLC also contributes to the reputation of the artsy neighborhood as being for students of color and may thus have an even greater clustering effect.

Interest groups make other residence hall floors more homogenous. The all-white floor we studied was in part a result of students of color selecting LLCs or other residence halls where they expected to be more comfortable. It was not just our floor that happened to be all white; we saw few students of color anywhere in the dorm, except for those who were working as employees in the food court. We noted that, "most of the people working at the various food stands look like they could be students (in terms of age). Four out of the 9 or 10 employees I can see from my central take-it-all-in post are African American. There is [only] one African American in the food court getting food" (Field Notes 9/1/04).

Race was only one of several dimensions along which special residential units were organized. Separate floors for honors students similarly segregated the most academically motivated students from the others. More academic students also turned to the alternative dorm and floors specifically designated as "quiet" floors. The absence of honors students on our floor was highlighted at the first floor meeting when the RA asked if anyone was in the Honors College. Only one woman—a senior who had received free housing for a semester because of university employment—raised her hand. She had no contact with anyone on the floor and graduated at the end of the semester. In fact, she was so removed from the floor that we do not even count her in our tally of fifty-three floor residents. Differences in the cost of on-campus residential options also sorted students by social class, with more working- and lower-middle-class students concentrated in "co-op" floors where students were expected to perform custodial duties.

Residential Reputations and Neighborhood Choice

Most freshmen end up in regular university housing, as they either do not apply for an LLC or do not get accepted into one. Although HPS does not allow students to indicate their preference for specific dormitories, students are allowed to request a neighborhood. HPS assigns students randomly within neighborhoods, usually granting neighborhood requests.

As a public institution, MU does not tolerate discrimination in housing, and the university does not acknowledge residence hall reputations. On the MU Web site, for example, residence hall descriptions offer only information about amenities, walking distances, and the presence of LLCs. Yet residential neighborhoods and particular residence halls have well-established reputations at Midwest University. The longevity of dorm reputations at MU is notable. We have only to utter the phrase "party dorm," and any MU grad, no matter when they graduated, knows which neighborhood we studied. Official sources do not tell prospective students about these reputations, but savvier admits consult older friends, siblings, online resources, or their parents. For instance, as one woman gleefully reported:

All the partiers from my high school have lived in [this neighborhood] and have always told the next [class to] live there and, there's just a really active, stay up late, like . . . everyone just drinks, parties, goes to frats. And the [other neighborhood] was just kind of more relaxed academically. (Whitney Y4)

The location of the dorms also plays a role in student preferences and in the development of dorm reputations. For example, the social neighborhood is located near sorority and fraternity houses, the stadium, and the playing field.

The practice of allowing students to select a neighborhood enables self-segregation by race and class. Yet it is unlikely that MU, or most public universities, will do away with student input in their housing situation. Not allowing students some control over where they live—especially given a freshman on-campus living requirement—may result in uproar. Indeed, when Elizabeth suggested to a student affairs staff member that MU do away with neighborhood selection, she was told that this would "be unrealistic, as admissions would be getting phone calls from parents all summer asking to have their kids moved to [a] desired residence hall. They would get 'beat down' from parental pressure" (Field Notes 11/3/04).

Fulfilling student (and parent) preference also advantages some students over others. Students varied in how aware they were of residence hall reputations and thus how successful they were in selecting dormitories filled with similar peers. Virtually all of the affluent women—even those from out of state—were well informed and intentionally sought residence in our neighborhood. As Tara, an affluent woman from out of state, put it, "I just heard it was a social neighborhood. . . . I just heard this was the neighborhood to be in" (Y1).

This neighborhood was known to be where partiers lived, but it also had a reputation as the place for wealthy, Jewish, and out-of-state students. Thus, when interviewed in her first year, Mara, an upper-middle-class Jewish woman from out of state, noted, "I chose to be in this neighborhood. [This dorm] is very Jewish." Our dorm in particular was highly sought after by this demographic. In fact, Naomi revealed that she and her roommate were originally supposed to be in another dorm but her mother "took care of it" (Field Notes for Y2 interview).

In contrast, less affluent students were hazier about dorm reputations. For instance, lower-middle-class Alana filled out her form quickly, jotting down whatever her stepbrother's girlfriend told her:

> I don't know if it was this one or which one it was but I didn't really request anything. I think I put something about smoking, but not that that matters. So I really don't know how they stuck me here. (Alana Y1)

Lower-middle-class Valerie was perplexed about her dormitory assignment and how the floor came to be filled with partiers. As she told us:

> I got stuck in [this dorm] where everybody is exactly the same and I was like, how can MU preach about diversity, more diversity, and here I am living in this dorm where every other girl [has the same name], and they have the same pink stuff, and they all look the same? . . . I hate to be stereotypical but this neighborhood especially is just like the big people who are into partying and stuff. If this is random, how did you

know? Like how did you know where to put these people? (Valerie Y1/Y2 combined).

Even if these women had known to avoid the social neighborhood, they were less likely to have parental advocates working to secure the perfect dorm placement. As a result, most of the affluent women on our floor ended up there intentionally, knowing what they were getting into, while the less affluent women landed there by accident.

The Puzzle of Dorm Preferences

The preference for party dorms by affluent, socially oriented students and their parents can seem puzzling as party dorms are not the prettiest, best resourced, or most comfortable residences on campus. For example, in contrast to the 1920s–1940s Gothic revival architecture of the alternative dorm, our residence hall was classic 1960s-era construction, with cinder-block walls, linoleum floors, and an institutional feel. Composed of six separate structures, it was more accurately a complex than a building. Laura's initial reaction to the lobby of the central building—where the more than 1,300 residents collected their mail—was that it felt "like a nice hospital lobby—sterile, easily washable" (Field Notes 8/20/04). Nothing about the floors where students resided was warm, intimate, or visually pleasing. They were each constructed around a massive central bathroom so that residents opened their doors to a wall rather than another student. As a result, it was like living in a maze. Even the amenities were lacking. Other residence halls had better food—for instance, the alternative dorm was known for its selection of healthy and vegan options—and semiprivate bathrooms. Dorms in the social neighborhood were also farthest from most freshmen classes.

In addition, our dormitory was governed in a top-down fashion, with the expectation that residents would, given half a chance, engage in every form of collegiate misbehavior possible. Every floor was locked at either end, and only the residents and the staff charged with servicing and policing the floor had access. We were given one special key, which meant that we could enter other floors on our wing, but typically residents could reach only the floors on which they lived. Over the course of the year, we frequently encountered locked-out residents attempting to contact their friends by cell phone to let them in. In fact, during the course of the research,

Elizabeth started to use her cell phone regularly for the first time, as it was so critical in coordinating research team members' access to the building.

It was not plausible that this policy was entirely to protect property as there was literally nothing valuable on the floor outside of the residents' belongings—and residents were expected to lock their rooms. From the RA's comments during the first floor meeting it seemed that the locking of doors was a contemporary version of in loco parentis: if it was no longer tenable to demand that women be home by a certain hour, at least there could be an attempt to regulate male access to women's living quarters. The RA made a point to let them know that unescorted men were not allowed on the floor. She justified this by talking "about a previous year where a girl's boyfriend was so drunk he wandered into another girl's bed." She also "said several times that if they were to get 'hurt' she would be 'very, very sad' (although she avoided saying what hurt meant)" (Field Notes 8/24/04).

The locked doors were only one part of the highly visible security arrangements. All residence halls were subject to peer police patrol. Our RA, with three years of experience in this dorm, expected particular problems. During the first floor meeting she launched into a series of warnings about drugs and alcohol. For example, she noted that "the best policy was to answer truthfully to the RAs and give them alcohol if they ask you if it's in the room. If they were not cooperative, the police would be involved and they didn't 'mess around.' They would cuff you and take you out. She told them then that if they drink to go off campus" (Field Notes 8/24/04). She also expected problems with noise, civility, and cleanliness. She spent time going over rules about quiet hours and discussing "vandalism and problems in the past with people writing homophobic, racist, and anti-Jewish statements on white boards." She told them that in previous years:

> People left hairballs in the shower. After a general ugh, the Resident Assistant told them to please pick up the hairballs. She also mentioned flushing toilets and joked that if any of them didn't know how to vacuum, "come to me and I'll show you." [The RA also told them about the] custodian for the floor and where she was located. She said that [the custodian] "is not your maid so be respectful." (Field Notes 8/24/04)

Indeed, we witnessed most of these behaviors over the course of the year. For example, one of the few sinks on the floor had a trash bag over it for an extended period of time because someone had stopped it up.

With its unappealing architecture, locked floors, authoritarian governance structure, expectation of bad behavior, and roving police with guns and walkie-talkies, the residence hall bore more than a passing resemblance to a prison—and not always a very clean one. If the residence hall were a K–12 school, many parents would have been fighting to get kids out rather than in. For some, the preference for this neighborhood may have been simply due to lack of information. But for most, the social and demographic characteristics of prospective dorm mates outweighed all other factors. These savvy students and their families knew that party dorms were havens for people with similar backgrounds, interests, and orientations toward college.

Affluent students in particular were often at MU because they were more socially oriented and had a strong desire to experience "college life." Our dormitory may not have been a nice place to live on the face of things, but party dorms had one major thing going for them: they channeled students into the party pathway, facilitating access to both the party scene and Greek life. In this way, both socially oriented students and Greek organizations benefited from the homogenous structure of residential life on campus.

Living in a party dorm made it easy to enter the party scene. All women had to do to get to a fraternity party was to stand out front. On weekend evenings, the front of the dormitory in which our respondents lived was transformed into a rowdy taxi stand. One Friday night at 9:45 we observed around a hundred women dressed in their party best, eagerly awaiting the arrival of fraternity men in their expensive sport utility vehicles. As one woman, who was rather perplexed by the whole scene, recounted, "So everyone's . . . getting ready for hours at a time before the frats come around and pick 'em up. . . . I actually remember being outside and just kind of laughing at the whole cattle show" (Brooke Y1). Sometimes referred to as "dorm storming," this delivery service (which was often one-way) enabled fraternities to fill their parties with underage, socially oriented women who were enticed by the free alcohol.

Living in a party dorm also provided a better site from which to participate in sorority rush. Sororities processed recruits in batches according to residence, and party dorms produced the largest groups of rushees. On our floor there was enough interest to allow information meetings to take place in our lounge. Women in other dorms often had to meet up with strangers on different floors in order to comprise a group big enough to warrant its own Greek representative. It was thus easier for both sororities and re-cruits if Greek-oriented women were concentrated.

Easy Majors

MU offers a vast array of academic options. This was not apparent when surveying the majors of women on our floor. Over two-thirds majored in business or communications (17 women, 38%), health or social services (7, 16%), or education (6, 13%).[15] These numbers include only those pursuing an applied medical or social service program not tracking to high-status professional positions, such as physician or dentist. Only thirteen (29%) women on the floor majored in a conventional liberal arts field and only two (4%) in a scientific or quantitative field.

This lack of diversity is not coincidental. Rather, it reflects heavy reliance on easy majors. As described in the Introduction, these majors are charac-terized by the ease of obtaining a high GPA; little evidence of general skills improvement during college;[16] and a heavy focus on appearance, personal-ity, and charm. Easy majors are a key feature of the party pathway. With-out them, partiers would not be able to divert so much of their time and energy from academics to the party scene. The academic infrastructure at MU is organized in a way that facilitates student involvement in these fields.

Like many public and private universities, MU offers a business school. According to the *2010 U.S. News & World Report,* the MBA program at the MU business school ranks in the top twenty-five. Undergraduate business school students can go straight through to the MBA or major in fields like accounting, marketing, management, or finance. Admission is competi-tive, and the program is demanding. Only two of the seventeen women on the floor majoring in business or communications went through the busi-ness school. We met Lydia and Erica in Chapter 1 and learned that both were cultivated for success before arrival at the university by highly involved parents.

The remaining fifteen women took one of the many "business-lite" op-tions that existed outside of the business school. At MU, arts manage-ment, sport management, recreational sport management, outdoor recre-ation and resource management, park and recreation management, and tourism management are some of the less rigorous business majors. One of our hardest partiers, who was enrolled in an arts management program in what was known as a business-lite school, told us, "I feel like [it] is a little easier" (Whitney Y4). Others gravitated toward communications as a way to gain less demanding training in marketing. For instance, one woman's advisor suggested telecommunications as "an option going around the Business School [to get] that same degree" (Sydney Y2). Of course, a telecommunications degree is not the same as a marketing degree—or else there would be no need to "go around" the business school. Classes in communications were notoriously easy. As a sport communication broadcast major admitted, "The classes I just don't think were that challenging" (Mara Y4).

MU also houses a School of Education. Historically considered to be vocational in nature, education is not a major available at many elite private or liberal arts schools. For example, Harvard undergraduates interested in elementary or secondary education must major in their field of expertise. Despite the importance of training future teachers, education majors at most universities have among the highest GPAs—a sign of less challenging coursework. Indeed, education majors at MU described their classes as filled with busy work:

> I don't think that education is that hard of a major. . . . It's just very time consuming. . . . Education gives you a lot of room to improve your grades, even throughout each course, because the teachers are very flexible with you, so that made it easier. (Melanie Y4/Y5 combined)

Some women, however, struggled to pass teacher certification tests. For these women, there was an easier option—human and family development— that prepared graduates to, as the Web site claimed, work in community services with children, the elderly, the disabled, and those with mental health issues in hospitals, schools, and group homes. Human development might be seen as an education-lite or social work-lite degree. It can be thought of as the modern-day equivalent of home economics—one of the most popular fields for female graduates in the 1960s, before sex segregation in field of study declined considerably.[17]

MU has also developed a number of majors that rely heavily on personal taste, appearance, and self-presentation. These majors allow women on the party pathway to use charm and attractiveness to their advantage in an academic realm. Such majors are almost exclusively filled by women and appeal to the particular kind of upper-middle-class femininity that they are simultaneously working to perfect in the party scene.

At MU there is a Department of Interior Design and Apparel Merchandising that offers two majors by the same names. No such department exists at elite private schools or even most top state schools. The school claims that these majors prepare students for jobs like merchandise buyer, residential interior designer, and showroom or manufacturer sales representative. Many of these jobs do not require a college degree.

Sport communication, along with telecommunications and communications and culture (in the College of Arts and Sciences) attracts students who see themselves as future media personalities. For instance, as one noted:

> I still do love sports. I don't play them as much as I used to in high school or middle school. But I mean I love going to baseball games and you know, being active and exercising and stuff like that. It's just a really important part of my lifestyle. I thought [about] doing something with like, ESPN. (Mara Y4)

Both men and women alike tended to pursue these majors, but for our residents an interest in communications broadcasting meant being the impeccably dressed, attractive, and bubbly woman that major networks would want to put in front of a camera. Students in these programs were, in a way, selling themselves—not their skills, academic knowledge, or credentials.

These majors were concentrated in the School of Physical Education. This school streamlined movement onto the party pathway by organizing a large number of easy majors under one institutional umbrella. The school's general focus is on recreation, leisure, sports, fitness, and nutrition—areas in which body, personality, and taste necessarily take front stage. Here one can find many of the business-lite options (such as tourism management and sports communication). The school also offers majors like athletic training/fitness specialist and human development/family studies. These students do not have to complete the foreign language requirement required of all students majoring in the School of Literature, Science, and the Arts. By dedicating an entire school to easy majors, MU ensures that the fields of study most popular among partiers are well publicized, easy to access, and treated as legitimate.

The institutional arrangements discussed above existed prior to any particular student arriving on campus. By attending MU or another similar school, young women entered a world in which the party pathway was organizationally supported. However, students are the lifeblood of this system and necessary to bring the party scene alive. If students arrived with other motivations, organizational arrangements would probably change. In Chapter 1 we met the women on our floor and learned that quite a few of them approached college with a social orientation. In Chapter 3, we delve into the peer culture that supported MU's party pathway. We focus specifically on competition for status in the context of sorority recruitment and the party scene.

Rush and the Party Scene

Chapter 2 provided insight into the university architecture that enabled the party scene. Yet without analysis of the peer cultures students produced in and around this infrastructure, the story is incomplete. A rich peer culture rewarding a gender style reflecting wealth, whiteness, and heterosexuality made participation in the party pathway compelling. Socially ambitious students invested heavily in the Greek system and the party scene as these were the prime venues in which social and erotic competition occurred. Women who accrued status among other women by winning spots in top sororities and who were seen as desirable by men in the party scene enjoyed themselves more, received more attention, and made more friends. However, in this fast world, fun, disappointment, and danger existed in exquisite tension—with marginalized or disadvantaged players at more risk.

Getting the Bid: Peer Hierarchies and Investment in Greek Life

MU recruitment does suck, I can't deny that, and I'm in a chapter now. Part of the problem is that many PNMs [potential new members] come in only wanting a [top house] rather than realizing that a "lower tier" chapter might be the best fit for them. Another part is that as much as women hate to say it, knowing active members really does help, they can fight for you and know you beyond a five minute conversation. The party structure isn't the best either . . . [so many] houses in two days in the middle of winter (I did my first day when it was snowing sideways and my second day it was approximately fifteen degrees out) is brutal, then waiting is horrible . . . not knowing if you have [a] chapter. It sucks.[1]

Sorority rush at MU typically begins between October and December, dragging into January. National Greek chat blogs are replete with MU sorority rush stories like the one above. A 2006 article in the campus newspaper even jokingly predicted that the weather during women's rush might generate a spike in flu cases. Although rush started early the year of our study—in late October—the first day brought "miserable pouring rain" that left the women "wet to their knees" (Field Notes 10/23/04).

Obediently dressed in their identical rush T-shirts (accessorized by the savvy with designer jeans, jewelry, bags, and heels), women met with their rush groups in the morning. Each group of approximately seventy women was assigned a Rho Gamma—a sorority woman temporarily disaffiliated from her chapter for the purpose of guiding "potential new members" (PNMs) through recruitment. Our Rho Gamma informed the women that she had a bag with all of the "essentials" they might need. (We assumed this meant Tylenol and Band-Aids, but the items she mentioned were hairbrushes and body splash—suggesting the importance of appearance over all else.) Women were also informed that they would not be able to eat until their first break at 3 p.m.

Rho Gammas led their groups from house to house, where the women waited outside, sometimes for fifteen to twenty minutes, for a sorority to welcome them in with loud chants. As we recorded:

> It was raining really hard at this point. . . . The women were lined up in front of all of the houses. When the house had some sort of covered porch, they were huddled together, sharing whatever protection it had to offer. At some of the houses, the women simply stood in long lines fanning out from the front door and waited, and waited and waited. . . . [At one house] we heard this drill sergeant order, "Put down umbrellas RIGHT NOW!" The major screaming started inside the house, but the girls hardly seemed excited as they filed in. (Field Notes 10/23/04)

Inside it was much like an intense and rule-bound speed dating match.[2] Many topics (like relationships with "boys," partying, and class background) were explicitly forbidden. Before heading out our Rho Gamma jokingly reminded the women not to mention "what your parents do. Your drug use, [and . . .] all the abortions you've had" (Field Notes 10/23/04). As nearly a thousand women came through each house during this stage, impressions had to be formed through brief conversations with two or three house members. Women looked bedraggled and drained upon completing this physical and social gauntlet.

After the two-day process, each woman ranked the houses from her most to least favorite. The houses also ranked the women. All rankings were entered into a computer program that matched the preferences of recruits with those of women already in the house. The women then waited months—until January—to find out the results. If all houses cut a woman, she would be cut from the process before the second round. The RA explained to us that this had happened to a woman on her floor the previous year:

> I had a girl who got cut after [the first] party and [was] really sad cuz none of the houses wanted her. It was the first round, no one wanted her. She came back early [before second semester to participate in the rest of the parties]. . . . Oh, it was horrible. She took it really hard. . . . She was like, "No one wants me. I'm a loser."

This time Panhell—the campus-wide organization regulating sororities—called those cut from all houses before they made the early journey back. PNMs invited back gave up part of their winter break to participate in three more rounds of evaluation with the goal of receiving a bid from one house. At each stage, the number of houses possible to visit gradually decreased, and women were allowed to visit only those houses that invited them back. Those women invited back to more houses than the maximum for that stage were in a position to cut houses.

The process was highly competitive. Although roughly 30% to 40% of women in each freshman class participate, only about 50% to 60% of rushees join sororities. A number of women voluntarily opt out along the way—sometimes out of a self-protective impulse—or are cut for failing to meet the GPA minimum. Direct rejection is also common. Our RA was acutely aware of this, as she ended up picking up the pieces when women were rejected:

> I think it's hard when you have the recruitment counselors here because . . . the residents look up to [them] and [are] like, "Oh, these girls are great," and then they don't get a bid and I'm left with them. It's just rough. The recruitment counselors leave after the bids. . . . It's just frustrating and I'm here [saying], "It's gonna be ok. There are other options. You can apply to be an RA. Look at the positive. You can have an apartment off campus if you want." So ugh. Most of them, it takes them awhile to get over it.

The potential for rejection was increased by the fact that women sought not only to get into a house but to be accepted into a good house. Sororities at MU are ranked hierarchically, based on the reputation of members as being sociable and "cute" and having "good personalities"—class-linked characteristics that we discuss below. There were three "top" houses, five other "good" houses, roughly eight "lower middle" houses, and three houses that were unambiguously at the bottom.[3]

The appeal of sorority recruitment, despite the possibility of rejection and discomfort, highlights the limitations of looking at the party pathway solely through an organizational lens: it is impossible to understand why so many women rush without looking at the role of campus peer cultures.

Greek Exclusivity

Exclusivity is part of the appeal of Greek life. It provides privileged access to college social life for a slice of the population—while explicitly excluding most students. One woman, who had opted out of rush her freshman year, described what it was like to be non-Greek during a major campus social event:

> It was all for the Greeks. Like if you weren't Greek you really didn't belong.
> So that really made me just be like, I really want to do this. It was fun and
> it was interesting to watch but it would've been a lot more fun if I would've
> been able to get involved. (Nicole Y2)

Her account of being on the outside looking in suggests that at MU student life was a bit like a movie set: Greeks were the actors and all others a forgettable and interchangeable crew of extras. The possibility of winning a leading role—rather than being an invisible, ordinary student—drew students into the competition.

It is no secret that sororities participating in the National Panhellenic Conference are composed primarily of affluent, white, conventionally attractive, single, heterosexually identified American-born women of traditional college age.[4] However, in contemporary American society—particularly in higher education—it is generally viewed as unacceptable to select people based on characteristics such as race or physical attractiveness.

This was cast in sharp relief in 2007 when DePauw University's Delta Zeta sorority hit the national news after twenty-two of its members were "put on alumnae status or told to leave because they didn't measure up in size or popularity. The only African-American, Korean and Vietnamese women were also told to go."[5] Although the role of weight, race, and physical appearance in the decision was unclear, the perception that these were grounds for dismissal was a public relations disaster. A national media storm ensued, DePauw kicked the sorority off campus and a number of the ousted young women filed lawsuits. The sorority responded by suing the university, demanding that it reinstate the sorority and "affirmatively acknowledge" that the decisions were not made on the grounds of "appearance or race."[6]

How do sororities end up with women who are so similar to each other without getting into trouble the way DePauw's Delta Zeta chapter did? To a large extent they rely on self-selection, as people generally do not want to join groups where they are likely to feel unwelcome. For some—particularly nonwhite students, those not born in the United States, older students, those with children, lesbians, others with unconventional gender styles, or individuals with disabilities—it was obvious that Greek life was not for them. When we asked a lesbian on the floor about rush, she thought the question was ridiculous: "Somebody asked me if I was rushing and I just laughed. You think a gay girl could get into a sorority? I don't think so, being as open as I am" (Brianna Y1). The implausibility of Panhell sororities for women of color was similarly obvious. As one of our more frank lower-middle-class women explained, "It's like a black person working at Abercrombie, not gonna happen" (Stacey Y1).

Sororities also subtly nudged those who would not fit to opt out before being cut. For example, the $60 T-shirt required for rush scared away the most economically disadvantaged students, as did publication of the substantial membership fees. The message was clear: if you could not afford the fees, you did not belong. Similarly, sororities generally did not discourage the impression that lesbians were unwelcome. For example, as a sorority woman recounted:

> This girl went to the [LGBT] meeting and the house told her not to wear her letters. And she went, and she spoke, and she said her house told her not to wear the letters to that. She didn't say her last name. Somehow the [campus paper] found out . . . and printed the whole story. . . . I guess it's not good. [Laura: Her house is like, treating her like shit now?] Yeah, just cause she's gay. . . . She doesn't feel welcome there anymore. (Abby Y2)

Stories like this served as a warning to lesbian, transgendered, or bisexual students who might have considered rushing.[7] However, self-selection went only so far. Homogeneity was also achieved through selection processes that took into account class and physical attractiveness, but in ways mysterious and subtle enough to avoid the appearance of discrimination.

Selection on the Basis of "Personality"

Sororities fostered the hope of membership among a far more heterogeneous group of women than they would actually accept by claiming to select on the basis of "personality" rather than parental income or other demographic factors. Women were advised to look for houses where they "fit" and were told that houses would be doing the same. As the recruitment chair of one sorority explained:

> We really stress with our members to look for people they think would, first of all, benefit our chapter and, second of all, be their friend. They have to live with them, they have to know them. Someone that they want to represent us. (Sydney Y4)

Those who made the cut tended to resemble the women conducting recruitment. Emma, a self-described "outlier" due to her (only) middle-class background and membership in an Elite Three house, explained:

> It just doesn't surprise me what girls they want in the house because they were the kind of girls I would expect [Top House] to get into the house. I don't think [Top House] is made up of girls like me, so I never felt like they should be picking other girls like that because I'm the outlier. So when they pick the girls I'd be like, "That's what I would expect from [Top House]." (Y4)

Not incidentally, during recruitment, Emma was pulled out of face-to-face rush (where she could theoretically select people like her) and placed on computer duty. It was while compiling the electronic database of desired recruits that she noticed the striking homogeneity of current house members.

Sorority women had to determine whether recruits could be friends on the basis of very brief conversations. Thus, shortcuts were used. If a PNM was already friends with women in the house, it was clear that she had a lot in common with house members. Current members often actively campaigned in the favor of their friends. As a sorority member explained:

> We have these things called rush crushes, and if you like someone and you've brought them over for dinner previously, people will make signs

and hang them up all outside the bathrooms. Just getting their name out there. 'Cause not everyone's gonna meet them, but you're gonna stand up and represent them if you like them a lot. You want people to hear the name so they vote for them. . . . Like you'd make up silly little rhymes. . . . They put them on the back of the toilet stalls. It was so dirty! So we have a girl named Alli Nebhart and some girl last year put "Shit and fart, Alli Nebhart." So people remember it! It's stupid stuff like that. (Whitney Y2)

This process ensured that a few recruits stood out and got special consideration. Indeed, several women on the floor were sponsored in this way, and virtually all who ended up in top-tier houses were. Legacy status—that is, when a recruit's mother, aunt, sister, or other family member had been in the sorority—was also taken into consideration in some houses.

Sorority women also told us that during recruitment they looked for women with "good personalities." What they meant by this was someone with whom they found it easy to talk. As Nicole—whose house ranked recruits from 1 ("I can't stand her") to 5 ("I definitely want her")—detailed:

If we had a conversation that was flowing really easily and it wasn't like pulling teeth. I didn't have to keep asking question after question. If we have a lot in common and were laughing and having a good time, then I would give the girl a five. [Laura: What are some of the things that you're like, "Oh, I'm going to have to give this person a one?"] For me, it was just girls that would be sitting there and she wouldn't ask me any questions about myself. I just have to be asking her things over and over again. Like when it got to the point where I had to ask her what her major was cuz we had nothing else to talk about. Then I knew it was bad. (Nicole Y4)

Nicole's comments suggest that sororities valued a particular style of femininity, defined by extroversion, niceness, and catering to the other (for example, asking questions, being polite). These ways of relating are strongly associated with an upper-middle-class gender style.[8] Conversation about academics signaled desperation.

Often, "personality" was read directly through social class markers that placed similarly affluent sorority members at ease. As Emma explained of successful recruits:

They bring their Chanel purses or their Prada purses, or whatever they are wearing usually gives it away. The way they present themselves gives it away. . . . [The house members] associate better with those people. . . . They can relate better to people with money because they have money. So it's kind of like they find the connection and it's easier for them to talk to people like that. I would just assume that's how girls like that keep continuously being brought into our house because they just relate better to each other. (Y4)

Emma points to ways that recruits signaled commonalities in social class—via the expensive accessories they paired with the rush T-shirt—and how these immediately fostered a sense of connection between affluent sorority members and privileged recruits. A similar signaling occurred in conversation about shared cultural tastes, such as favorite places to shop, vacation spots, and clothing brands.

Sororities were also on the lookout for women who could damage the sexual reputation of the house. An ideal sorority woman was attractive to fraternity men but did not cross the line from sexy to slutty. Selecting women who did not demonstrate what sorority sisters viewed as appropriate sexual restraint had consequences. Nicole explained:

People have called a bunch of the new girls [in the house] slutty. . . . A lot of it has to do with them not knowing their limit when they drink and then just going way too far and doing things that were just not acceptable. . . . Or rumors that some of them ran around a fraternity naked and got banned from that house. That [they] slept with a certain amount of guys in that house. . . . We're just hoping to rush in a pledge class that is more representative of us [as] opposed to the new girls because we don't really like how they've been acting and the way that they represent our house. (Y4)

Recruits with bad reputations were thus subject to rejection. In most cases, however, sorority members knew little about the sexual reputations of recruits and had to rely on impressions formed during rush.

Social Class, Race, Religion, and "Cuteness"

Sororities have the reputation of selecting on the basis of attractiveness. In interviews, sorority women acknowledged that looks mattered, but they did not expect every successful recruit to be beautiful. Sorority women were, however, expected to be "cute." Cuteness referred to what a woman did with what she had. Although it was not possible for all women to have perfect features or bodies, it was, in the estimation of sorority women, possible for everyone to be well dressed and well groomed. For example, Hannah noted:

> When I was rushing I just remember it was just so gross and rainy out and our Rho Gamma was like, "No, the girls aren't gonna judge on . . . how you're looking." Of course they are! Oh my God, that's the first thing that everybody looks at. How they're dressed, what jewelry they're wearing, what kind of shoes they're wearing, what jeans they're wearing, and this and that and this. Yes, it's the first thing. (Y4)

Hannah suggests that judgments were based on clothing, jewelry, shoes, and the like. All are tightly linked to class, unlike purely physical attributes, which are more loosely related to class (through the expense of athletic participation and access to high-quality nutrition).

Accomplishing "cute" required the sustained investment of money, time, and cultural know-how. Women who most successfully navigated sorority recruitment tended to be those who had long made their appearance a project. They knew what to wear and had the money to buy fashionable clothes. They also watched their weight and went to the gym. As another sorority woman remarked, "I'm not trying to take a stance, no fat people, but . . . I mean, we need to have, I mean we are a sorority. We can have some standards" (Abby Y2).

Failure to present a "cute" appearance effectively screened out most of the less privileged women. When they managed to slip through, they often did not last long. One woman described of her former sorority roommate:

> She deactivated. . . . I don't know why she was in [Top House]. Like you could never see her in [our house]. She was really different from the other girls. Like she just, I mean, she wasn't as cute as a lot of the girls and she definitely wasn't very well off. . . . You can tell [she was] just kind of like blue collar, just kind of like country, hickish type. (Tara Y3)

Judging on "cuteness" also had racial, ethnic, and religious implications. The privileging of "blondeness"—meaning blue eyes, white but tanned skin, and straight hair—disadvantaged women of color and Jewish students. A Jewish woman complained, "Some people [are] only letting in blondes. Like [Top House,] it's like all blondes" (Abby Y2). Another woman observed that it was a virtual requirement that Top House members be "blonde, have big boobs, and are tanned. You know?" (Taylor Y4).

Women with money often enhanced their blondeness with expensive hair coloring, colored contacts, hair straightening, trips to the tanning salon, and sometimes cosmetic surgery. Jewish women—some of whom had dark hair, brown eyes, and thick or curly hair—often had to spend more time and money to achieve a blonde look. Such alterations were viewed as necessary to be high status on campus. As one Jewish woman noted, "The girls at home, the Jewish girls aren't really that cute. . . . I probably got it more from camp and just being interested [in] . . . high society, entertainment, like high status type of things" (Tara Y3).

At the top of the sorority hierarchy women were almost all affluent, "blonde," and "cute." In these houses, sorority women typically did not have to account for why they ranked a woman poorly, making it easier to cut undesirables. These houses won the recruits who had "perfect rushes" (that is, were called back to all of their preferred houses at every stage). The benefits of being in this type of house were considerable. As a woman described of her highly ranked sorority:

> If you look around, there are like, very pretty girls . . . but other than that, a lot of them have really great personalities. I think that we're considered a really fun house. And [fraternities] want to pair with us for certain things, because we're so outgoing and fun and we know how to have a good time. We just had our philanthropy and we had so many people show up. I think it says a lot about our personality. People really like hanging around us, and not just 'cause these girls are pretty, but because they actually have life to them, and love to party, and . . . just like to have a good time. (Mara Y4)

There were, however, potential costs of getting into a top house—namely, unrelenting social anxiety and difficulty prioritizing academics. We will explore these issues in later chapters.

In contrast, at the bottom, sororities did not begin to select desired recruits until "later parties, when these are the people that continue to choose us to come back" (Sydney Y4). They were forced to be much more lenient. As Abby, who worried about having "some standards," noted, "There's this girl, I don't want her in our house cause she's really fat. . . . But I think everyone in the house is still gonna be like, give her a chance. You know, just 'cause she's fat, doesn't mean like she's not nice. And they're gonna let her in. . . . [But] people are gonna see her and be like, I can't be in this house" (Y2).

Women were often reticent to join low-status chapters even when they had no other choice. When they did join, they garnered less status from being Greek. A member of one such house told us, "I never really like to wear letters. . . . It has a bad reputation. Everybody's like, oh, the Jewish sorority, likes to eat and some of the girls are really not pretty" (Hannah Y3). As she suggests, being in a Jewish sorority was, in and of itself, low status in a system based around Waspy "cuteness." Yet for those willing to tolerate the low status, there were benefits to membership in a less highly ranked house, as the social competition and expectations of participation were reduced.

Overall, peer-driven screening and ranking mechanisms—centered on social ties, personality, sexual reputation, and cuteness—effectively ensured the top slots were filled with extroverted women who had successfully created an upper-middle-class, white, and heterosexual style of attractiveness. These students also fueled the party pathway. The lack of transparency in selection processes made it seem like the failure of individual women to measure up, rather than a systematic sorting on social class and other characteristics. Competition did not stop with getting the bid. Women who went Greek became invested in improving the collective reputations of their houses, as their status on campus was so intimately linked to these rankings. This motivated continual investments in appearance, charm, and sociability—rather than academics—making it hard for Greek women to get off of the party pathway.

Pleasure and Peril in the Party Scene

By definition, everyone has to participate in the academic side of college; similarly, a vast majority of the women we studied also passed through the party scene. In fact, out of fifty-three residents, forty-nine attended at least one college party—typically a fraternity party—in their first year. Over half could be said to be "regulars." For sixteen women (around a third of the floor)—whom we classify as either socialites or wannabes in Chapter 5— partying was nothing short of a vocation. Although these numbers were likely higher because of our location in a party dorm, they still suggest the extent to which the party scene was central to college life at MU.

Indeed, on Thursday through Sunday nights, after the flurry of hair drying, makeup applying, and outfit borrowing died down, the silence on the floor was deafening. The only people left were isolates. As one such woman bemoaned, "There is a group on [this] side of the hall that goes to dinner together, parties together, my roommate included. I have never hung out with them once. . . . And, yeah, it kind of sucks" (Linda Y1). Linda's quote suggests the extent to which partying was central to making friends—particularly early on. Women like Linda, who did not engage in this college pastime, were seen by others as "weird," not worth associating with, and potentially contaminating. Linda's roommate even chose to switch rooms halfway through the year to room with someone she saw as more compatible.

By choosing not to party, Linda missed out on a critical opportunity to build status on campus. In the party scene, women could advertise the personality, "cuteness," and shared cultural tastes that would land them a spot in the Greek system. However, status was not only derived through evaluations by one's same-sex peers; women's place in the campus hierarchy was intimately connected to men's perceptions of them. As the main heterosexual marketplace in town, the party scene was the place to gain erotic status. This function ensured that the party scene remained central to campus life, even when it predictably produced disrespect and danger—especially for the most vulnerable women on campus.

Erotic Status and the Role of "Hooking Up"

In a 2010 article in a newspaper devoted to Greek life, a fraternity member described "the trusty 1–10" system for rating girls. He described a one as "as bad as it gets. Lucky enough these girls hardly ever go out in public." A three "is the first girl that might get a little action from time to time. Granted the guy who falls for her will be wasted beyond belief." A five is "the first girl on the list that can be acceptable to bring around your friends. . . . A five may be in a sorority, but it will be an ugly one so don't get excited." In contrast, an eight "can make it into almost all the sororities and can get away with being a you know what. She's got a lot of guys texting her and she's texting a lot of guys." A nine "will get you mad bro points out the wazoo . . . raise your self-esteem, popularity, and other girls will suddenly find you more attractive." Finally, a ten "get[s] what they want, when they want it. Guys want them, girls want to be them."

This commentary highlights some similarities in how men and women gain rank within peer cultures: Both derive status via the type of erotic attention that they can attract. The more attractive, desirable, and popular

they are considered by their opposite-sex peers, the more likely they are
to have a powerful position—and vice versa. There is thus considerable
incentive for men and women alike to constantly try and do "better" and
exchange "up" the hierarchy. Not much can be gained from a long-term
romantic coupling unless one is able to pull a "9" or "10" off of the erotic
market—hence the reason that the author describes "nines" as the first
women to "make ideal girlfriends." In contrast, casual sexual encounters,
particularly when initiated in the public social venue of the party scene,
are more amenable to the type of visibility and quick turnover necessary
for the pursuit of status.

Paula England's survey of over 14,000 students attending twenty-one
different colleges and universities indicates that about 70% of today's male
and female students report hooking up at least once by their senior year.[9]
Men report an average of ten hookups by their senior year, while women
report seven. Most hookups do not involve intercourse—only about 40%
report intercourse in their most recent hookups. However, among the 80%
of students who had intercourse by the end of college, roughly 67% had
done so outside of a relationship.

With the help of youth media, alcohol, and spring break industries, hooking up has become a normalized and institutionalized activity, something
that "All . . . the people who came to college to have a good time and party"
do (Nicole Y1). Women were insistent that this was not just something that
men wanted. As one noted, "I know so many girls who honestly go out on
a Friday night and they're like, 'I hope I get some ass tonight.' They don't
wanna have a boyfriend! They just wanna hook up with someone" (Erica
Y2). Thus, particularly among the more privileged youth who participate
in the party scene, hooking up was built into notions of what the college
experience should be.

This represents a departure from college peer cultures in the 1980s,
when, at least at some schools, women gained status through boyfriends.[10]
As Dorothy C. Holland and Margaret A. Eisenhart describe in *Educated
in Romance: Women, Achievement, and College Culture*, women's investment
in a "culture of romance" distracted them from the academic side of college.[11] In contrast, we found that the most socially ambitious women
thought of boyfriends as social liabilities who pulled them out of the party
scene.

For example, when asked why she thought some people on the floor
were unhappy, a woman explained, "A lot of them still date boys [they

knew in high school] . . . so they are obsessing over that, and all they do is sit on the phone. We go out all the time, go out as much as we can. It's so fun. I think they hold themselves back a lot" (Whitney Y1). Even women who had boyfriends sometimes tried to hide this fact. Tara, in her quest to make friends, found out the hard way that boyfriends were not to be advertised:

> We went to [a fraternity] and hung out and then I was so excited to get to know Nicole. . . . [I said], "So, tell me about your boyfriend." She snapped at me. She goes, "Oh my God! You can't talk about it when we're hanging out with guys, cause then no one will wanna hang out with me." Never talked to her since. . . . I see her a lot, but we don't say "hi." (Tara Y4)

This mention of a boyfriend caused such a rift that the two women harbored a dislike for each other throughout college. Eventually Nicole dumped her boyfriend. She told us that not doing so before coming to MU was her only regret about college:

> I would not have had a boyfriend at all, ever. I would have just broken up with him before I got to college. . . . I think everything would have been totally different if I was on my own the entire time throughout college . . . which is so sad now that I think about it. (Nicole Y5)

Hooking up—or at least being present in the erotic market—has thus usurped the role once played by dating in determining college women's erotic status. Although men have historically gained status among their peers by demonstrating their sexual prowess, it is only recently that women's ability to get sexual (as opposed to romantic) attention from men has been viewed so positively among their peers. This has cemented the importance of the party scene on campus and made the party pathway that much more compelling for men and women alike.

An Uneven Playing Field

Although women and men engaged in the same status game in the party scene, the playing field was far from even. Because men were often the party hosts and women the guests, men dictated who got into the party, what their guests wore, and even how much they drank. For example, when we observed the fraternity pick-up scene at the front of our residence hall, Laura noted:

> They would either pick up girls they knew . . . or recruit girls. . . . The
> two . . . girls near us, for example, were told by a [fraternity] guy . . . to go
> to the front of the curb to catch the cars. Clearly, he was selecting some of
> the more attractive women. (Field Notes 8/27/04)

The themes of fraternity parties also placed men in more powerful positions over women, who were required to be the scantily clad subordinates—
playing "secretary ho" to the male's CEO, sexy student to the male's school
teacher, or Playboy bunny at the Playboy Mansion party (which required
two or more bunnies for every Hugh Hefner).

At the party, women needed to be alluring, friendly, and flirtatious in
order to be included in the fun. As a woman noted, "I flirt with guys. . . . I
just pretty much do that so we can go play flippy cup [a drinking game] or
get free beer" (Crystal Y1). Not all women were willing to make this exchange. As one described of a party:

> I was uncomfortable . . . in the sense that all of the girls kind of have to
> compete with each other to get the alcohol, and it just screams so much
> like prostitution to me. You know, even if they're not literally having sex
> with the guys, it's just like they're . . . selling their flirtiness for beer or
> something, and that's just so not me. (Leah Y1)

She indicated that women were expected to trade on their erotic appeal to
gain access to resources that men monopolized.

Sorority members sometimes even kissed other women to get attention
from men. One noted, "Guys said, 'Do it, do it!' just screwing around. . . .
[They] were like, 'These girls are going to kiss!' So you think you're cooler
and guys think you're cooler" (Hannah Y1). However, the women insisted
that "it's totally different if you're into it. Like lesbians" (Whitney Y1). Most
assumed that "real lesbians" were too "boyish" or "mannish" to be attractive to men.[12]

When women failed to appeal to men's sexual interests, they reported
feeling scorned. One vividly recalled a bad evening out, when her "secretary ho" outfit was a little too secretarial (including a knee-length skirt and
blouse) for the occasion. She received a sarcastic thumbs-up gesture and
mocking "nice outfit" comment by the fraternity door gatekeeper (Emma Y1).
Another woman with a similarly unsexy outfit lamented, "I was like the
little conservative, country bumpkin in my outfit. I was like, no, I'm not
going to get any of the attention. They're not going to waste their time with
me" (Brooke Y1).

Another way in which the playing field was uneven was the fact that women, unlike men, encountered the belief that "good" women were not interested in casual sex. As one woman described of this sexual double standard, "Guys can have sex with all the girls and it makes them more of a man, but if a girl does then all of a sudden she's a ho and she's not as quality of a person" (Mary Y1). Women also encountered what we have called the "relational imperative"—the notion that normal women always want love, romance, and commitment.[13] Such beliefs contradicted the more gender-neutral pressures to hook up and actively participate in the erotic market of college, putting women in a difficult double bind: while they gained status from garnering male sexual attention, too much of this attention put them at risk of a bad reputation. Their experiences of being judged were painful; one woman even waited two years to tell us about being called a "slut" because it was so humiliating (Erica Y3).

As a consequence, women's erotic status was also influenced by the skill and ease with which they navigated the fine line between "sexy" and "slutty." What was seen as slutty in one situation was sexy in another. As a woman explained:

> [Halloween is] the night that girls can dress skanky. Me and my friends do it. [And] in the summer, I'm not gonna lie, I wear itty bitty skirts. . . . Then there are the sluts that just dress slutty, and sure they could be actual sluts. I don't get girls that go to fraternity parties in the dead of winter wearing skirts that you can see their asses in, shirts that don't even cover. (Becky Y1)

She makes a variety of subtle distinctions—between women who dress provocatively when it is viewed as acceptable to do so and "actual sluts" whose dress is presumably reflective of their character. She hints that the difference has to do with the ability to match self-presentation to context. An even trickier rule had to do with the relationship between dress and deportment. One woman noted that it was considered acceptable for women to "have a short skirt on" if "they're being cool" but "if they're dancing really gross with a short skirt on, then like, oh slut. You've got to have the combination" (Lydia Y1). These and other rules made successfully navigating the party scene without being labeled as a "slut" a performative minefield for college women.

The Costs

The party scene predictably produced both fun and danger. Women participated because they genuinely enjoyed the ritual of partying, which started with getting dressed and pregaming (that is, drinking before the party) with friends. This was a time to bond over shared makeup, clothes, and clandestine shots of hard liquor. At the party, alcohol, music, attractive people, sexy outfits, and flirting created an erotic energy. As one woman described, "Everyone was so excited. It was a big fun party" (Tara Y1). Women "loved" it when they had an "excuse to just let loose" and "grind" on the dance floor. Women reported turning on their "make-out radar" (Morgan Y1), explaining that "it's fun to know that a guy's attracted to you and is willing to kiss you" (Becky Y1). After the party, getting home was sometimes an adventure in itself.

That said, there were troubling downsides of the party scene. Men's control over fraternity parties put women in potentially dangerous situations. For example, women reported that men used a home-turf advantage in the attempt to extract sexual interaction. As one described, "Every guy [says] you wanna drink, you wanna . . . oh come see this. Oh, let's look on my computer. Oh, let's close this, and closes the door and I just get so annoyed" (Abby Y1). Women also reported feeling pushed to drink. As one explained:

> I've seen boys [at a fraternity] pressuring girls to drink who don't want to drink, or not even who don't want to drink . . . but who just don't feel comfortable drinking with them. Sometimes boys are creepy. You don't want to sit and pound shots with them. (Erica Y1)

In addition, although fraternity members happily transported women to the party, they were not exactly eager to provide rides home. One woman told us, "we were at this frat and they wouldn't give us a ride home. . . . They were just dicks" (Taylor Y1). The lack of reliable transportation home sometimes left women walking home in the dark, drunk, in stilettos.

Women also complained that men at parties showed a lack of respect for their feelings—treating them solely as "sex objects" (Blair Y1). This soured interactions that might have otherwise turned into mutually agreed upon hookups. For example, one woman reported:

> This guy that I was talking to for like ten/fifteen minutes says, "Could you, um, come to the bathroom with me and jerk me off?" And I'm like, "What!"

I'm like, "Okay, like, I've known you for like, fifteen minutes, but no."
(Hannah Y1)

When hookups occurred, they were sometimes colored by disregard. As one woman described, "The guy gets off and then it's done and that's all he cares about" (Lydia Y4). Another complained of her efforts to get a recent hookup to call, "That wasn't me implying I wanted a relationship—that was me implying I wanted respect" (Erica Y2). In her view, casual sex did not mean forgoing all interactional courtesies. Women told us that men at parties acted as if only girlfriends were worthy of decent treatment. One noted, "If you're talking to a boy you're either going to get into this huge relationship or you are nothing to them" (Sydney Y3). This either/or situation often frustrated women who wanted men to treat them well regardless of the level of commitment.

Virtually all women who partied reported the occasional encounter with a "creepy" frat guy and told at least one story of things gone wrong. Yet not all women were equally likely to experience the most serious consequence of the party scene—sexual assault. Affluent women arrived at college well versed in a long list of practical party rules imparted by mothers and older siblings. For example, in a conversation with Laura about partying during the first year, Nicole "said that her mom also warned her about drinking at fraternities. She told her never to take drinks from anyone or do shots when they were sitting out" (Field Notes 9/15/04). Nicole reported that she felt "silly" for not drinking the shots since all the other women did, but she followed her mother's advice and abstained. In addition, several women had even been to fraternity parties in high school. Most had enough experience with alcohol to know their limits. Having a high rank in the campus social scene also protected them, as men were held more accountable to well-connected women. Indeed, insulting a highly ranked woman in a top sorority was akin to affronting her whole sorority, and disrespecting a girlfriend or friend of a fraternity member was equally risky.

In contrast, women from less privileged backgrounds entered into the party scene less prepared and more vulnerable. With less party experience, they were unaware of fraternity men's tactics. They did not have the extensive (and protective) networks that more privileged women developed. They were lower on the status hierarchy, if only by virtue of exclusion from the top sororities, and less likely to be afforded the respect granted elite sorority women. Less privileged women also tended to lack the detailed knowledge and resources necessary to pull off a "sexy" rather than "slutty" appearance. For instance, two working-class women on the floor often broke the rules of dress—wearing garish makeup, bright clothing, and tube tops with miniskirts. This immediately marked them as non-girlfriend material and therefore as less deserving of male respect. The two women who told us about experiences of sexual assault in fraternity parties were also from less privileged backgrounds.

Experiences with assault were, unfortunately, far from unusual. One might expect the risk of assault to deter women from participating. Yet rather than recognizing and challenging women's victimization, women blamed others who were assaulted for being "immature," "naive," or "stupid." In discussing a sexual assault of someone she knew, a woman explained:

> She somehow got like sexually assaulted . . . by one of our friend's old roommates. All I know is that kid was like bad news to start off with. So, I feel sorry for her but it wasn't much of a surprise for us. He's a shady character. (Julie Y1)

The implication was that the woman was partly to blame as she should have never been with such an untrustworthy male. Julie dismissed sexual assault as nothing to worry about " 'cause I'm not stupid when I'm drunk" (Y1). Vulnerability to sexual assault thus became yet another way to reinforce hierarchies among women. Affluent, socially savvy women benefited from their position at the top of the social heap by being less vulnerable to sexual assault and disrespect, then used this protected status as proof of their worth.[14]

The importance of the party scene for the production of fun, status, and belonging also meant that women tended to gloss over, or not take seriously, some of its other costs. For instance, the centrality of alcohol and drugs to partying pushed partiers to consume more than they would have otherwise. One woman described how she began to drink:

> I think freshman year basically I'd have a drink in my hand so people wouldn't bug me all the time. I wasn't really interested in like woohoo let's get wasted. More of the social oh I'm meeting people thing. . . . Over the past couple of years . . . going out with girls in my house. I just feel like I, and it sounds bad, I've really conformed to what they do. I just think it's the atmosphere that I'm in. (Blair Y3)

Another woman's parents pulled her out of school as she got heavily involved with drugs. These stories—as well as those above—point to the role that peer cultures play in creating the headlines that colleges and parents fear. Alcohol is often blamed for sexual assaults, hazing, academic failures, and even student deaths. However, the high-stakes status competition that fuels drinking and leads to other problematic behaviors is less well understood.

In this chapter we examined the rules of the game in the sorority system and the party scene. These are not the only venues in which status competition occurs, however. In Chapter 4 we draw on our ethnographic observation to describe competition for status on the dorm floor. Just over a quarter of the women on the floor entered the university interested in a primarily social pathway through college. Yet, as we will show, living in a "party dorm" meant that all who lived there were swept up in the system of evaluation. This had consequences for who was socially dominant on the floor and who was virtually invisible.

CHAPTER 4

The Floor

I hyped college up so much and I got here and I'm kind of lonely, doing the depressed freshmen thing. . . . I like the environment around me. It's pretty. . . . I came here for classes, and I really do like the classes. But in terms of the people I'm having a little difficulty being with some, not with a certain person or anything, but just in terms of people being friendly. I thought people would be a lot more open and college was just going to be a great place where I have all these friends.

(Alana Y1)

Alana's first year at college was miserable, but not because of her coursework; in fact, she was one of few women excited about her studies. Our field notes recount Alana sharing information from her sociology class and moves from her belly dancing class. Even though her finite math class presented a challenge, she claimed that there was "nothing like the satisfaction of solving a difficult math problem" (Field Notes 8/31/04). During her first-year interview, she queried Elizabeth about a sexuality class offered at MU and excitedly remarked, "There's just so many cool classes" (Y1). Indeed, as the quotation at the beginning of the chapter suggests, there was little Alana did not like about MU—except for the social experience.

Our first clue that Alana was lonely was the sheer amount of time she spent hanging out with us instead of her floormates. Her lack of connection with the other women on the floor was not for lack of trying. As a research team member described:

Friday night she was getting ready to go out. When I arrived around 8 p.m. she was freshly showered, blow-dried, and all done up in makeup. . . . She said that she had met some girls down the hall and they expressed interest in going [out]. Periodically she would go to talk with the girls, but she never stayed long (if she's going out with them, why not hang out now?), and by the time I left she was saying something about them getting delayed, or how some of the girls had already left. . . . Whatever happened, when I left she was hanging out in her room, fully dressed and ready to go. Just waiting for the girls. (Field Notes 9/4/04)

Later in the year Alana finally managed to "get out and do something" with two of her floormates. However, this did not turn out as expected. She explained:

> They had been drinking. And we were gonna go out to this fraternity. So we load up, them and their friends in my car. And I'm the only one who's sober. . . . I think it was probably the worst night ever just because I was babysitting. Like I wanted to hang out with them because I thought they were cool. But really again I think they were just using me for the ride. . . . I wasn't having any fun. I'm wanting to leave and I'm trying to stay just a little bit longer for them. . . . It was so God awful. I did not like any of the people at the party where I was. They weren't friendly. It was not a good time. (Y1)

We liked Alana, as she was lively and easy to talk with, and we found her poor treatment heart-wrenching to watch.

By the end of the year, Alana's isolation had taken its toll. We were worried when, near the end of the year, we realized that she had made no concrete plans to return to MU for her sophomore year:

> We asked Alana about next year's living situation. Alana said she had no clue. . . . As the conversation progressed, it was clear that this decision is connected to a variety of other unresolved issues. She continues to be lonely. Her mom and aunt visited this weekend. They had a good visit. . . . Alana said . . . that she feels left out of life [back home]. . . . Her boyfriend is there (and said that he would not consider moving to Fairview). Her mom is hinting for her to come home, to transfer. . . . She said that she feels like she is having to choose between "my family and me." The pull of her family is strong, but she seems to realize that she cannot fully grow into herself there. But here it is very hard, and so far there does not seem to be any obvious payoff for dealing with what seems to be a hard/depressing/lonely struggle. She has no idea what she wants to major in, another decision that is keeping her up at night. [Also] she doesn't know . . . whether to live on or off campus. She doesn't know where to live on campus if she does live on campus. I suggested [the alternative dorm]. She didn't dismiss this idea, but hasn't been there and doesn't seem to know much. As she

lacks friends, she hasn't had the opportunity to visit very many places around campus. (Field Notes 2/20/05)

To make matters worse, Alana's grades had also slipped as she grew more depressed over the course of the year. She started to "drink [and] smoke more," which made it harder to focus. As she managed to piece together, "Maybe the lack of social environment that I was looking for kind of interfered with my schoolwork" (Y1).

Isolates

Alana was not alone in her misery that first year. In fact, an astonishing twenty-five women—nearly half of the floor—could be described as social isolates.[1] We defined isolates as those who, by the end of the year, could claim only one person on the floor (outside of a roommate) as a "friend." Our designation was heavily informed by friendship data collected from the women during the first-year interviews; however, we also imposed our own definition: a friend was someone who willingly socialized with another woman and regularly included her in activities like going out for meals, doing laundry, watching TV, and partying (if so inclined). Isolates contrasted sharply with other floor residents who were networked into at least one of three cliques on the floor.[2]

Eighteen isolates were from less privileged families, including all working-class and lower-middle-class women on the floor and a few middle-class women. As discussed in Chapter 3, these women were less likely to have the funds, time, social tastes, and knowledge necessary to successfully engage in college social life. Several, including Mary, Valerie, Amy, and Megan, found the party scene to be off-putting. For example, Valerie was appalled by the fraternity transport system operating in front of her dorm. She explained:

> All those girls would stand out there at the circle drive and just like, no joke, get into these big black Suburbans driven by frat guys, shoving themselves in there, wearing like seriously no clothes, piled on top of each other. This could be some kidnapper taking you all away to the woods and chopping you up and leaving you there. How dumb can you be? (Y1)

Others, like Alana and Becky, struggled to fit in and make connections when they attempted to party. Most of these attempts eventually failed, even if they seemed successful at first.

For example, Stacey and Heather started at the center of a highly social clique but were abandoned when they could not follow Whitney, Mollie, Chelsea, Nicole, and Brenda into sororities. The sorority recruitment process we described in Chapter 3 sorted almost perfectly along class lines. Only one lower-middle-class woman and not a single working-class woman from our floor ended up in a sorority. As Heather later noted of her former friend Whitney, "I hardly ever talked to her after, after she got in her sorority" (Y3). Similarly, Carrie, who watched as Hannah, Blair, Karen, and Sydney joined sororities, was left so isolated that midway through college she told Laura, "Last year I didn't have any friends, and I came here and I realized that I have nothing to do, and I have no one to call because I don't talk to anybody, but I wanted to" (Y3).

Seven isolates were from upper-middle-class or upper-class backgrounds. Several just did not fit socially. Linda, for instance, was an affluent woman who arrived "cultivated for success," but she was entirely opposed to drinking, which meant that even the balanced partying typical of achievers (see Chapter 7) was not an option for her. Linda instead tried to make friends by knocking on open doors and asking people if they wanted to play cards. As she noted, "It was really scary. And no one wanted to play cards. I went around the first three days with a packet of cards I have never touched since then" (Y1).

Brooke, Morgan, Natasha, and Leah were more socially aware than Linda. Brooke was our budding sociologist, as she perceived the status games occurring on the floor. Morgan and Natasha identified as alternative. They hung out with a skater crowd in high school and found fraternity parties mostly "creepy." They were not interested in conforming by going Greek— but did not have a strong network of friends from home at MU to compensate for this decision. Leah's identity as lesbian put her outside of the social world of the floor, as suggested by her distaste for flirting in exchange for beer discussed in Chapter 3.

In a rather idiosyncratic occurrence, Julie was shunned by the floor in response to her treatment of her initial roommate, Brianna. Julie was from a conservative Christian community and arrived at college with no exposure to sexual diversity. Within the first week, Brianna came out to her as a lesbian. Julie was completely freaked out and proceeded to tell others about Brianna's sexual identity and her negative reaction to this information. Her homophobia offended a number of women on the floor (and the research team). Even those who chose not to associate with lesbians themselves

shunned Julie—and her new roommate, Angela—because of her politically incorrect response.[3] As Julie explained:

> Even to this day a lot of the people on the floor don't say "hi." Don't smile.
> Don't acknowledge [my new roommate and me] because they think I'm
> this bad person. . . . And now I have this bad rep, and Angela's being as-
> sociated with it. (Y1)

Despite their best efforts, these two women could not overcome their initial reputation.

Thus, isolates were a varied group, defined by a wide array of individual
characteristics—for example, a disinclination to party, quirky and non-
mainstream interests, and religious conservatism. None of these are obvious sources of social marginalization. Even social class does not cleanly
predict isolation. It is in the context of the floor that these particular
women struggled socially—although this set the tone for the rest of their
time at college. Had they started in a different residence hall or on a different campus, they may have made friends. Our efforts to steer Alana toward the residence hall housing alternative students were based on this
possibility.

The social dynamics of the floor made it difficult for isolates to see where
they might fit elsewhere on campus and to feel like they belonged at MU—
or even at college more generally. Below we describe these interactional
dynamics in detail, the responses of isolates, and the effects on those who
suffered as a result. If isolation only meant a hard first year in college for
students, it might not be as critical to understand. However, as Alana's example hints, students' social experiences are deeply intertwined with their
academic success.

Social Dynamics of the Floor

In the first weeks of the semester, our field notes were filled with women's
complaints about the "unfriendliness" of the floor and their difficulties getting to know people. We were initially puzzled by some women's problems
connecting. Expecting friendliness in a "party dorm," we sought explanations for its absence. We considered architecture: as Figure 4.1 demonstrates,
gigantic shared bathrooms effectively broke up the floor into two long halls
of eight rooms facing an empty wall and two short halls of seven rooms
across from each other. Yet floor geography did not account for women's
lack of ties to others in the same vicinity. Similarly, we were concerned that

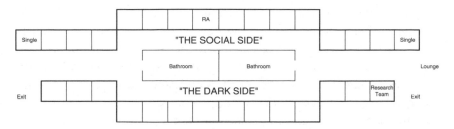

Figure 4.1. Layout of the floor

our presence hampered social interaction. But when Laura asked Alicia if she thought it was "us being here that made it quiet," she responded:

Alicia: No. 'Cause y'all weren't here the first day, were you?
Laura: We were here.
Alicia: No one knew of it.

Theoretically, more extensive Residence Life programming might have also helped women to get to know each other better. However, sparse attendance at the few floor events suggested a bigger problem.

Eventually we came to the conclusion that unfriendliness on the floor was not primarily the result of architecture, our presence, or limited programming. Mary nailed the issue when she compared life in a party dorm with other dorms on campus:[4]

> [In some other dorms] people are more friendly, people are less concerned with appearance, less concerned with social status. Drinking is not such a big thing. . . . They know each other on the floor better than people do here. It's just more open, more friendly. And they're definitely more academically focused. (Mary Y1)

In a context defined by the exclusive, hierarchically organized peer culture described in Chapter 3, open friendliness and concern with status were at odds. Socially ambitious women's efforts to establish a high rank for themselves—most immediately by gearing up for a successful rush—created a chilly social climate for everyone else.

Dissociation and Status

In *Freaks, Geeks, and Cool Kids: American Teenagers, Schools, and the Culture of Consumption,* Murray Milner applies his theory of status—developed through study of the caste system in India—to American high schools. Outlining basic principles, he notes, "*Disassociation* is important: The status-conscious avoid people and objects that are low status, and may even try to publicly denigrate them."[5] This task was challenging in the close living quarters of the dormitory. The socially ambitious were placed in intimate daily interaction with individuals they did not view as desirable associates (for example, nerdy students, poor students, and researchers). Even worse, without background information, it was sometimes not obvious which associations were valuable and which were not.

The high potential for risky mistakes led the status conscious to very narrowly define those worthy of association. Meeting people did not mean getting to know just anyone; it meant those who were fun, attractive, and connected. They had little use for new kinds of people. Most simply looked for more people like themselves. As Naomi explained, "I kind of stuck with people that are similar to me. . . . I left home to meet new people, but at the same time I knew that the people I was gonna meet were gonna be similar to my friends from home" (Y1). They did not view the dorm floor as a potential community, or even as a place to make friends, but as a temporary residence until they got into sororities. Thus Chelsea deemed even her "friends" on the floor just "livable" (Y4). She later admitted she had no intention of forming her closest ties on the floor. "I knew, freshman year . . . I knew they weren't going to be my best friends. Like you could just tell" (Y3).

These women often selected roommates strategically to ensure they were paired with the right kind of person, who could accompany them everywhere until they got more established. For instance, Naomi decided to room with Abby, whom she knew from home, even though she did not anticipate a close friendship. As Naomi admitted, the two were "very similar, [in that] her family is extremely wealthy. . . . I knew we were gonna have completely different friends, but it was nice to have her around at the beginning when we were just meeting people" (Y1).

Socially ambitious women, in fact, arranged how they lived on the floor so as to minimize contact with new types of people. They avoided the dorm lounge, kept their doors shut, or—if open—failed to look up from their screens when individuals walked by their rooms. When moving through common spaces, they deflected the interactional overtures of strangers by appearing to be perpetually engaged in interaction. Laura noted when observing in the main lobby:

> I decided that a major rule (at least for now) was NOT TO BE ALONE. People always wandered around with at least one other person. Which is probably

why I got a few stares. And if you are alone, the cell phone seems to count (or at least prove that you do have friends, family). (Field Notes 8/25/04)

Association with floormates could not be entirely avoided, however. Social climbers perfected what we dubbed "being mean nicely." That is, most found ways to shut down interactions without being directly rude. Alana's first attempt to go out with others, as described at the start of the chapter, provides a perfect example. When approached socially by a lower-status individual, women were often vaguely agreeable so as to end the interaction quickly and without confrontation. Later they would fail to follow through with social plans or, if pressed, offer excuses.[6]

Refusing Acknowledgment

The most extreme form of dissociation that we witnessed on the floor was a refusal to even acknowledge the existence of those deemed unworthy. For example, Evie and Aimee—a graduate and undergraduate researcher pair—encountered Whitney and her roommate Mollie early in the semester. Evie was a sporty, attractive, late-twenty-something sociology graduate student. Aimee was a confident, attractive, blonde member of an upper-middle-tier sorority with an evident interest in fashion. Evie and Aimee independently reported on this encounter. Aimee noted:

Whitney was carrying a Dooney and Bourke pink purse and seemed to be in a rush to get out the door. However, she stated to us that no one had been by her room yet, as though she was feeling left out in our research. I found it weird that she made that comment but couldn't stay and talk to us for more than a minute. Before she left she also told me, "Nice top. Nice shoes. Wow, cool purse. Do you live here?" It was as though I had proved myself to her through my outfit. (Field Notes 8/31/04)

Evie also picked up that Aimee had scored points with her fashion sensibility:

Whitney seemed to immediately identify Aimee as someone of interest. Aimee's clothes provided important cues. In complimenting her, she demonstrated shared tastes—a knowledge of what's hip. I felt invisible in the interaction with Whitney—presence restored when Mollie came out of the room. Aimee and the other undergrads will be a real asset in generating the interest of residents who may not want much to do with old grad students. (Field Notes 8/31/04)

In this brief interaction, Whitney conveyed to Aimee that she was worthy of notice and managed to make Evie feel old and invisible.

Laura and Elizabeth were both also on the receiving end of Whitney's snubs (although over the years Laura built a connection with her). Despite the fact that our social worlds were far removed from the floor, we were hurt. Laura tended to react with anger. For Elizabeth, attempts to interact with Whitney unearthed long-buried feelings of middle school inadequacy: "I always feel like the biggest loser around her. In general I feel totally over being intimidated by the popular girls that I never was, but she is something else" (Field Notes 9/21/04).

Whitney's practice of refusing to recognize the existence of others was even more hurtful to her peers. For instance, Carrie recounted a painful experience to Laura and her good friends on the floor. As Laura described:

> Carrie saw Whitney enter into The Express. Carrie started walking over that way to say "hi." About that time Whitney walked out and looked directly at her. Carrie was waving and saying "hi," and Whitney moved her eyes, pretending like she didn't even know her. (Field Notes 1/27/05)

The interaction—or rather the avoidance of interaction—occurred in front of Carrie's sister. Whitney even told Alicia, a friend of Carrie's on the floor, that she saw Carrie "but just did not want to say hi to her."

A conversation between Whitney and Aimee suggests that Whitney's rudeness was, in part, fueled by social anxiety. As Aimee reported:

> Whitney turned away from her computer and actually gave me her undivided attention so I knew she needed to talk to me about something that was important to her. . . . She asked me how my rush went and I told her I had a perfect rush all the way through but got my second choice for a house. She was like, "Oh my God, you're so lucky. How did you get everyone to like you?" (Field Notes 9/21/04)

In Chapter 5, we learn that Whitney had some cause to be nervous. Although she was pretty, blonde, slender, tall, socially connected, and outgoing, her parents were divorced and she did not have quite the financial—or cultural—resources for the social status that she sought on campus. She was, as we learned over time, very bright and acutely aware of what she lacked. It may have been these deficits that made Whitney so careful to tailor her interactions on the basis of status—women who were more comfortable in their position had a greater margin for error.

Communicating Popularity

Just as it was important to cut low-status ties, affiliation with high-status individuals was central to social success.[7] High-status social ties operated like currency: women could use these ties to procure more, in the same way that money is invested to make more money. As a consequence, an individual's value as a potential acquaintance rested in large part on how well she advertised the quantity and quality of preexisting social connections.

Hannah arrived knowing relatively few people on campus and roomed blind—ending up with working-class Alyssa, who did not offer much socially. However, she brought with her mounds of photographic proof that she was worth getting to know and widely advertised this fact. For example, one day she showed Laura her photo album:

> The pictures got Hannah talking about her HUGE album from high school and how it was busting at the seams. I asked to see it. After flipping though a few pages I was quite surprised. Hannah was clearly part of the popular crowd at her high school. In picture after picture I noted that she was surrounded by "beautiful" people who would fit quite well here—tan, many blonde, several with dark hair and petite bodies. The guys were quite built for eighteen years old, most with dark hair and dark eyes, almost no skin problems. . . . Many of the pictures were of parties—Hannah doing shots, Hannah drinking beer with some guys and girls, other friends drinking, guys kissing Hannah on both cheeks. This girl clearly drank and partied hard in high school. Other pictures were of her with girlfriends—one or two, or in large groups. There were tons of pictures of her with the track team and meets. She pointed out some guys that she had "hooked up" with, both very cute. She mentioned that they were on the wrestling team and that she really liked wrestling guys since they were in such great shape. (Field Notes 9/23/2004)

The pictures indicated that Hannah's initial lack of ties was situational. In showing that she had friends to spare—of precisely the "right" kind of people (blonde, attractive partiers)—she conveyed entitlement to status in the college scene and that she would eventually prove a useful connection for others.

Because they attended in-state feeder high schools, some women knew literally hundreds of other MU students the day they set foot on campus.

A number of out-of-state students had their own ties through travel and camps. Perhaps without conscious calculation, women made sure to advertise this—immediately getting in touch and hanging out with existing friends and acquaintances. For example, Blair's older brother lived off campus and often threw parties. Blair built friendships on the floor by offering access to these parties. Hannah even reported that she and Blair had become friends after she received one such invite:

> We were talking for a half an hour and [Blair] says, "Listen, my brother's having a party on Friday." This was all about a month and a half ago. She said, "Come on by," so I got her number. We called and we went by and ever since then she's become one of my good friends. (Y1)

Similarly, knowing men in fraternities also helped get invitations to socialize outside of big anonymous parties.

As socially oriented women on the floor made new friends at college, they made sure to document the process. Every night out, every tie formed, every experience acquired was captured through photographs, which could then be shared widely. In 2004–2005, Facebook was just taking off, providing a new way to display popularity. Women also tended to relive their nights out, partly to solidify bonds with the friends they had shared them with, but these conversations also provided evidence that they were someone others should get to know.

The Vampire Effect

Initially we assumed that floor isolates would find each other and create their own friendship groups. However, the interactional strategies of socially ambitious women made this difficult. For example, those who moved into the dorm who were genuinely open to meeting people, quickly acquired the impression that everyone else on the floor had a million friends. Linda, for example, believed everyone was like her roommate, who was "extremely intimidating. Bailey already knew hundreds of people here. Her cell phone was going off from day one, like all the time." She was thus "too shy to ask anyone to go to dinner with me or lunch with me or anything. I ate while I did homework" (Y1). Some even believed that they were alone in being excluded from a floorwide friendship group. As Alana explained, she was less lonely in her one-bedroom second-year apartment than the dorm: "I would hear things going on a lot more and kind of feel left out because all the other women were friends. Here I don't feel as left out because everyone's not hanging out together at the end of the hallway and excluding me" (Y2).

Isolates shut down as most came to realize that openness to friendship would be read as desperation. Amanda and her roommate Madison learned this the hard way. They went around the first day and wrote their names on everybody's white boards expressing openness to interaction. When no one responded, we figured out that they had committed an embarrassing faux pas—their willingness to befriend just anybody marked them as low status and unaware of the fact that only some ties were valuable. Amanda, in particular, rapidly overcorrected and became one of the most withdrawn women on the floor, to the point that even Laura did not connect with her until her second year.

Those marginalized on the floor also found it hard to locate each other because the louder, more visible roommate (virtually always from the higher social class background) typically defined the pair. Others treated the quieter roommate as sort of a sidekick or an invisible appendage. For example, Carrie and Valerie—quiet, lower-middle-class women interested in music and the arts—lived across the hall from each other first semester. They had a lot in common, but Valerie did not like Carrie's more socially ambitious roommate, Blair. She thus never bothered to talk with Carrie, who was too painfully shy to reach out to her.

As the year progressed, those who were not included became quieter (we worried that one was becoming clinically depressed). They became even less visible on the floor, quietly slipping in and out of their rooms and always keeping their doors shut. The most socially integrated women on the floor typically did not even register the existence of the isolates—something we learned in interviews when we asked women about their relationships with all the other residents on the floor.

As the isolates became invisible, socially integrated women took up more and more space—shrieking, literally climbing the walls, coming back loud and drunk in the middle of the night, even at one point in time rollerblading around the floor. In doing so, and inevitably interfering with the sleep and study of the other women, these women communicated their social dominance and sense of entitlement. This dynamic intensified over the course of the year.

The work of Randall Collins and Erika Summers-Effler helps makes sense of what was occurring on the floor.[8] Building on Collins, Summers-Effler argues that in a confined group, emotions can be understood as operating as a system. Dominants absorb energy from subordinates, while subordinates become depressed, resigned, and passive. In this case, social climbers sucked up the emotional energy on floor while the others became emotionally drained, in a sort of vampire effect.

Isolates' resignation to their fate is best illustrated by the failure of all but two to leave the floor. Linda, for example, was placed in our dorm by mistake. When Elizabeth asked about whether she thought about transferring, she said:

> It never really went through my mind. I don't want to move. Well, I don't want to move all my stuff; I don't want to meet another person. Bailey is not my best friend or anything like that, but she . . . isn't scary, doesn't bring people over in the night, doesn't do a lot of the horror things of roommates. (Y1)

Her expectations were quite low, considering that she had overheard Bailey's friends discussing—in her room—how much they disliked her. The incident even caused Linda to leave in tears. In contrast, nonisolates had no qualms about requesting roommate switches or moves to different residence halls. Bailey, for instance, moved out of the room with Linda at the end of the fall semester because staying there was so socially stigmatizing. Similarly, Hannah left her working-class roommate Alyssa behind because she was no fun (see Chapter 1). Sydney moved away from Leah, seemingly because of Leah's sexual identity.

In late spring of 2005, the RA posted a blank board on the hall intended for the recording of floor memories. Not surprisingly, the most dominant floor clique, spearheaded by Whitney, took over the board with all of their own memories. They also made reference to the "dark side" of the hall (see Figure 4.1), which they used as shorthand to refer to a cluster of floor isolates—including Amanda, Amy, Michelle, Megan, Brooke, Mary, Julie, Angela, and—at a later point—Valerie. This came in contrast to the "social" side housing most members of Whitney's clique. Amanda later found out about this insulting label from someone who did not even live on her floor. As she described:

> You know how they always like decorated their hall and [would] be like up until all hours of the night? Like hanging out and partying together and then like we didn't do any of that. So they called us the Dark Side. (Y2)

This incident was so salient for her that years later she would create a Facebook group intended to reclaim the name; however, all but one woman ignored her request.

As the "dark side" example suggests, the vampire dynamic made it difficult for women who were excluded or mistreated to even indirectly confront those who were not nice to them. Although many harbored private resentments, most found the thought of saying or doing something about the situation to be unthinkable. During that first year, public challenges were so rare that we were aware of only one—what we came to call "the shaving cream incident."

Floor isolates Michelle and Valerie were surrounded by affluent partiers—Naomi and Abby on one side, and Melanie on the other. Despite repeated requests to quiet down, the partiers next door were "Really loud. . . . Valerie and I could not sleep. There were nights where [we were] up until 5 a.m. just waiting for them to shut up." However, it was not just that Naomi, Abby, and Melanie were loud. As Michelle explained:

> They were just obnoxious. Like they would walk by and we would hear them talking about things . . . like, "I don't have anything to wear," when you know their whole closet is full of things to wear. But they would talk about it for a half hour. They'd be like, "No, seriously, I don't have anything." And me and Valerie would be like, "My God, go to the mall and shut up." You know? (Y5)

Valerie, who was paying her own way through college, also found her neighbors' lack of academic engagement utterly baffling:

> They stay up until 4:00 in the morning. Do you guys go to class? Do you not have classes? What's your deal? . . . You're paying a lot of money for this. It's not like high school where you're forced to go. If you even want to be here, then why aren't you trying harder? If you fail this class, it's like 500 dollars gone [laugh] and the books too. Why are you wasting your time? . . . I can't understand why people would come to college and fail. I guess if you're not paying for it yourself, you can just take it for granted. (Y1)

Michelle and Valerie cared about their grades, and when Melanie and her boyfriend "had a yelling match all night long" during finals week quiet hours, it was the last straw (Michelle Y5). Finally, they reacted. Michelle took "a big manila envelope and filled it with shaving cream and slid it under the door and stomped on it" (Y5).

Michelle and Valerie's ability to engage in retaliation depended on their solidarity—they had known each other since childhood. Had Michelle been entirely alone, she probably would have suffered quietly. Even so, as a senior, Michelle realized that the practical joke was not the most direct way to address the situation. She reflected: "I don't think I would do that now. I would just walk over there and be like, 'Shut the fuck up'" (Y5). At the time, however, she did not and could not do that. Michelle was not aware that nearly half of the floor shared her sentiments about loud, affluent partiers, as most isolates kept such a low profile on the floor. Nor did she feel entitled to demand that her preferences—which were in line with actual dormitory rules—be respected. The vampire dynamic ensured her silence until the very end of the year, when it was too late to change anything.

The Consequences of Social Isolation

To flash forward briefly, only 38% of women who were socially integrated into the floor were, five years later, either at risk of a failed mobility project or downward mobility. In contrast, 64% of social isolates were, and the number would be even higher if leaving the university had not turned out to be a positive for many less privileged women, as detailed in Chapter 6.[9] These numbers suggest a link between social integration in college and later stratification processes, a finding that is supported by higher education research.[10]

Below we identify mechanisms through which social isolation in the first year of college set students up to struggle at the university, potentially leading to troubles down the road.[11] In some of the cases we discuss, there is a "chicken or the egg" puzzle: it is impossible to know if social isolation generated the problem, or if the problem contributed to the social isolation. Regardless, placement in a party dorm increased the odds of certain students finding themselves without social ties, and this, for some, reinforced or intensified existing issues.

Limited Social Networks Later in College

Social isolation in year one had strong and lingering effects on network tie acquisition throughout the duration of college. This was in part due to the structure of housing. Freshmen, who were required to live on campus, took up most slots in university housing. Although not explicitly stated, first-year student housing is expected to feed students into other arrangements. But this works only if one makes friends in the residence hall. First-year housing is thus perhaps the most critical space for the formation of college friendships.

The process worked for socially integrated women on the floor. Not one of those who moved into a sorority their sophomore year was a floor isolate. Sorority members were immediately integrated into large and dense network structures, gaining "insta-friends" as outsiders sometimes derogatorily commented. Other socially integrated women moved into apartments or houses, typically with at least one person they met on their first-year floor. For example, Brenda, Nicole, and Bailey—all part of Whitney's clique on the "social side" of the floor—lived in an apartment together as sophomores. Here they made friends with those in the apartments nearby, as well as with each other's friends from high school and college. Two of these women rushed as sophomores.

In contrast, students who left their first-year dormitory as isolates had to start the process of making friends over. For example, Crystal, Valerie, and Olivia all spent their sophomore year in college on largely freshmen floors. Crystal and Valerie, who moved to dorms where they fit better, both made a few friends. Olivia, who stayed another year in the same dorm on the same floor in the same room, experienced the same outcome—another year of social isolation. Linda secured a single room in one of the few dormitories designed for older students. However, the suite layout, designed for greater privacy (presumably for students who already had friends), did not facilitate much interaction. As Linda noted in retrospect, "Unless you know . . . the people who live there, you're not going to meet your neighbors . . . which is what I wanted to do. So [it was] not a great fit" (Y5).

A few isolates had first-year roommates that they continued to live with their second year in off-campus apartments. Yet in all of these cases the connection existed prior to arrival at college. For instance, Julie and Angela were childhood friends, as were Heather and Stacey, and Morgan and Natasha. Pairing with a longtime friend did not offer a new network tie. In addition, these women did not benefit from each other's social networks as they overlapped so extensively and, when considering ties with other MU students, were impoverished.

Given the barriers to forming new ties in college, many isolates relied more heavily on high school friends, family, or friends from work. This pulled them further away from their MU peers and made it less likely that their paths would cross. For instance, as Morgan noted, "I haven't grown apart from any [of my friends from home] at all. . . . [My friends and] my boyfriend came up a lot and I went down to Capital City every weekend. It was kind of bad cause I didn't make friends here" (Y2). Similarly, over time, Amanda grew more deeply tied to the people at the big box store where she worked. As she explained, "They need me there, and I have like responsibility there, and I've connected to people there" (Y3). Olivia, who at year three had only one friend at MU, was very dependent on her family—driving home virtually every weekend to be with them. Over time it grew even more unlikely that these women would form friendships on campus.

Lack of Goals and Interests

The initiative and clarity that lead to decisive action often derive from social networks through which ideas and encouragement flow. Particularly in moving from the structure of high school to college—which is more self-directed—students rely on other college students to get them interested and get them going. For example, a woman may talk to a professor because someone else encouraged her to do so, join a club because acquaintances pushed her to come to a meeting, or get the courage to study abroad if several friends are also going. Even after leaving the floor, a few isolates continued to display high levels of passivity in part because they lacked access to others who could motivate them into action.

Two of the most frustratingly passive women were upper-middle-class Morgan and Natasha. As suggested above, they spent most of their free time with friends who "just kind of stayed home" after graduation (Natasha Y2). Lacking interactions with other MU students, Natasha and Morgan remained inert, adopting the lowest effort path in every aspect of their lives. They lived with each other throughout the entirety of our study, never engaged in any sort of college activity not required by their classes, and remained in majors in which they were dissatisfied. Even a year after college, neither could identify even a general area of interest. As Laura inquired of Natasha:

Laura: And you don't have any idea of what you might be really interested in?
Natasha: I really don't. That's kind of my problem. I just don't really know what my thing would be. (Y5)

While others had undergone considerable transformation in college, these two seemed not to have changed. As Morgan put it, "I think I'm still the same person . . . as the first time you interviewed me" (Y5).

The women were aware that something had not gone exactly right with their college experience, although they were not particularly upset about it. For instance, Morgan answered that her biggest regret in college was not studying abroad. When Laura asked why she never did, Morgan responded, "I don't know. I didn't know how to figure out having a house and room-mates for half a year and what I would do with the rest of it" (Y5). We saw this as in part about a lack of college friends to provide a model, push her along, and fill in some of those alternate half-year slots. In trying to piece together how things might have been different for her, Natasha told a story about one of her few college-going friends with the opposite experience: "She went to Villanova. . . . I went out there and I loved the environment out there. She had the small school and she had the group of friends; she knew everyone" (Y5). Natasha's friend had what Natasha did not—college friends.

Academic Disengagement

As Steven Brint and Allison Cantwell argue in "Portrait of the Disengaged," most college students require interaction with fellow students (as well as professors) in order to absorb and engage with classroom material. When social networks are not in place to facilitate interaction, academic commitment and performance often weaken. They refer to this specific form of academic disengagement as "interactional."[12] Because of their lack of social ties on campus, isolates on the floor were far more likely than others to display interactional disengagement.

Here we return to Alana who, as we noted at the start of the chapter, arrived with a thirst for knowledge. Our notes from the start of freshman year document Alana processing her course material with others:

> Another topic of conversation with Erica, Taylor, and Alana concerned the research project. Alana is in Jacobson's intro class, and he does a session on, as Alana aptly put in, "sociologists gone bad." She explained to us about research involving electric shocks, untreated syphilis, etc. We responded by explaining that, yes, sociologists really did these things, and incidents such as these motivated developing rules to protect human subjects, which we now have to follow. We talked about the human subjects issues related

to our project. Erica was very interested, and quite intrigued about the possibility of this someday being a book. This conversation was positive on many levels. It allowed Alana to display and gain additional mastery over course material. It gave us a context to talk about the human subjects issues related to our work in more depth than we have yet—generating a deeper level of informed consent on their part. . . . It also modeled intellectual engagement as a normal topic of conversation for a Saturday afternoon. (Field Notes 9/4/04)

Even though several of her floormates were in the same classes, Alana had few opportunities like this—most of which were orchestrated by us.

Alana was aware that she never wanted the college experience many of those on her freshman floor sought out. She described: "They're the ones that I see in class texting all the time. And bitching about class being boring when I'm actually enjoying it" (Y4). Connecting with them may not have offered her much. However, she realized that not interacting with others who shared her vision of college caused her to pull back academically that first year. As she recalled:

It was very lonely and hard. Really hard. I didn't do so well academically. You'd think if I was a social recluse that I'd be really good at academics, but I think I got some C's that semester. . . . I wish more than anything in the world that I would have made more friends that year. (Y4)

Certainly, there were other factors that contributed to Alana's early academic performance. Yet the lack of peers with whom she could discuss her coursework limited her learning.

Mental Health Issues

Social ties are one of the best predictors of good mental health.[13] It is thus not surprising that those without them would be at risk for depression and other issues, such as alcohol and drug abuse. We found this was particularly true of isolates who, at one point or another, tried desperately to fit into the social scene at MU.[14] Rather than seeing the structure of social life at MU as the problem, they tended to put the burden on themselves to make the situation work—and take the blame when they failed.

In this case, Carrie's story is illustrative. Carrie had the misfortune of rooming with one of the more aggressive social climbers on the floor—Blair, a friend from her hometown. This meant that Carrie was often close enough to high-status individuals to be evaluated by them, if not included. For example, as she noted of Blair's sorority: "I don't really go down there, people aren't that friendly in the house. Most people just like ignore me, just like I am not there" (Y3).

Carrie was not a partier in high school and was quite shy. She had to make herself drink in order to tolerate social situations, especially since Blair would often run off with friends, leaving her alone. Soon her drinking got out of hand. For instance, early one morning, at 3 a.m., she received a call from a guy who claimed to have made out with her. Yet Carrie could not recall who he was. As she explained, later "someone said they saw me asleep on the couch [that night] with some guy." She also told Laura about "one night that I [had] gotten so sick that I really don't remember. I remember hitting my head on something and then going outside and then throwing up, but everything between I don't . . . [remember]" (Y1).

Carrie's concerns about fitting in were so intense they started to inhibit her movement on campus. She would walk long distances in the dead of winter, or not leave at all, rather than take the bus. As she explained:

> I don't like taking the bus [because] sometimes the other people look at me weird. . . . I don't like this winter coat that I have. [Laura: So when you're on the bus you feel like people are looking at your coat?] Yeah it's so different from everybody else's. I don't like it. [Laura: What does everybody else wear?] A puffy coat. . . . I want a puffy coat. (Y1)

As Carrie withdrew, she began to get more depressed, and in order to feel comfortable around others she had to drink—a vicious cycle that, as the quote above suggests, was complicated by her lack of resources (that is, money to buy the "right" clothing). By her senior year, Carrie still saw her lack of friends as primarily her fault. As she noted, "It's hard to make friends. . . . For me it is. It's really hard" (Y4).

Limited Access to Information

Social networks are one of the most critical conduits for information. Students without many friends are less likely to learn about an exciting major, a critical deadline, fraternities to avoid (due to reputations for sexual assault), good places to park, or opportunities for internships. For instance, Julie and Angela—who were ostracized on the floor—experienced what was, from their perspective, a second social disaster because they were not tapped into peer networks. As they described:

Julie: We knew before we even came here that we wanted to rush, and our moms were both in it and our dads and so, like . . . it was really something we wanted to do. But I don't even know how it worked out. . . . We heard about a deadline after it had already passed. You had to sign up to do it, so we missed that. We tried to contact a ton of different people, but it was a pretty strict thing. It was pretty upsetting just 'cause none of it had started.

Angela: That was one of the things we regret.

Other isolates did not learn about living situations on campus where they might have felt more comfortable because they lacked ties to others. Thus, as we described at the beginning of the chapter, Alana did not transfer to the alternative dorm because she did not know anything about it. She realized how well it would have worked for her only in retrospect:

I should have lived in [the alternative dorm]. . . . I should have put in for a dorm transfer because I was very unhappy and lonely [in my original dorm] and I didn't make any friends that year. The type of people in [the alternative dorm] would have been more accepting. It's more social there. . . . I would have had friends. (Y4)

Alana also missed out on joining a multicultural Greek organization, which offered a more diverse and studious group of students—exactly what she was seeking:[15]

I thought there was gonna be a sorority for people like me. . . . And it wasn't gonna be all like sorority-like. And that wasn't true. I found out that was just something I made up in my head [laughs]. (Y1)

Such a group did exist. However, without talking to others, Alana did not learn of it. These alternative living arrangements and social groups provided protective segregation for students who did not fare well on the party pathway. Yet these niches were not easy to locate, particularly for isolated students who started college in a party dorm.

Leaving the University

In Chapter 6 we show that being a less privileged student significantly increased the likelihood of transferring from or dropping out of MU. Setting aside, for now, whether leaving was a good thing, social isolation was one reason why students left MU. Ten isolates left before graduation (and an additional two strongly considered it), in contrast to only two women who were socially integrated that first year. Isolation on the dorm floor was also one of the few experiences that less privileged and more privileged leavers shared.

As we detail later, there were a variety of factors that led less privileged women to leave the university. Many were interrelated. For example, Alyssa noted:

> If that whole [boyfriend from home] situation wasn't going on, I definitely think I would have made a better attempt at getting to know people and to stay at MU. But I also know that where I was living I don't think that I was real comfortable with the girls. So I think without him and without . . . being [in our dorm] and maybe [in a different] neighborhood, getting to know more people, and money would have been my last issue as far as living in Fairview. But people do it all the time money wise. I'm sure I probably would have [stayed] if given those three factors. (Y5)

It is interesting, however, how often their narratives ultimately hinged on belonging. As Alyssa suggests, she probably could have made the money situation work, likely by taking out more loans. She left because she did not know anyone at MU and her social ties were elsewhere—primarily with her boyfriend in her hometown.

If students generalize from the experience of not fitting in at a given school, they may decide college in general is not for them. This seemed to be Leah's problem, one that was compounded by leaving MU for a more highly ranked public university, where she found strong parallels in the college scene. In her final year of college she explained:

> The older I get, the more I realize that I'm the kind of person that's not really cut out for the college life. I'm not into the whole binge drinking thing. I'm ready to be an adult in the world, so that's something that I wouldn't find at any college.

Leah managed to get her bachelor of arts, due in part to resources associated with her upper-class background; we return to her story in Chapter 7. However, when working-class students Monica and Heather came to a similar conclusion, they left the four-year system entirely.

Exceptions to the Rule

Not all floor isolates experienced the negative consequences of social isolation identified above. A few managed to leave their freshman year of college unscathed. Why were they spared?

Perhaps the most unharmed was Brooke, a very pretty upper-class woman from out of state with a strong high school academic record. When in high school, her family had moved cross-country, requiring her to break into a new social world:

> I had a lot of friends. I was social, so I never felt like a loser. Ok, so then I moved to a new state and I'm just completely on the outside. I could see every group, every clique, from the perspective of an outsider looking down on it. I'd meet certain people and I could feel them looking up and down, just judging me. (Y3)

Eventually Brooke managed to join the popular crowd in her new high school. However, this experience allowed her to approach college with a detached and analytical eye. One of her first days at MU, she decided to try and interact with some new people:

> I was like, alright. Everyone should still be wanting to meet people, right? I'm just gonna sit down with some people and I'm gonna meet them. And I did, and it was the first and only time I've ever been completely, completely blown off. They just wanted nothing to do with me. . . . I was like, that's horrible! Why? Why would they just shun me off the bat? What? And then I was just like, I don't want to try. Those aren't people I wanna be friends with. (Y3)

This interaction provided a lot of information: she registered the game in play, knew from experience that she could figure out how to break in if she wanted to (as she had the looks, social skills, and money), but decided that she had no interest. She viewed the behavior she observed as immature and, from a position of superiority, extricated herself: "I looked down on a lot of people there that wanted to go to frats all the time and dress up and just make such a big scene about going out. I would just be like [sound of disgust]. . . . I knew by two weeks that I wasn't gonna stay" (Y2).

Brooke moved within the first few weeks of school. Her boyfriend, who lived in another dorm, and her sister, who was on campus and had a car, facilitated the process:

I wouldn't have probably done it but I had seen how nice the rooms were, how nice the people were at my new dorm. And then my boyfriend was like, "I'll move your stuff for you!" [Laughs] I was like, "Okay!" That was a huge step. My sister had a car here, and he was promoting it. That took a huge burden off.

She smoothly transitioned into her new housing unit—known primarily for a heavy concentration of international students from diverse cultures. A year later, when we asked how the move panned out for her, Brooke told us:

Overall I loved it, and ended up with good grades and a lot of friends, and it's perfect. I'm really glad I moved. I talked to Megan, and she, I don't think she came back. I haven't talked to her since. (Y2)

As Brooke's case demonstrates, to evade negative consequences isolates had to exit the floor immediately and rapidly enter another social world. Moving was the most obvious way to do this, but it could also be done by forging strong social ties elsewhere on campus. In order to relocate, a student had to be aware that she was not happy and that she did not fit. She had to have the confidence to realize that the problem was not with her but with the situation. She had to have an expectation that she should be included, optimism that there was a place on campus where this could happen, knowledge of where that place was, and the resources to make it happen (for example, a car to make a move and other friends to help). All of these things are hard to pull off for a lonely student in a new place, especially if they are from a less privileged background.

That Brooke's situation was an exception challenges the vision of college as a collection of diverse social worlds that all students can easily navigate. Some students are able to rapidly move both physically and socially toward places where they fit better. But many of the students who most need social alternatives are the least equipped to find them. As the following chapters detail, fit—at a given university, between students' resources and their pathways, and within one's peer group—is perhaps the most crucial ingredient for success in college. Most floor isolates thus started out on shaky footing. Many did not recover.

CHAPTER **5**

Socialites, Wannabes, and Fit
with the Party Pathway

The Socialite Experience

During college: I'm proud of myself that I made a whole entire network of friends and I made a whole entire sorority. That's so crazy.

(Hannah Y5)

After college: It's fun because we go out all around here . . . down by the Murray Hill area [in Manhattan]. . . . I see a lot of people from MU. There are a lot of girls from my sorority here so that's nice.

(Hannah Y5)

The Wannabe Experience

During college: I just never fit in. I don't know if it was personalities. I think it was mainly because I felt like they all had a lot of money. All their dads were doctors and lawyers and I just didn't fit in. I never felt like I did.

(Blair Y5)

After college: I'm young and I want to be on my own and everything. Ideally, I really would love to move to the city, but because of money right now I just can't. . . . I wish someone told me that college was like Disneyland. It's just not real.

(Nicole Y5)

Socialites and wannabes included ten women who arrived "primed to party" and six who came to MU by default but quickly became party pathway recruits. For these sixteen women, college did not officially start until Greek life was in full swing.[1] Most partied at least four days a week for stretches of college and perceived such participation as obligatory. As one woman put it, "I went out a lot freshman year, but now I don't. I mean, I go out Wednesday through Saturday night. *Sometimes take a night off in the weekend"* (Melanie Y4, emphasis added). Academics were a means to staying in school and accessing college life. Easy majors aided in this task. Seven women majored in some form of communications or journalism, four in education or human development, three in business-lite majors, and one in apparel merchandising.[2]

However, the party pathway did not result in the same journey or have the same consequences for everyone. Disparities were patterned by the level of resources available to the two groups. The seven socialites were from upper-class and upper-middle-class families who effortlessly supported their acquisition of a "college experience" and continued a high level of financial support, combined with active social and career engineering, after college. The nine wannabes were from families who had to dig deep in order to support their daughter's sorority fees, spring break trips, and bar tabs. They included four women from middle-class backgrounds, as well as five upper middle-class women whose parents had stretched beyond their means to afford an out-of-state education. Wannabes often had to rely on raw beauty, and determination to play the same game as socialites. The rewards of the party pathway—fun, social status, a career based on personality and appearance, and a secure upper-middle-class existence—were far less likely to materialize for this group.

Social and Erotic Status

Both socialites and wannabes were among the most socially and erotically successful on the floor. Most got into sororities; some even made it into top houses. They engaged heavily in the party scene, enjoyed hookups, and formed relationships with high-status men on campus. This description, however, hides many of the ways in which class resources mattered. For example, there was an ease, naturalness, and entitlement to socialites' experiences in the social scene, whereas wannabes' experiences were marred by a painful sense of never quite measuring up (see Table 5.1).

The Socialite Experience: Comfort and Ease in the Social Scene

Blonde, blue-eyed, slender, bubbly, and stylish Tara embodied the socialite experience. Tara came well educated about "designers and labels" and attributed her sense of style to her extremely wealthy grandmother.

Table 5.1. Socialite and wannabe college experiences

Descriptor	Socialites (7)	Wannabes (9)
Class background	Upper class or upper-middle class	Upper-middle class or middle class
College arena		
Academic	Low effort, less demanding approach	Downgrade from pragmatic approach
Social	Privilege confers status and fun; overrides deficits	Rely on raw beauty and savvy; struggle to measure up
Romantic/sexual	Primed to hook up; status and networks are protective	Encumbered by hometown boyfriends; no protection from negative experiences

Women	Upper class (4):
	  Abby
	  Hannah
	  Maya
	  Melanie
	
	Upper-middle class (3):
	  Naomi
	  Tara
	  Bailey
		Upper-middle class (5):
		  Mara
		  Nicole
		  Sophie
		  Sydney
		  Alicia
		
		Middle class (4):
		  Chelsea
		  Whitney
		  Blair
		  Karen

Before college she had moved in elite social circles in her moderately sized Southern city, attending balls and other social events with older, distinguished "gentlemen." Being charming and perfectly dressed came easily for Tara. Seemingly endless financial resources helped her pull off her look.

At college, Tara had a "perfect rush." As she explained, at "every round" she got "every single house back." This appeared to happen without much effort on her part. She noted:

> I just kept talking and asking questions and being friendly and with every house there seemed I had something in common. . . . Even in a house I didn't like there was something that I could relate to. (Y1)

When we inquired, she explained that she did not really think about what to wear to rush events. She told Laura, "I like fashion a lot, and clothes, and looking cute. . . . I didn't have to do that [plan ahead]. I just knew that I wanted a cute outfit" (Y1). Given the extent to which she fulfilled the criteria valued on campus, it was not surprising that Tara was empowered by—rather than at the mercy of—the rush process. As she explained, "I just kinda had to eliminate houses that I liked. A lot of 'em were pulling for me" (Y1). With the decision in her hands, she selected a house in the Elite Three because "They kinda have like a classy image. Are known to be classy, and I like that" (Y1).

Not every socialite, however, came to college as perfectly packaged as Tara. Two were even chubby by Greek standards. Both had curly hair that they often left unstraightened. Neither of these women worked particularly hard to impress. For example, one had a Grateful Dead wardrobe that was generationally out of style. She was also so unfriendly during rush that an undergraduate researcher reported she was getting a reputation for being a "bitch." Both of these socialites were aware of what one should do in order to get into a good house. Abby even noted:

> You see the people on our floor, what they're doing, wearing their pearls and stuff. I'm like, no I'm not gonna do that. I mean, I have pearls but they're for black tie. I'm not gonna wear them to rush in a sorority. I didn't blow dry my hair or anything. I didn't care. So I did not get a good look-back. (Y1)

Although both women went Greek, neither made it into a top- or even middle-tier house. What was surprising, however, was that they made it into any house given their indifference to the process and unwillingness to work at cuteness.

We initially could not understand how they managed to flout social expectations. In fact, before people knew who Hannah was, she was so lonely she considered transferring. However, the mentions of exotic vacation locals, piles of designer clothing lying unworn in her closet, and—as we noted in Chapter 4—stacks of party photos with hordes of obviously affluent high school friends conveyed to everyone on the floor that she, like Abby, was very wealthy. Both women also exuded a sense of entitlement to a place in the Greek system, to the extent that Abby—as suggested above—did not even try to impress during rush. What saved these two was a combination of extreme privilege and the self-assuredness that came with it.

Social success was also about having fun, making memories, building friendships, and having a "best time of your life" experience. For socialites, college was invariably this, regardless of how their sorority ranked. Tara, the socialite with a perfect rush, told us:

> I'm glad I joined because I like having activities. I grew up that way and I like the dances and all the functions and stuff. It was fun, like I say, especially during events. Everyone probably felt that way during MU Game Week. It was fun having all your parties that week and welcome week and organized events. You felt really a part of it during the race and stuff. Those were fun times being in a sorority. (Y5)

Being a socialite also made it possible to have a similar experience without being in a sorority. For example, one woman who was cut from rush because of poor grades moved to a new luxury apartment complex near the bars that had developed its own elite party scene. It housed out-of-state women who did not need to join a sorority because they were so rich and connected.

Socialites' standing on campus also translated into positive sexual and romantic experiences with high-status men, and these experiences reinforced their position at the top of the hierarchy. As described in Chapter 3, much of the erotic ranking on campus occurred via the party hookup scene, in which socialites arrived primed to participate. They saw hooking up as a normal part of college life. As Tara put it, "It just happens. It's natural" (Y1). Thus, virtually all socialites arrived at college without boyfriends, although Abby—who had a boyfriend back home—did not let this stop her. She noted of hooking up, "I just kinda leave him clueless. It's better that way" (Y1).

With hundreds of ties on campus, socialites rarely hooked up with men that they or their friends did not know. Closed networks were protective. They held fraternity men accountable for their actions, which reduced the likelihood of encountering negative treatment. As Tara noted, "I've never had experience with guys harassing me. I hear so many girls saying that they were harassed or guys were so disgusting with them, and I never had that experience" (Y1). Socialites were also typically secure enough to reject disrespectful sexual advances, regardless of the man's status. As Naomi reported of a late-night text message from a potential hookup, "It was totally perverted and gross, but it involved hot sauce. . . . I remember showing all my friends and I was just like I am not answering any more of his phone calls" (Y3). Naomi—with the support of her friends—simply ignored the man.

Over the course of college, socialites spent time in committed relationships. However, they were highly selective about whom they dated. For

example, Hannah activated her information network before even considering a relationship. She explained, "I told my friend Steven, who's in
[his fraternity house], about him. I'm like 'Can you get information on this
kid?'" (Y1). Socialites often pulled men in top fraternities—or college
athletes—off the market. For example, one woman dated a football player
for most of her time at MU. Dating athletes, who were surrounded by eager
groupies, brought status. Her packed social life revolved around his sporting
events, parties with other athletes, and hanging out with the girlfriends of
other players. Similarly, Tara dated a guy in a respected fraternity. This afforded her special benefits in his house. She noted, "Everyone knows we're
boyfriend girlfriend so it's just like my home now, it's not like a fraternity
house" (Y1).

The Wannabe Experience: Not Measuring Up

As a cheerleader in her in-state high school, middle-class Whitney was no
stranger to the top of the pecking order, but in college she was out of her
league. When a new acquaintance from the East Coast jokingly called her
a "hick," Whitney claimed that she teased her about "bumping around in
your Gucci and your Diors, your Christian Diors!" (Y1). Although the point
of the story was to convey her friendships with wealthy out-of-state students, she also revealed awareness of the class differences that separated
them. Whitney could not afford to buy a complete designer wardrobe and
set about building the right look piece by piece—for example, buying a few
accessories (like a Dooney and Bourke purse) that would allow her to signal
greater wealth than she actually had. Still, Dooney and Bourke (at roughly
$150 dollars a purse) was a far cry from Dior purses—which could easily
cost thousands—and one purse could carry you only so far. As Whitney
noted, "Once rush is over . . . it's like, all over. That's like, the one purse that
[you] have" (Y1).

Aware that she was lacking vital information about how the social system
worked, Whitney set out on a quest to figure it out. Aimee—an undergraduate research team member and member of a good sorority on campus—
was recruited for this task. Her research notes state: "I don't think Whitney
necessarily likes me but rather uses me as a good source of information for
her regarding sorority life" (Field Notes 9/28/04). Whitney repeatedly
pestered Aimee for details on the reputations of various houses and, as
we suggested in Chapter 4, on ways to impress during rush. Her thirst for

information paid off. Although she did not achieve Tara's perfect rush, Whitney also made it into a top house.

The comparison between Tara and Whitney highlights the extent to which wannabes had to work to achieve what was seemingly second nature to socialites. The wannabes who reached the top were highly savvy and able to skillfully read their environments, extract the necessary information, and act on it despite limited resources. For example, Blair—a homecoming queen in her small in-state town—went from wearing no makeup, without a tan or highlights, and lounging in her church group's "What Would Jesus Do" T-shirt, to a passable sorority member in a matter of months.

Whereas socialites could break into the Greek system without being per-fectly qualified, wannabes were in the opposite situation. There was little variation in their "beauty." All could be described as attractive and several as drop-dead gorgeous even without makeup or the right accessories. Blair had the bone structure and body of a beauty queen. Beauty was not enough, however. Other similarly pretty women were hampered by a lack of cul-tural or social know-how, went into rush unprepared, and found it to be harrowing.

Field notes recount the first rush experience of Karen, an attractive, pe-tite, blonde, blue-eyed wannabe who would try again sophomore year:

> She was pretty bummed out about the houses she got back. . . . She looked me in the eyes with a really disbelieving look saying, "I swear they look at your clothes. I know they do." . . . Apparently she got many compliments on her pants and her top. . . . [But] she said that . . . at a certain point [she] didn't switch from her [rain] boots back into her [more fashionable] shoes. . . . She pulled them out to show me, saying that they were her [in-state] boots—a dead give-away of where she is from. . . . [She] also said that she felt like they were looking at her body at one house. A girl in [one house] stared at her stomach the entire time they talked, making her really conscious of her body. She said that it wasn't like she has a huge belly or anything. (Field Notes 1/5/05)

Her sense of being judged and found wanting comes in direct contrast to the self-assured awareness displayed by socialites. Another wannabe simi-larly recounted:

> It was really intimidating, the whole rush experience. . . . I think my rush would be completely different if I went through now because I know so

much more and I feel like I was really naive and didn't know anyone when I went through before. (Sydney Y5)

Both of these women eventually ended up in the same low-ranking house, seemingly as a result of fairly minor social mistakes (like wearing rain boots instead of cute shoes on a rainy day). Looks did not always make up for lack of money and lack of savvy.

Despite their struggles with rush, some wannabes reported stories of fun and belonging once they got in their Greek houses. Notably, these were mostly women whose parents had enough money (or pulled out enough loans) to help their children live like socialites during college. For example, as Nicole explained, sorority life helped her to obtain the college experience she had heard so much about:

All I knew was like movies that I saw about crazy college parties and stuff. And there are crazy parties, but I think it's about a lot more than that. . . . I wanted to join a sorority. And now I'm in a sorority and I love it. . . . We all just get along so well and I'm just having the best time. . . . It sounds so stupid and I know everyone says it, but it really feels like you're part of a community. (Y3)

Ironically, obtaining this type of social experience would make the realities of wannabe life after college that much more painful.

Most wannabes, however, suffered from feelings of inadequacy throughout college. Blair, for instance, managed to strategize her way into a top house. However, she quickly realized that getting in was not the same as fitting in. As she explained:

I think the whole sorority thing was kind of disappointing. Like I thought I would meet a lot better friends. I hoped, and that just never happened. . . . I was happy to get into [Top House] but I remember even that first day I felt so uncomfortable. (Y4)

Blair also recognized the large gap in resources:

We have this pledge class giving out awards and of course I didn't win any. . . . It was like, Julie wins the cutest clothes award. And I was like, her clothes are really cute but then, no one in [my hometown] would ever think to wear stuff like that. You know? It was just completely different. How much people spend on clothes or jewelry or things. . . . I mean, on dad's credit card and just swipe it and it'll be fine. It just boggles my mind.

[Laura: Were there other people more like you?] Um, no, not really [laughs]. . . . All of my roommates' dads have always been like some kind of surgeon, doctor, this or that. . . . Well there's this one girl in my pledge class but she deactivated because she couldn't afford it. (Y4)

No matter how hard she tried, Blair never felt like she quite measured up. As she noted:

I think that in a way that I'm not good enough. . . . I just didn't fit in. You know? . . . And not just like clothes and jewelry and stuff like that but just girls who knew each other. It just never worked out. (Y4)

Although Blair's experience of social failure was particularly intense, most wannabe women had a sense of themselves as outsiders looking in. Mara told us:

I come from a single mother household. Like I'm not flashing jewelry. . . . It's just, there is that money thing there. Because all these girls have all these designer handbags, and jewelry, and it's like okay, like this is normal [laughs]. You know, no, it's not normal. You're just living in a house where it's normal. (Y4)

These women were unable to display the same sense of entitlement that characterized socialites' consumption of the full "college experience." They were often struck by things that others simply took for granted. As Whitney remarked wonderingly:

It's funny. I was just looking around the other day and we had chapter. . . . I was just looking at everyone's jeans and there were thousands of dollars of denim in that room. I was just thinking about it, 'cause almost everyone's wearing designer jeans. (Y2)

Sometimes they even sounded like sociologists. One woman noted, after reading about peer dynamics in middle school for her sociology of gender class:

This whole like cycle of popularity. . . . I feel like it's kind of the same type of thing [in my sorority]. . . . A lot of it is heavily, I feel like based on appearance, and looks, and materialistic things. (Mara Y4)

It is thus perhaps not surprising that our most insightful critiques of the Greek system came from less affluent members.

Wannabes' position in the erotic market of the party scene was also more precarious than that of socialites. Although most did not realize it in advance, seven out of nine came with a handicap—serious boyfriends, the majority of whom were (or would be) attending college elsewhere. It was in this context, as reported in Chapter 3, that wannabe Nicole snapped at socialite Tara for revealing to others that she had a boyfriend. It is possible that part of the reason why Tara did not see this as damaging information was because her own boyfriend, in a fraternity on campus, enhanced her status. In contrast, Nicole's hometown boyfriend only posed an obstacle in her pursuit of status. As she noted, "I don't need to be tied down to my high school boyfriend for two years when this is the time to be meeting people" (Y3).

Like Nicole, all wannabes eventually broke up with their boyfriends and moved into the hookup scene—at least for a time. Their experiences, however, were markedly less positive than that of socialites. Even the few who made it to top houses were never as well networked and well known as socialites, giving men fewer reasons to treat them well. Blair described:

Oh my God I hate telling about this. So I hooked up with Alex twice. . . . The first time he was kissing me and stuff like that. But last—let's see, not this past weekend but the last weekend—let's just say oral sex. Oh my gosh! But, okay, I haven't talked to him since that night. . . . I mean I just don't hear anything from him anymore. I even went over there and he did not say hi to me. So, but it's fine 'cause I've learned my lesson. (Y2)

One wannabe was even the victim of an attempted sexual assault at a fraternity party. Experiences like these soured wannabes on hooking up. Blair even started searching for sexual and romantic connections elsewhere. She noted, "When I saw Rob at church I just was like this kid is cute. . . . He's not in a fraternity, which I love, because I hate frat guys. He goes to church. I mean, hello?" (Y2).

Though more relationally oriented than socialites, wannabes could not afford to be as selective—particularly if they were interested in dating high-ranking guys. For example, one wannabe even stayed with her boyfriend (in a top fraternity) after he cheated on her and gave her a sexually transmitted disease. Wannabes seemed more desperate for their relationships to work out, even if they were less than ideal. For instance, although Karen was full of complaints about her brief relationship with a campus athlete (who was from her hometown), she was hopeful that it would rekindle. As she explained, "I'm not ever gonna give up on the opportunity [to be with him]. Maybe he still wants me. If I still have two more years of school left, could be a possibility. Who knows?" (Y2).

Striving for social and erotic status often took its toll on wannabes. There were higher personal costs given how much they had to transform themselves. For example, field notes recount a moment of crisis that Blair had during her first year:

> She said that [her boyfriend from home] said something to her the other day that was hard to hear but maybe true. He told her that maybe she is just trying to be something she is not. He said that ever since she got here she has been different, trying to be "Miss Big U sorority girl." Blair said that she didn't feel like herself anymore and that she thought maybe he was right. . . . [She] now thinks that everything she once wanted was not who she is. (Field Notes 3/29/05)

This tension between who she believed she had to be to fit in and who she felt more comfortable being characterized Blair's time at college.

Perhaps in response to the stress, some wannabes drank so heavily that their habits were deemed excessive even in this hard-drinking social world. Blair's dormitory friends began to wonder whether she was an alcoholic. Similarly, Whitney admitted drinking massive quantities of alcohol. As she noted, "You just build up a tolerance. I'll take twenty, thirty shots and I'll be fine. . . . It's to the point now that I have to, or I don't even get drunk." She told us that during spring break she "passed out in a port-a-potty. Which was kind of unsafe." Another time, after a night of drinking Mountain Dew vodka shooters, she reported:

> I think something bad happened to me and I couldn't move, and the next day I was throwing up yellow stuff. It wasn't like your normal throw up, get sick morning. . . . And I would start foaming, but not really foam. That definitely sucked, but it wouldn't stop me from going back. (Whitney Y1)

Academic Success

Socialites arrived at college with the intent to play hard and work only as hard as necessary. In contrast, wannabes took a similarly low effort academic approach by default. What the women could not see from their position—nor even could we, until years later—was that this approach would be logical and effective for some but rob others of needed skills and knowledge.

The Socialite Experience: Making a Low-Effort Approach Work

Five of the seven socialites arrived with interests in media, sports, fashion, or entertainment. As Naomi noted, "I've always been focused more on entertainment, like dancing, TV shows, than reading books" (Y1). She wanted to be in "the entertainment field," specifically "in public relations or something with fitness" that could lead to a job in Chicago or New York City (Y1). In these fields, personality, appearance, social skills, and charm—traits that she, like most socialites, had perfected—were highly valued. Socialites did not expect to devote too much effort to developing academic knowledge and credentials. Naomi explained:

> I mean I like entertainment, but I also wanted to stay in [the School of Physical Education] 'cause I don't have to take a language. I struggle at languages. I just never, I mean I don't even got—I don't even got!—I don't even have my English down straight (Y2).

Though a bit lazy and ever the joker, Naomi was far from stupid. Like other socialites, she just opted not to expend unnecessary energy.

In fact, even exceptionally smart socialites arrived at college with an aversion to intellectual heavy lifting. Abby immediately selected psychology, which is a challenging major at MU and favored by students in the Honors College. For her, however, this major was anything but demanding. As she explained:

> I never go to my psych classes and I have a B+ in one and A+ in the other. . . . I have a 9 a.m. No, I'm sorry. I'm not gonna go. It's stupid. It's experimental psychology. You learn about interviewing and hypotheses—stupid things. . . . I'm not saying that I know everything, but . . . there's not really been any hard concepts [in college] to grasp except for calculus last semester. (Abby Y1)

Instead of switching to a major that would require her to exert herself, she later revealed that sticking with psychology was part of her low-effort strategy. She told us that she always aimed for a "3.0, about an 80 percent," which she could achieve with minimal effort:

> In classes where I knew I would get an 80 percent, at least a B, a B–, I would not care as much. . . . It's not worth the 80 percent stress for the 20 percent grade increase. For me, it wasn't. Half the reason I was in college was not because of school. (Abby Y5)

Socialite GPAs hovered between 2.8 to 3.0 mostly because academics were irrelevant to their overall orientation to college. Naomi even accurately predicted that her GPA would dip below a 3.0 by the spring semester of her freshman year given all of the social demands. As she noted, "My parents aren't gonna be very happy but they'll understand. . . . I mean, I'm living in a very social dorm, always things going on. It's very hard to sit there and focus on your work." Similarly, at the end of college Tara reported of her then 2.8 GPA:

> I have a really low GPA. . . . I never took it seriously. I never thought about it. 'Cause I'm, like, not an intellectual. I mean, I go to class. I have my responsibilities, but I'm more social. . . . Not book oriented, you know? (Y4)

Given who they were and what they wanted to do, grades, work ethic, and major did not matter much for socialites, as long as they graduated. All were strategic about staying in good standing in order to remain at college and at the party. Despite occasional dips in GPA, none of these women ran into classes they could not pass or ended up on academic probation. This was, in part, because they were linked into a grapevine of information about the least demanding majors and how to pass difficult classes they could not avoid (such as taking them during the summer or at community colleges).

What did matter—particularly in entertainment-oriented fields—was industry experience and networking. Socialite families had excellent contacts and provided their children with opportunities of which wannabes could only dream. For example, one of Hannah's father's "best friends at work grew up with [Tom,] an owner of [a major sports team]." He secured her a summer internship in a top media studio in New York. Hannah recounted:

> I was in the studio the whole entire summer. . . . I became like good friends with a bunch of the anchors and a bunch of the producers. I would sit there and I would go into the editing room and watch them edit and cut highlights, and how they did it on the machinery and everything. (Y3)

Similarly, the summer after her sophomore year, Naomi did an internship in New York for the sports division of a major network. She got the internship through her sister:

> My sister works for [music company] and they do a lot of barter situations with [major network]. . . . She met a girl [who] worked in human rela-

tions and she just mentioned, "I've been doing a lot for you guys. Can you help my sister out?" And they were like, "Of course." . . . I worked on a floor [with] like the chairman of [major network], and the VP or something. . . . I learned about clips, I learned how to put together a clip packet and press packets and writing many paragraphs that go into press releases. And I put together a [sports league] media guide, and I learned a lot of faces. (Y3)

Although these internships were sometimes not easy—also involving a lot of "bitch" work as Hannah called it—they gave women opportunities to mingle with top executives, learn important skills, and acquire valuable recommendations from powerful people.

Only affluent, well-connected families could help their children land such opportunities. This was particularly obvious in the case of poorly credentialed socialites. For example, when Naomi arrived at the network, she was the most junior in the office in terms of year in school, age, length of tenure in the office, and school selectivity (the others were all from elite private schools). It was apparent that she had gotten the internship not on the strength of her resume but the strength of her ties. In fact, internships in her desired industry seemingly dropped in her lap as a result of her social location. The summer after her junior year Naomi got another amazing opportunity that she turned down, preferring to spend the summer relaxing, traveling, and shopping with her mom.

Socialites' internships were often unpaid and involved living in expensive metropolitan areas for the summer. As Naomi described of her time in Manhattan:

I didn't get paid this summer. . . . [Laura: Did your parents pay for costs of living?] Yeah. But it was expensive. And I feel bad. I felt awful, 'cause New York's expensive. And it wasn't like I had a food plan or something. Every day I had to eat out. (Y3)

For most wannabe families, this additional financial burden—on top of college tuition—was unmanageable. However, experience living in big cities before graduation was valuable. Naomi left her internship knowing where in the city she wanted to live and the importance of bringing friends with her because "it's hard, especially in such a big city like that" (Y3).

With these advantages, the stakes of both failure and success were relatively low for socialites. This fact informed their academic approach. For example, one socialite explained, "When I get married and start having kids, I think I'll . . . I hope I can stop [working]. Of course, I have to marry someone successful" (Melanie Y4). When Laura asked how she planned to support herself before marriage, pointing out that her lifestyle was more expensive than her career would afford, she agreed but noted, "If I ever need help my parents will obviously help me and they live in [big city] anyway so I can just tell them to come down for every dinner, so I can get a free meal." Or, she remarked, she could "go home and ask my mom to go shopping" (Melanie Y4).

The socialite approach to college was thus rooted in a great distance from necessity. That these women did not envision a future in which they ever needed to be fully—or even primarily—self-supporting enabled them to elect an easy major. They assumed that their affluent lifestyles would be uninterrupted, irrespective of however much or little money they personally earned. Career-building post-college was something to do because it was fun and glamorous, what a twenty-something woman of their social class was supposed to do, at least for a while.

The Wannabe Experience: Downgrading by Default

Wannabes often arrived at college with more practical and ambitious educational goals than socialites. Three aspired to go into business (two via the business school), two into nursing, and two into education. All three majors—although not as demanding as the sciences or liberal arts—led to solid jobs that were less dependent on class resources and more contingent on academic performance. However, within months, most wannabes realized that they were caught in a bind: they needed to select pragmatic majors and earn good grades, but it was nearly impossible to do so while trying to keep up with their more privileged peers in the party scene. Most downgraded majors and career goals as an unintended consequence of the party pathway.

Take Karen, for example. Her two rush attempts took a toll on her academic performance. As she recalled, "I did really bad in that math class, the first Elementary Ed math class. And I was like if I can't do the first one there's no way I'm going to do the others. There's three math classes required" (Y4). She soon ended up with the same major as Naomi—sports communication and broadcasting. Her story suggests the seductive appeal of majors that facilitated the socialite experience. She described:

I'm from a really small town and it's just all I ever really knew was jobs that were around me, and most of those are teachers. And so when I got there, [a girl] from my floor, she was Sports Broadcasting and I was like there's a lot of majors I never thought about. So many people go to MU for fashion. I would have never thought about that. And so I saw hers, and I was like that's something that I really like. One of my interests is sports, watching them, playing them. (Y5)

No one that Karen encountered on campus helped her assess whether a career in this field was plausible for her or suggested that maybe she should not give up a well-considered career plan after one difficult course. With this major, her plan was to work in

media relations with a sports team, preferably the Cubs or Colts. . . . I would be in charge of getting all interviews ready, like press conferences. I get to be on the field talking to players all the time. I could be a sportscaster on ESPN if I really wanted to but I don't know if I wanna do that 'cause I'm kinda shy in front of the camera. (Y2)

Her parents, who expected Karen to graduate from college with a recognizable, marketable skill, were horrified by her change of major. The family had no useful industry ties and did not support her decision to major in what her mother called a "hobby."

Unlike Naomi, who had so many internship possibilities that she turned some down, Karen was unable to find an internship in the field. When interviewed as a junior, she mentioned that she wanted to intern at

a Triple-A baseball team that's [near my hometown]. It's like twenty-five minutes from my house. And since I'm doing all this sport stuff I might as well. . . . I emailed them actually last summer, but they already had someone. But I think this year they want two interns, 'cause they normally only have one. So it's a better chance. (Y3)

Although this was far from the prestigious big city internship that Naomi was handed, even an internship of this quality never materialized for Karen.

Two years into her new major, Karen realized that a career in sports was unrealistic. It made an impression on her when one of her teachers told the class that "he had switched like twelve different jobs. . . . That's how it is until you get out there. Ok now, I don't want to move around. He lived in twelve different cities. That's not for me" (Y4). Whereas for Naomi and other upper-class women it was inevitable—even desirable—that their careers and social lives after college would take them to major metropolitan areas, for Karen leaving the Midwest for life in New York or Los Angeles was simply unthinkable. Pursuing a career in sports broadcasting or media was never a realistic option for Karen given where she came from, both in terms of geography and family background.

Thus, to her parents' great relief, Karen decided to switch back. However, returning to elementary education also proved difficult. Her GPA was too low to do so at MU. In order to complete an education degree, she had to transfer to a regional campus. Even at the regional campus, she had to bring her GPA up before she could get into the education program. In addition, the courses that she took for sports broadcasting did not fulfill any requirements, which, she explained, is "why I still have to go the extra two years" (Y5). Yet the move extracted her from MU's social scene, enabling her to concentrate on her schoolwork. That her parents were willing and able to pay for six years of college sheltered her from the potentially devastating consequences of her major change and poor academic performance.

Features of Karen's academic trajectory (diversion to an easy major, low performance, and delayed graduation) were shared by other wannabes. However, Karen had one of the rockiest college experiences. We suspect that the high costs faced by Karen had to do with a significant misreading of social location. Though from a middle-class family, in her small, predominantly working-class, in-state town she was at the top of the social class ladder. What Karen did not realize quickly enough was that she lacked the resources to run with the national elite—whether socially or in her career.

At the opposite end of the spectrum were wannabes from larger cities who were more aware of their respective class locations. One was Whitney, whose savvy had translated into a spot in a top sorority house. She recognized the need for college to translate into tangible returns, although she was still drawn in by the social scene. She arrived at a compromise: rather than adopt the socialite low-effort approach, she would work moderately hard while partying hard.

This meant giving up dreams of entering the competitive business school. In this sense, her strategy was in line with a typical wannabe response to the social demands of college. Although Whitney noted in her second year, "School's important to me. . . . Academically I just wouldn't be satisfied if I graduated with a [business-lite] degree," ultimately she opted out of the business school and into a less difficult school. She explained this choice, telling us, "It's really important for me not to have classes on Fridays. It just doesn't work for me. . . . Everyone always goes out Thursday, Friday, Saturday" (Y3). Even though she was taking an easier path through college than the business school, hers was still more challenging than the communications and media-based majors favored by socialites. So Whitney partied Thursday to Saturday, and she "work[ed] all Sunday night, Monday night, Tuesday night, Wednesday night" (Y3).

For Whitney, the results were good. She managed to leave with a 3.85 GPA. Given just how hard Whitney partied—recall she claimed to drink twenty shots on a party night—this was hard to believe. In fact, it struck both her parents and peers as remarkable that Whitney was so successful in school:

> I've always gotten good grades, but I always go out, so it's hard to balance it. I just think [my parents] were more impressed with the fact that I can do it. We have the academic banquet every semester at our house, to get rewards for your grades. In May there were four people that got 4.0s. . . . There were three people that [when I got one] [we]re like, are you serious? 'Cause I go out all the time, and I don't think people expect it. I probably don't seem super smart. (Y3)

What saved Whitney was the fact that she was extremely bright, highly organized, and in a major that demanded less than her full capabilities. As she explained:

> I think I'm really good with time management. I get a lot of stuff done. . . . A lot of people have to spend a long time studying. But I almost always go to class and that's a lot of studying for me. Once I hear it once and write it, it just kinda sticks. (Y4)

Whitney's combination of characteristics—extroversion, ferocious energy, a near perfect memory, an iron constitution, and an uncanny aptitude for strategic planning in all aspects of life—were quite unusual.

Indeed, Alicia's largely failed attempt to work moderately hard while partying hard illustrates that this approach was unrealistic for most wannabes. Like Whitney, Alicia entered MU intending to apply to the business school. Unfortunately for Alicia, she followed the advice of an advisor rather than tapping the student grapevine, ending up with a heavy schedule of classes plus Finite Mathematics her first semester—something that savvy

socialites (and perceptive Whitney) knew to avoid. Alicia blamed the resulting 2.25 GPA on her advisor, convinced that the intent was to extract
more tuition from her:

> My advisor freshman year was horrible, God awful. I thought she was just
> stupid. She had no idea what she was doing. . . . I think they care so much
> about the money that they screw you over so you stay in longer. . . . They
> told me to take Finite—first of all, you don't take Finite your first semester
> of college, you just don't. No one told me that. So if I would've known bet-
> ter, I probably would've started off a little bit better, but the classes I took
> were so hard. (Y3)[3]

This academic disaster had huge consequences for Alicia both socially
and academically. Her grades were so low that she did not make the grade
cutoff and could not rush her first year, putting her on our freshman floor
as a sophomore. This was the social equivalent of flunking a grade in school.
She was also forced into the management program in the same school as
Whitney. Unlike in Whitney's case, this was not a calculated decision. She
also had to devote the rest of her college years to a not very successful attempt to repair her GPA. By her junior year she had brought it up to a 2.98,
ultimately graduating with a 3.2. She explained:

> I'm in [a business-lite school]. It's not like hard, but it is harder than peo-
> ple give credit for. [They say,] "Oh it's easy business." It's not easy. It takes
> as much studying as business school. . . . I'm at the library a lot. I study a
> lot but it takes me . . . a long time to understand things. (Y4)

Success after College

The differences between socialites and wannabes were starkest after college. Parental funds and ties gave socialites tickets to the big city, where
jobs valuing charm, personality, and appearance waited—along with opportunities to meet well-heeled potential mates. In contrast, when "Disneyland" was over, wannabes did not have the right currency to exchange
for a secure life (Table 5.2).

The Socialite Experience: Living the Glamorous Big City Lifestyle

Perhaps the most basic—yet most critical—marker of success after college
is employment. Despite entering into the labor market in 2008–2009, right

Table 5.2. Socialite and wannabe post-college trajectories

Descriptor	Socialites (7)	Wannabes (9)
Class trajectory	Reproduction (into upper-middle class)	Upper-middle class downwardly mobile; middle-class mobility at risk
Dimensions		
College performance	"Easy" majors	Diversion to "easy" majors
	Moderate performance; graduate on time	Performance varies; risk of delayed graduation
Career prospects	Parental connections secure media jobs in big cities	Limited credentials = unemployment, more schooling, job dissatisfaction
Marital prospects	Parental support delays need to marry; socializing with high-earning men	Unsuccessfully searching for high-earning mates

in front of the Great Recession, within a year of graduating all seven socialites were employed. Five were in full-time jobs that they loved, and two were in part-time jobs—although one intentionally limited her work hours to increase leisure time. Their ability to get these jobs was dependent on heavy parental support in the transition out of college. That is, their parents moved them to glamorous cities (for example, New York, Los Angeles, Chicago), put them up in nice apartments in popular neighborhoods, used their connections to help them secure jobs, and continued to subsidize their lifestyles.

Here we return to Hannah, whose CFO father had gotten her the spectacular internship. After graduation, Hannah's parents put her up in a converted two-bedroom apartment in Manhattan with a sorority friend of hers for $2,400 per month. The neighborhood in which the apartment was located sat below the wealthy Upper East Side, to the east of Central Park, and just north of an area full of restaurants, bars, and youthful nightlife. The apartment boasted wooden floors and spacious bedrooms; Hannah's room was large enough for a bed and a separate sitting area.

Like her internship, Hannah's job was obtained through her father's contacts—in fact, Tom, the same friend of a friend who was an owner of the sports team in New York, happened to be "very, very good friends with the CFO of the [sports league]." After spring break her senior year, Hannah e-mailed her résumé to Tom, who then sent it on to the CFO. As she noted, "Literally a day later I got a phone call from the production department." She interviewed via phone and was told "when you get home from school give us a call. We would love to see you." Upon graduation, Hannah went on an international trip and then called the sports league. Given the hard times, they had "gutted the whole company" (Y5). It took them a few months, but they did eventually find a position for Hannah—even though there were no other openings.

This did not happen without another round of action on the part of her father. As she noted, "My dad is crazy about [getting me a job]." The sports league CFO responded to her father's "pressure" (via Tom) to "get her in" by creating what Hannah described as a "permanent" freelance position specifically for her (Y5). The position was in productions management and involved the backstage planning for broadcasting games and special segments with players. It paid $250 a day, or roughly $60,000 a year—one of the highest incomes of any of the women on the floor. Being freelance, Hannah did not receive medical benefits; however, her parents were covering her through private insurance. Hannah had been given reason to believe her employers would extend her contract until they could create a salaried job for her. As she told us:

> I met with the CFO who has this huge office, a corner office overlooking all of 6th Avenue and it's just gorgeous. It's so nice. He's like, "Oh Hannah, I've heard you've been doing such terrific things downstairs and everybody really likes you." I was like, thank God. It's really nice to hear that. He's like, "The next thing we're trying to work on is getting you here permanently." (Y5)

Although Hannah's situation was unique in the level of pay and the extent to which her father intervened, three other women got jobs in part due to family connections, and a fifth could have done so, although she refused her father's offer. Even when family connections did not secure a job, they mattered indirectly via the internships socialites had completed in college.

GPA and major, as the most quantifiable measures of the college academic experience, had little bearing on socialites' abilities to get jobs. In fact, when we asked Tara if her 2.8 GPA mattered in her job search, she noted:

I didn't really find that to be an issue. I didn't put [my GPA] on my résumé and if they asked then I would tell them, but honestly no one really asked. That's the thing from being out here and actually having a job and seeing my company hire people. . . . I hear them saying that they don't even want to look at the education first. MU taught me to put your education at the top, and then you go into your other objectives. But instead they were like you should put that at the bottom. So I guess a lot of them just wanted your experience. They just want to know what you've done. (Y5)

Similarly, Naomi—who became an executive assistant for a large media company in Manhattan—told us, "I think I graduated with a 2.9. No, they don't [care]. They had my résumé. They never asked for my GPA. I don't think that matters at all" (Y5). When asked if she thought they considered her major in the hiring process, Naomi explained, "In the world I'm working in, it doesn't matter" (Y5).

Naomi's story of how she got the job illustrates the type of qualifications that did matter. She told us that when she was in the waiting area, she "noticed that they had a [home state college] sign" (Y5). She used that as a jumping-off point for the conversation because she assumed—correctly—that getting the job hinged on "being able to communicate with them and just have a good conversation where I walked out and they remembered me" (Y5). After her years in the sorority, Naomi was confident about her social skills: "I can keep a conversation going with people, and I can engage them. Nothing's made up, it's all true, and I always have something to talk about" (Y5). Part of the reason that Naomi meshed so well with her interviewers had to do with similar backgrounds and social networks. As she discussed:

[One boss] grew up in [my home state], about forty minutes from where I grew up, and his sister is married to a guy in my town. So, we had someone in common. My other boss, he had worked with my sister in the industry a couple years back. Her company had done some promotional product placement with [the company]. (Y5)

These shared experiences were not incidental, as Naomi's affluent suburb was more strongly tied to media industries in New York City than a small in-state town like those from which several wannabes hailed. Not only did such similarities facilitate conversation, they led to the discovery of dense network ties that likely helped seal the deal.

As in Greek recruitment, displaying a good personality in such workplace settings was in part about enacting the right kind of femininity. Tara explained, "They want you to be outgoing and bubbly and down to earth and polite and respectful . . . [and] just put together. You just show up and want to make a good impression" (Y5). Her answer points to the skills socialites honed in college.

These women fared well in the labor market considering their grades and majors, but they would not follow their fathers to the executive suite. Naomi, for example, ran up against a wall when she took a math test for her current company and failed miserably, barring her from all positions requiring this skill set. Similarly, another socialite—an assistant manager at a high-end clothing store—had gotten her $30,000 position in part because she was a loyal customer with considerable knowledge of designer clothing. Yet she could not easily break into better-paying management positions because she had chosen to major in apparel merchandising instead of going into the business school.

For most socialites, the fact that charm, personality, and taste could go only so far hardly mattered. Two tapped into trust funds upon graduation and five others received substantial monthly support that made up for the difference between their expensive big city lifestyles and their income. In fact, two women were employed only part-time, but their standard of living did not show it. One was Abby, the intelligent psychology major who never pushed herself. Instead of utilizing family connections on the East Coast to land a good-paying job, she decided she wanted to be in a major city out West. She had specific requirements for her job: it started at 9 a.m. at the earliest, allowed casual dress, included at least an hour-long lunch, and fit within her ethical standards (for example, no companies with a negative impact on the environment). She ended up taking a part-time, $10 per hour position working as a secretary for a small massage company, as few decent-paying, full-time jobs fit her criteria. Her parents funded not only her rent but her car (a brand new BMW SUV), medical insurance, and cell phone. They even sent her on a pleasure trip to Europe. When asked whether she thought they minded, she noted:

No, not really. Thankfully, they're able to. I don't feel like I'm being a huge financial burden, just a financial nuisance. They definitely could think of some better ways they could be spending their money, but I don't feel like I'm putting them in the hole. (Y5)

With this level of financial support, virtually all socialites experienced life after college as an extension of the social college experience they had just left. Certainly, it came with more responsibility (for example, showing up at work), but for most it was a new, fun stage of life. Socialites were instantaneously networked into the youthful city social scene as large numbers of their sorority sisters also lived and played in these areas after college. Their evenings were packed with social events—dinners and drinks out with various groups of friends. Being close to the action helped. As Naomi noted, "There's tons of bars near me. And after work, they're packed, Monday through Friday packed. It's a good area. I like it. I like it a lot" (Y5).

The erotic market of the city also put socialites in contact with successful and high-earning men. Indeed, most had not taken the men they met at MU seriously as mates, waiting for men who had already proven themselves. As Naomi told us:

> [I am] waiting until late 20s, early 30s, 35 [to marry]. I mean, I just don't think I'm gonna find that person here. . . . I'm looking for an older guy now. . . . Guys our age, they're not as mature. . . . I'm clearly looking for someone probably similar to my dad. . . . He's a hard worker. He started his own business when he was young. . . . He worked really hard, and he made his own money. And I think that's important. (Y4)

Similarly, another remarked, "I don't feel like there's anyone that special here. Maybe after college. I'm gonna move back to Chicago, so then there's plenty of options" (Melanie Y4). In order to access these options, they had to be socially visible and rely on the presentation they had refined in college to attract someone with a better career trajectory than their own.

From all accounts, most socialites were meeting and mingling with men whom they expected would eventually support them. For example, as Hannah described:

> Ellen was also in my sorority too. Ellen hooks up with this one kid and one night when we were out he was with one of his very good friends . . . Jack. [We] hit it off and we had a great time. We had dinner and he took me out for dinner the next week. *This kid has money flowing out of every single angle of his body.* He's originally from California and his parents are divorced and his mother is an architect. She designed different [buildings] in California and his dad now lives in England. Whatever. The kid is like a genius. He

went to [top school] and graduated from the business school and is an investment banker here now. . . . I've gone out for dinner and drinks with
him a whole bunch of times and he has taken me to such great nice places.
The time we went out he spent over $100 and I was like wow, on dinner
that's not bad, and then we went to this great place two or three weeks ago
and that was another $200. I'm like, Jesus, this kid. He's twenty-three years
old but he's very sophisticated. (Y5, emphasis added)

Although Hannah ultimately rejected Jack after realizing that "all he did
was talk about work and money," her father had been pleased with this
suitor. She noted, "He was really happy when I was dating Jack, the
I-banker. . . . He always says to me marry rich, marry rich" (Y5).

The Wannabe Experience: Underqualified and Unsatisfied after College

Whereas all socialites were employed at the time of the last interview, four
of the nine wannabes were employed, with only three in jobs requiring a
BA. Entering the real world after college was a shock for wannabes, who—
lacking access to compensatory parental resources—soon realized how
sorely they needed the credentials they had forgone.

After college wannabes ran up against a lack of funds. Although many
did not know this until after college, their parents had exhausted financial
resources in paying for the party pathway. Whitney was even surprised to
find she had loans:

I didn't know I did [have loans], but thanks, mom, for taking that out
in my name. Just $2,500 a year, so it's like $10,000. But they deferred
payment . . . so I think I'm going to have to start paying it in a couple
months. . . . I didn't even know she did that until I got one of those free
credit reports. I was like I'm just curious. It was Stafford loans. I was like
what is this, what is this? (Y5)

Similarly, sending Nicole out of state was more than her parents could afford. She had been told they would pay for college, but ultimately she owed
15% of the total cost. Staying in state could have left Nicole debt free. In
Whitney's case, more than $2,500 a year would have been recovered by
not joining a sorority. She was left paying for her college social life long
after it was over.

Without parental financial assistance, most wannabes could not follow
their socialite peers to the big city. As Nicole lamented:

I really would love to move to the city, but because of money right now I just can't. . . . Every time I talk about it, I think [my parents] don't take me seriously because all they want me to do is just get a job. And I tend to kind of lose my head about things and get lost in the big idea of moving to the city and being on my own. And then I have to kind of get back down to earth and be like I need a job, I need money, I need to be able to support myself to do all that stuff. (Y5)

Unlike socialites, wannabes often faced the prospect of finding a job that could then finance a move to the city. Unfortunately, it was hard to do things in this order. Living in the city provided a New York City address—a fact that employers considered. It offered easier access to the industry jobs these women desired, as well as ties that could lead to employment. At home, wannabes were far from their ideal job markets.

With the right parental social ties, wannabes might have found city jobs. Nicole had assumed that her father had such connections, as he worked at a public relations firm in New York City. However, there were no openings in his firm, and he lacked the clout of Hannah's father, who was seemingly able to make jobs appear out of nowhere. Others had no hope of parental intervention, regardless of circumstances. Blair watched her brother fail to get a job after graduating from MU. A year later he was working part-time in a local restaurant. She, in part, blamed her parents:

They're great parents, but I don't think they were very supportive. . . . When I saw how much [my boyfriend's] parents were so supportive of his interviews [and] job search, stuff like . . . I have a connection here, I'll e-mail them. Then when I saw this summer how upset my dad was, he was like why doesn't he have a job? It's like, he has no connections, he lives in [a small, in-state town], and he's supposed to figure [it] out? (Y4)

After seeing this play out, Blair did not expect her parents to provide help in getting her a job.

Major and GPA might not have mattered for socialites, but for wannabes they were everything. Virtually all expressed considerable regret upon realizing this. As one such woman explained, employers often screened out applicants without at least a 3.0:

[My GPA] was a 2.8, which I'm a little upset about because I totally could have had a 3.0 if a few semesters in there I would have worked a little harder. [Laura: Do you think it matters at this point?] I think for some job opportunities it does because some places I looked deny you right away if you don't have 3.0. (Sydney Y5)

Sydney also found her telecommunications major to be a limitation and regretted having allowed herself to be "intimidated" by the business school. As her job search dragged on, she became depressed about the choices she had made in college. After seven months of looking for a job, she was ready to go "hide in the closet" at family functions (Y5).

Once they recognized the extent to which they were behind in the job market, some wannabes considered graduate school. However, their low GPAs were an obstacle there as well. Blair, for instance, was working as a cold caller for a technology company after college. The job was uninspiring, did not require a college degree, and paid on commission (which meant she made barely anything to start). Blair had considered graduate school. Yet as she explained:

At first I thought about applying for school counseling. . . . My advisor said you won't get accepted anywhere [because my GPA] was 2.6 or something. She said if you work for a while and you have really good references you might be able to get into an okay school. (Y5)

Unfortunately, Blair was unable to get the kind of job that would provide "really good references." Indeed, such a job would have, in her mind, eliminated the need for graduate school.

Two women whose GPAs hovered above 3.0 did go back to school to improve their odds on the job market. One was Nicole, whose hopes of a glamorous public relations job had been dashed. She decided to fall back on the teaching degree that she had managed to obtain despite her switch in career plans. In order to be employable in her home state she needed more schooling, leading her to apply for a master's program at a local college at the cost of an additional $5,000 per year. Another out-of-state student went back to school for nursing. To enter a fifteen-month fast-track program, she had to take a year of undergraduate science and math courses her communications major had not required. This time, however, she was focused on her school work:

I don't have the distraction of MU . . . wanting to go out Wednesday through Saturday. . . . Also different [is] the fact that I'm paying for my classes because now it's like I don't want to skip a class that I'm paying for. (Sophie Y5)

Both women found they had to seek more schooling to be employable—in one case repeating portions of her undergraduate degree.

The three wannabes who were able to land jobs requiring a BA had higher GPAs; however, they too had struggled. For example, one of Whitney's first interviews was for a sales position with a large wine company in which her lack of cultural sophistication was painfully apparent:

> It was an interview weekend and I was the only non–East Coast person. I didn't fit in at all. I stuck out like a sore thumb. And there's all of these wine receptions because they do wine, and I don't know anything about wine, so I looked like an idiot. And there was this big dinner presentation and everyone wore suits, and I didn't know, and I walked in with no suit. I looked like an idiot, and I was late, which I'm never late. . . . Everyone's already sitting down at this presentation, I'm like hi. Maybe that's why I didn't get the job. (Y5)

Contrast this with socialites' intuitive understanding of what to say, act, and wear. Whitney's experience suggests that even one of the most sophisticated wannabes—who, after all, scored a top house on campus—could not compete on a larger social stage.

Alicia's exclusion from the business school was most painful when it came time to look for a job. Alicia resented that business school students were offered separate career planning and placement services. From her perspective, "People in the business school have it so easy. . . . They just kind of place you with a potential job and you pretty much get it" (Y4). In contrast, her job hunt was a self-directed marathon. She applied to over 300 jobs, heard back from twenty, had five interviews, and only one offer—for a merchandise coordinator position in a large department store in her home city. She eagerly took it despite misgivings about the job.

The few wannabes with jobs requiring college degrees received salaries on par with many of the socialites, but there was a distinct difference in how much this mattered. Without parental help, wannabes needed every dollar they could get. For Alicia, who made $30,000, money was tight, and she was frustrated by her working conditions. She explained:

> Everyone in my job is hourly. They will never change that. But, my boss . . . said you can't have a single minute overtime. . . . To them, 100, 200, dollars isn't a lot. To me it is. That's my groceries for a month (Y5).

Though Whitney was outearning the other wannabes, her salary went only so far. As she noted, "It's more than a lot of people I know. But forty [thousand] in the city, it's still paycheck to paycheck." She even ran into problems with the dress code because of lack of funds. She was "pulled into HR . . . and they said something to me. I was in tears. . . . It's suits all the time, but I can't afford a lot of suits" (Y5). She soon lamented her down-graded academic trajectory:

> I have friends in finance that make $60,000 already. I'm like, oh my gosh, I picked the wrong occupation. . . . Sometimes I kind of regret it because . . . I could have gotten into business school easily, and I know I should have, I know it. (Y5)

Employed or not, wannabes faced a rude awakening upon graduation. The fun social lives they had had in college were over. Nicole perhaps put it best when she said:

> I wish someone told me that four years ago I was going to have the best time of my life but none of it was going to be realistic, and then once I graduated everything was going to change. . . . Living in a sorority was not realistic. I will never live like that again with 100 of my best friends. . . . We didn't have to cook for ourselves. We didn't have to clean for ourselves. We had events planned for us. . . . I feel like it was living in a retirement center. (Y5)

Nicole highlights the gap between the experiences that wannabes had (or tried to have) in college and the reality of their lives afterward. In particular, those stuck at home after school struggled to readjust. As Sydney described:

> It's like I fell into a black hole because I moved home and I started job searching and getting really frustrated because it was awful. . . . My friends . . . were in grad school or working or had totally different lives. So I never saw them and I didn't really have anyone else around to hang out with besides my parents. (Y5)

Things were not much better for the few who made it to the city. They talked about moving back home. Whitney told us:

> [In-state Capital City] was perfect, perfect size, everything's accessible, things are easier. . . . Lincoln Park [in Chicago] is so wealthy, which I really like but I don't fit in. . . . It just doesn't feel like home. (Y5)

Part of the problem was the lack of dense social networks that facilitated socialites' social lives. Wannabes, even those in sororities, often did not leave with the same tight friendships. Alicia, for instance, could no longer relate to her sorority friends who lived in her home city. She noted, "They're still really immature, and just want to party all the time, and you just can't when you have a job" (Y5). As a result, Alicia rarely went out.

Their limited social lives had romantic consequences. Nicole, for instance, was looking for a boyfriend but was unable to find one who was not similarly stuck at home:

> I don't want to be single. I really, really want a boyfriend. . . . It's really hard to meet someone at home. It's people from high school pretty much. . . . When I go into the city, I have met people every single weekend that I've been here. So, that's another reason I want to move, to meet people. (Y5)

This situation was particularly frustrating for wannabes who were often actively searching for more serious commitments. Socialites like Naomi could afford to play in the city and wait until "early 30's, 35" to marry, allowing them to be more selective (Y4). In contrast, wannabes were more desperate for someone to help them economically, and few options were coming their way.

Consequently, most wannabes were (sometimes rather unsuccessfully) trying to get men to commit. One had met a medical student, but he did not seem interested in getting more serious. Alicia had been dating someone from her home city for a few years. His parents were rich, but over the years he had partied his way out of a flagship school into a regional one. She wanted to move in together and start heading toward marriage, but he refused. Blair was the only wannabe engaged by the final interview. Although from an upper-middle-class family, her partner was a wannabe like her. His media-based major and lack of credentials meant that he made even less money than she did.

Thus, a year out, the returns of college for wannabes were low. Unlike socialites, who coasted through college unscathed, wannabes were at risk of downward mobility. Their stories suggest the party pathway was a viable route to success for only a small, highly affluent segment of the MU population.

CHAPTER 6

Strivers, Creaming, and the Blocked Mobility Pathway

> My friends, they're like, "I don't know how you do it" because there for a while last semester, I worked and I was a TA for Psych 100, which I loved doing. . . . So I was taking fifteen credit hours but it was like I was taking eighteen because I had to go to that class also. . . . Then every Friday, Saturday, and Sunday, I worked [at a restaurant a half hour from my house]. Friday night, I worked. Saturday, I would get up at five or sometimes earlier, depends if the roads were bad, and I worked until whenever the next person came in. Then, on Sundays, I worked all day from 7:30 to 3. So I didn't get home until about 4. And then I would have class every day. So, I had papers due, and it was a lot, and I've just never had time to go out and do stuff. . . . [And] I have to feed [the horses] every morning, so that's even earlier. The way we have our barn, we don't have water out there, so I have to carry it in buckets. . . . So, add that to the plate.
>
> (Megan Y5)

The life Megan describes above, filled with studying, wait-ressing, and domestic work, bears little resemblance to the lives of the so-cialites and wannabes described in the previous chapter. Although some-what extreme in her work ethic, the centrality of paid work to Megan's life was shared by virtually all of the working- and lower-middle-class women on the floor. These women, whom we call strivers, could not afford to treat college as a luxury vacation.[1] In fact, with little to no parental financial support, they could barely afford to be there at all.

United by their financial circumstances during college, not everyone on the mobility pathway landed there in the same way. Eight strivers were direct recruits. They came "motivated for mobility," making it to college despite considerable odds and leaving behind communities where college attendance was far from the natural next step in life. Five others landed at

MU by default, following the flow out of their large, in-state feeder high schools. The experiences of these thirteen women converged at MU. Limited resources placed the party and professional pathways far out of reach, leaving only the crumbling mobility pathway—the organizational machinery devoted to serving disadvantaged students.[2]

All but one woman found the mobility pathway to be underdeveloped and blocked by seemingly insurmountable obstacles. Valerie—the exception—was channeled into a special program designed to help the most talented students from disadvantaged backgrounds navigate the academic and social terrain of college. We refer to such programs as "creaming" programs. Based on the idea that the cream is the best part of milk, the expression "the cream of the crop" is a colloquial way to refer to the identification of the best of any group. In this case, these programs cull the best and brightest strivers while the rest are left to their own devices. We contrast Valerie's story with that of the other strivers who were not "creamed" and thus did not have access to such extra assistance.

Creaming

Valerie was the exception to the rule (see Table 6.1). She was the only striver on the floor invited to participate in a program designed to help disadvantaged students succeed at the university. Certainly, Valerie was bright. Her high school GPA was a 3.8, and she had taken gifted or accelerated classes; she even came in identifying as a "nerd." Her first-semester class schedule was difficult—including Informatics, Finite Mathematics, second-year Latin, and Classical Studies. She tested out of the remedial classes that filled many of the other strivers' schedules and got credit for some introductory classes (for example, first-year Latin) on the basis of her high school accomplishments. Upon arrival she was already thinking about graduate studies—initially a master's degree in human-computer interaction.

Valerie was not the only academically accomplished striver on the floor. At least two others, both from working-class backgrounds, had similar high school records and motivation. However, Valerie's father—unlike the parents of other bright strivers—had some college education and was aware of programs like the one that Valerie joined. Valerie was advantaged simply by knowing that such programs existed. Her father helped her hunt down the information online and apply. It is unlikely

Table 6.1. Striver college experiences

Descriptor	Creamed (1)	Blocked (12)
Class background	Lower-middle class	Lower-middle or working class
College arena		
Academic	Scholarships reduce need to work; challenging classes; faculty attention	Work cuts into study time; remedial classes; inadequate advising
Social	Opportunities to network with other less privileged students	Isolated; no ties to other students; overwhelmed by diversity
Romantic/sexual	Reject party scene; develop orientation to later marriage	Uncomfortable in party scene; troubled relationships with hometown men
Women	Lower-middle class (1): Valerie	Lower-middle class (6): Alana Michelle Carrie Crystal Andrea Stacey Working class (6): Amanda Megan Alyssa Heather Monica Amy (no interview)

that Valerie, without his involvement, would have realized that she should apply.

Once she was accepted, Valerie received immediate financial benefits, totaling $4,000 in her first year of college. As a result, she was spared working the long hours that, as we discuss below, filled the other strivers' schedules. She needed only to keep her part-time work-study job in residential food services, which otherwise freed her to study. In the spring semester of the first year, she received a 3.9, making her eligible for a range of merit-based awards. She told us:

> Because my GPA was really high last year my scholarship increased $1,000 per semester. So now I get $6,000 for the whole year so that pretty much covers my tuition. And then I got a $1,500 scholarship last year from the classical studies department. And I got a Bailey Grant. I don't know why I didn't have that last year, or if they just instituted it this year but it was for having an honors diploma in high school. And that was like $1,700 or something like that. And then I got a Pell Grant too. . . . So I didn't have to take out any additional loans besides the Stafford Loans. It really turns out I didn't need to take that out. . . . I'm living in the [academic] co-op and it's like half as [much as] it was to live in [other dorms]. So it's a lot better this year. And I have a job, but I only work five hours a week, so that doesn't really count. (Y2)

The boost in scholarships and grants reduced her need for employment, thus enabling her to continue to earn extremely high grades. This process demonstrates how the investment of resources early in the process shapes academic outcomes. Others, without access to scholarship assistance, would toil long hours, which brought down their GPAs and made it even less likely they would be recognized as candidates for merit-based scholarships.

Valerie's early academic experiences at the university also ramped up her ambitions. By her third year—when many of her striver peers were finally finishing entry-level classes—she was in seminars with twenty people or fewer, requiring heavy reading and long research papers. As she noted, "I'm in a class now and it's, like, almost all graduate students" (Y3). Being in small, advanced courses brought her into the line of vision of faculty, who took an interest in her. Faculty encouraged her to study abroad in Italy—something she could afford to do with the increased aid. (She could, however, afford to go only for a summer rather than for the entire academic year that her more privileged peers spent abroad.) Her professors also pushed her to consider pursing a PhD in classical archaeology, steering her away from the more practical MA route.

Socially, her experience was also different than that of other strivers. Hailing from a larger in-state city and being lower-middle class as opposed to working class, Valerie knew people on campus from high school, and at least two women on our floor. She initially roomed with Crystal and when that did not work out moved in with Michelle (of the shaving cream incident detailed in Chapter 4), who was one of her best friends from childhood, although the two women had attended different high schools. Valerie also started dating a friend from high school who lived on campus in another dorm, allowing her to recognize that her floor was not representative of the whole university. The social programming in her scholarship program was limited, but it also helped her to meet other people like her. These ties allowed Valerie to reject the party scene, rather than questioning why she could not fit in. She explained:

> I'm supposed to go to parties every weekend, to frat parties, and I'm supposed to enjoy it like everyone else. But it just doesn't appeal to me. That's what made me question like why do you [everyone else] enjoy doing this? (Y1)

By offering money, enhanced academic experiences, and social opportunities, the scholarship program that creamed Valerie improved her time on campus (although, as we discuss later, her transition out of college suggests some limitations of this sort of programming). Her academic preparation, intelligence, self-identification as a nerd, and strong ties with people elsewhere on campus also protected her. Her experiences were far from the norm for disadvantaged students.

The Blocked Mobility Pathway

The twelve other strivers found that MU's mobility pathway was blocked. Strivers arrived at MU with limited financial, cultural, and social resources. In an educational environment tailored for students like them, these initial deficits need not have posed insurmountable obstacles. The social and academic infrastructure at MU was, however, designed to serve other, more privileged students. This context presented these students with five major obstacles.

Financial Worries and Adult Realities

Strivers were constantly trying to figure out how to pay for the necessities of everyday life. For instance, at one point, Heather explained that she was counting on holiday gifts from family members to make her next rent payment. In an extreme case, Carrie even worried about going hungry. As she described, "I have no money and I have no food. I don't eat breakfast, I don't really eat lunch. . . . The only thing I've bought is milk in the past two weeks" (Y2). Even with the assistance of student loans, staying at MU was a constant struggle. Carrie told us:

[Rent is] $455 and then we have to pay electric and cable and some other stuff. I can't afford it at all. I thought about leaving the whole school. Just going to [college near home] and living with my friends over there . . . at my best friend's house because her family is like my family. That would be a lot cheaper. (Y2)

Not surprisingly, strivers worked simply to make ends meet. As Amanda told us, "If I didn't have a job I wouldn't have a cell phone. I wouldn't have gas. I wouldn't have food" (Y5). The jobs they took were physically and emotionally demanding. For example, Megan did a stint in a factory where she put glass jars in boxes and screwed on lids. Monica worked in a daycare her first year of college. Amanda was a full-time checker at a big box store and also tended bar at a bowling alley at night. Stacey described herself as the "Miller Lite girl," as it was her job to promote the beer. Often this work seemed futile, as they were paid so little. As Heather described of her waitressing job:

I had a table of twelve last night and each one of them wanted separate checks. . . . Each of them left me a dollar or less for a tip. . . . After I bust my ass trying to get the kitchen to hurry up and make all their food so it isn't cold . . . I still don't get crap for it. This makes me so mad. . . . It's just frustrating, like I feel like I'm wasting my time. I could be doing other things instead of sitting there and waiting on people hand and foot and not getting anything for it. (Y2)

Many strivers also spent time working in the dining halls or libraries on campus. The jobs were helpful in that transportation was not necessary, they were less physically demanding, and they brought in much needed money. At the same time, though, they placed disadvantaged students in a second-class position—literally performing service for more economically advantaged students. For example, the RA on our floor (a job that came with a housing subsidy) was a working-class woman. She had much to say about the privilege of her charges:

I'm not gonna sit there and be like, oh, my life is so much harder than yours, but sometimes I get frustrated 'cause some of these girls don't work.

I'm like, all you gotta do is go to school. I pay for school by myself. Your parents are paying for your education. All they [are] telling you to do is go to school and get good grades, and you don't even work. And you're talking about your life is hard? (Y1)

She was particularly frustrated by the extent to which these students expected others to meet their needs. As she continued:

Today I was in the café. . . . I look over and this group of kids ate and left all their trash sitting on the table and I just, I don't understand how. . . . I couldn't even think to leave my stuff on this table so someone else can pick it up for me, but that's how some people here think. . . . They always think people are always gonna be here to clean up after them. (Y1)

Although strivers had realized that it would be difficult to afford college, they did not anticipate how isolated they would be in their struggles. They did not have the time or resources to share in the college social life that occupied socialites. As Amanda explained:

If I didn't have a job in college I think it would have been a completely different experience. It would have been completely different because freshman year when I wasn't working every week I would go out to parties, and I'd go out all the time. . . . If I had my parent's credit card I could just go to the bars whenever I wanted, or if I just had to work during the summer and that money wouldn't be used to pay my bills over the summer. (Y5)

That other students were able to party so much frustrated many strivers. As we discussed in Chapter 4, strivers were forced to confront the leisurely and noisy lifestyles of their more affluent peers, at least when they lived in the dorm.

At times these peers were also condescending about strivers' heavy schedules. For instance, Amy was offended when a wealthy roommate's friend noted that she "admired her" for working two jobs. Amy thought it weird that working hard was something to admire, as "everyone my age where I come from works" (Field Notes 9/22/04). For Amy and other strivers, adulthood had arrived well before college. Megan noted, "Starting in fifth grade [with my parents' divorce], I had to rely on myself a lot. . . . I was just forced into adulthood. I really didn't have much childhood after that" (Y5). Burdened as they were with real-life responsibilities, strivers lacked the same license for focusing on the self as the majority of their peers. In the college environment, especially in a party dorm, these women were oddities—so remarkable that others felt the need to comment.

In many ways the "college experience" at MU can be likened to a luxury cruise. Less privileged students often witness and provide luxury but do not have the experience that the cruise is designed to provide. The MU college environment is set up to best serve the interests and desires of students who are unmarried, childless, not working for pay, and receiving considerable parental support—individuals who are not quite adults. Strivers, who arrived on campus as adults, were not its primary constituency. Instead, they were employed serving those who were—for example, as cheap on-campus labor and in mixing drinks for wealthy socialites at famous college bars.

Even the academic side of college life seemed stacked against those with adult responsibilities. Strivers had to work for pay around a class schedule packed into the hours between 9 and 5, when more lucrative and secure employment could be had. This left them piecing together hours at multiple, low-paying evening jobs. For example, the semester that Amanda worked fifty or sixty hours per week at her two jobs, she got "lazy" and did poorly in her classes:

> It ends up I'm going to end up being here for 5½ years anyway because I got lazy [that] semester. . . . I just didn't go to my classes. So I have to retake them. . . . I just didn't do well. . . . My GPA went [down] but I still qualify to graduate. (Y5)

Heather had problems attending review sessions and devoting time to studying during weekends, which are typically free for most students. She explained:

> Sometimes it's a little stressful, like this week. I feel like I don't have enough time to study cause I know I'll be working all day Saturday. I still don't know if I'll have Sunday off, and I have a review on Sunday. . . . I don't even know if I can go to that, then I have a test on Monday. [In] chemistry I have a quiz due, then [another] test, it's just so overwhelming right now. (Y2)

Even those strivers like Megan, who miraculously managed to keep their grades up, were bothered when they realized how different the situation was for other students. She told us:

> This one girl I met, she was in a sorority, and . . . she was like, "I work real hard and all I have to do is get a good GPA and my parents pay for

everything." . . . And then she goes, "All I have to do is go to school, I don't really have to work, and my GPA is a 3.2 so that's good." I'm like all you have to do is go to school and you only have a 3.2? Are you serious, what do you do? I just can't be around those kind of people. (Y5)

Academic Roadblocks

Strivers also encountered academic roadblocks inadvertently created by the university. Just as there are many MUs socially, there are also many MUs academically. Academically talented students from affluent school districts arrive with AP credits. They are direct admits into the prestigious business school, work in biology labs as sophomores, or study abroad as juniors. They participate in the Honors College, reside in Living Learning Communities, and take small seminars, even as freshmen. However, this is not the university most strivers encountered. As products of underperforming in-state high schools, with little parental know-how to help them navigate MU, they arrived barely prepared for college and at the mercy of the university machinery.

For example, Heather and Stacey came from an in-state high school where "we had a lot of people who dropped outta class. Drugs and gang-related stuff" (Stacey Y1). Upon arriving, Heather was enrolled in Introduction to Media, Basic Composition (a course students are exempt from taking if they score 670 or better on the SAT), Ballroom Dancing, and Basic Algebra (a remedial math course that did not offer college credit). Strivers described the instruction in their courses as really poor. For example, field notes detail one striver's first few days of class at MU: "[She] told me that on one day she had a professor that did not show up, one professor that was so old (came out of retirement to teach) that they thought he was going to drop dead in the classroom, and a third who did not speak much English" (Field Notes 8/31/04). Another described the majority of classes she had as "worthless" (Crystal Y3). Even if we assume that the instruction was not as terrible as the students perceived, and that their frustration was partly a result of their lack of preparation, the picture is still not inspiring.

Research universities like MU are designed to select, nurture, and revere academic excellence. Delivering remedial instruction is challenging, low-status work not often sought by the most experienced or charismatic of instructors, who have a great deal of discretion over who and what they teach. They often opt to teach upper-division undergraduate courses or graduate seminars—if they are in the classroom at all. Faculty are trained to "cream"—to identify and cultivate the best students (who are often also the most prepared). The hierarchical nature of the curriculum and how faculty are sorted into the classroom means that students who could have gone to elite private colleges can get an excellent education at schools like MU.

Good advising could have gone a long way toward providing strivers with the same knowledge about how to succeed at the university that was available to students with college-educated parents. This is a goal of programs targeted toward "first-generation" students. However, at MU these programs were tiny, restricted to the exceptionally academically talented, and unknown to the vast majority of less advantaged students.[3] Large numbers of working-class and lower-middle-class students—many of whom are not technically first generation, as one or both parents have some postsecondary education—just fall through the cracks.

Standard college advising did not meet these students' needs. Heather reported that by sophomore year she had been through four different advisors: "My first semester [advisor] quit. Then I got a new one first semester. Then they switched me over to [a] different guy second semester, and now I have a new woman this year but I haven't met her yet" (Y2). Without consistent advising, Heather was blindsided by the fact that her two remedial pass/fail classes did not count for college credit.[4] As she explained, "They don't tell freshmen that pass/fail classes don't count. Like, we didn't know that . . . It can only hurt you" (Y1). She and her roommate Stacey also took several major-specific classes that did not fulfill general education requirements. Upon changing majors, these classes were no longer necessary. When Laura asked what they would do differently if they could redo their first year, they answered:

Stacey: Classes. I'm gonna recommend my kids take general classes like psychology. Stuff that you're gonna need for a lot of different majors. And do not declare major till . . .
Heather: Your sophomore year.
Stacey: I regret taking so many classes last year.
Heather: For what? Like we're never going . . .
Stacey: I'm never gonna use them. They're not even, doesn't have anything to do with my degree. (Y2)

We suspect that part of the problem was that advisors were accustomed to advising more affluent students—those with the means and interest to have a more social experience. As a result, strivers often got advice seemingly tailored for affluent socialites. Stacey noted:

> I just saw [my advisor]. I was sitting and waiting for him and this homeless looking guy . . . walked past and . . . I'm like, that's probably my advisor, and then he called my name. . . . He's really nice, though, [he] told me stuff I already knew but, "Study everyday for anatomy before five. Yes study everyday for anatomy before five." . . . 'Cause at five it's time to drink or something, I don't know. (Y2)

It is possible he had surmised that she might need to work after five; however, our interpretation, as well as the student's, was that he assumed she would be out partying. As she continued, "Maybe they need to educate them more of like what's going on? . . . 'Cause like, I don't know, they're just they're not in our shoes so and it's like when they tell us that it's just like . . . [fades off]." (Y2)

Amanda's experience exemplifies how poorly MU served the strivers on our floor. She wanted to be a teacher, but after visiting a few elementary schools in early courses she was turned off by the less glamorous aspects of the job. At the same time, she heard about "wedding planning." She explained:

> I took a freshman seminar about how to be in college. We all had to talk about our majors. I was still undecided at that point. There was a girl in there who wanted to be a wedding planner. I found out that that was a job and I was like, wow, that would be a ton of fun. I like doing that anyway. I might as well make that my job. I looked it up and found that they put event planning in with tourism. So then I applied and got in. I realized later that I probably should have not done that. (Y5)

The fact that MU supported a major in event planning led Amanda to believe that this was a practical career choice. It is not clear whether she consulted an advisor during her decision making. However, it seems no one explained to Amanda the classed nature of certain jobs. People hire wedding planners to help them with decisions about aesthetics, and given her background, she lacked the right cultural tastes and social networks to be hired by the sorts of people who could afford this service. Thus, Amanda, along with several other strivers, was channeled into a major better suited for more privileged students. These majors would become stumbling blocks as they attempted to secure employment.

Being the Wrong Kind of "Girl"

Strivers wanted to make friends, fit in, and—to the extent possible given their schedules—have fun in college. As we saw in Chapter 3, a social hierarchy that relegated less privileged students to the bottom thwarted their efforts. Without the necessary money, time, or cultural knowledge, strivers were typically unable to perform the type of upper-middle-class femininity that would buy them social status. Consequently, as we discussed in Chapter 4, they consistently found themselves on the receiving end of social rejection.

Amy's story perhaps most vividly demonstrates the social experience had by many strivers. Recall from Chapter 1 that Amy was a working-class woman from a small farm town. Like other strivers, she identified as "country." There was an unmistakable twang in her voice, and she had a tendency to use bad grammar. Amy did not have expensive highlights in her hair, go tanning, or get her nails done. At one point, Elizabeth walked in on Amy and her one friend from home engaged in the process of dyeing Amy's hair—a task that, in the eyes of the affluent women on the floor, should have been done only in a salon. Amy's clothing selections were also much more limited. When we first met her, she was wearing a white "Hooters" T-shirt, which was perhaps as far from designer as one could get. After overhearing a discussion about someone having fifty-something pairs of a certain kind of pants, she told us, "I'm lucky if I have five pairs of jeans" (Field Notes 9/22/04). Her possessions were also all wrong for the type of commercialized upper-middle-class femininity displayed on the floor. Instead of hot pink, she had a few lime green possessions and a Scooby Doo comforter.

As we noted earlier, Amy was intensely lonely at MU. This experience was shared by most strivers. Among the few to make it out of their small towns, they often arrived without any connections to other students. In Amy's case, she felt that her fate had changed when she found out she was getting a new roommate to replace the one who never showed up. Unfortunately for Amy, Melanie was the worst possible roommate that she could have gotten. Melanie was affluent, knew a ton of people on campus, and was gearing up for sorority rush. Around sixty-five people from her out-of-state high school were at MU, including ten of her closest friends. She was not worried about moving onto the new floor, and within days—possibly hours—she was friends with other affluent women on the floor.

Upon moving in, Melanie took charge of the room, purging it of undesirable décor, reflective as it was of Amy's working-class style. She reorganized it around a pink color scheme. It now seemed to be all Melanie, no Amy. There was much more stuff, and it was much nicer and lusher. After this redecoration effort, the room was more like the others on the hall—with everything in matching pink: a furry pink rug on the floor, a pink rope light, and a variety of other pink accessories. One day Amy found her lime green rug under her desk and the pink rug out in the middle of the floor. Melanie had moved Amy's rug without asking.

Amy reported that Melanie was always on her computer while Amy futilely tried to strike up conversation. Not only did Melanie take to ignoring Amy when they were alone together, but she began bringing friends back to the room, where they collectively ignored Amy. At one point, we observed Amy returning to her room, occupied by Melanie's friends. "She maneuvered around the crowded room. The route to her desk was strange, going through the most obstacles, but avoiding any contact with any of the other girls. . . . They had a huge presence all sprawled out over her space. The girls were not exactly mean to her, they just did not pay attention to her" (Field Notes 9/22/04).[5]

Amy's situation was much like that of other strivers. At the end of the year, when we asked women to report on their friendship ties, strivers were more likely than other women to be unknown by their floormates. As we noted in Chapter 4, a group of highly social women had dubbed one particular block of rooms—containing a high proportion of less privileged women—as the "Dark Side." Although some affluent women were interspersed throughout the Dark Side (for example, Melanie and a few of her friends), the reference was intended to describe those who were not actively participating in the social side of college life. Unfortunately, strivers were so isolated that they were unable to form ties even with their potential allies—each other.

Social ties to others on campus were often just as nonexistent. For example, when asked whether she had made any friends at school, Megan noted that she had met "a couple people but we don't ever go out and do stuff together, it's not like you can talk to them, and I don't know. Not really" (Y1). As it turns out, the acquaintances she was talking about were fellow workers at the library—other less privileged women also working for a living. Similarly, by the end of college, Amanda's social network consisted almost entirely of friends made at the big box store in which she worked, many of whom did not attend college.

Strivers found campus social life unfamiliar and confusing. As Megan naively noted, "I was curious to see like what do they do, these sororities and fraternities, I mean what's the big deal?" (Y1). Because they were lonely, some forced themselves to make forays into the party scene. One described:

> I tried so hard to fit in with what everybody else was doing here. . . . I think one morning I just woke up and realized that this isn't me at all, I don't like the way I am right now. . . . I didn't feel like I was growing up. I felt like I was actually getting younger the way I was trying to act. Growing up to me isn't going out and getting smashed and sleeping around. . . . That to me is immature. (Monica Y1)

Monica's ultimate refusal to accept partying as a normal part of college reveals the fundamentally classed nature of this idea. Strivers did not arrive expecting that college would be a never-ending party and could not afford to avoid "growing up" for as long as their affluent peers.

In the case of Heather and Stacey, the promise of college fun and social integration proved seductive for longer into college. At first it seemed that they had made friends with some of the more social women on the floor. However, as we described in Chapter 4, these relationships did not last. Early on, there were hints that a falling out would occur. For example, field notes recount an evening in which Heather and Stacey were getting ready to go out:

> Both were in tight pants (one black, one brown) and tight tops. They had plenty of makeup on (this was clear from far away) and tall heels. Whitney asked them why they were wearing tube tops to go visit some boys. . . . I can't remember exactly what the girls said (I was down the hall anyway) but they very loudly yelled something about going to "whore around" in their tube tops. (Field Notes 9/15/04)

Whitney had registered that their dress was all wrong—such sexual attire would be appropriate only for a theme party, in which women were given license to dress "slutty." Her subtle questioning suggests that Heather's and Stacey's out-there, direct, and sometimes crude gender style set them apart. They did not embrace the style of femininity performed by most, although not all, of the women on the floor. Publicly stating that one was going "whoring around" was not something that most privileged women, who were constantly monitoring their sexual reputations, would say, even in jest.

When time for rush came about, all but one striver opted out. Although most simply noted that it was "not for me," their decisions seemed to be rooted in a sense of self-preservation. Indeed, Amanda—the only one who rushed—dropped out in the first round because she was so uncomfortable. Heather and Stacey looked on as most of their friends joined houses and began spending time with their Greek friends. Soon their floor friends no longer had time to spend with them. As Heather put it, "A lot of the girls that were on our floor that got into sororities changed a lot, even like the first week that they were in it. They all thought they were better than everybody" (Y3). Their bitterness was palpable.

The perils of trying to fit into the social scene went beyond peer rejection. Strivers were more likely to receive negative sexual labels, despite having fewer sexual partners than more privileged women. For instance, Heather's and Stacey's forthright manner was often interpreted as evidence of promiscuity, even though neither was hooking up at all. One was involved in the only incident we witnessed where a woman was directly called a slut without it being an obvious joke. Similarly, another working-class woman had been seen kissing her middle-class roommate. She was labeled a lesbian while the other was presumed to be performing for men's benefit. This same woman also faced backlash at home for her attempt to party at college: She was the subject of a virulent sexual rumor that even reached her parents.

Although the social snubs strivers experienced can be attributed to peer cultures, the university plays a role in setting strivers up to have these experiences. For instance, the placement of working-class students in party dorms, with little meaningful adult supervision, no protection from their affluent peers, and few ways of bonding with each other likely generates the same interactions floor after floor, year after year. Organizational support for the party pathway not only caters to the agendas of privileged students, it undermines the experience of less privileged students.

Encountering Diversity and Difference

Perhaps one of the most uncomfortable features of the college environment for strivers was the extent of diversity on campus. Religious differences in particular were an explosive source of division on the floor. For some strivers, college was literally the first or second time they had ever even met someone Jewish. Amy's exposure to Judaism, for example, was limited to a Jewish music teacher who moved to her tiny town but was so badly treated that he quickly packed his bags and left. This lack of familiarity with those from other religions only added to strivers' sense of MU as overwhelming and foreign.

Some lashed out at the Jewish students on the floor. For example, a Jewish undergraduate research team member recorded this anti-Semitic incident in field notes. She was walking down the hall when it occurred:

> We walked by Stacey's door and I have absolutely no idea how this got started but I guess Stacey had never met a Jew before and started asking us if we wore crosses. We were shocked by this question and I said "No." She was like so, "Do you believe in God?" Before we could respond she was like, "Well, what about Jesus?" We said we didn't believe in Jesus. She went ballistic. "WHAT, WELL THEN WHO IS YOUR SAVIOR? GOD? You are going to go to hell if you don't have a savior." Mollie started laughing and said, "We don't believe in hell and we don't have a savior." At this point, I was completely appalled. I asked Stacey if she was aware that there were Jews on her floor. She crinkled her nose as though Jews are bugs and said "Yeah." . . . It is one thing to not know about someone's religion or understand it for that matter, but to attack it in front of two Jewish people as though her religion is better was just inappropriate. Also, her tone of voice and facial expressions led me to believe that she seriously had a dislike for Jews. (Field Notes 9/14/04)

The researcher's feelings about this incident hint at how other Jewish students on the floor must have felt living with strivers who seemed so hopelessly ignorant and bigoted. It is in the context of a very real threat of anti-Semitism that Melanie (who was Jewish) closed off the possibility of any authentic interaction with Amy (the striver profiled earlier).

On MU's campus, religion is associated with both class and geographic difference. There is a substantial population of Jewish students, most of whom are also wealthier, out-of-state students, primarily from the East Coast. Thus, for many strivers who had little experience with Judaism, it was hard to separate religion from the wealth and big city interactional style that they found so alienating. For example, Amy wished that there were more Jewish holidays so that Melanie—who was making life so difficult for her—would leave more often. Similarly, Megan's description of why she did not fit in at MU bundled all of these things together. She did not explicitly mention religion, but the reference to New York was often used as a shorthand for Jewish:

> It was so weird at MU. Like, it was crazy [laughs]. I cannot believe that . . . those girls in [our dorm], their cars and they're from New York and New Jersey and I'm like, "How do you afford this?" I couldn't even imagine how they afforded it. And, I was like, oh my God, I work and all my money goes to tuition and you girls are around, you know, and . . . [Sighs] I don't know. I felt so out of place. (Y3)

Stacey, who offended our research team member, also used geographic shorthand:

> All the East Coast bitches, it's like, "Mommy and daddy just pay for me to go here and it's not a big deal if I fail out. Who cares? I'll still have money and they'll still give me money, so it doesn't matter whether I fail or succeed." They're going to have financial support anyway, so it doesn't really matter if they get their fashion merchandising or apparel degree. (Stacey Y3)

The layering of difference upon difference made it difficult for strivers to make connections. It did not help that some affluent Jewish students from out of state arrived with little interest in extending their friendship networks to those from different backgrounds—leading many less privileged women, like Stacey, to feel painfully excluded. However, singling out East Coast (and, implicitly, Jewish) students was unfair. Affluent, out-of-state, non-Jewish women from other areas of the country also had little interest in relating to those different than themselves. It was not religion or region at the root of the problem but class disparities. The anti-Semitic language used by strivers only contributed to the invisibility of social class inequities at the university.

Sexual orientation was another stumbling block for strivers, who had rarely encountered openly gay or lesbian individuals. MU, with its relatively large lesbian and gay community, was a shock for some. Whereas privileged students typically dealt with their own prejudices in subtle ways, strivers were often blatantly homophobic. As Heather and Stacey noted:

Heather: We've kinda been sheltered around diversity . . .
Stacey: So we're not used to all this gay pride stuff, and it's just like, what are they doing? Read the Bible. (Y1)

One evening, another striver told a researcher and some of her floormates how tired she was of looking at "that" (the Gay, Lesbian, Bisexual, and Trans-gendered Rainbow Week bulletin board just outside her door). She said vehemently, "I just want to take a big black marker and write straighten up . . . straighten up your future" (Field Notes 2/1/05). For these women, the constant presence and reminders of foreign views on sexuality felt invasive and offensive.

These reactions to diversity marked many strivers as different, having not learned the upper-middle-class political correctness that pervades higher education. Although many of their peers also held less-than-tolerant views, these women were more restrained about how and when they expressed them. For example, most were okay with differences in sexual orientation as long as they did not personally have to befriend lesbians. Strivers violated the social contract by explicitly stating that they believed sexual diversity to be unacceptable.[6] Had the environment that they lived in been more racially diverse, we have no doubt that similar dynamics would have played out around issues of race.

These tensions made strivers feel threatened and uncomfortable but were also extremely detrimental for students who held marginalized statuses. Yet the university provided only limited programming designed to foster acceptance of diversity. Students on our floor received the message, in cursory fashion, only twice. The first occurred at the initial floor meeting, in which the RA made a brief attempt to explain the importance of respecting people's differences, including religion, ethnicity, sexuality, and place of origin. Second, there was a "Celebrate Diversity" board on the dorm floor, designed to promote tolerance for others. This was the same board that had so provoked one of the strivers. However, in no instance was there discussion involving student participation or a safe space in which students were forced to encounter, learn about, and deal with each other's differences. Class differences were not addressed at all by university programming.

A Fast Track to Family Formation

Strivers approached sex and romance differently than affluent women.[7] They did not have the luxury of setting aside time exclusively for academic and career development. Thus, there was no need for hooking up—privileged women's way of delaying relational commitments until schooling was completed and employment established. Indeed, most strivers viewed hooking up as "gross." As one woman put it:

I just don't see myself doing that kind of thing [hooking up]. . . . I'm not that kinda girl. Not saying that there's a kinda girl that, you know, goes out and does whatever she wants, but I think with my history and the things that's happened in my life, I'm not the kind of person that would do something like that. (Alyssa Y4)

Instead of postponing serious relationships, strivers treated building relationships as part of a three-pronged approach to economic security. These women invested in potentially permanent relationships, a labor market track record, and academic credentials simultaneously. This was a reasonable approach, given their economic circumstances and need for immediate stability. However, it was sometimes incompatible with being at a four-year residential university, where being a student was supposed to supersede all else.

Most strivers arrived at college involved with working-class men at home. In order to maintain these mostly long-distance relationships, women spent what little free time they had either driving home to visit or on the phone with them. For example, Alyssa explained that this played a major role in her discomfort at MU: "I think if I hadn't been connected with [my boyfriend], I think I would have been more strongly connected to Fairview" (Y4).

As her quote implies, strivers often felt they were confronted with an either-or choice—either put roots down at MU or build the romantic relationship. Boyfriends exerted pressure on women to do the latter. One described of her hometown boyfriend, "He'll be like, 'I want to see you. Come home.' . . . The stress he was putting me under and me being here my first year. I could not take it" (Stacey Y2). Women often reached a breaking point, prompted in part by a fear of losing their boyfriends. For some, leaving MU was a good decision—even if the relationship ended. However, these decisions were not easy. Megan noted:

I kinda wanted to stay down there [at MU] but like I know Tom would've came [back home] no matter what and he was really homesick. . . . He didn't have any money, and I thought, well if I come back I'll save myself a lot of money, then I'll be with him and I'll still go to school and get the same type of education. . . . *I could put what I wanted to do second.* (Y2, emphasis added)

Many strivers started college on a far more rapid path toward family formation than their privileged peers. For instance, although this would change, Amanda noted, "I actually want to have kids, be married and have a kid by the time I'm twenty-five. Like one or two" (Y3). Her mother, who married young herself, also pushed her. As Amanda described:

> She's like you're in college and there's twenty thousand guys on campus. I'm sure you will be able to find somebody. And I'm like, well, I don't know anybody right now. And she's like, come on you have to find somebody. [Laura: Does she think that you're going to find your husband at college?] Yeah, I think that's what she probably was planning on. She's like you're going to meet a nice guy at college . . . hang outside the chemistry building [laughs]. (Y2)

From the perspective of her privileged peers, this was not normal college student behavior: They were busy avoiding commitment while waiting for a chemistry major to prove himself after college or earning those science credentials on their own. This fundamental difference in life timelines made it hard for strivers to connect to others on campus.

As Amanda's quote also suggests, strivers found it hard to locate good potential mates because of their limited college networks. They did not meet many people at college—men or women. Attending MU did not expand their pool of possible romantic partners, keeping them tied to dating men from home they already knew. These men had little ambition. As Alyssa described of her ex-fiancé:

> Not one single part of his body is driven unless it's something he really, really wants to do. But if it's something he doesn't want to do, it's going to not get done. One area of concern for me was always schooling. . . . I don't like school, but you have to do it to get done, and he didn't. He would just take class after class after class over again, and I was like, do you not understand you are wasting money? This is not funny. If you don't pass the first time, make a change. . . . Meanwhile you're unemployed. . . . It's not cool. (Y5)

Alyssa's ex-fiancé was somewhat unusual in that he had, for a time, enrolled in a local college. Most of the men strivers dated had no education past high school. They were also more likely to espouse traditional gender views. Some even seemed threatened by their partners' educational and career advances. As Megan noted of her then husband:

> He wants me at home. . . . He wants to have control over me and . . . to feel like he's the dominant one. . . . The fact that I'm going to school and he

knows I'm smart and he knows that I'm capable of doing anything that I want . . . it scares him. (Y4)

Megan's relationship ended as emotional abuse increased and her husband turned physically violent, forcing Megan to flee for her safety. She was not the only striver to be in such danger. Three others also dealt with relationship abuse and former partners who stalked them. Heather, for example, had moved in with a controlling boyfriend, and when she moved out he "went crazy," slashing her tires "every night for two weeks straight." She got a restraining order against him, but "he violated the order the day he got served the papers" (Y4). Further complicating the situation, her work schedule was so demanding and unpredictable she could not make the court dates necessary to keep the restraining order in effect.

These failed and traumatic attempts at mate selection took their toll on strivers. As Heather noted, of all the difficult things she experienced in the college years, dealing with her boyfriend was the worst. She told us, "That was the hardest thing I've ever had to do. I do not wanna go through that again" (Y4). Similarly, it took Megan several months to get her life back on track after leaving her husband. She lost at least a semester of coursework. Alyssa, tired of supporting her nonworking and eventually noncollege-attending fiancé, had to temporarily sever ties with her family when she left him. Her family simply could not understand why she had ended the engagement. As she noted, "They had a hard time with it, and . . . it was like they were more concerned about him and I wasn't doing it right in breaking it off" (Y5). Alyssa's relationship with her parents had not recovered by the time of the last interview.

Stayers versus Leavers

Although they all faced financial, academic, social, cultural, and romantic obstacles, strivers differed in how they dealt with these challenges. Those who managed to stay at MU were primarily from lower-middle-class families and bolstered by greater financial resources. Indeed, not one of the working-class students graduated from MU within the time frame of our study. The great irony was that, for most, leaving MU meant a better shot at mobility than staying. With the exception of Valerie, who was creamed, the most successful of all the strivers were those who transferred to regional campuses (Table 6.2).

Table 6.2. Striver trajectories: stayers versus leavers

Descriptor	Stayers (6)	Leavers (7)
Class trajectory	Mobility at risk, except for students in creaming programs	Potential for upward mobility, but leaving poses threat to pursuit of BA
Dimensions	If not creamed:	If stay on path to BA:
College performance	Diverted to socialite major; low to moderate performance; risk of delayed graduation	Pragmatic majors; good performance; delayed graduation
Career prospects	Struggle to secure job requiring BA; record not sufficient for graduate school	Enter into well-paying occupations related to degree
Marital prospects	Unsuccessfully seeking solid earner for financial assistance	Unable to locate desirable mate but self-supporting
Women	Upwardly mobile (1): Valerie Mobility at risk (5): Alana Michelle Carrie Crystal Amanda	Upwardly mobile (4): Andrea Stacey Megan Alyssa Mobility at risk (2): Heather Monica Unknown (1): Amy

The Stayers

Class advantages, relative to their working-class peers, helped most of the six stayers remain at MU. For example, one of these women had a parent on staff—effectively cutting her tuition in half and leaving her with only $8,000 in loans. Another woman's stepfather had a PhD and her mother was an educator. They discouraged her from leaving MU for a regional campus, where they feared the quality of instruction would be lower. As we noted in Chapter 4, Alana was in danger of leaving MU after her first year, as she did not know how to find housing. Her father found her a safe place to live and paid for it. Meaningful advantages in the form of parental funds, education, and intervention thus combined to secure these women an MU education.

One of the stayers was Valerie—the only striver able to utilize MU's tiny creaming program. She left with a 3.8 GPA, a 1220 on her GRE, great faculty recommendations, applications to top PhD programs in a humanities field, and minimal debt. However, in the transition out, Valerie's fate became less certain.

Valerie was accepted only to the least prestigious school on her list— without any funding. She noted:

> It surprised me that I didn't get accepted to any of them except for [safety school]. I was surprised and then I was like, no, maybe that's just you being full of yourself; but it surprised my professors that I didn't get in. (Y5)

As a result, Valerie turned to what she knew:

> I worked for [MU's residential services] all through college, so I just got a job as an assistant manager. . . . I was just trying to find different jobs in July. I applied for a few jobs like teaching high school Latin in private schools, and I didn't get one so I was like I guess I'll just stay working for [residential services] for a while. (Y5)

The pay, at $28,000, was solid and the employment secure. However, it seemed as if her life had not changed. She was still serving (albeit at a higher level) the affluent students she provided for during college. She was living in a one-bedroom apartment "pretty close to where I used to live last year" (Y5). Her boyfriend had attended her high school, but he never made it to college.

Valerie had been prepped for what was, realistically, not a viable career for someone with her profile. Admission to an elite PhD program in the humanities was a long shot. She was competing against Ivy League and elite liberal arts graduates, all with similar GPAs but with likely better test scores and more research experience. It mattered that financial considerations had pushed her to MU rather than to a more prestigious school with more undergraduate research opportunities. The fact that faculty encouraged her to aim for the humanities PhD instead of the more applied master's degree she intended when she started jeopardized her chances of making it to the upper-middle class.

Luckily, Valerie's scholarship program had helped her to develop aspirations and credentials that were transferable. Her academic experiences reinforced her initial inclination that graduate school was for her—while a working class life was not. As she explained:

I know that I want to do graduate school or do something different obviously. . . . I think I would just, I don't know, jump out of a window if I had to do it [work for residential services] more than two years. . . . I'll probably end up going to law school. . . . I think I would do well at law school, because I'm definitely competitive and I think I would really enjoy that kind of environment. (Y5)

Given her strong record, Valerie was able to devise a plan to enter into law school:

I've looked into scholarships for law school, and my GPA is high enough that if I get over a 164 on the LSAT I'll have [MU's] scholarship—which is everything, full ride paid for. I could apply to other law schools, I will apply to other law schools, but if I get into MU and get that scholarship, that's where I'm going to go. (Y5)

Valerie's ambitions also made it unlikely that she would get too tethered to her current boyfriend. As she explained:

A lot of the reason why the people that I went to high school with are getting married, especially the people who didn't really go away to college, is they're bored. They're like, okay, I haven't really done anything since high school graduation, that's the last time people were like "good job," or something. What's the next big thing in my life? (Y5)

This orientation to a later marriage, after building a career, made her more similar to her privileged peers. Law school would also offer an additional opportunity to extend her social and dating networks beyond her hometown.

One working-class woman, Amanda, stayed at MU. Unlike other stayers, idiosyncratic family dynamics—rather than family resources—kept her there—she supported her brother, his girlfriend, and a baby when they were kicked out of the family home. Moving during this time period would have been problematic. Amanda's story puts into extreme relief the problems faced by all other strivers who attempted to persist at MU without the benefits of a creaming program.

Recall that Amanda was diverted to a tourism major when she heard that she could become a wedding planner. It took her a while to figure out that event planning did not require a college degree. She explained in her fifth year:

> I just got on Monster [a job search Web site] just to see how many event planning jobs are actually available. All of them are like one to two years experience. . . . None of them [say] oh you need a degree in this. Most of them are like you need a [high school] diploma and experience. I'm like oh that's great. I didn't even have to go to college for this. (Y5)

As we discuss in Chapter 7, parents of achievers knew not to let their daughters make such disastrous changes in major. They paid careful attention to their progress through school and nudged them back on track when they were tempted to transfer to majors viewed as less appropriate. In contrast, Amanda's mother's initial response was supportive. Amanda told us:

> My mom and I talk about it all the time. I should have just stuck with education and got my teacher's license and I would be out and I would be working. . . . She's like, "You could be teaching." I was like, "Shut up. You should have told me not to switch." (Y5)

Even worse, from Amanda's perspective, was the fact that "event planning" is folded in with "tourism," meaning that most of Amanda's classes did not focus on her core interest:

> It's stupid because I want to do event planning and promotion. The tourism management degree there [has] two event planning classes. . . . I have to take recreation classes and tourism classes and hotel classes and all this other stuff. You know, I'm sure that's great for somebody or for outdoor rec people or for tourism people, but . . . I really don't need to know how to run a recreation facility because I don't want to. I really feel like it should be in a different school. . . . I think it would go better in business. (Y5)

Her insight that "event planning" might fit better in business suggests that she was beginning to figure out, much too late, that she might have been better served by a more general degree. She had no advising that might have helped her realize this.

With her heavy workload, combined with family issues, Amanda was still in school at year five. Including the internship criteria, she would be there well over six years upon graduating, and keeping her GPA above the

2.0 required to graduate was a struggle (she was at a 2.1). Assuming she did graduate, she would be carrying an estimated $35,000–$40,000 in loans, with few employment prospects. Realizing this, her plan was to revert back to teaching—which was her initial goal before she had gotten seduced by the possibility of being a wedding planner. However, to do so she would have to go back to school—likely at the local community college—and spend even more money. As she noted:

> I tried to look into it but I just kept getting sent in circles on a Web site about still getting my teaching certificate and then having that to fall back on too. You don't necessarily have to have a teaching degree. As long as you have a degree you can get a license. . . . With a degree in tourism I don't know what they would really have me teach, but I have a ton of English credits that I'm not using for anything. . . . I figure I could . . . go to [community college] for a couple of semesters and get, I don't know if [community college] has English degrees or anything. Just get an Associate's in English and then I'd have a Bachelor's and Associate's degree to teach English somewhere. (Y5)

Although Amanda's inability to graduate was exacerbated by a heavier work schedule than was carried by lower-middle-class stayers, such an academic trajectory was common among stayers. Indeed, most were sorted into majors that were a better fit for socialite women. Two others were also tourism majors. Neither was qualified or connected enough to get jobs that required a BA. Crystal became an "activities, events, and party coordinator" at a gated community, getting paid $13 an hour. With $200 monthly loan payments, she was barely making ends meet. Alana was a part-time ski instructor at the time of the final interview. Carrie started in interior decorating, a socialite major. Several years in, her parents pushed her to switch to education. This initial diversion cost her an extra year and a half of schooling, not to mention additional loans. Upon graduating she could not find a teaching job in her area (being unable to afford to move elsewhere) and was working in childcare.

Most stayers had little hope of augmenting their situation with financial support from a partner. College had not extended their social networks— although most dated college men, only one dated a man not from her hometown area, and he was similarly less privileged. Even the few who did not return to their hometowns after college found it hard to meet good men. For example, Crystal was a virgin not because of any religious or moral convictions but because she could not find "someone that has their life to-gether, is out of college, graduated, has a career, can make me laugh" (Y5). The only guy she talked to was her coworker, and he had a girlfriend of three years. As she noted, "If I had found someone that I really liked and had been dating for a while I would [have had sex] but that just hasn't hap-pened" (Y5).

This was problematic given that many strivers wanted to build families alongside careers. As twenty-one-year-old Carrie explained:

> I feel so old. . . . I feel like I'm already getting to the point where I'm gonna be, like, an old maid. It's true [laughs]. It's just, like, my sister . . . well, when [she] married, they obviously had more money together. And they're building a house and all the stuff is really appealing. . . . You know, [they] have nice cars and I've never had that. (Y4)

Having stayed at MU, stayers were typically unwilling to dip into the pool of unemployed high school graduates readily available in their home-towns. With few viable options, they sometimes jumped at potential mari-tal prospects, even if they were less than ideal. Amanda, for instance, was dating and talking about marrying a fellow employee at the big box store where she worked—despite the fact that he was still married to another woman.

It is possible that it may take a few more years for these women's economic trajectories to smooth out, given the rocky nature of the striver experience. However, at the time of the last interview—with the exception of Valerie—stayers actually seemed worse off for their time at MU, having spent four (sometimes more) years of their life accruing debt. Without the right cre-dentials, parental support, or access to marriageable men, their mobility was at risk.

The Leavers

Seven strivers, five of whom were from working-class backgrounds, left MU in their first three years.[8] As most lacked the resources available to stayers, remaining at MU was fiscally and socially untenable. Leavers fell into two distinct groups: those who (at least temporarily) exited the pathway to the bachelor's degree and those who transferred to regional campuses.[9]

The two women who stepped off the trajectory to a four-year degree were from working-class backgrounds. Both had been lured into the party scene for a time, with disastrous results. As Monica described, "I went a little crazy and I started partying and that kind of stuff. . . . I was afraid if I continued down there that I would just go crazy and either not finish school or get myself in trouble and I just didn't wanna do that" (Y5). She left at the end of her first year. Heather was similarly drawn to partying and exited MU at the end of two years with a 2.0 GPA and only a few transferable credits. Leaving MU made sense for these women, as they attempted to minimize financial and personal costs.

However, in the transition out, both women downgraded their educational trajectories. Monica, for instance, went to a beauty school in her hometown, and—as she described, "worked in a couple different salons. And it was one of those things where I loved doing it, but I woke up every morning wishing I had finished my nursing degree" (Y5). Heather had followed her lower-middle-class roommate Stacey to a regional campus, where they were both planning to switch to associate's degrees in an effort to speed things up. However, Stacey's parents intervened. As Stacey noted, "[They] influenced me not do dental hygiene. 'Cause they want me to go for a bachelor's degree instead of an associate's degree" (Y2). Without such advice, Heather opted for an optometry associate's program.

It was unlikely these women would break into the upper-middle class, but their fates were hardly worse than those of the stayers. If Heather could graduate as planned (her progress was slowed by waitressing on the side), it seemed certain she would have a job. Companies frequently called the optometry school asking for optometry assistants, as there was not enough supply to match the demand. In many ways, this degree had more promise in the job market than the tourism degrees pursued by stayers.

Several years out, Monica's situation had also changed. Returning to the familiarity of her community and safety net of her family helped her to heal from her painful experience at MU. Back home, she was also able to find a stable, although not college-educated, mate with a good paying managerial job. As he was on a similar early timeline, they married when she was twenty. This provided her with financial independence from her family. Her husband was supportive of her attending a local community college for an associate's degree in nursing. The entire course of study would cost less than half of the total bill for her first year at MU—the loans for which they were just beginning to pay back. Monica's story suggests that for some strivers, early marriage can offer the kind of stability and financial support that facilitates rather than hinders schooling. However, in the context of a flagship school like MU, there is little room for moving into the family formation phase of adulthood.

The most positive outcomes for any of the strivers, however, were for the four women who left MU to finish their bachelor's degrees at less prestigious regional campuses. The irony of this was not lost on us, as we assumed that the decision to transfer would limit, not facilitate, their mobility. This assumption—that going back home was a step backward—had some merit.[10] It meant returning to parental households and the "black hole" towns they had tried to escape. Even as bad as their experiences at MU were, these strivers looked wistfully back on their time in Fairview. As Megan noted:

> I miss [MU] so much. I like [my new school] but MU is just, I don't know. I like it a whole lot better. I come back home and feel like I haven't left high school. I've always pictured myself being away from home, doing my own type of thing. Having to come [back] is really not my cup of tea. (Y2)

Coming back home often felt like failure and meant returning to the worlds they had hoped to leave behind. Transferring also resulted in the loss of credits that did not satisfy requirements at new schools, extending the time to degree.

Nonetheless, considerable benefits were to be had from leaving MU, for those who summoned the initiative to make the move. These strivers managed for one of two key reasons. First, two of them—both working-class women—were highly intelligent and quite pragmatic. They, along with a third, had arrived strongly "motivated for mobility." The last woman had the same level of resources as most stayers, but her parents "wanted me to come back 'cause I was going home a lot anyway" (Andrea Y5). This turned out to be the best thing she could have done.

Although not necessarily true of all regional schools, these campuses offered smoother avenues to mobility for strivers because they were designed with such clientele in mind. The mobility pathway was the primary pathway available. Students were less affluent, and many were commuters living at home. Fewer came from out of state, and a much larger proportion needed to work while in school. Here strivers could find more students "like them"—students who were balancing adult realities with study. The needs of the modal student were more pragmatic, and the campuses—with less developed party scenes—reflected this.

The most obvious benefits of transferring to such a school were economic. Megan, for example, saved an estimated $6,000 a semester by transferring.

For another woman, the cost of being at MU for one year was more than the four years she spent at her new school. By living at home, although far from an ideal situation, women also saved considerable money. In addition, the cost of driving back and forth to visit hometown boyfriends was no longer an issue.

The interlinked social and academic benefits, however, seemed to matter the most. Women often talked about the importance of being with other strivers. Megan told us:

> There's more people who have practical majors. Like, more farmers and more kids who have lower social economic status. . . . You know, they can work for their school . . . There's more of those kids. So I feel more comfortable because I can relate to them. Because I've never had any money growin' up, so I can relate to that. (Y4)

Similarly, as Stacey explained:

> [Regional campus] doesn't have any fraternities or sororities. It . . . only has, like, ten buildings. . . . I just really love it and, like, nobody cares about it 'cause they're there just to graduate and get through. (Y3)

Being part of a student body in which they felt more comfortable and included was critical for these women, particularly after being at MU. No longer were they isolated in a world full of people who did not understand where they were coming from. Here they could relate to other adults with similar responsibilities and priorities.

Not getting distracted by a myriad of majors and social pursuits tailored for socialites tended to translate into better academic outcomes for striver women. As Stacey noted:

> I was [at MU] for two years and I was flipping through so many majors 'cause I didn't know what I wanted to do. Finally figured out what I wanted to do at [the regional campus]. (Y4)

There were simply too many options at MU, and the most readily available options were ill-suited to someone like her. The lure of MU's social life contributed to her inability to get on track. She continued:

> Our freshman year we partied every weekend and during the weekday. Went to the fraternities. Went to all the house parties. Had fake IDs. Went to the bars. . . . Then you finally, it just snaps. Like, oh my God, OK, I need

to get done with school. . . . After the first two years I was just over it. And
that's what I loved about [the regional campus]. (Y4)

For Stacey, a regional campus offered the opportunity to focus and avoid
the risks and seductions of the party scene. Others had similar reports. As
a nursing major explained:

[Being in] Fairview and living in the dorms and class being so far away, it
was easier to not wanna go. And [at the regional campus] since you have to
drive there, and then once you're there, you're there and you'll go to every
class. . . . When I got to [the regional campus], I knew I was competitive to
get into nursing school, so I tried a lot harder. So, I mean, I was getting A's
and B's. . . . I'm pretty sure in Fairview it was, like, C's. (Andrea Y5)

Her story highlights the extent to which the regional campuses served different, more practical purposes.

However, these transfers cost time. The four leavers who moved to regional
campuses each added a year or more to her time to degree. Most finished
college with GPAs above 3.0, resuscitating them after receiving low grades
at MU. All graduated with majors that they would turn into practical careers. For example, Megan's psychology major prepared her for a master's
program in school counseling. Alyssa went through a tough accounting program and was considering becoming a CPA. After five total major switches,
Stacey went into health service management. Andrea, as noted above, became a nurse. None of these majors or their associated jobs depended
heavily on connections and all required college degrees.

Like many stayers, most leavers were marriage oriented and desired mates
with whom they could combine earnings. Their options—having returned
home—were perhaps even more limited. These women did a lot of sifting
through the available alternatives, which made them susceptible to traumatic experiences with controlling, unmotivated, or nonsupportive mates.
Stacey eventually managed to find a supportive, older hometown guy who
owned his own home and earned a considerable amount at the local chem-
ical plant. However, others vowed to remain single for a while. Megan, who
had just left an abusive marriage, noted, "I'm not dating and I don't want
to date" (Y5). Yet unlike for stayers, the solid and practical career trajectories of these leavers ensured that they could stand on their own if they
needed to.

The positive stories of the four leavers, particularly in comparison to the
outcomes of the stayers, raises questions about the viability of the mobility

pathway at MU and perhaps at other similar four-year, residential state schools. Although our sample size is small, it is damning that not one of the working-class students graduated from MU in five years. It is instructive that the women had to leave in order to graduate and that they ended up with less debt and more useful degrees when they went elsewhere. The experiences of these women suggest that schools like MU may be failing to educate the students who most need college skills and credentials for economic security.

CHAPTER 7

Achievers, Underachievers, and the Professional Pathway

An Achiever

I feel like when you do accounting, the business school and my dad too, they just try . . . There's, like, a big four accounting firm . . . [and] that's kinda where they try and steer you. That's where you wanna work, so that's kind of what he's been doing. [Laura: Trying to push you?] Yeah . . . cause, it's like, I think when you start there having that name of that company can kind of set you up to wherever you want to go. All the people I [interned] with said if they ever didn't like what they're doing, they have the headhunters calling them all the time. Just cause the name is good.

(Lydia Y4)

An Underachiever

[Laura: What drew you to teaching?] Actually nothing. I never wanted to do that. I actually wanted to be a pediatrician. I was so set on that. I was so bummed out when I knew I needed to quit premed. It's just really hard and a lot of time that you need to put into it. And the classes and everything. And I need to take that test my junior year and I just knew that it was just going to be a bomb waiting to hit. I talked to my parents about it and they said if you want . . . get out of it.

(Olivia Y4)

Thirty-eight percent of women resembled Taylor and Emma, the two dentistry hopefuls profiled at the start of the book. They all attempted, with varying levels of motivation and preparation, to use the professional pathway as a means to achieve a lucrative professional career.[1] Generally less affluent than socialites and more affluent than strivers, women in this group were perhaps more typical of college students at MU than those

180

discussed so far. Many spent their time in ways that most hope college students will—engaged in academics while socializing moderately.

Just as not all on the party pathway fared equally well, not all of these women were equally successful. We call the seven most accomplished women "achievers." All but one—including upper-middle-class Taylor—arrived at MU "cultivated for success." As we noted earlier, Taylor graduated with a 3.6 and was enrolled in a top dental school one year after graduation. In contrast, middle-class Emma was one of eleven underachievers, all but one of whom arrived at MU by default and struggled on the professional pathway. Emma graduated with a 3.0 GPA, ended up living with her parents, and was working as a dental assistant—making $11 an hour in a job that did not require a bachelor's degree.

Here we take a look at why Taylor's and Emma's lives diverged so drastically. Our explanation requires understanding the nature of the professional pathway at MU. It was dense and resource-rich but also narrow, fast-paced, and zero-sum. There were, for example, only so many spots available in top academic programs, only so many merit awards, and a finite amount of attention from ladder-rank faculty to go around. Resources were thus far from evenly dispersed, generating fierce competition. This competition was set in a larger institutional landscape defined by an alluring party pathway, creating a lot of distractions and opportunities to go astray. Unfortunately, the professional pathway left little margin for error. Students who made missteps were simply left behind.

By rewarding only those who were already polished, the professional pathway effectively outsourced to parents much of the work involved in producing professionals. Achieving success was a family endeavor that had to start well in advance of attendance at MU. However, not all families were equally equipped for such a project. Class resources were necessary—only upper- or upper-middle-class parents had the knowledge of higher education, money, and time to serve as effective navigators for their children. Class background alone did not guarantee success. The parent-child duo had to align on numerous criteria—for example, motivation, communication, and navigational skills—and any disruption (for example, family illness, parental death, or divorce) could threaten the entire project.

Achieving Professional Success

Successful students on the professional pathway were often those who could immediately move into selective academic programs. Using the highway metaphor, there were few on-ramps for these programs, and they came up very quickly. Entry was gated and monitored. Students needed to fulfill specific (and strict) requirements to proceed. If they missed the on-ramps or were not prepared enough to enter, then they could not break into these programs.

The competitive business school provides an example. Direct admission required students to identify business as an intended major before college, score a 1270 on the math and critical reading sections of the SAT combined, and be in the top 10% of their graduating class. After arriving, students could petition for direct admission if they did not meet one of these criteria, so long as they exceeded another. Yet anyone who did not meet all standards would not be considered for freshman business school scholarships. There was standard admission for students who later decided on the business school or whose records did not qualify for direct admission. However, they had to complete at least one semester at MU, take a number of difficult courses (including Finite Mathematics or Calculus), and get no lower than a B across all courses (no B-minuses). Students with more than seventy course hours (typically completed by the end of sophomore year) could not gain admission, effectively cutting off late attempts to transfer into this school.

A similar level of early focus and preparation was required for those desiring eventual admission to graduate programs. Here a detailed look at Taylor's and Emma's academic and extracurricular experiences is instructive (see Table 7.1 for a more general comparison of achiever and underachiever college experiences). Recall that both arrived at college expressing interest in dentistry. In her first interview, Taylor spoke knowledgeably about what she needed to accomplish at MU to be a viable candidate for dental school admission. First and foremost was joining the Dental Club to fulfill her target schools' prerequisite of forty-eight hours of shadowing. Second was a 3.5 GPA, and third was a résumé attesting to her engagement in community service. Taylor knew this before arriving at MU, allowing her to start working on accomplishing all of these things from day one.

Taylor's inside knowledge was not the result of independent efforts. After graduation, Laura asked Taylor, "How did you know to do all that stuff?" Taylor acknowledged:

Table 7.1. Achiever and underachiever college experiences

Descriptor	Achievers (7)	Underachievers (11)
Class background	Upper class or upper-middle class	Upper class, upper-middle class, middle class, or lower-middle class
College arena		
Academic	Clear goals; selective majors; career-building extracurricular activities	Poor fit between goals, major, and abilities; few, irrelevant extracurriculars
Social	Balanced approach: moderate partying declining over time; networked with ambitious peers	Overinvolvement in partying or social isolation; ties to noncollege peers
Romantic/sexual	Friendship hookups early on; committed relationships later	Sustained commitments to noncollege men; isolation from college dating scene

Women	Upper class (4):
	  Brooke
	  Brenda
	  Lydia
	  Tracy
	
	Upper-middle class (3):
	  Erica
	  Taylor
	  Madison
		Upper class (1):
		  Leah
		
		Upper-middle class (6):
		  Linda
		  Lisa
		  Julie
		  Brianna
		  Morgan
		  Natasha
		
		Middle class (2):
		  Mary
		  Emma
		
		Lower-middle class (2):
		  Becky
		  Olivia

[My parents] played a big role in it, and my mom always encouraged me to really get involved, and my dad, too, both of them. They helped me a lot in my process just in terms of researching and things I needed to do. [Laura: When you said researching stuff, would that be like the extracurricular?] Yeah, they would look on all these [dental] schools' Web sites and just see.

> They have all these recommended things you can do with a freshman to
> start building [a résumé]. I mean it's really creepy. (Y5)

Taylor's mom (a professor) and dad (who had his MBA) had begun this
process with Taylor in high school. Because Taylor had researched dentistry
from the start, she quickly gained a sense of what was involved and was able
to confirm that it was the right fit for her. As Taylor joked in her second year,
"[It] sounds so stupid, but I love teeth!" By her third year she was shadowing
her second dentist. Her senior year she was president of the Dental Club.

Emma's parents, though college-educated, were less familiar with academia than Taylor's. Emma's mom was a high school teacher and her dad
was a former businessman recovering from a major illness that left his
family in considerable debt. Thus, Emma's first years in college coincided
with a hard time for her parents, who might have been able to serve as more
effective navigators under different circumstances. They took her proclama-
tion that she wanted to be a dentist at face value and, given her stellar high
school record, left the task of figuring out what this entailed to her. It was
not until junior year that Emma realized this career was not a good match:

> I said I wanted to be a dentist for so long that they were like . . . well, my
> daughter's going to be a dentist. And I got into college and I saw the people
> I was going up against, trying to get into dental school, and I was like, these
> people are hard-core, and I'm not. And the more I saw of dentistry and what
> it entailed, the more I was like, ew, I don't wanna do that! [laughs] (Y3)

Emma briefly settled on zookeeping (a much lower paying profession) and
interned at a local zoo. Her mother vetoed this choice, telling Emma it was
not "serious." Without a viable new goal, Emma was adrift as she began her
senior year.

These stories highlight the central role that achiever parents played in
helping their children identify a field that fit their interests and abilities.
Students who did not arrive focused could easily get lost, lured into sexy
alternatives, or delayed by bouncing around from major to major. It was
not enough to simply pick a field. Like Taylor, other achievers had parents
who pushed them to engage in self-discovery early rather than find out too
late—as Emma did—that it would not work. Lydia, for instance, found her
love of accounting because of a high school class that her dad, a CPA, had
pushed her to take. She described herself as "smart as hell in math" and was
a direct admit into the business school upon arrival at MU.

This level of early clarity, however, was not always possible. Two achievers were rescued by their parents' willingness to fund more than four years so that they could move to programs that better suited them. Although—as we saw with Emma—late transfers could be risky, they tended to work when students were well informed and focused. Brenda, for example, took five years to graduate because she moved into MU's nursing program her junior year; however, she and her parents had researched the pay, availability of jobs, and working conditions for nurses before she made this move. Madison, the only in-state achiever, transferred to another residential state school where smaller class sizes and a slightly less robust party scene helped her to complete her anthropology-biology double major successfully. Her situation suggests that it was possible for students who did not arrive "cultivated to succeed" to get on a professional pathway—although, for her, it turned out that this occurred more easily elsewhere.

The most common problem for underachievers was a never-resolved mismatch between their aspirations and their preferences or abilities. For example, Olivia was a premed major and English double major until sophomore year, when she realized that she did not actually enjoy science classes. By then her GPA had dropped to an unrecoverable 2.5. One might think that an advisor could have prevented this. However, no one had suggested dropping the premed major. Olivia found that advisors were not helpful even on the basics, like what classes were required for her majors. As she noted:

> I find it pointless. . . . They're just there. . . . I don't see them [much] . . . and a lot of times they're wrong about what you need and what you don't need and I just don't want to fall on them . . . for everything that I need. (Y2)

Achievers were not getting any better help from their advisors. The difference was in their parents' abilities to provide sound advice. Parents of underachievers often had limited knowledge of what graduate programs or jobs really required. For example, Mary doggedly pursued an ambitious plan to get both a PhD in psychology and a law degree, despite modest academic abilities. Her middle-class parents were her biggest fans, but they did not understand what pursuing multiple graduate degrees entailed—or that the plan was doomed for failure.

In other cases, high-resource underachiever parents were tone-deaf to their children's interests. For instance, Morgan sought guidance from her father, who pushed business:

Morgan: I'm probably not a business person.

Laura: I remember you had a hard time in math last year.

Morgan: It took two tries, but I finished it.

Laura: Do you think your dad knew that you weren't necessarily in love with business?

Morgan: He doesn't even know. He's like really successful. I think he thinks that's the only way you can do it. (Y3)

Morgan chose to focus on the humanities, as these classes were easiest for her and she could see no viable alternatives. She later lamented the lack of a direct career application for her major. The combination of a strained relationship with her parents and her passive approach to career development (also discussed in Chapter 4) made it hard to get on a fruitful career track at MU, where decisive action was required.

As these examples suggest, finding the right match for a student's ability and interests mattered for academic achievement. Achievers had GPAs ranging from 3.4 to 3.7, while underachievers, with one exception, had GPAs at or well below 3.0. Quite simply, it was easier for students to do well if they liked and cared about their classes and if there was a good match between their abilities and the coursework.

Preparation for professional careers also occurred outside of official university curricula. For instance, all but two achievers participated in internships that helped them in graduate admissions and on the labor market. None of these opportunities were set up through MU. Like socialite parents, achiever parents often helped their children to locate and land these positions. For example, Lydia's father used his influence to secure a paid internship in a high-status accounting firm. As she explained:

I think [my dad] played a big factor in me getting the internship. He had given my résumé to someone and he said that if people refer you in the office, that's like a huge deal. . . . They really take that seriously, so, I mean, I don't know if I could've maybe gotten it on my own. I'm not sure, but . . . I think that made a huge deal in helping me. (Y4)

Unlike Lydia's, most internships were unpaid, as were valuable shadowing and intensive volunteer experiences. Most students who could take these opportunities relied on the funds of parents. For example, as Brooke described of her first (unpaid) internship:

D.C. is really expensive . . . so [my parents] are like, "Well, we can help you." And even living in a dingy dorm at George Washington, I was paying

$250 a week. So $1,000 a month for two months. . . . And then they gave me spending money. . . . People obviously have to have enough money to be able to live in D.C. and work for free. . . . And pretty much all D.C. internships are unpaid. . . . There was one girl who . . . worked at a bar at night, so she came into [her internship] a mess. She was, like . . . the worst intern. Like, they'll never hire an intern again for that position because she was so bad. (Y4)

While Brooke was able to translate this experience into a second (paid) internship, it is unlikely that her less privileged peer received the kind of recommendation she would need to do so.

Parental financial support paved the way for other forms of résumé building and self-enhancement. For example, study abroad programs tended to cost considerably more than equivalent time at the university.[2] The programs achievers selected were often more immersive and academically serious than those frequented by socialites. Erica, for example, elected to live with a Spanish-speaking family in an economically impoverished city in Spain rather than enroll in a "party abroad" program in a major city with other American students. This was a calculated and expensive family investment in Erica's future. Funds also had to be devoted to Erica's side trips around Europe. As she noted, her otherwise frugal parents "were so amazing about money, you know, they just were like, 'Go live.' After five months, I was ready to come home" (Y4).

Achievers were also spared from the need to work for pay during the school year. Only Madison worked, as she wanted the retail experience, and her parents supported this decision under the condition that she maintained good grades. In some cases, summers were also devoted to travel and study—like Tracy's mission trip to Africa or Taylor's summer prep for the dental exam. In contrast, underachievers lost time for self-enrichment to paid employment. Mary, for instance, was an RA on a dorm floor for two years during college—a particularly time-consuming job. Morgan, although she did not need the money, worked during the school year as a hostess and had a short stint in a grocery store. It is possible that even experiences like these could be parlayed into usable credentials (indeed, Madison's dad would help her to do so); however, as we will see, underachievers did not have the same help in selling themselves to graduate programs and employers.

Navigating the Tightrope

As we noted in the Introduction, young women today are held to exacting standards across multiple arenas. It is not enough to perform well academically and accrue a variety of career skills and credentials. Successful professionals have to develop the social skills, networks, and shared experiences necessary to slide into upper-middle-class worlds. Romantically, they must learn to identify a match who is supportive of their achievement and contributes to the success of the couple—and find ways to wait until the best mates will be ready to commit. In short, they need to figure out how to do it all and in just the right ways.

Success can thus be envisioned as a tightrope walk, where tipping in any one direction can lead to a fall. This task is tricky for women at any university to achieve. However, walking the tightrope at a large middle-tier research university presents a particular challenge. The well-developed party pathway structures the available social and romantic options in ways that best meet the needs of socialites—not achievers. It can exert a heavy pull on otherwise academically oriented students and cause them to lose their footing.

In such an institutional context, students who finish largely unscathed operate with a safety net in place and are aided by an ever-present coach: their parents, who provide academic guidance and help them navigate the other interconnected aspects of their lives. In this way, students' families (with all of their varied resources and dynamics) become inserted into the university as strong predictors of student success or failure.

A Balanced Social Life

Navigation of the professional pathway required learning to balance the social and academic arenas of college. The tightrope metaphor is particularly apt here. Destroying grades through too much partying was undoubtedly a failure, yet so was not developing a rich on-campus social life. The nature of the social scene at MU, somewhat ironically, made both types of failure likely among those seeking the professional pathway.

Women were often torn—wanting to be out partying while simultaneously trying to juggle a challenging (and, in this context, potentially isolating) workload. As Lydia complained:

> I feel like some majors are a lot less work. Like [my friend] . . . she is sports
> marketing. . . . I feel like I never see her study. She's maybe gone to the

library once. At least twice a week I will be at the library for like five hours straight, just studying. . . . [Also, the] 9 a.m. class pretty much cuts off my going out Thursday nights. I had midterms all last week, so I hadn't gone out like two weeks before that because we have tests on, like I had [a] test on Friday night. [And] I have [a] test on Saturday night. Yeah, the business school does it that way. Like our last test on Friday night ended at ten. (Y3)

Devoting oneself to this sort of rigorous academic schedule, especially when surrounded by peers who derive status primarily from participation in the social scene, could be a serious impediment to integration into campus life. At the same time, abandoning it completely for an easier major could have serious career consequences.

One of the more revealing moments came when one woman realized that at other more elite campuses it was easier to both study and party without the two coming into conflict. As she described of her visit to a top public university:

I was so just fascinated by how every single person had gotten up on a Friday to go to the library and do work and, like, got their stuff done. And I loved it. You know? It was great. When I go to the library . . . my friends are like, "Really? You're going to the library again?" . . . Everyone [at the other school] was studying and I was just like . . . This is crazy! I mean, MU is a party school and I like to go out and have fun and, you know, I can do that here. But you could do that [at the top public school, too]. [And] everyone wakes up the next morning, hung over or not, and goes to the library. (Erica Y3)

Erica's disbelief that such a place existed—where partiers were also good students who studied—suggests just how radically different it was from her experience at MU.

Given the constraints of their environment, achievers had to develop coping mechanisms that helped them to strike a balance between the social and the academic. Four went Greek (several after being advised to do so by parents)—but in middle- or lower-tier houses. Participating in Greek life ensured they would not be nerdy isolates. As Lydia described:

[The first few weeks of school] all I was doing was studying and stuff, and I was like I kind of want to get involved, do at least something, so I knew that. And then I wanted to meet more people and like, I've met so many people since I've joined like it's ridiculous. (Y1)

Because achievers' houses attracted a more diverse membership than elite houses, they also worried less about being entirely swept away in a social whirlwind. In fact, Taylor's sorority was so known for being studious that she considered declining:

> I was so afraid that I was joining this house that, you know, all they do is study. But . . . it was one of the best decisions because I was able to do everything I wanted and still get good grades. Because my friends would study, too, you know? (Y4)

Though all achievers guiltily acknowledged partying more than they "should have," particularly in their first two years, they were careful about not letting their grades slip too much. Their parents often played a critical role in helping them learn just how much effort their classes required and how much energy this left for other pursuits. For instance, when juggling the demands of her upper-level classes, keeping up with her friends, and trying to manage a serious relationship, Taylor consulted her mom:

> I had like a long talk with my mom today. I wrote it down. Homecoming week is this week and my roommate plans everything. . . . She's all pressured. She's planning all these activities with one of the frats. And I have this really busy week next week and it's Owen's twenty-first birthday and then one of my other friend's twenty-first birthday, so I planned to study study all week and then I could celebrate those. But then my roommate is like "why doesn't anybody come out?" My mom was like "just try to stay out of her room as best you can during the day." (Y3)

This sort of interaction was crucial to achievers' abilities to successfully balance their social and academic lives. Rather than simply telling Taylor that school should come first, her mother coached her through competing demands and offered concrete advice.

Even with the more moderate social demands of the less elite houses, achievers pulled back as academic pressures increased. As we discussed in Chapter 2, not one achiever actually lived in her sorority house during her senior year. Parents were often behind these moves as well. Taylor and Brenda, for instance, received encouragement to opt out of their houses and into apartments with close friends.

In contrast, underachievers often erred on the side of being too social. Because of what Laura called her "sparkly and fun" personality along with good looks, Emma was accepted into a top sorority (Interview Notes Y2).

As we noted in Chapter 3, with her middle-class background she was something of an anomaly in her sorority. Earning a place in this house had consequences for Emma's academic performance. As Laura observed, the atmosphere in the sorority was not conducive to studying:

It is pretty apparent that these girls party A LOT. Certainly, for a Tuesday night there was a ton of commotion going on. Loud music, hairdryers going, talking in the halls. And we were doing the interview in a study room. I can't imagine really getting any work done in that house. (Interview Notes 10/25/05)

Emma's efforts to strike a balance in this house did not work. She found that when she insisted that she needed to stay in on a Saturday night to study for a test on Monday, her sorority sisters would "look at me kind of funny, like it's Saturday night. Monday's not for another day" (Y2).

Unlike Taylor, Emma received little advice about how to deal with these competing demands. Recall that her parents were less informed about what it would take for her to actually make it to dental school. As she described of her parents' response to her slipping GPA, "I got my first C ever in my life. And my parents were like, you're in college, you know. It's something totally different than high school" (Y2). This left Emma confused about how to balance academics with her burgeoning social life, which was her real issue—not the increasing difficulty of her studies. She continued, "But college, I think what is most difficult about college is not necessarily the school work. It's organizing my time. Like applying the right amount of time, giving the right amount of time to what's [important] and prioritizing" (Y2).

Sometimes, however, even parents' best efforts were not enough to keep women from sliding deeply into the college social scene. Brianna was a straight-A student and an athlete in high school. She self-identified as lesbian, had a masculine style, and initially avoided fraternity parties. As she recognized how women garnered status on campus, she changed:

[Some of my old friends] were talking about . . . where are your big boy shorts, and your sports bra, and your wife beater, and your boy shoes, and your hat? . . . I know this sounds bad, but . . . I suddenly changed my group of friends. Kinda went from kind of attractive to really attractive. . . . Everybody was like, you could be so much prettier if you were just girly. (Y3)

Along with her reinvention came heavy drug and alcohol use. Brianna's parents realized she had a problem. They pulled her from MU, brought her home, enrolled her in community college, provided her with a job in their law office, and monitored her schoolwork. Ultimately, even this approach failed as Brianna continued to party with her newfound MU friends (who were within driving distance). Time in rehab and jail effectively dashed her hopes of achieving even an associate's degree during the period of our study.

While being too social posed issues for some underachievers, not being social enough was a problem for others who did not fit (or did not want to fit) into MU's Greek scene. It was possible to develop a balanced social life without going Greek. Tracy, for example, built a network of friends by combining existing ties with those of her roommate. However, as we learned in Chapter 4, living in the midst of the party scene (especially in a party dorm) shut down interaction with potential friends for many women. Locating alternative niches was also difficult, as it required initiative and was facilitated by class-based resources that many did not have.

Instead of branching out, a few relied on preexisting ties with friends from home or family members. For instance, as described in Chapter 4, Morgan and Natasha never disconnected from their shared hometown friends—very few of whom were headed for upper-middle-class professional careers. As Natasha explained, "I think most of them probably won't get any sort of degree or anything. They're more focused on working and finding a job instead of getting into school" (Y2). These friendships, while valuable to the women, modeled—and normalized—a pattern of downward mobility that Morgan and Natasha would later follow.

Sexual and Romantic Relationships

In some ways, achievers shared romantic concerns with socialites. Boyfriends threatened socializing (for socialites) and career development (for achievers). Both groups adopted a reserved approach to relationships. Lydia, for example, intentionally started college without a boyfriend:

> I came in single. . . . I wouldn't want to come in with a serious relationship. . . . I feel like now I'm so busy I don't even have time for anyone. I don't know how people do relationships in college because I just feel like I

don't have time for anyone. I guess if I did have a boyfriend, I couldn't really be going out with my friends as much. (Y1)

Similarly, Erica was still not ready to deal with a boyfriend in her second year of college:

I feel like I do want a boyfriend, but not yet, you know? . . . I think having a boyfriend is hard because it's hard to . . . be really excited about it and still not let it consume you and like still not lose track of keeping touch with your girlfriends and . . . just not letting it take over. Which I think is hard for anyone to do. (Y2)

Yet unlike women on the party pathway, those on the professional pathway were uncomfortable with using hookups as the primary means to postpone serious romantic commitments. That this was the dominant mode of relating sexually on MU's campus posed some frustration for achievers and underachievers alike. For instance, achievers Taylor and Brenda described hooking up as "gross" and "kind of meaningless and stupid," respectively (Y3, Y2). Similarly, underachiever Olivia noted, "I would rather be a virgin for as much as I can than go out and do God knows who" (Y1). Such an orientation meant less exposure to the risks associated with hooking up; however, it also required women to devise other sexual and romantic strategies.

Five of the seven achievers rather creatively experimented with a different model of sexual relations that combined the benefits of hooking up (for example, low commitment) with the benefits of a relationship (for example, mutual respect). As Erica described:

I personally would want someone to constantly be with, but not a relationship. You know what [I] mean? Like that's what I want. Someone you can constantly hook up with, hang out with—that's great. That's like utopia. That's perfect. But I don't necessarily want all the baggage of a relationship. (Y2)

What we call "friendship hookups" are sexual liaisons between individuals who know each other beforehand and engage in sexual activity over a period of time, sometimes accompanied by "hanging out" or doing other social activities together. Instead of becoming an official couple, the two stay "just friends" or allow the liaison to remain undefined. Although some socialites also experimented with friendship hookups, achievers expressed the most interest in them. This occurred, in part, because other existing sexual options were so far removed from what achievers desired, especially early in college.

All achievers did eventually enter into relationships, particularly later in college. However, they often slowed their progression to preserve independence. As Brooke explained:

> I won't let myself think that [I love my boyfriend]. I definitely don't say that. He's sort of serious. The person he loves is the person he is going to marry. I don't want that to happen. . . . I don't really see the point of rushing into anything. I mean, at the age we are at now I feel like I don't want anything to be more serious than it has to be until it is. (Y3)

Even one year into a relationship, Erica held back. She noted:

> Not that I think I could do so much better, I just think it would be silly to not see what else is out there before making a commitment. And twenty is so young. I have so many more experiences, so many more people to meet that I couldn't imagine saying, okay, this is the person I'm going to marry. It just seems ridiculous. (Y3)

This space was critical for keeping focus on self-development, and not closing off options (for example, the study abroad program that Erica did her junior year, despite having a boyfriend).

Achievers' willingness to limit commitment reflected their life timeline. They planned to first build a career, establish financial independence, and only then marry and start a family. Their parents helped to cement their views about the appropriate timing of family formation. As Taylor noted, "My mom's always saying things are so different now. . . . People are living longer, getting married later, having kids later. . . . [My parents] are like you're so young still" (Y4). If necessary, achiever parents gently intervened. Brenda told us:

> They didn't want me to get married young. . . . I mean, my mom thought for a while that I was gonna marry [my first boyfriend] and she was getting nervous for a while. But then they're like, we don't regret [getting married so young], but we don't want . . . we want you girls to go and live your life and then get married, you know? Go do things you wanna do. (Y4)

Similarly, when Madison was conflicted about ending a relationship she felt was moving too fast, her mother reassured her this was the right decision— giving her the confidence to move on.

The parents of achievers also helped women learn to identify men who not only had the potential to contribute economically but would not threaten their careers. For example, when Taylor began dating Owen during her junior year, she was flattered by his attention and awestruck by his wealth. However, the relationship became combative when Taylor experienced pressure to put her career ambitions on the back burner. Taylor's parents interceded, not strong-arming a breakup but planting the idea that this was not a healthy relationship. Her mother, for instance, helped to identify features of emotional abuse:

> My mom was like, you know, it's like the battered woman's syndrome. She goes back Hoping this time. And, he never touched me, but mentally it can be almost the same thing. Have almost the same effect, you know? (Y4)

Her parents also forced her to think seriously about the relationship: "My mom and dad were just like, 'What are you doing?' They knew I [had to] make the decision myself" (Y4).

Through this experience, Taylor learned that she was best served by an equal marriage—not a traditional, gender-complementary marriage. As she described:

> I was supposed to just go to these functions and stand there and try and look pretty and not really talk, and that was obviously an issue for me. That was doomed for failure. That made me nauseous, that whole circle of people, the debutantes and their bachelors. . . . It's so outdated. A lot of people can't even believe that still exists. (Y5)

Her experience underscores the importance of careful mate selection for achievers and the central role that parents—even from afar—can play in this. As Taylor noted (in agreement), "My mom said, 'I don't even know if you would have succeeded with everything if you stayed with him'" (Y5).

Underachievers were not as effective as achievers in protecting their autonomy. These women were even less likely to see hookups as viable options. Only one—Lisa—participated in a friendship hookup. Five spent most of their time in college in relationships that continually escalated in seriousness. Some even had parents who seemed to hope for a more traditional and early marriage for their daughters. As Natasha described (after a breakup):

> My mom tells me to find someone successful who can support me. . . . So she's been telling me that she started praying, and she said six to eight

months I'll find a guy [laughs]. [Laura: Six to eight months you'll find a guy, you'll marry this guy?] She says she has her line [to God]. (Y4)

Similarly, Emma's parents and siblings had all married young, so when her military boyfriend was pushing Emma to get engaged "when he's back from Iraq next year," her parents did not raise any concerns (Y3).

The partners that underachievers selected also tended to have less career promise. Emma's boyfriend, for instance, was a working-class military recruit from her small hometown who had no desire to attend college. Similarly, Morgan's boyfriend worked a low-paying job and did not plan on going to college. Like the hometown boyfriends of strivers, he began to stand in the way of Morgan's academic progress. As she noted during her junior year:

He's becoming needy and controlling and I've talked to him about it, like, he doesn't understand why I can't just pick up and go to Capital City and see him all the time. I have school. . . . I feel like I always have to explain myself, like why I wanna stay here. . . . I just kinda wanna be a college kid. (Y3)

The tense relationship between Morgan and her recently divorced parents meant that they were unable to artfully intervene like Taylor's or Brenda's parents. Her mother tried a forceful approach in which "he wasn't allowed to sit on our couch. He wasn't allowed to park in our driveway, and he was not welcome," but it backfired (Y4). Morgan even entertained plans to get engaged in part "to piss my mom off" (Y4). She only ended the relationship after a long three-year ordeal that defined much of her time at college. Her experience highlights the fact that not only class resources had to be present for parental navigation to work. (Morgan was from a college-educated, upper-middle-class family living in an affluent suburb). Trust, open communication, and a secure relationship between parents and children were also key.

Rather than getting enmeshed with the wrong match, two underachievers tipped too far in the other direction. For instance, Linda's insecurities and fear of sex made it difficult for her to find a relationship. As she described:

I still have never been kissed and I'm still a virgin. I have some friends who have relationships and some who don't, some like to tease and some feel pity. . . . Actually it's very odd, I don't know if this is clinically insane or not, but kind of a relationship in your head? Like you've met a guy and you liked him and he was funny. You might not have even talked to him that much, but you had kind of like a fake relationship. I don't even have that this year. (Y2)

Similarly, late in college, Mary's virginity started to become a dating liability. As she explained, "You almost feel like you need to put it out there because if it's going to be an issue, I just don't wanna bother with dating you. Which is why I think I've dated a lot less people in the last two years" (Y4). These women's limited romantic experiences placed them out of sync with their peers and could make it difficult for them to locate a high-earning spouse in the future.[3]

The Transition out of College

Achievers were the products of successful social reproduction: Parental resources—time, money, social connections, and familiarity with college and the professional world—helped them to extract the credentials and experiences they needed from the university's professional pathway. Whatever they could not get from the university, they sought from special off-campus opportunities. In a marked contrast to the socialites discussed in Chapter 5, they left college economically self-sufficient. Admission to the upper-middle class was fairly certain (see Table 7.2). All that remained was getting to market—selling their solid profiles in the right locations, where the best opportunities could be found. In this regard, achievers benefited from exclusive university job placement services, as well as critical instances of parental support.

The task for underachievers was more daunting. Their experiences on the professional pathway were less rewarding, leaving them unfinished. The burden remained on their families to create self-supporting professionals in the face of less than ideal academic records. In the transition out of college, the fates of underachievers diverged. Compensatory efforts by high resource parents pulled one group back on track toward an achiever profile. The second group, although similarly privileged, was unable to make this move, setting women on a path for downward mobility. The final group had low-resource parents who could not help.

Table 7.2. Achiever and underachiever trajectories

Descriptor	Achievers (7) and redirected underachievers (3)	Underachievers (8)
Class trajectory	Reproduction (into upper-middle class)	Lower-middle and middle class: mobility at risk Upper and upper-middle class: at risk of downward mobility
Dimensions		
College performance	Reasonable GPA in respectable major	Low GPA in major with limited entry-level job prospects
Career prospects	Rapid entry into professional job or grad program; parental assistance for relocation	Unemployment or underemployment; GPA limits access to graduate school; continued dependence on parents
Marital prospects	Access to or in committed relationships with potential peer marriage partners	Limited access to upwardly mobile potential partners
Women	Achievers (7): 　Brooke 　Brenda 　Lydia 　Tracy 　Erica 　Taylor 　Madison Redirected underachievers (3): 　Leah 　Lisa 　Julie	Downwardly mobile (4): 　Linda 　Brianna 　Morgan 　Natasha Upward mobility at risk (4): 　Mary 　Emma 　Becky 　Olivia

Achievers: Moving Smoothly into Professional Careers

The professional pathway offers a bridge between college achievement and post-college opportunities for many top students, particularly those enrolled in selective programs. Their success reflects on their respective programs, raises the national profile of the school, and facilitates recruitment of high-achieving high school students willing to cross state lines for the right academic curriculum. There are thus strong incentives for universities to invest in placement services for this subset of students and to take the steps necessary to position them well in job and graduate school markets.

The business school at MU, for instance, has been assigned a grade of A+ by *Businessweek* magazine for its stellar job placement services. These services are typically open only to business school students—even though business-lite majors across the university are looking to land similar jobs. The business school puts considerable effort into building relationships with well-respected employers who are located in major cities nationwide. The school sponsors recruiters to come to MU to participate in exclusive job fairs and on-campus interviews. Business school students watch this process for years before they go through it themselves and even engage in mock interviews beforehand. This socialization, as well as help constructing résumés, ensures that they will be "packaged" in a favorable way.

For the business school students in our study the job search unfolded smoothly and without issue.[4] Take Erica's description of how she got her job:

> I hate to sound like such a jerk but it was like, I don't want to say an easy process, but it certainly was not the hardest thing I've ever done. The business school really set it up nicely where everything was done online. I clicked the companies that I was interested in and got the interview scheduled. . . . I went in and it was a half an hour interview. Then I got a second interview and they flew me to [my home city]. They got me a hotel. They offered to extend my trip if I wanted to stay at home with my parents. Things kind of just fell into place for me, which I'm very lucky for that. But the business school really had a nice system of getting people interviewed. . . . It was nice knowing before Thanksgiving my senior year what I was doing. (Y5)

Her account highlights ways that the university can automate aspects of the job search that are most likely to go awry for job candidates (for example, locating jobs in distant geographic locations, making contact with employers, and getting to the interview). By providing this help only for those in select programs, the university gives an edge to those who least need it.

Indeed, achievers rise to the top of the pile, regardless of university assistance. For instance, as noted earlier, Taylor—a biology major—landed a spot in a top fifteen dental school. As Taylor acutely realized, she enjoyed a distinct advantage over other candidates:

> It's becoming pretty competitive. . . . A lot of people in these schools are older than me. I think the average age in my class is twenty-five or something, because a lot of people just don't know to do that [focus on the extracurriculars], so it takes them two or three times to apply. So I guess I was lucky that I knew that and was able to start [early]. (Y5)

Here Taylor's parents' coaching, inside information, and efforts to keep her on track academically paid off. These benefits, however, were invisible to those evaluating her, as they were instantiated in her record. Taylor—like Tracy, who ended up in law school—simply looked more intelligent, accomplished, and suited for the profession than most applicants.

Achievers' parents also had the resources to step in as information brokers, coaches, and agents for job-seeking children if necessary. In many cases, much of the hard work was done well before graduation. For example, Lydia's employment at a top four accounting firm was anticlimactic—a result of the internship her father helped her to land:

> I'm just gonna [work for] the company I interned with this summer. . . . With business for the most part I feel like their internships, the point of it is to recruit for full time jobs. 'Cause I didn't really do that much on my internship. It was, like, they're just trying to make us have fun and want to be there for full time. (Y5)

Others would need more help. Madison's dad, for example, coached her on how to interview:

> My dad gave me a lot of advice. . . . He just said make sure you have questions. Make sure you know about the company before you go in there, and make sure you don't stutter and say 'like' a whole lot, and just make eye contact. . . . It went really smoothly. (Y5)

He also suggested that Madison frame her retail experience during college as a résumé builder, a move that underachievers, who had also held similar jobs in college, did not know to make.

Parents also provided critical financial support that enabled achievers to be geographically mobile, seeking the best opportunities in large cities around the United States. Brooke's case is typical. She took a job with the federal government that required moving to a new city. As she described of her parents:

> They really set me up. Granted, it's only a studio apartment. They only had to buy so much [furniture]. But they were so generous about that and then paid my first month's rent. That was huge, obviously. I really didn't save money during school because I didn't work during school and the money I made during the summer was just enough to pay for what I was doing in the summer. Now I have enough money to do all the basics. (Y5)

Without her parents' help, it is unlikely that Brooke could have managed to take a job more than eight hours from home. Once she was situated in a safe and comfortable place to live, they were able to rein back their investments, as Brooke could support herself.

Achievers were, in fact, well positioned to move into the upper-middle class. All started their lives post-college with a major advantage: no debt. For example, as Taylor noted, "I'm really lucky that I don't have college loans. That would just keep building up" (Y5). Without this burden, the $40,000–$60,000 entry-level salaries associated with their jobs would go much further. Many of their positions also came with promise of considerable advancement, to over $100,000, within five to ten years. All achievers had benefits and could cover their own medical insurance. Their jobs were ideal career-launching sites rather than stopgap situations. As accountants, managers, dentists, and other professionals, achievers would have greater autonomy and control over their time than their underachiever peers.

By the fifth interview, it was apparent that achievers had learned how to identify ideal candidates for a peer marriage. Able to support themselves, they were willing to wait until better options were available. Most realized that "meet[ing] more promising young men" in the context of college—especially at a party school—was challenging. As Brooke explained:

> College-age girls, they just assume [that] they're looking for what we have here, but . . . the smart guys here try to pretend they're not as smart because people see it as dorky. . . . There's so much emphasis on drinking and partying and being that way that they don't come across respectful. They

come across like drunken pigs even though they're not . . . because [otherwise] they won't be cool. It's like high school. . . . I wanna go to a good grad school so I can meet a mature guy. . . . I wouldn't really want to date a guy unless he's really smart. Not a genius, but smart enough. That's really attractive to me whereas at least one of my roommates wouldn't find that as a particularly attractive quality. . . . I'm like, that's ridiculous, you're never gonna do well if you don't want someone intelligent. (Y2)

Brooke understood that it would probably be necessary to go higher up the educational ladder in order to get the quality of man she desired, who was ready to be serious about his career and a relationship. She also rejected the notion that being smart was "dorky," realizing the economic potential of pairing with an intellectual equal.

Lydia had perhaps come the closest to this ideal. Through most of college, Lydia did not date anyone because she was "super picky" and not interested in a relationship (Y4). Thus, Laura was surprised to find during the senior-year interview that Lydia had been casually dating a guy named Ethan for four months. However, Ethan was not just any guy—he was a good-looking informatics major, with lucrative career options. He also happened to belong to a fraternity that paired with Lydia's sorority for a social event. When Lydia landed her CPA job in a major city, Ethan followed suit, securing an even higher-paying business consulting job in the same city.

It was at this point—and only at this point—that Lydia allowed the relationship to get more serious. As she explained, "I wouldn't date someone unless I really saw myself marrying them. And I found someone I liked" (Y5). Moving slowly, Lydia told Ethan that she wanted to live alone for a year before moving in together. This would afford her some independence as she got her career off the ground. After saving for a year, combining their resources allowed them to live in a desirable area of the city:

> The place Ethan and I got, we're paying a good amount more [than we do now]. It's going to be $960 each because it's a lot farther south. It's more expensive when you get closer to the city. . . . I was afraid that the application wouldn't go through or something. He's like between the two of us we have a good amount of money. They're not going to deny us. I was like,   . yes, that's true. (Y5)

The next logical step would be engagement. Lydia was "not in any rush to get married." Yet ever the planner, she told Ethan, "I don't want to be that girl who five years down the road, we're still living together and I'm not engaged. . . . That's not going to happen. He's like no, no, no. He's like within a year I really want to seriously look into talking about this and seeing if this is what we want" (Y5). Lydia and Ethan married in 2011, three years after graduation.

Lydia's romantic trajectory—individual achievement, career establishment, and then serious commitment—is distinctly characteristic of economically secure professionals and likely reflects the future of the other achievers. Her cautious approach allowed her to assess whether Ethan could hold up his side of the bargain while she continued to develop her own earning potential. At the same time, Lydia was clear that she wanted the legal and public recognition of marriage, should all signs remain positive. Just as their coupling allowed Lydia and Ethan to upgrade to a nicer apartment, their marriage would consolidate their privilege and bring significant financial and status benefits.

Underachievers: Getting Back on Track

The fates of underachievers were split. Many of these women were from privileged families. Their stories highlight just how difficult it can be to ensure success on the professional pathway at a school like MU, where a whole team of cooperating individuals is necessary for success. Most of these women had academic profiles at the time of graduation that were not stellar, but neither were they irrevocably damaged.

The first group of three women managed a major redirection late in the game. Leah's case, which we briefly touched on in Chapter 4, is illustrative. Leah had struggled on all fronts because of her general discomfort with the college environment. Part of this was the result of living in a party dorm as a self-identified lesbian, with a roommate who rejected her, and in the shadow of the college party scene. Her social isolation and exposure to socially oriented peers made it hard for her to see what she could get out of college. As she told Evie, a graduate student research team member:

Leah: I'm ready to just kind of be an adult. And I'm sick of having work to do, like homework, grades, I'm just ready to move on with my life.

Evie: What about missing college social life?

Leah: I don't feel like I need to be at college to be doing like the type of socializing that I do. I'm not like, going to frat parties every night so it's not like [I'm] going to miss the opportunity to do that. (Y2)

This ambivalence about the academic and social components of college life was unusual for a student from an upper-class family, and it posed barriers to Leah's success in both arenas. We might have expected her affluent parents to intervene perhaps much earlier than this. However, Leah's father had recently passed away, and her relationship with her mother was strained, as she did not accept Leah's sexual identity. Leah managed to move to a stronger flagship in her own state but left college with a social work major and a 3.0 GPA. Her record was not strong enough to get into a competitive graduate social work program.

After college, Leah planned to move to San Francisco and join Ameri-Corps. AmeriCorps is a prestigious federal program that places individuals with nonprofit service groups. The program pays very little (for Leah, it would be $22,000—not enough to live in a city like San Francisco). Although still emotionally distant, Leah's mom kicked in the substantial financial support Leah needed to make this happen, plus more. As Leah noted:

> She helped me with the initial moving and all of the moving costs because I just didn't have that, and I think she helped me with rent. . . . Then this summer, so I got my last paycheck, living stipend, whatever, mid-June and I ended up actually going to Australia for a month and traveling, so I wasn't getting a paycheck and I was spending money, so she ended up helping me pay this summer. (Y5)

Leah's AmeriCorps experience resuscitated her record enough to place a good graduate social work program within her reach. Leah's mother was also prepared to help pay for graduate school. These critical financial infusions would pull Leah back on track not only academically but socially and romantically. For the first time in years, she formed new friendships with other college graduates and started to seriously date a highly educated woman like herself. In this case, post-college investments made it possible to align all realms of her life with an upper-middle-class trajectory.

Resolution of the family issues that derailed women during college could also recalibrate their chances for economic stability. For instance, Lisa's relationship with her parents (especially her mother) was strained by a divorce at the end of high school. Knowing her ability level and interests, her mother suggested education as a likely major. Lisa resisted, selecting the easier—and less directly transferable—human development. Over time, Lisa's relationship with her mother began to heal (as she noted, "Oh my

God, we get along so much better!" [Y5]). After college—and struggling to use her degree—Lisa was in a place to take her parents' advice. She entered graduate school to get her teaching certificate and her master of arts. Lisa refused further parental financial aid but benefited from a lack of undergraduate debt, as paying off loans could quickly eat away at a teacher's salary.[5] Her situation illustrates the ways in which class advantages could facilitate a shift in trajectory.

Underachievers: Failure to Change Course

The second group of four underachievers was not as successful in changing course. As we saw with Brianna's descent into substance abuse, inserting certain individuals in a school with a heavily resourced party pathway can set into motion a chain of negative events that even the most involved and informed parents could not reverse. For others, class resources simply could not overcome strained parent-child relations.

Upper-middle-class Morgan provides a good example. Just before college, her parents had undergone a messy divorce, dismantling what seemed to be a picture-perfect family life. Both parents quickly formed new families, leaving Morgan feeling unanchored. Her father remained distant, offering career advice without really listening. Morgan also found it hard to turn to her mother, who (despite Morgan's slender frame) was critical of her weight and her "loser" boyfriend. Instead, Morgan sought support from her roommate and longtime friend Natasha. Recall that both women arrived at MU by default and lacked ties to college peers to motivate them. Morgan and Natasha graduated with 3.0 GPAs—too low for graduate school in English/history or audiology, majors that lacked direct routes to employment.

As Leah's case suggests, records like these can be salvaged. However, the efforts of Morgan's parents to redirect her were ill-informed. For example, her dad suggested that she take three months of sales training classes with a for-profit firm run by his friend. The goal was to place recent graduates in internships, but Morgan rejected the internships because "It was just sitting in a cramped room answering phones. It was basically like telemarketing" (Y5). Perhaps beholden to her dad, the firm took her on as an "executive assistant," but this really meant "cleaning up after a bunch of forty-year-[old] men all the time" (Y5). After a series of similarly unhelpful interventions, Morgan took a $12-an-hour job as a bank teller. Natasha—living with Morgan again—was in much the same boat, working at a hotel answering phones for $10 an hour. Neither job had benefits or required a college degree.

The women did not seem bothered by the situation. Laura even noted, "I had to be careful not making it sound like I assumed [Natasha] would see this as a problem" (Interview Notes Y5). When Laura asked Morgan what jobs her friends from home had found, Morgan indicated that they were working at "restaurants and CVS [drugstore] or not working at all and living at home and not doing anything" (Y5). Given this basis of comparison, it was no wonder that their jobs seemed adequate. These friends also formed the basis of Morgan's and Natasha's dating pool, making marriage to an upper-middle-class man unlikely.

Without a change in personal motivation, Morgan and Natasha seemed slated for downward mobility. In the context of MU, features of their biography (for example, a lack of direction, fraught relationships with their parents, and discomfort with the Greek party scene) translated into serious deficits. The result was isolation from their peers, an aimless academic experience, and a limited ability to take advantage of other class resources—like time and money—that were in their favor. These young women may have struggled in any institutional context. However, they would have had greater odds of success in a place where the party scene was not so dominant, the professional pathway not so zero-sum, and greater efforts were made to made to offer all students the sorts of assistance that some parents were able to provide.

Underachievers: Barriers to Rescue

The last four underachievers came from lower-middle-class or middle-class families. During college, they had positive relations with parents who aimed to help, but limited financial, cultural, and social resources stood in the way. After college, their parents could not compensate for inadequacies in their daughters' academic records. These women struggled to get jobs requiring a college degree.

Here we return to Emma. As we saw, Emma started college with considerable promise—a dream to be a dentist and a high school record suggesting this was possible. However, Emma got sidetracked by admission to an elite sorority, where she lost her balance on the college tightrope. Her parents were unable to help her regain equilibrium. Emma's GPA of 3.0 was high for the underachievers, but too low for her biology major to translate into a job requiring a college degree.

After graduation, Emma had hoped to leave her hometown—a working-class city hard hit by the recession. She quickly ran into problems. As she described:

> I have a biology degree, so I knew when I got out it's not like a business degree where you can go straight into utilizing your degree. You kind of have to specialize in something. . . . There's not really any jobs that just require biology degrees because it's such a broad subject. But I applied to jobs in Capital City. . . . I got to the point where I was applying to just anything. (Y5)

Her parents did not have job connections in Capital City, nor were they able to assist financially by setting her up there as she hunted for work. Eager to help, they offered her free room and board at home. This had the unintended effect of further restricting her job opportunities. She noted, "It's tough because there's not really a whole lot in [my home city]. . . . If I wanted something in my degree area, I was probably going to have to leave" (Y5).

As noted in the Introduction, Emma's 3.0 GPA was not sufficient for graduate school, given competition with premed majors who did not make it into medical school. She had tried, and failed, to enter a clinical laboratory scientist program. She knew, however, that "there are ways to kind of circumvent the GPA thing, you kind of have [to have] an in" (Y5). Unlike achiever parents who themselves were in fields or sectors that their daughters were hoping to break into, Emma's parents had no ties to hospitals in state. Nor did Emma want to "get a job at the hospital like phlebotomy, doing blood and stuff like that" to try and work her way in (Y5).

With few other options, Emma took a position as a dental assistant. She described:

> You don't actually have to have any sort of degree to be a dental assistant [in this state]. . . . All you have to have is a high school diploma. My boss told me this, I am the most qualified, overqualified, dental assistant that works there. I'm actually the only dental assistant that has their bachelor's degree. (Y5)

When Laura asked whether this position was like a dental hygienist, Emma explained:

> Dental hygiene would be higher up in the dental world because you have to go to school to be a dental hygienist and you have to take a state board.

I've got more of a degree than anybody where I work minus the doctors. Hygiene school is only a two-year degree, and besides the doctors I've been in school the longest. (Y5)

She made only $11 an hour, but her job came with benefits. This, sadly, placed her a step above the other women in this group who were, respectively, unemployed, working at a pizza chain, and waitressing at the time of the last interview.

In the Introduction, we also suggested that Emma's limited career options made it harder to resist her boyfriend Joe's push to marry young. As she described, "[In the military] Joe's surrounded by relationships that are . . . based on the fact that they get more money if they're married. . . . Like that really disgusts him, but he's still surrounded by it, so he gets in this mentality like, we're old enough, we can do this too. It's fine" (Y4). She had planned to wait for several years in order to develop her career before getting engaged. As her career did not take off, the necessity of waiting disappeared. Instead she suddenly found herself dependent on Joe's relatively limited resources.

Emma's story highlights the difficulties of using the professional pathway as an avenue into the upper-middle class without having a similarly privileged family background. Emma was smart, motivated, and charming. There was nothing that suggested she was less capable than Taylor. Her struggle and the struggles of others like her reflect the ways in which the university depends on family resources and intervention to smooth the way for students—both during college and in the transition out.

CHAPTER **8**

College Pathways and Post-College Prospects

It was a little deceptive, you know, in what they said and then what they produced. It's kinda like the stuff that works on TV and then you get it home and it doesn't really quite live up to the expectations.

(Father of a striver)

The words above reflect the disappointment of a striver's father with his daughter's experience at Midwest University.[1] From his perspective, the university did not deliver on its promise. Indeed, for most students like his daughter—and some from far more privileged backgrounds—MU did not provide what is often expected of and promised by large research universities: a ticket into the upper-middle class.

Below we look at women's trajectories as they left college. We explain why some left MU on track for either class mobility or reproduction of privileged class status and others did not. Successful women were able to locate a pathway at a school (not necessarily MU) that matched their needs and the resources they had at their disposal. The three pathways required varying levels of class resources to translate a college experience into socioeconomic success.

Trajectories at College Exit

We interviewed forty-six women between five and six years after they started college.[2] At this point we assessed their class trajectory. As discussed in the Introduction, we avoid referring to "outcomes," which suggests that change in direction is foreclosed. The women were still in the thick of establishing their careers, relationships, and post-college lives. At the same time, the concept suggests that the direction of most lives flow from previous circumstances and opportunities.

We classified women from relatively less privileged backgrounds (that is, working class, lower-middle class, and middle class) into two groups: those who exited college upwardly mobile from their original class positions and those for whom mobility was at risk at the time of the last interview. Similarly, women from privileged families (that is, upper-middle class and upper class) are categorized based on whether they were poised to reproduce affluence at least into the upper-middle class or whether they were at risk of downward mobility.

Class trajectory was based on the intersection of three aspects of women's postcollege life. The first was the quality of employment after college. Here we took into account salary, benefits, growth potential, whether the job required a college degree, occupational status, geographic location, and whether it afforded women the ability to live on their own. We also considered the degree of direct parental subsidies, that is, how much debt the student was left servicing after college and how much financial or material assistance they received and expected to receive into the future. Finally, we considered the marital prospects of the young women at the time of the last interview. We based this on the likely class trajectory of serious boyfriends and men with whom they socialized.[3]

Reproduction of Privilege

Table 8.1 displays the projected class trajectories of the privileged women in the study. Around two-thirds of upper-middle- and upper-class women (seventeen out of twenty-six) left MU having seemingly secured their class futures. All but three of these women were from out-of-state. This group included the seven achievers discussed in the last chapter, the three underachievers who changed course shortly after graduating, and the seven socialites discussed in Chapter 5. All graduated from college (although two transferred to other universities), and all but two graduated within four years. None were saddled with loan repayment. Virtually all lived apart from their parents in major metropolitan areas (for example, San Francisco, Chicago, Washington DC, Los Angeles, or New York). All were employed or in graduate school, although the quality of their jobs varied. Achievers were headed toward lucrative professions. Most socialites had lower-paying jobs, yet heavy parental subsidies allowed them to maintain a comfortable existence.

All women in this group were embedded in social worlds in which they socialized with successful, single men. A few, like Lydia and Brenda,

Table 8.1. Trajectories at college exit of privileged women

Descriptor	More successful trajectory: Reproduction of privilege	Less successful trajectory: Risk of downward mobility
	Socialites, achievers, redirected underachievers: 17 (65%)	Wannabes, underachievers: 9 (35%)
Dimensions		
College performance	All graduated GPA varied: achievers around 3.5 socialites around 3.0	All but one graduated Lower GPAs Easy majors
Career prospects	Employed/graduate school: achievers in professions, socialites in glamour fields	Unemployed or in jobs not requiring degree; not competitive for grad school
Debt	No loans	About one-third had loans
Living situation	Most on own in large cities	Five living with parents; not in desirable cities
Marital prospects	Engaged/strong dating pool	Limited access to dating pool
Women	Achievers (7): Brooke: UC Brenda: UC Lydia: UC Tracy: UC Erica: UMC Taylor: UMC Madison: UMC Underachievers (3): Leah: UC Lisa: UMC Julie: UMC Socialites (7): Abby: UC Hannah: UC Maya: UC Melanie: UC Naomi: UMC Tara: UMC Bailey: UMC	Wannabes (5): Mara: UMC Nicole: UMC Sophie: UMC Sydney: UMC Alicia: UMC Underachievers (4): Linda: UMC Brianna: UMC Morgan: UMC Natasha: UMC

Note: UC = upper class; UMC = upper-middle class.

were engaged to such men. Achievers were positioned to partner with similarly successful men, thus consolidating privilege in a relatively gender-neutral fashion. Socialites socialized with wealthy men whom they stood a chance of marrying. It was likely that their future husbands would be the primary providers and they would exit the labor market when children arrived. For example, in Chapter 5 we learned that one of the men Hannah dated after college was Jack, an investment banker who had "money flowing out of every single angle of his body" (Y5). Given the weakness of their undergraduate credentials and first jobs, women were not grouped in this category unless their families were capable of directly transferring wealth to their daughters, should jobs fail to rapidly increase in salary or marriage partners not materialize. Tara, for instance, stood to inherit a substantial trust fund.[4]

It is not clear, however, that even the most successful or well-married privileged women will manage to be as affluent as their parents—most of whom were extremely wealthy. Brooke was one of the few aware of just what extreme outliers her parents were and how unlikely it was that she would reproduce her parents' circumstances. As she explained:

> I have this disadvantage. . . . My parents worked all the time when I was little but they sold their business five to six years ago. Since then, they have not worked at all, and they live in an over a million dollar house. They bought a house for a million dollars and sold it for two. They made a million dollars in three years doing nothing, so my perception is so off. . . . It's just unrealistic. (Y2)

That we studied women also adds additional uncertainty. Virtually all of the affluence in their families of origin was due to fathers' earnings in male-dominated positions such as corporate leadership and finance. Few were on track to reproduce this. Thus, we use the term "reproduction of privilege" to mean entrée into the upper-middle class—not necessarily exact replication of parental class position.

Risk of Downward Mobility

A third of upper-middle- and upper-class women (nine out of twenty-six) left MU at risk of downward mobility. This group included five wannabes and four underachievers, all from upper-middle-class families. Six of the nine women were from out of state. Only one failed to graduate from col-

lege, but many could not find good jobs with their low GPAs and easy majors. Five of these women were stuck living at home and all were unable to
move out of their hometowns to destination cities. Three were working in
positions that did not require a college degree, and two went back to school
on their own dime in order to construct a viable career plan. Others had
jobs that paid as much as most socialites earned, but they felt the low salary acutely without the cushion of parental support. Marriage to a wealthy
man was not an option for most: They were geographically blocked from
the best marital markets, and the men they knew were in equal—or
worse—economic positions.

Mobility at Risk

Table 8.2 displays the projected class trajectories of the less privileged
women in the study. In striking contrast to those reproducing affluence, a
majority of less privileged women (fifteen out of twenty, or 75%) left MU
with their mobility projects at risk. This group included strivers, wannabes,
and underachievers. All but one of were from in state. Given the range
of class backgrounds—from working class through middle class—what was
necessary for economic mobility varied, but none of these women were
poised to move upward. In fact, those who started relatively higher in the
class structure were at a potential risk of falling.

Among the twelve middle-class and lower-middle-class women in this
group, only one—Whitney—had found a job with benefits that required a
college degree.[5] The others had jobs delivering pizzas, waitressing, teaching preschool, cold calling for a sales company, and working as a dental
assistant. Two were in school: one still finishing her BA, having lost years
to an easy major, and another had gambled on a risky (and expensive) advertising portfolio program that would not provide an established credential. Virtually all were servicing substantial debt. Seven had moved back
home out of necessity. Most were lonely or unhappy being thrust back into
lower-achieving high school networks. Several of these women actively
sought men who could help support them. A handful of women were in
relationships but mostly with men whose economic prospects were no better
than their own. Others struggled to find ideal candidates who were willing
to commit.

Consistent with research on the social class gap in college completion,
the mobility of the three working-class women in this group was limited

Table 8.2. Trajectories at college exit of less privileged women

Descriptor	More successful trajectory: Upwardly mobile	Less successful trajectory: Mobility at risk
	Strivers: 5 (25%)	Strivers, wannabes, underachievers: 15 (75%)
Dimensions		
College performance	One BA in 4 years from MU; other BAs at regional campus within 6 years; GPAs: 3.0–3.8	Eleven BAs at MU (3 took 5–6 years), one late regional transfer, two associate's degrees, one still at MU; GPAs low (except Whitney)
Career prospects	Practical majors and/or realistic career plans but still in school	Mix of majors; majority had jobs not requiring a degree; some returned to school
Debt	Substantial loans	Substantial loans
Living situation	About half living with parents	About half living with parents
Marital prospects	Struggle to locate desirable mate	With men like themselves or struggling to find ideal candidate
Women	Striver who stayed at MU (1): Valerie: LMC Strivers who left MU (4): Andrea: LMC Stacey: LMC Megan: WC Alyssa: WC	Strivers who left MU (2): Heather: WC Monica: WC Strivers who stayed at MU (5): Alana: LMC Michelle: LMC Carrie: LMC Crystal: LMC Amanda: WC Underachievers (4): Mary: MC Emma: MC Becky: LMC Olivia: LMC Wannabes (4): Chelsea: MC Whitney: MC Blair: MC Karen: MC

Note: MC = middle class; LMC = lower-middle class; WC = working class.

by not completing their bachelor's degrees.[6] Only Amanda had stayed at MU; however, given her struggle to maintain a passing GPA, it was unclear whether or when she would graduate. Monica and Heather, who left MU for associate's programs, were doing better. Neither would likely leave the working class given their income, geographic location, and cultural identification; however, they did not carry nearly as much loan debt as Amanda and were heading into medical professions in which there were jobs to be had. Monica also had the financial support of a spouse with a factory job.

Upward Mobility (in Leaving MU)

The great irony is that among the quarter of less privileged women on track for upward mobility (five out of twenty), four left MU for regional branch campuses. Here they found lower costs (for one, four years at her new school cost less than one year at MU), a less alienating and distracting campus culture, and more strivers like themselves. A transfer and the need to work for pay lengthened the process, but they managed to improve their academic records and select practical majors that translated directly into jobs. Alyssa— who graduated from an accounting program—was one of the few women on the floor to break into a field that, particularly at the senior levels, is still male dominated. Megan moved into a graduate program for school counseling. Two other women went into the health professions, one as a nurse. All were from in state.

These women had hoped to marry early to financially stable men, but their options were limited. Given the mismatch between the men they knew—typically less educated men with traditional gender beliefs—and their own credentials and ambitions, it looked like upward mobility might mean forgoing serious commitments.[7] Women's own income and occupational status were enough to move them up the class ladder, especially without carrying the weight of an economically and emotionally draining relationship.

One striver—Valerie—managed to achieve mobility via her college experience at MU. As we described in Chapter 6, she was the only woman to benefit from a small and exclusive creaming program. With faculty encouragement, Valerie ramped up her academic ambitions and applied for a PhD program in classical studies. When she was unable to qualify for a top program—even with a stellar record—it seemed that her mobility was threatened. However, the aspirations and credentials that the creaming program built resulted in a solid plan to apply for law school. Valerie had also developed an orientation to later marriage that would facilitate her career.

Pathways and Inequality

MU was far from a class equalizer in the lives of the women we studied. With the exception of one case of upward mobility and a significant minority of potentially downwardly mobile affluent students, women who stayed at MU were on track to land roughly in the same class location from which they started. Most upward mobility occurred among less privileged women who transferred from MU to regional campuses: These women were upwardly mobile despite their experience at MU, rather than because of it. The difference in circumstances among the women was smaller at the close of the study but mostly because of the downward mobility of some affluent students. Two-thirds of the women from out-of-state graduated with more successful trajectories as compared to one-third of the women from in state.

What distinguished women poised to reproduce affluence or become upwardly mobile from the less successful was a good fit between their resources and their pathway through the university, sometimes not MU. Those at risk of downward and failed mobility could not find a way through the university that fit their needs or means.

Pathways have expectations about the characteristics of the people they serve built into them. They vary in the class resources necessary to have a positive experience during college and to translate that experience into a way of life beyond college. Class resources mattered in the transition out of college because what kind of job a degree garnered cannot be predicted by the quality of the credential alone.[8] It mattered for some credentials more than others, who attempted to redeem them: women with family ties in media firms had better luck finding jobs in those fields. Both during college and in the transition out, an inequitable pathway is one in which few individuals have the resources to ensure success. In contrast, the most equitable pathway includes the resources necessary to level the playing field for all who seek to pursue it.

The organization of the university shaped whether students found a pathway that worked for them. As we have discussed, the party pathway was the most developed at MU and the mobility pathway the least—with the high stakes professional pathway falling in the middle. The structure of the university is thus at the heart of stratification processes.

Fit with the Party Pathway: Socialite Success

The party pathway, the most visible and highly resourced pathway available at MU, required the highest level of class resources to pursue without negative consequence. This pathway worked well for the seven socialites who exited college situated to reproduce their parents' upper- or upper-middle-class status. These women came out on top of hierarchically organized peer cultures as they had the time, money, and know-how to perfect gender- and class-specific interactional skills, appearances, and cultural tastes. They used these positions to extend their social networks with similarly affluent people. Easy majors offered time to socialize and to refine feminine, upper-middle-class selves. When asked what she learned in college, stylish Naomi insisted that she became a more sophisticated dresser. Hannah pointed to her ability to acquire "a whole entire network of friends" (Y5).

This pathway does not produce impressive academic credentials. Yet deficits in their academic records mattered little, as women set their sights on industries in which networks, charm, and fashion sense were more relevant than GPA. They found employment through their own connections or those of their parents. Their parents set them up in apartments in hip, happening neighborhoods in desirable cities. This level of parental support would likely be forthcoming at least until they married.

Misfit with Party Pathway: Wannabe Downward Mobility

The party pathway was a poor fit for anyone not advantaged in every possible way. Nonetheless, the party pathway, as a main artery through the university, attracted a number of students who would have been best suited for, and may have otherwise selected, another pathway. Being pulled onto the party pathway contributed to the downward mobility or failed mobility of all wannabes and some underachievers and strivers.

The nine women we classified as wannabes pursued the party pathway full-time and suffered the most from their involvement. From middle- and upper-middle-class families, they were able to pull together the financial, social, and cultural resources to participate while in college. A career in the glamour industries seemed within reach—at least at first. Thus, they graduated with the same low GPAs and easy majors as socialites. But their experiences both in college and in the transition out differed in key ways. While in college they typically did not land at the top of the social pecking order and they did not start with—or develop—the same expansive networks or refined feminine presentation of the socialites.

The most serious problem, though, was that wannabes' parents lacked the resources to help them translate this portfolio (for example, good looks, social skill, and fashion sense) into a life beyond college. Their parents did not know people in glamour industries to call to get them jobs, nor were they able to set them up in apartments in major urban areas. A number offered support by allowing their daughters to move back home, but this isolated them from the best labor and marital markets. Wannabes did not understand that graduating with a low GPA in an easy major was a luxury that only the extremely affluent could afford.

Fit and Misfit with the Professional Pathway

Success on the professional pathway required high levels of class resources as well. The timing and form of parental investments differed from what was required for success on the party pathway: They were concentrated earlier in the life course and were directed more toward skill and résumé building and less toward consumption. The achievers—seven women from privileged backgrounds who had strong relationships with highly involved parents—were well served by it. They exited college positioned to reproduce their parents' privilege. In contrast, eight women who did not have such relationships—the underachievers—exited at risk of downward mobility or with mobility projects at risk.

Relative to the other women, achievers arrived with higher high school GPAs and a much better understanding of how the university worked. The way they talked about their relationships with their parents alluded to a high degree of involvement prior to college. Strong preparation and parental support enabled them to track into stronger undergraduate programs. These women did not have to work for pay in college, as their parents funded them at high levels, allowing them to study and engage in résumé-building extracurricular activities. Their parents provided academic, social, and romantic advice throughout college. Achievers graduated with high-quality credentials that required little further parental involvement to translate into good entry-level jobs or graduate school admission. Yet even at this point, parents provided assistance with the job hunt or graduate school admission process—reading applications, providing funds to sponsor moves, paying for cell phones and cars, and drawing on their own network ties for job leads.

Underachievers did not have such relationships with parents—either because their parents lacked knowledge of the university or because the quality of the parent-child relationship was such that parental advising was ineffective. These women had less information about what was required for graduate school admission. They made errors such as taking difficult courses as freshmen or getting too involved in the party scene. As a result, they graduated with lower-quality credentials that were more difficult to translate into good jobs or graduate school admissions. Their parents were also ineffective in helping them compensate for their weak records.

The outsourcing of guidance to families leaves those without college-educated parents at a disadvantage. However, the professional pathway tends not to consider how or why students land at the top of pile, but simply rewards those who do.[9] Class disparities become invisible, embedded—at every stage of achievement—in the credentials themselves.

The Absent Mobility Pathway: Leaving MU to Get Ahead

Life at MU was not easy for strivers. They started college right at the heart of MU's vibrant party pathway, yet they lacked the resources to participate. The professional pathway was not an option either: Only a fraction of this group had the necessary high school academic records. Even those with the best records had to work for pay and lacked highly educated parents. Strivers needed organizational arrangements to compensate for a lack of financial support and parental guidance. They were looking for skills and training directly transferable into jobs. MU maintained a few small creaming programs to provide exceptional disadvantaged and minority students with financial, academic, and social assistance. These programs were not, however, generally available to all in need of them. Only one woman was recruited into a program of this type. The others were less academically exceptional, just over the financial cutoff, or unaware of the programs. They did not find a mobility pathway at MU.

In part as a result of organizational arrangements, working- and lower-middle-class students encountered serious roadblocks. They struggled financially, sometimes lacking funds even to eat or pay their bills. They received little assistance dealing with diversity on campus or making sense of the vast class disparities they encountered. They lacked time to study, particularly given incompatible work and school schedules. Some found the Greek system and related hookup scene seductive. These women attempted to participate briefly but exited quickly when they experienced sexual assault, alcohol violations, social exclusion, or shock at the level of sorority fees. Others simply found the party scene alienating.

One response to MU's failure to address their needs was to leave the university. Six of the twelve strivers whom we tracked over the duration of the study left MU before graduation. Four of the six leavers transferred to a regional campus and got on track for upward mobility. Of the six who stayed at MU, five ended up with their mobility projects at risk. Valerie, the striver who was creamed, was the only stayer to leave college on an upwardly mobile trajectory. In general, those who transferred to regional schools fared better than those with stayed at MU.

The finding that regional schools facilitated mobility more than the state flagship is at odds with existing research. In *Crossing the Finish Line: Completing College at America's Public Universities,* William G. Bowen and colleagues use longitudinal survey data to conclude that students are best served when they attend the most prestigious school that they can.[10] Our findings suggest a qualification: If the more prestigious school available is a party school, students from less privileged backgrounds may be better off going to a less prestigious school, as long as it has a strong mobility pathway.

Specific features of our case helped us to arrive at this determination. The flagship university in the state we studied was only moderately selective and had a reputation as a party school, while regional schools were not known to be party schools. Young women's accounts regarding the seriousness of the regional schools—particularly from those who simply could not a resist a party—confirm this. We would not expect our findings to apply to state systems where the flagship is highly selective and academic, or where regional schools are known to be party schools.

Our study suggests that institutional prestige is not the only factor to consider when predicting student success. How developed the mobility pathway is on a particular campus matters a great deal. Moving toward a stronger mobility pathway could involve going up or down the prestige ladder. For Valerie, attending a more selective school likely would have increased her chances of mobility. Indeed, Valerie's dream school (for which she was well qualified) was Northwestern. As she explained:

> There were some other schools that I would really like to go to, like Northwestern. But that's really expensive. Two of my really good friends go to Northwestern, but their parents are doctors. It's like 35,000 or something a year, and they're just like, "Oh I'm failing chemistry tests left and right." I'm just like how can you do that? Like your parents should adopt me because I would appreciate it. (Y1)

Although she managed to, by a narrow margin, get on track for upward mobility, we think her journey would have been less rocky had finances allowed her to aim higher.[11] For most of the less privileged students we studied, however, going to Northwestern was simply not an option. In their situation, going down in prestige made sense if it meant finding an organization better equipped to meet their needs.

The Party Pathway and Gender

Embedded in each pathway is a model of family formation composed of notions about the ideal age of marriage, sequence of life events, and gender relations. Given the centrality of the party pathway, we focus on the way in which gender is built into this pathway—and its consequences. The party pathway supports a traditional model of gender relations that is not sustainable for anyone but women from the wealthiest of families.

The party pathway (described in Chapters 2 and 3) focuses women's attentions on refining the traditionally feminine tastes, personality styles, appearances, and interactional skills heavily valued in the party scene. For example, the university offers a variety of majors in which being good at being a "girl" (for example, bubbly, engaging, and attractive) is reinforced, as well as majors in fields heavily occupied by women (for example, education and healthcare). At the same time, this same style of femininity is highly valued in peer cultures. It is arguably the central criterion to receive a bid from a high-status sorority.

These structural supports make it possible for women who arrive at college with gendered interests to devote time to further cultivating traditionally feminine tastes and skills.[12] Furthermore, the party pathway may actually encourage those without such interests to develop them. For instance, Hannah refused to wear designer duds—much less makeup—at the start of college. By year three she noted:

> I feel like everything more is about name brands here. . . . I'm much more conscious of that. I feel like every—not like anything is a competition— but I mean I feel like it's more. . . . Now I like to wear like makeup. I don't really like to go out without like mascara on. I feel like I'm albino, like my lashes. (Y3)

These transformations go deep, practiced as they are in virtually all aspects of the college experience—from the social to the academic—to the point that they feel natural.

Heavy investments in femininity can come at the cost of academic knowledge, job skills, and career credentials.[13] In the model of family formation with which the party pathway meshes, this is not a problem. A privileged, feminine self is cultivated with the intent of ultimately marrying a high-earning man and eventually moving out of the labor market to be a wife and a mother. This model is different from the past, in which engagement before college graduation was the way to earn the MRS degree. Today's elite marital markets do not swing into action until after college graduation, and men and women both circulate in these social worlds throughout their twenties, having fun before settling down.

This approach may be risky. Success requires being in close social contact with men likely to be economically successful up to and through the time they are ready to marry. Such men often spend their twenties and even thirties in MBA programs or in law or medical school, where they meet women with whom they may have more in common. Indeed, the surplus of "perfect women" may lead men to prefer to marry a woman with similar earning potential.

The continued viability of a gender-complementary approach is called into question by a 2007 Craigslist exchange forwarded so extensively that it has reached the status of urban legend.[14] No one knows whether either side was sincere or whether the entire exchange was faked. Its authenticity is irrelevant. What matters is that it hit a nerve. A woman supposedly drafted an ad in which she referred to herself as twenty-five, "spectacularly beautiful," "articulate," and "classy." She indicated that she was "looking to get married to a guy who makes at least half a million a year." The response, reportedly from a man in the desired income bracket, replied that her offer

> is plain and simple a crappy business deal. Here's why. Cutting through all the B.S., what you suggest is a simple trade: you bring your looks to the party and I bring my money. Fine, simple. But here's the rub, your looks will fade and my money will likely continue into perpetuity . . . in fact, it is very likely that my income increases but it is an absolute certainty that you won't be getting any more beautiful! So, in economic terms you are a depreciating asset and I am an earning asset.

Tellingly, he also suggests, "You could always find a way to make your own money and then we wouldn't need to have this difficult conversation."

Research suggests that men's preferences may indeed be changing. Women with a lot of earning power now have better chances of marrying and of marrying men with considerable occupational prestige and earning potential.[15] The earnings of husbands and wives have converged, and since the 1980s, high-earning men are increasingly coupled with similarly high-earning women.[16] The patterns suggest that women's economic contributions are now not only valued but expected by men.[17]

Still, the gender-complementary approach might work for socially oriented women from wealthy families. If it does not work, they have other avenues open to them. The gendered attributes that they have to offer in the marriage market (looks, cultural savvy, networks, social skills) also have value in the labor market. They may build successful careers in media or fashion, where traditional femininity is important to success. Naomi, for instance, admitted in the last interview that she was now more focused on "my career and seeing where that path leads first" than on meeting a guy (Y5). Regardless, these women always have family wealth as a safety net.

For everyone else, however, this approach is problematic. Without parental support, they cannot live in the cities where the men they want to marry live and socialize. Back home, as Nicole put it, "None of the boys have steady jobs. . . . One just got a job at a delicatessen at a ShopRite kind of place, a supermarket" (Y5). These same financial limitations make infinite parental support improbable. In addition, as we learned with Whitney's failed interview at a Northern California vineyard, less privileged women lack the same polished femininity of the upper classes that might assist them in acquiring some jobs.

By supporting the development of traditionally gendered selves, the university nudges women toward an approach to family formation that serves most poorly. Most women need credentials and skills for personal economic security and marital success.[18]

Individual Characteristics in Organizational Context

Could class background and other individual characteristics (in particular, motivation, ability, and initial orientation to college) account for our findings? How do we know that what happened in college—the sorting of students onto pathways—had an effect on social and economic location after college? Individual characteristics matter. Some students are more likely to succeed no matter what college they attend and regardless of the organizational environment. However, individual characteristics are not deterministic. For most, the probability of success depends on organizational context. A closer look at three groups of students illustrates this point.

Upward Mobility: Smarts, Drive, and Organizational Characteristics

Stratification scholars speculate that the few individuals from disadvantaged backgrounds who make it through college are, on average, more motivated and intelligent than those for whom college attendance is an assumption.[19] Although such characteristics are difficult to measure, our observations suggest that this was indeed the case in our study.

Four of the five women who experienced upward mobility shared a constellation of characteristics. Relative to the others, they were strikingly intelligent, as evidenced by either higher levels of verbal facility or the ability to earn better grades under more adverse situations. These women were grounded. They never lost sight of the basic realities of their lives. Financial constraint was, for these women, the core theme of their interviews with us. They were resilient in the face of obstacles: Megan, for instance, went to school, worked several jobs, had responsibility for a horse, and took care of her father's house (and kids) while carrying a full academic load. All the while these women remained optimistic about improving their circumstances.

Yet these characteristics alone did not predict upward mobility. In fact, a few women much like Megan ended up with mobility projects at risk. Conversely, one who was less academically inclined and not as driven appeared on track for at least the middle class. What united the five strivers who left college on clear upward trajectories was their success in locating a mobility pathway while in college. This group includes Valerie, who was swept into MU's creaming program, and four others who had to leave MU for regional universities in order to find the mobility pathways they needed.

It is possible that the leavers shared some hard-to-observe characteristic—like an ability to read the organizational environment and the oomph to drive a change that generated their success. Even if this is true, a shift in circumstances might have kept them at MU, as it did Amanda (who had family members in need of help living in Fairview). The fate of similar women suggests they would have fared much worse had they stayed at MU. That their success was made more likely by leaving MU suggests the importance of the institutional context.

Downward Mobility: Personal Failings in Organizational Context

Each of the downwardly mobile women suffered from at least one "fatal flaw." A couple were just not very smart: While an initial round of bad grades can be attributed to poor strategy, the inability to earn solid grades in college when putting forth a great deal of effort suggests cognitive limitations. Some lacked the drive, energy, motivation, and resilience of the upwardly mobile women and seemed to passively accept whatever came their way. A few lacked focus. Other issues were more idiosyncratic: Linda's social skills were low. Brianna, whose downward spiral was most dramatic, had problems with drugs and alcohol.

There were also women who were situated to reproduce affluence that had one (or a few) of these issues. Yet most of these women also had parents who could help them to mitigate these challenges. For example, less intellectually gifted students received advice about taking hard classes over the summer at community colleges or transferring to easier majors. Those who were not motivated had parents who pushed them. Women who were not focused had help finding a passion. Downwardly mobile women were more likely to lack the type of trusting and communicative parent-child relationships necessary for this sort of mediation.[20]

We do not believe, however, that any of these individual or family traits in and of themselves explained the women's trajectories. Their issues arose in the interaction of such traits with MU's organizational context: For example, Morgan and Natasha did not succeed at MU. They would have had a better chance had they attended a school where the party scene was less dominant and the professional pathway more forgiving. Similarly, Brianna may have struggled with addiction anywhere, but this was much more likely to happen at a school with a hard-to-avoid party scene.

The Malleability of Young Adults

Young adults, particularly those who have been shielded from adult responsibilities, are in the thick of what Ann Swidler describes as an "unsettled" period in their life.[21] During this time, they are trying on different selves. Indeed, college students often switch majors, pursue seemingly contradictory goals, and reenvision their futures. They are thus particularly likely to be influenced by the organizational environments in which they find themselves.

Nearly half of our floor arrived at MU without a clear focus on either the party scene or academics. Whitney is a good example here, as she was initially adamant about both partying and entering the competitive business school. Given that she was undeniably sharp and had an impeccable academic record—as well as looks and social savvy—Whitney could have easily gone either way. However, at MU, where the party pathway was the easiest and most visible avenue, she opted for a more social approach.

It is wrong to assume that even those with the most seemingly established orientations to college—women who arrive primed to party or are cultivated for success—will not, under any circumstances, switch course. Even motivations and ability (if measured by achievement) can shift, as students respond differently when they locate a passion. A student who was academically disinterested can become engaged if she takes the right class or has the right professor.[22]

For instance, near the end of college, Laura was surprised when Mara—a woman who was initially so socially oriented and status conscious that she barely acknowledged Laura's existence—started to spontaneously analyze her sorority experiences by drawing on an academic paper assigned as class reading.[23] As it turns out, Mara had taken a sociology class, loved it, and decided to take upper-level sociology classes even though these were not required. As she noted:

They kind of just count as extra classes, and people probably think I'm crazy because they're really hard. . . . Like, you're crazy. You're taking a

300-level. I mean, there's some probably really easy ones, but those two are not. . . . I think that they are really great professors. I would definitely recommend them to anyone. (Y4)

We cannot help but wonder how different Mara's college experience might have looked had she been exposed to classes that she found interesting and challenging much sooner in her college career. The party pathway made it possible, even easy, for her to avoid them almost entirely.

The Equalization Argument

On the face of it, these findings contradict the quantitative findings of stratification scholars such as Michael Hout and, more recently, Florencia Torche.[24] These researchers found that college graduation significantly weakens or erases the relationship between social class origins and social class destinations.[25] Admittedly, the women we studied were too young (just turning twenty-four at the conclusion of the study) to assess ultimate class outcomes. Over time we might see class trajectories converge, particularly if those from less privileged backgrounds simply take longer to see the benefits of their MU education. Their paths through college were bumpier and less linear than those of privileged women.

Yet, for example, we found it difficult to imagine how the class fate of Megan (who was pursuing school counseling) would converge with that of Lydia (in an entry-level job as an accountant). We offer three general explanations for why our findings differ. Extending the arguments above, we suggest that features of the type of school in which we were embedded mattered: Particular aspects of the organization of student life at MU (and similar schools) reinforce and even exacerbate inequality. We also point to the historical context of our study: That is, the college degree may equalize less now because of changes in the economy, class structure, and the labor market. Finally, we argue that a more nuanced measurement of social class might find less equalization.

University Organization and the Amelioration of Class Difference

As discussed in the Introduction, large public universities try to serve multiple populations—hence the need for multiple pathways. With a large undergraduate population and only moderately selective admissions, there is substantial heterogeneity among students at the point of admission. There is likely overlap between academic preparation and class background, meaning that, on average, more affluent students admitted to MU likely have stronger academic profiles than less affluent students. The gap in need of closing is large.

In contrast, a selective admissions process may reduce heterogeneity in academic preparation and potential. While few individuals from less advantaged backgrounds are admitted to more elite schools, they have been screened for traits that suggest the potential to perform at a high level. Individuals from less advantaged backgrounds who have demonstrated the ability to overcome adversity and to take advantage of opportunities tend to be recruited. In short, elite schools may appear to be doing the work of closing a gap, while instead they have already selected the most exceptionally talented individuals from that group.

Small private schools with explicit commitments to integrating students into a shared student culture may also do a better job than large public schools at closing preexisting class gaps.[26] These schools can require students to live on campus. They can engage in more social engineering, integrating students by class and race. They have more resources for student affairs programming. They can select students who endorse the mission of the school and who signal openness to associating with those different from themselves. Students at these schools are more likely to believe that other students at the school are appropriate friends, particularly if the admission process is highly selective.[27] These schools may also be more aware of their heritage as elite institutions and may be more intentional about enacting organizational initiatives to integrate students from disadvantaged backgrounds.[28]

The size and diversity of student bodies at MU and similar schools make integrating students into a shared community a challenge. We did not observe an effort on the part of MU to do so. The constellation of pathways provided reflects an undergraduate student culture bifurcated between affluent students participating in Greek life and everyone else. Although not quite 20% of students participated in Greek life, this 20% included a sizeable share of the most affluent students on campus.

At MU, social worlds were largely segregated by social class. After the first year in the residence hall, the less affluent students we observed had little social contact with more affluent students. (And as we saw in Chapter 4, the cross-class interaction that occurred that first year was not successful.)

Lack of cross-class interaction extended to the romantic sphere: Few less privileged women reported dating a man from a more privileged background. No woman in the study not in a sorority reported dating a fraternity man. Thus, the overall social organization of undergraduate life at MU mapped onto preexisting differences among the students and reproduced them.

We suspect that both ends of the four-year university spectrum—more elite institutions and broad-access schools—may do a better job leveling class differences than large, flagship public schools like MU. Given the different populations of students that form the bread and butter of these institutions, the party pathway is less likely to be as central. At elite schools, for instance, the professional pathway is often richly resourced and accessible, and—as many of our less privileged transfer students found—broad-access schools tend have mobility pathways that are in better repair.

The Equalization Argument Today

Finding that higher education serves to equalize at one point in time does not mean that it does so at another. Recognizing this, Florence Torche's used data collected on more recent cohorts to test Michael Hout's findings.[29] Although more recent than Hout's data, the data that Torche used were, by and large, collected from individuals born between 1951 and 1975—and thus graduating from college between roughly 1973 and 1997. Although she confirms Hout's finding that class background does not predict future earnings for those with just a bachelor's degree, she finds that class background does predict future earnings among those with advanced degrees. Moreover, she also finds that "the strong intergenerational association among advanced-degree holders is a recent phenomenon, which sharply departs from the substantial mobility opportunities of those who attained an advanced degree a quarter century ago."[30]

Until data are available to replicate her analyses for cohorts born in the 1980s and beyond, it is impossible to know whether the prior patterns still hold. There are reasons to suspect that they may not. As the higher education system continues to expand, there is increasing differentiation in the quality of bachelor's degrees awarded.[31] We have seen a dramatic increase in social inequality in society more generally. Elites have responded to an increasingly competitive and polarized society by increasing financial and time investments in their children, especially in college-age youth.[32]

Consequently, the academic achievement gap between children from low- and high-income families has risen considerably in twenty-five years.[33] The role of parental involvement in helping college graduates get a job or get into graduate school may have also escalated in a tight labor market— particularly during the Great Recession. Thus, it is an open question whether higher education still works as an equalizer.

Measuring Equalization

The way in which we measure class trajectory may also lead us to see more reproduction of inequality. Were we to use only income and occupational status instead of including parental support, differences in class trajectories would appear smaller. But given increasing dependence on such parental support well into adulthood, we found it critical to take this into account. A woman with a $30,000 per year job that includes no benefits, $20,000 in loans to service, and no parental support is in a much worse position than another with the same income who has no loans and parents paying for rent, car, cell phone, and health insurance. Someone with less parental support may also be less likely to make a risky but high-return career move or attempt to relocate to a location with better job prospects.

Also, we studied women, whose mobility is less understood than that of men. Women have more varied routes to mobility, with marriage remaining more central to class destination. Stratification research also typically assesses class origin by using only father's class standing, not accounting for maternal resources. Both of these features may obscure intergenerational patterns.[34] In fact, Torche's analyses across different data sets produced slightly different results, with analysis of the Panel Study of Income Dynamics suggesting that among women with a college degree a significant link between class origins and destinations remains.[35]

Moving beyond Class Trajectory

In this chapter we have examined the returns of college primarily through its effects on future class location. However, this is not how all women evaluated the worth of their college experience. It presumes that everyone strives for an upper-middle-class existence and values economic success, occupational status, and marital prospects above all else.

One woman in particular made us acutely aware that not everyone desires to move up the class structure. Monica grew up in a small, rural in-state town and was from a tight-knit working-class family. As we discussed in Chapter 6, she dove into college life upon arrival, attempting to fit in with her more privileged peers. However, she soon "realized that that's not the person that I wanted to be. I was just afraid that if I stayed, I would get, like, so far into it that I would . . ." (Y5). Here she trailed off, but the implication was clear: for Monica, staying would mean transforming her identity and leaving her family, small-town, and working-class roots behind.[36]

Others would make this trade. All of the upwardly mobile less privileged women did. Monica, however, hoped to use college to improve her economic circumstances without having to reshape her values or social ties. This was not easy at MU. Monica wanted to marry early and build a life together with a partner. Her desire to marry and have children young was viewed as so puzzling by her privileged peers that it contributed to the severing of friendships. As one former friend complained:

> She would always talk about how she couldn't wait to get married and have babies. She's so ready and it was just like, whoa. I'm eighteen. . . . Slow down, you know? Then she just crazy dropped out of school and wouldn't contact any of us. . . . The way I see it is that she's from a really small town and that's what everyone in her town does . . . is get married and have babies. That's all she ever wanted to do maybe? (Sydney Y4)

Monica ultimately got some of the economic security she desired—without the other class trappings—but she had to leave MU to do so. As noted earlier, we think it likely she will stay in the working class. Yet marriage allowed her to pool resources enough to buy a small house, and her husband encouraged her to leave her job at a salon to get an associate's degree in nursing.[37] Assuming all goes according to plan, she will have a financially stable future.

Despite her frustrations with the experience, Monica was glad she attended MU, if only for a short time. Her assessment highlights the fact that there are other ways to determine the value of a college experience:

> I definitely don't regret going to MU for a year. I think it was a big growing experience for me, getting away from home and being on my own for a while. . . . I have a really big family and we don't do anything without the

entire family and so it was kind of nice for me to be away and just kind of find out who I was by myself. . . . Around here I'm still known as Adam's daughter. Or, oh, you're Milton's granddaughter or so-and-so's niece. It was kind of nice to just be, oh, you're Monica, you know? And [to] just know that I am my own person and, yes, I love my family, but, you know, I can survive. (Y5)

She highlights important benefits: self-efficacy, independence, self-awareness, and self-esteem. Monica even attributed her interest in nursing to academic experiences had at MU, explaining:

Had I not [attended MU], I probably wouldn't have ever gone back to do nursing, you know? Cause I had spent that first year there when I really loved it, and so I think had I not ever experienced some of the med classes I took, I really wouldn't have ever thought about going back. (Y5)[38]

Monica was far from alone in having many positive feelings about what seemed—at least with regard to mobility—to be a failed project. Most of the less privileged women viewed their time at MU positively. For instance, Alyssa, who transferred to a regional campus after one year on the Fairview campus, told us:

I loved Fairview. I'm so thankful that I at least got the one year at Fairview and got away, just to see things differently than what I'm used to. (Y4)

Alyssa even found her inability to relate to the wealthy women on the floor to be a learning experience:

Just coming from where I come from and not really being able to relate to some of the girls that were there really made it hard, but it was learning and it was different. I wouldn't take it back for anything. I loved the MU experience, and school, and the campus, and just seeing the different things that I know went on, and it [was], like, a true university and stuff. That was just awesome. (Y4)

Alyssa's comments suggest that she acquired a better understanding of the American class structure and her place in it. For a woman whose father was a mechanic, it was eye-opening to live with Hannah, whose father was a CFO of a major corporation. Alyssa's reference to the pleasure of attending a "true university" also hints at a widely shared cultural reverence for state flagships. For Alyssa it was "awesome" to be a part of this world for a year—even though the debt accumulated from that year will follow her into the future.

Monica's and Alyssa's stories suggest the importance of not reducing the benefits of college to economics. Yet their accounts must be interpreted cautiously. As they could not undo the decision to attend MU, they may have simply been putting a positive spin on it. The fact that they and most other strivers identified positive aspects of what was a painful, difficult, and costly experience speaks volumes about their resilience and drive.

CHAPTER 9

Politics and Pathways

I needed to get away from Fairview, just get away from going out all the time, get away from all of those other negative things that were coming at me, and come to the regional campus so I could refocus on what my goal was for this part of my life.

(Karen Y5)

Karen, a middle-class wannabe profiled in Chapter 5, got on track academically only after she left Midwest University and transferred to a regional campus back home. She was not alone. In previous chapters we learned that four of the five women from working- and lower-middle-class backgrounds who were headed toward upward mobility also transferred to regional campuses. Their experiences suggest that many students would be better served by Midwest University if the party pathway was less prominent and other pathways more developed.

In this chapter we outline ways to challenge the party pathway, revitalize the mobility pathway, and broaden access to the professional pathway at MU and similar schools. These changes threaten powerful constituencies and are thus politically difficult to implement. Yet it is not just the fate of individuals at stake here. The vitality of the four-year residential college experience at public universities may depend on these schools doing a better job of meeting the educational needs of less advantaged students.

Challenging the Dominance of the Party Pathway

Serving students like Karen first means making sure that those like her continue to be represented at Midwest University and similar schools. This means resisting—and even reversing—the move toward recruiting more affluent out-of-state and international students and refocusing on serving in-state residents, including those of modest means. For this to occur, tuition and fees must be affordable and financial aid accessible and generous, ideally in the form of grants rather than loans. A less privileged and more

234

diverse study body (along lines of class, race, and age) should, without any other intervention, reduce demand for the party pathway. However, additional steps are necessary to change existing infrastructure, which, in turn, would help in the recruitment of a more diverse student body.

Dismantling the Party Pathway

Eliminating the Greek system would be an obvious step toward dismantling a party pathway. Some small liberal arts colleges have already done so.[1] For example, Colby College, located in Maine, abolished fraternities and sororities in 1984. According to the senior associate dean of students Paul Johnston in 2011, "Rushing, pledging, perpetuating and initiating activities by fraternities and social organizations are strictly prohibited." Colby's policy, per Johnston, is based on the view that "exclusive, single-gender organizations are divisive and out of step [with] Colby's mission and values."[2] To our knowledge, no large public university has taken this step. Short of elimination, close oversight of fraternities and sororities could keep social excesses in check. Education might help these organizations revamp recruiting processes to be less exclusive along lines of race, class, and sexual orientation.

Another option would be to level the playing field among existing Greek houses. As described in Chapter 2, historically white organizations participating in the North-American Interfraternity Conference and National Panhellenic Conference tend to have the greatest resources—and thus the greatest power—on college campuses. Black organizations—along with other racial- and ethnic-based and multicultural Greek organizations—are far less likely to have houses on campus, funds to host events, and special ties to university administrators.[3] "Cultural interest" Greek organizations, as some have referred to them, are often marginalized, in part because of these resource disparities. If all Greek organizations on campus—or, ideally, none of them—had access to special organizational membership benefits, the status hierarchy that privileges affluent, white, heterosexual, and traditional-age students might shift.

These same students, particularly when housed together in large residence halls with minimal programming and adult supervision, contribute to a party culture. In contrast, the party culture is attenuated by housing students in small, academically oriented Living Learning Communities, overseen by actively involved faculty and integrated by year in school.

Congregating students by academic interest, especially when there is no Greek system to compete for student loyalty, is likely to make students more open to forming community in the residence halls. Designing dormitories to facilitate interaction both on the floors and in other areas—particularly the dining hall (ours was dominated by a large television that killed conversation)—would also foster ties among students. More intensive training for RAs (particularly geared toward helping students navigate diversity), residence life programming of activities not viewed as hopelessly nerdy, and adult engagement in residence hall life might also help.

On campuses with a diverse student body, it is possible to integrate students demographically in university housing. This directly dilutes the concentration of students that sustain a party culture.[4] This would not be advisable on a homogenous campus, as full integration would mean that students of color would be isolated in entirely white living environments. This isolation may threaten the experiences of students of color and others who are more marginal to the mainstream of college life—particularly if other students were as intolerant of difference as those we studied. For example, full integration of Midwest U with the current composition of students would require dismantling existing identity-based Living Learning Communities—destroying spaces that allow students of color, academically oriented students, and other groups to flourish. On a more integrated campus, these forms of protective segregation would be less necessary.

Increasing time spent studying is presumably straightforward: make easy courses and majors more difficult or eliminate them all together. In *Academically Adrift*, Richard Arum and Josipa Roksa find, not surprisingly, that courses requiring more reading and more writing are associated with more growth in critical thinking.[5] This would necessitate smaller course sizes and more time on the part of instructors correcting papers, meeting with students to discuss writing, and reading revisions. Stronger academic advising would also help some students to clarify their academic interests or career goals before they got pulled onto the party pathway.

Scaling back college athletics is also another logical corrective. Others have suggested this—most famously Murray Sperber in his book *Beer and Circus: How Big-Time College Sports Is Crippling Undergraduate Education.* Collegiate men's football and basketball, in particular, are central to the party pathway.[6] They attract socially oriented students and generate school spirit, social events, rivalries, and reasons to drink. However, these sports are more than moneymakers and party starters. They link groups of schools that compete with shared identities and similar levels of prestige.[7] Indeed, several of the women we studied came to MU because, as they told us, it was a school in a particular national conference. Membership in a shared organization made these schools, in their eyes, largely interchangeable. There is reason to suspect that these schools reinforce each other's investments in a party pathway: In competition for visibility and tuition paying students, they come to more closely resemble each other.

Conversely, incorporating a larger proportion of the student body in demanding, well-organized intramural competition—as is typical at small liberal arts colleges—could absorb some of the time and energies that current students devote to partying. Many of the women on our floor were serious high school athletes. Few succeeded at getting involved in similarly demanding physical activities in college. They were used to the way competitive athletics structured their time and their social lives and helped them control their weight. Without this structure, they were bored and at loose ends. Partying provided them with a way to spend their time.

Implementing these changes would contribute to building a mobility pathway because, as we have seen, a vibrant party pathway serves either to seduce or to alienate students looking for a mobility pathway.

Building a Mobility Pathway

In the Introduction, we outlined characteristics of a mobility pathway. Most centrally, provision of this pathway requires the university to do much of the work in moving students from where they are to someplace better. For example, courses need to pick students up at their existing level of mastery—which in many cases means provision of high-quality remedial coursework to compensate for prior educational deficits.

A mobility pathway is, ideally, streamlined—offering direct routes from coursework, to skills, credentials, and finally careers. As time and money are scarce, each course should be necessary, well taught, and substantive. High-quality, personalized advising—perhaps resembling what highly educated parents would offer their own child—should ensure that students do not take courses they do not need or pursue a major or line of study unlikely to lead to employment.

As James Rosenbaum, Regina Deil-Amen, and Ann Person suggest in *After Admission: From College Access to College Success*, the organizational arrangements of the party pathway should eliminate the possibility of costly mistakes (for example, courses that do not transfer).[8] Although practical, this pathway should not track students into low-paying occupations. It should be possible to transfer into more demanding and prestigious programs at multiple junctures. Also, as affluent parents provide resources that enable young people to bridge graduation and employment (for example, money to finance moves and network ties that secure employment), a comprehensive mobility pathway would ideally compensate for parental inability to provide support after graduation.

Broadening Access to the Professional Pathway

A more equitable professional pathway will require recognition of the processes that convert class advantage into merit. This is a challenging task, given the truly American adage that anyone can succeed with enough hard work. Indeed, the success of today's "new elite" in seemingly meritocratic competitions has made their privilege invisible, and they expect others to "earn" their status in the same way.[9] The American educational system, from kindergarten on, operates as a system of contest mobility.[10] That is, every level is presumed to be an open contest, in which anyone can win. Inequities in starting position are not taken into account, and winning is the only thing that matters. College is the accumulation of many inequitable contests, in which the affluent have presumably justified their position at the top of the heap.

Broadening access to the professional pathway means the meticulous unraveling of the often invisible advantages that accrue to wealthy and highly educated families. Perhaps the most egregious example comes in legacy preferences, which provide an admissions advantage for children of university alumni. This policy quite obviously disadvantages first-generation students, but it also hurts underrepresented minorities.[11]

The most select university programs should also provide more clearly marked on-ramps—and offer ways for students whose academic performance improves sharply over time opportunities to enter these programs as they get up to speed. Increasing the number of spots available in such programs, as well as providing additional support for students who struggle (rather than "weeding them out"), will open them up to a more diverse group of students. All students should have access to high-quality programming—small classes with invested faculty—as well as other advantages (for example, better connections to internships and research opportunities) that often accrue to a select few.

A more accessible and equitable professional pathway would overlap with the mobility pathway. The two should actually share considerable academic programming and flow easily from one to the next. Students should not have to opt for vocational training because they cannot get on the professional pathway, nor should they stay on the professional pathway if they prefer to pursue teaching, nursing, social services, or other similar careers. Given that many of the motivated students who start on the mobility pathway will, ideally, end up on the professional pathway, compensation for differences in family resources—economic, cultural, and social—is key.

Entrenched Interests and Other Obstacles to Change

Many university staff—particularly those engaged in frontline work with students—support policies such as those proposed above. Yet administrators find them difficult to implement—even when they would like to, particularly in the context of declining state support. By taking the fun out of college and increasing the work required of both students and faculty, the above policies risk alienating affluent families and research faculty—two groups critical to the solvency and prestige of the university.

Solvency, the Upper Classes, and Tuition Dependence

Four-year residential colleges and universities have long depended financially on the patronage of upper- and upper-middle-class families and have consequently provided the social experiences desired by this constituency. The benefits of doing so extend beyond the hefty tuition these students pay. Students who participate in Greek life donate more than others to their alma mater after graduation. Encouraging college life tends to generate a politically docile student body. On many campuses, fraternities and sororities also house and feed large numbers of students.[12] Nonetheless, academic leaders have long been ambivalent about heavy socializing on campus, often attempting to rein it in.[13]

There have been historical moments in which the revelry was successfully tempered. During what Clark Kerr referred to as the Golden Era of the American research university (circa 1940 to 1990), federal and state governments invested heavily in higher education.[14] Marked by low tuition and the availability of financial aid, these years saw the influx of more diverse and less advantaged populations into the university.[15] Evidence suggests that the party pathway grew weaker in response. For example, historian Blake Gumprecht, writing about the history of Greek life at Cornell University, noted: "Many [fraternities] closed during World War II and struggled to regain their previous stature in a postwar era during which veterans dominated campus life. Fraternities boomed again during the 1950s, only to come under attack in the nonconformist Sixties. Membership declined and some two dozen fraternities and sororities at Cornell closed."[16] Helen Horowitz and Michael Moffatt, in their historical and ethnographic accounts of college life, also both discuss the fading of "original college-life culture" in the wake of the 1960s. Horowitz concludes by touting the ascendance of the academic over the social on American campuses, and Moffatt describes what he saw as a "common classless, internationally defined youth culture."[17]

However, the state support necessary to curb the party pathway has been steadily eroding since the Reagan era.[18] Clark Kerr refers to 1990 through the present as an era of "constrained resources."[19] Universities have compensated by raising tuition (particularly out-of-state tuition), increasing the numbers of out-of-state students, engaging in aggressive fundraising, and pursuing research grants. Tuition now accounts for the biggest share of revenues.[20] The University of Michigan started moving in this direction in the 1980s, with other public universities following suit.[21] The University of California's adoption of this model has been particularly abrupt and politically contested.[22] Midwest U has operated in step with these other public universities: Its recent pursuit of affluent out-of-state students has been so noticeable that it has been written about multiple times in the national media.

Schools seeking to enroll affluent students looking for a social experience have had little choice but to compete for this small, mobile population. These students seek the best "college experience" when selecting among universities. For example, Nicole explained her choice of Midwest U rather than her own state university by comparing the social life at the two schools:

> Northern U doesn't have a football team, first of all. . . . And at Northern U I think the kids would be inside more often just 'cause it's always so cold there. [And] I heard there were a lot of parties at Midwest U. . . . I met someone who said that he loved it here and everyone was so spirited. (Y1)

Abby and Naomi could have saved money by attending their in-state party school instead of Midwest U—and may have done so if residence life had not responded to their complaint about residence hall assignment by moving them to the dorm of their choice.

This competition drives the expansion of party pathway infrastructure. For example, MU is building a new residence hall complex designed for students who prefer—and can afford—more luxurious private accommodations. On four-year residential campuses around the country, increases in spending for student services—including recreation and athletics—have far surpassed those for academic instruction and financial aid (which has actually decreased since 1998).[23] The result has been what some scholars have labeled the "country-clubization of the American university."[24] Such spending is likely to increase as pursuit of affluent out-of-state student tuition dollars intensifies.

Prestige, Faculty Interests, and the Research Imperative

Public universities are dependent on the research activities of their faculties for prestige. The last half of the twentieth century saw a research "arms race," in which a larger proportion of faculty at more institutions were expected to produce more research.[25] This speedup was particularly pronounced at middle-tier universities.[26] The focus on research is embedded in graduate education and in standards for tenure, promotion, and salary setting. With little attention to pedagogical training in graduate school, tenure-line faculty members are often not prepared to teach well and do not develop strong commitments to undergraduate education. Graduate students receive the message that teaching is simply something one has to do—preferably as little as possible—in order to access the time and resources required to do research. Faculty members who become skilled and committed teachers are frequently not rewarded.[27]

Some types of teaching are more consistent with research productivity and the pursuit of prestige than others. The more directly students contribute to faculty research and reputation, the more likely they are to receive attention from tenure-line faculty. Postdoctoral research fellows, doctoral students, undergraduate honors thesis students, and undergraduates in small, upper-division seminars get the lion's share of the time that research faculty devote to teaching. An orientation toward excellence—which is built into the university—makes it logical to focus on the students with the most promise. With the exception of administrative time required to deal with problem students (those who plagiarize, do not show up to class for weeks on end, stalk their peers, and so forth) faculty pay relatively less attention to average or weak students. Yet faculty see their calendars chockfull of meetings with students, not realizing that these students often represent only a fraction of the students at the university.

Challenging the party pathway means not only focusing more faculty energies on instruction but attending to the students who are more challenging to teach. This requires placing the least prepared students with the most talented teachers and working hard to interest socially oriented students. These students arrive at college lacking respect for the intellectual endeavor, motivation to learn, or a stake in earning high grades. It takes skilled instructors, like the one that Mara encountered (see Chapter 8), to reach them. University initiatives that reduce time available for socializing also work. For example, research suggests that holding classes on Friday reduces student emergency room visits by effectively eliminating an evening per week of partying.[28] Given expectations for faculty research, however, there is little incentive for faculty to support initiatives that require greater investment in students and teaching.

Declining Public Commitments to Equity

As we learned in the Introduction, public universities were founded to provide an avenue for mobility to qualified state residents. State governments continue to be invested in universities fulfilling this mission: They want universities to provide a measurably high-quality education for low cost, while preserving access. Yet by scaling back state appropriations year after year, the power of state governments to insist that schools fulfill this mission is reduced. In a number of states, legislators have cut funding so much that states provide only a small fraction of university revenue.[29] In 2011 the *Chronicle of Higher Education* reported Robert M. Berdahl, president of the Association of American Universities, as saying that

> many state legislatures have long since abdicated their important roles in nurturing the major research institutions that should be a cornerstone of any sound higher-education policy. . . . If lawmakers abandon their vital policy function and starve universities of resources, major research universities will necessarily look even more to the federal government for

support through contracts and grants, while also increasing out-of-state enrollment to bolster tuition revenues.[30]

Reliance on the tuition of affluent students protects both solvency and prestige—at least in the short run—and is thus an understandable response to the challenges facing many public universities today.

The Vulnerability of Public Research Universities

This solution is, however, problematic not only for less affluent college-goers but for the future of public universities.[31] It is on these campuses where elite and mass education intersect. As Steven Brint notes in a recent essay, "Beyond the Ivy Islands":

> Since their inception in the mid-19th century, [public universities] have been open to students from a variety of backgrounds, and they have always provided training in practical occupations, as well as education in the arts and sciences. . . . The idea that college is a place for realizing one's full potential remains strong in these institutions, as does the belief that higher education matters (or should matter) for something more than a job qualification.[32]

Education at public universities has historically been both vocational and idealistic, offering both preparation for work and a place for self-discovery.[33]

When universities focus their energies on recruiting and serving the most affluent students in the country (and, in some cases, the world) while turning away or underserving others, access to the more idealistic vision of college closes for less advantaged members of society. They are not blocked from higher education altogether but are directed to mass options, such as community colleges and online courses. As economist Ronald Ehrenberg recently observed, "With privatization, we run the risk of public higher education's becoming even more stratified, with upper- and upper-middle-income students studying at relatively wellfunded flagship campuses and lower- and lower-middle income students studying at less well-funded public comprehensive institutions and two-year colleges."[34] As a result, an already highly stratified sector becomes even more so. In fact, Steven Brint coined the term "Ivy Islands" to highlight that a few elite schools—where the children of the affluent will continue to enjoy expensive four-year residential experiences—are separating from the rest of the higher education sector.[35] It is not surprising that the straddling of elite and mass education has become more difficult, as higher education is not spared from the increasing class polarization in society at large.[36]

If we imagine a chasm opening up between elite and mass higher education, public universities are being forced to jump to one side or the other. Try to join the Ivy Islands? Or become part of the mainland? Schools like MU are attempting to land on the elite side of this emerging new divide. This is a risky strategy, however. Even the most casual look at the composition of those currently in and approaching higher education suggests that only a small number of schools, mostly private, will successfully land on the elite side of the chasm.

The majority of those entering postsecondary education today are not traditional students but are instead what Arthur Levine refers to as "new majority" students.[37] Many do not attend school full-time. A number are adults, both with respect to age and financial responsibilities. Some are parents or have other caretaking responsibilities. Many live off campus with parents or other family members. A sizeable fraction needs remedial coursework. Increasingly these students will not be white, born in the United States, or native speakers of English.[38] Experts also predict a decline in the number of well-prepared students with affluent, college-educated parents in the national college-going pool.[39] In short, there is—and will increasingly be—a shortage of students who are willing and able to go out of state for their college education.

Those trying to land on the elite side of the divide are competing for a tiny and shrinking segment of the population. MU fares reasonably well in the competition for affluent students, but mostly for those seeking a more social experience. The parents of academically oriented affluent students tend to be savvy, informed consumers of high education. They know better than to send their offspring out of state to a public university (unless they receive a huge price break or identify a specific, high-quality program appropriate for their student). Although recruiting socially oriented out-of-state students can keep the university afloat, the provision of the party pathway necessary to recruit them comes with a cost.

It is difficult to make a claim to elite status when the most visible aspects of the undergraduate culture involve tailgating and beer pong. It is not just the size of the tuition payments parents make but what happens on campus that constitutes a school as elite. As we demonstrated, a highly visible, dominant party pathway tends to bleed over and encroach on other pathways. The failure to provide either a high-quality intellectual experience or a well-designed vocational experience—the two primary models of college that various constituencies endorse—places a school in a vulnerable position. Indeed, as we have suggested throughout this book, in an era of climbing tuition, debt, and an uncertain payoff, it is not clear whether it is worth it to support college as a playground for the young—and an expensive, exclusive one at that.[40]

While declining state appropriations have contributed to the problem, raising tuition does not generate good will with the legislators who determine future funding. In fact, Patrick M. Callan, founder and president of the National Center for Public Policy and Higher Education, has expressed concern that a reliance on out-of-state tuition will make it difficult to justify obtaining state support in a better economy.[41] In the meantime, universities that stray from the mission of the public university may find that state support declines even further. For those few universities who can afford to cut financial ties with their states and fully privatize, this is perhaps not a problem. The fate of most public universities, however, is still linked to the goodwill of the state legislatures.

Though perhaps efficacious in the short-term, hiking tuition, recruiting affluent out-of-state socialites, and provisioning the party pathway generate a host of long-term problems. It pulls the university away from its mission, which risks further loss of support by the legislatures. It reduces access to a four-year residential college experience, contributing to the polarization of higher education. It places the university in the precarious position of relying on a shrinking, highly mobile proportion of the population. Critically, it also neglects the biggest market in need of postsecondary schooling—the new majority.

Educating the New Majority

While MU and similar schools compete for the tuition dollars of the affluent, major foundations, venture capitalists, and educational entrepreneurs of all varieties are rethinking mass education.[42] The higher education mainland is on the cusp of an organizational transformation.

As we have learned, four-year public research universities are playing a smaller role in the education of the new majority. The public institutions devoted to serving these students—regional campuses and community colleges—have been even more starved of state support than the flagships.[43]

This is unfortunate, as these institutions may offer mobility pathways not present at state flagships. Yet public willingness to invest in such schools is low, in part because community colleges in particular have uneven track records—with low rates of transfer and graduation.[44] Like four-year residential campuses, regional and community colleges still rely primarily on face-to-face instruction—which is inherently expensive.

The price of instruction is the biggest factor driving the escalating costs of higher education. William J. Baumol and William G. Bowen have referred to the "handicraft" nature of higher education as the source of what they call the "cost disease."[45] Until the present, the laborious nature of teaching was simply taken for granted. Education required teacher and students to be together in physical space. Virtually the entirety of the higher education system in the United States rests on this simple and enormously expensive fact. It is not only the compensation of instructors that is expensive. Building and maintaining the massive physical plants of today's colleges and universities requires utilities, custodial services, sidewalks, roads, buses, snow removal, landscaping, and so on. Bringing people together in space and time also requires transportation and the establishment of all the services necessary to preserve health and welfare. On a residential campus, the housing, feeding, disciplining, and entertaining of students requires a veritable army of student affairs staff.

It is around the issue of cost reduction that interests converge. New majority students want affordability, convenience, and quality—what Arthur Levine refers to as "a stripped-down version of higher education." As he suggests, such students do not need rock-climbing walls in state-of-the art gyms, majors that will never lead to a job, gourmet dining options, or thousands of extracurricular activities. If new majority students cannot get what they want from four-year residential schools, they are willing to seek it elsewhere.[46] A group Steven Brint refers to as "educational industrialists" (including philanthropists such as Bill Gates) are also on board, as they seek to graduate the greatest number at the lowest cost. The goal is to give graduates access to the credentials they will need to get jobs without going broke or getting sidetracked by the rest of the college experience.[47]

What is different now, as opposed to the past, is that new digital technologies offer new possible solutions. In a recent report William G. Bowen optimistically exclaimed, "The time may (finally!) be at hand when advances in information technology will permit, under the right circumstances, increases in productivity that can be translated into reductions in the cost of instruction. Greater and smarter use of technology in teaching is widely seen as a promising way of controlling costs while also reducing achievement gaps and improving access." These comments were made in a report on a randomized experimental study comparing student learning in an interactive online course (with limited face-to-face instruction) versus traditional instruction. The study found no difference across the two contexts.[48]

There is, of course, a great deal of skepticism about the quality of online instruction—with good reason. The quality of much that currently exists is low. Some players in the arena are more interested in profit than education. Yet the potential of this technology is, some think, as of yet largely untapped. Educational innovators such as Candace Thille are, at this writing, sought after for consulting and speaking.[49] Discussions of MOOCs (Massive Online Open Courses) are gradually making their way from the imaginations of visionary educational entrepreneurs to the everyday language of ordinary citizens. It remains to be seen whether digital education will mostly take the high road—free or low cost, high quality, focused on serving low-income and underserved populations—or whether it will take the low road—organized around the aggressive pursuit of profit, low quality, characterized by fraudulent claims about the market value of degrees, and engaged in predatory financial practices.

Whichever direction it takes, signs suggest that rapid change is coming. Mitchell Stevens and Roy Pea identified the core issue in a proposal for a 2012 seminar series on "Education's Digital Future" at Stanford University:

> The delivery and consumption of formal education are still largely accomplished face-to-face in physical space. This must, and will, change radically in the near future. It must change because face-to-face instruction is too costly and inefficient to deliver at quantities demanded. . . . It will change because digital delivery opens up vast new markets for educational products and services.[50]

Some even question whether the residential university will survive.[51] In "Can Colleges and Universities Survive the Information Age?" former president of the University of Michigan James Duderstadt predicts a restructuring, not unlike that which recently hit the publishing industry, which will relegate many higher education institutions to cyberspace.[52]

The 2012 firing (and rehiring) of Teresa Sullivan from her post as president of the University of Virginia foreshadows the disruptions likely to be experienced in the upcoming decades. Sullivan clashed with Helen Dragas, head of the board of trustees and a graduate of the UVA business school, over key issues facing higher education today—including how quickly and comprehensively universities should adopt online education. Sullivan's defense of the traditional academic model put her on the outs with the board of trustees.[53] In the *Chronicle of Higher Education*, Kent J. Chabotar (president of Guilford College) indicates that the University of Virginia's quick determination that Sullivan was incapable of handling the challenges facing the university reflects a sense of urgency among trustees nationwide. Given declining state support, new technologies on the horizon, and worries about the sustainability of four-year residential education, he notes that "most boards are running scared."[54]

It is no wonder that boards of trustees are "running scared": Technology is moving quickly and the cost issues will not be resolved with short-term improvements in the economy. It is unclear whether universities will lead the digital revolution or be relegated to history by it. It is likely that we will see rapid growth in digital education and an accompanying decline in the numbers of lower-income students at four-year residential universities. Some public universities may find themselves out of the business of undergraduate education, out of business entirely, or resorting to the mass side of the chasm, providing education entirely online.

"It's Like Painting Your Whole Room Yellow"

Rather than conclude with a forward-looking endorsement of digital learning's potential or an impassioned defense of the four-year residential experience, we offer a story from our data that captures the conundrum.[55]

We met Alana in Chapter 4. Lower-middle class, from an industrial in-state city, her first year of college was not easy for her socially or academically. Like other less privileged women, she did not make friends on the floor—a failure for which she initially blamed herself. Alana nearly left the university after her first year as she had no one to live with at the start of the next. Her father, compensating for long absences from her life as a child, came to town, helped her find an apartment, and paid for it. With a stable living situation, she eventually adjusted to college. She got involved in the hiking and outdoor excursion club on campus. As she noted, "I really started to enjoy college. Like everyone else. And find my place and find my friends" (Y4). Her involvement in this group introduced her to two central loves of her life—nature and a man who was similarly devoted to the outdoors.

Telling a romantic story of passionate love, Alana describes how she and Michael tried to resist each other, but after a car accident where Michael was nearly killed she realized: "Oh my God, I think I love this man. What am I doing? Why am I trying to lie to myself? This man is amazing" (Y4). They finally got together on a university trip to Colorado:

We kind of decided to hang out, just go on this trail. And we ended up walking down this trail and we went swimming in the stream. We take off our clothes. And it was beautiful! We were in the middle of these can-yon walls and there was this trickling stream of the Colorado River and it was gorgeous. It was beautiful. I've never felt more alive. You just feel so alive and so just full of energy and connected to the earth. That's the kind of feeling and moments that I live for, and the whole trip was like that. Just really, like, amazing, wonderful, unplanned, intense, like, natural experiences, you know? There's no cell phones or TV. Everything's just so real. Like, so we have this amazing trip and there's definitely something going on between us. We really took this whole thing in, the beginning of our relationship, we just spread it out really far. Like, we moved really slow. We got to know each other so well. (Y4)

This fully embodied experience is in part what the affluent are seeking for their children when they send them off to college. And Alana managed to get it at Midwest U, despite her disadvantaged background and isolation in the party dorm. It transformed her life for the better and altered her tra-jectory permanently, although it did not shift her toward a middle-class life.

Her love of nature and Michael led her West after college into a series of minimum-wage, seasonal jobs that did not require a BA or offer benefits (for example, tour director and ski instructor) alongside her boyfriend, who fought wildfires. Although this placed her in the "mobility at risk" category because of the lack of a clear economic payoff from college, she was happy:

I'm really glad I went to college. Well, I might change a couple things, but I like where I am right now so I guess I wouldn't mess with it. . . . I would be miserable in my hometown because it's just like nobody does anything or goes anywhere. It's just horribly boring and awful high school memo-ries and stuff. . . . I feel really lucky a lot of the times. My mom's side of the family has never really left the state before. I just feel lucky because they'll probably never get to travel or live anywhere else. I really like California. I like the mountains. A lot of people have the same views that I do, a lot of things that I think are important, gay rights issues and just they're just kind of more liberal. And having just really pretty surroundings I think makes me just more positive or keeps me happier. It's like painting your whole room yellow as opposed to black. (Y5)

MU brought Alana wonderful things—a chance to see the world and a partner with whom to see it. She was unconcerned about money, status, or class position and just happy not to be trapped in her hometown. College brought beauty, joy, and love into Alana's life—a chance to live her life in a room painted yellow. Her experience at MU offered her what Andrew Delbanco, author of *College: What It Was, Is, and Should Be*, claims that college should provide: "the opportunity for young people to make a pause between adolescence and adulthood, to reflect on life, on their choices, on who they are or want to be."[56]

Alana could never have gotten what she needed from college sitting at home at a computer terminal. For her, and for a number of the women in our study, moving from a small, provincial town to a larger, more cosmopolitan small city was a main benefit of college. For Alana, the move to Fairview and her travel experiences while in college enabled the much bolder move after college. Her time in Fairview weakened the link with her family and community of origin, exposed her to beautiful places, and enabled her to meet a companion with whom to make this move. We are not alone in identifying geographic movement as a central aspect of mobility. In *Hollowing out the Middle*, Patrick Carr and Maria Kefalas vividly describe the ways in which the most talented young people in small Midwestern towns are pulled toward larger cities—to their benefit and the detriment of these communities.[57]

Our research led us to be highly attuned to the embodied aspects of the college experience. The formation of social skills, physical styles, cultural tastes, and social relationships requires shared residence, which generates skepticism about whether even high-quality online education will translate into employment. Optimism in its payoff rests on the belief that higher education offers pure human capital and that people can and will move anywhere to deploy it. This is not what we found. We found that the ability to translate a degree into a job rested on a host of factors beyond the skills themselves. Online education may not pay off for those stuck in remote locations with poor labor markets and limited network ties. Despite the mobility of the population and the possibilities of more jobs being done remotely, both people and jobs are still deeply entrenched in place.

While online education would likely have done little for Alana, it is hard to get past the reality that MU did not provide Alana access to the upper-middle class—or even a job requiring a college degree. Granted, she did not look for such a position, as her heart took her to the mountains with Michael. It is not clear, however, that had she searched for such a job, with her tourism major and no family connections, that she would have found it, even with a very good GPA.

From a purely utilitarian perspective, it is hard to justify a four-year college experience that appears to have generated limited intellectual engagement, no pathway toward a professional career, and little hope of earning a middle-class salary. If Alana were unique, this would be less concerning. But as we saw in Chapter 8, only a tiny fraction of the women on the floor—perhaps just the seven achievers—exited MU with the kind of credentials or human capital that many expect all college graduates to acquire. This makes it difficult to engage in a wholehearted defense of the four-year residential experience in its current form.

We are thus left deeply worried about reduced access to the four-year residential college experience but are just as concerned about whether that experience pays off for many students. Delbanco, in his defense of it, captures the dilemma in another way. He argues:

> It's very hard for me to imagine how distance learning of any kind could re-create what the small class, at its best, can provide. The chance to have civil discourse and debate with people with whom you disagree, to learn to listen and consider arguments rather than just put forward opinions.[58]

This description of "the small class, at its best" does not describe the academic experiences of the women we studied. If college in reality resembled the ideal that he describes, of course it would be worth defending. Given how poorly some students are served by the four-year public residential university, a carefully crafted education involving online courses and no requirement to be in residence might, under some circumstances, actually come closer to the ideal.

We remain hopeful that reforms like those proposed earlier in the chapter will improve the four-year residential public university experience. Yet as we have discussed, the current state of higher education is a result of political priorities—as is its future. Unless priorities shift, four-year public universities remain vulnerable. The fortunes of the women we studied suggest that these organizations may not be delivering on their promise. If the experiences we document are common rather than atypical, the chorus questioning the value of a four-year college degree may grow louder. Some observers have even begun to talk about a "higher education bubble," hinting at the vulnerability of many colleges and universities should Americans lose confidence in higher education en masse.[59] It is not possible to know what the future holds for American higher education, but it seems likely that massive changes lie ahead.

APPENDIXES

NOTES

REFERENCES

ACKNOWLEDGMENTS

INDEX

APPENDIX **A**

Participants

Table A.1. Study participants

Study participants	Social class background	Residency	Orientation to college	Floor isolate	Class trajectory
Party pathway					
Socialites, *n* = 7					
Abby	UC	Out	By default	No	Reproduction
Hannah	UC	Out	Primed to party	No	Reproduction
Maya	UC	Out	Primed to party	No	Reproduction
Melanie	UC	Out	Primed to party	No	Reproduction
Naomi	UMC	Out	Primed to party	No	Reproduction
Tara	UMC	Out	Primed to party	No	Reproduction
Bailey	UMC	In	By default	No	Reproduction
Wannabes, *n* = 9					
Mara	UMC	Out	Primed to party	No	Reproduction
Nicole	UMC	Out	Primed to party	No	Downward
Sophie	UMC	Out	Primed to party	No	Downward
Sydney	UMC	Out	Primed to party	No	Downward
Alicia	UMC	Out	By default	No	Downward
Chelsea	MC	Out	Primed to party	No	Downward
Whitney	MC	In	By default	No	Mobility at risk
Blair	MC	In	By default	No	Mobility at risk
Karen	MC	In	By default	No	Mobility at risk

Mobility pathway

Strivers: Stayers, *n*=6

Valerie	LMC	In	By default	Yes	Upward
Alana	LMC	In	Motivated for mobility	Yes	Mobility at risk
Michelle	LMC	In	Motivated for mobility	Yes	Mobility at risk
Carrie	LMC	In	By default	Yes	Mobility at risk
Crystal	LMC	In	By default	Yes	Mobility at risk
Amanda	WC	In	By default	Yes	Mobility at risk

Strivers: Leavers, *n*=7

Andrea	LMC	In	By default	Yes	Upward
Stacey	LMC	In	Motivated for mobility	Yes	Upward
Megan	WC	In	Motivated for mobility	Yes	Upward
Alyssa	WC	In	Motivated for mobility	Yes	Upward
Heather	WC	In	Motivated for mobility	Yes	Mobility at risk
Monica	WC	In	Motivated for mobility	Yes	Mobility at risk
Amy	WC	In	Motivated for mobility	Yes	Unknown

Professional pathway

Achievers, *n*=7

Brooke	UC	Out	Cultivated for success	Yes	Reproduction
Brenda	UC	Out	Cultivated for success	No	Reproduction
Lydia	UC	Out	Cultivated for success	No	Reproduction
Tracy	UC	Out	Cultivated for success	No	Reproduction
Erica	UMC	Out	Cultivated for success	No	Reproduction
Taylor	UMC	Out	Cultivated for success	No	Reproduction
Madison	UMC	In	By default	No	Reproduction

(continued)

Table A.1 (continued)

Study participants	Social class background	Residency	Orientation to college	Floor isolate	Class trajectory
Underachievers, n = 11					
Leah	UC	Out	By default	Yes	Reproduction
Linda	UMC	Out	Cultivated for success	Yes	Downward
Lisa	UMC	In	By default	No	Reproduction
Julie	UMC	Out	By default	Yes	Reproduction
Brianna	UMC	In	By default	Yes	Downward
Morgan	UMC	In	By default	Yes	Downward
Natasha	UMC	In	By default	Yes	Downward
Mary	MC	In	By default	Yes	Mobility at risk
Emma	MC	In	By default	No	Mobility at risk
Becky	LMC	In	By default	Yes	Mobility at risk
Olivia	LMC	In	By default	Yes	Mobility at risk
Incomplete data					
Angela	UMC	Out	Primed to party	Yes	Unknown
Eva	UMC	Out	Primed to party	No	Unknown
Meredith	UMC	Out	Primed to party	No	Unknown
Joanna	MC	In	Cultivated for success	No	Unknown
Mollie	LMC	In	Primed to party	No	Unknown
Rose	LMC	In	Motivated for mobility	Yes	Unknown

Note: UC = upper class; UMC = upper-middle class; MC = middle class; LMC = lower-middle class; WC = working class.

Table A.2. Interviews collected by year

Study participants	Interviews						Discussed in Chapter					
	Y1	Y2	Y3	Y4	Y5	Total	1	4	5	6	7	8
Party pathway												
Socialites, *n*=7												
Abby	1	1	1	1	1	5	1	1	1			1
Hannah	1	1	1	1	1	5	1	1	1			1
Maya					1	1	1	1	1			1
Melanie				1	1	2	1	1	1			1
Naomi	1	1	1	1	1	5	1	1	1			1
Tara	1	1	1	1	1	5	1	1	1			1
Bailey	1	1	1	1	1	5	1	1	1			1
Wannabes, *n*=9												
Mara	1				1	2	1	1	1			1
Nicole	1	1	1	1	1	5	1	1	1			1
Sophie	1				1	2	1	1	1			1
Sydney	1	1	1	1	1	5	1	1	1			1
Alicia	1	1	1	1	1	5	1	1	1			1
Chelsea	1	1	1	1	1	5	1	1	1			1
Whitney	1[a]	1	1	1	1	5	1	1	1			1
Blair	1	1	1	1	1	5	1	1	1			1
Karen	1[b]	1	1	1	1	5	1	1	1			1

(continued)

Table A.2 (continued)

Study participants	Y1	Y2	Y3	Y4	Y5	Total	1	4	5	6	7	8
			Interviews						Discussed in chapter			
Mobility pathway												
Strivers: Stayers, *n*=6												
Valerie	1	1	1	1	1	5	1	1		1		1
Alana	1	1	1	1	1	5	1	1		1		1
Michelle			1	1		2	1	1		1		1
Carrie	1	1	1	1	1	5	1	1		1		1
Crystal	1	1	1	1	1	5	1	1		1		1
Amanda		1	1	1	1	4	1	1		1		1
Strivers: Leavers, *n*=7												
Andrea					1	1	1	1		1		1
Stacey		1[a]	1[a]	1	1	5	1	1		1		1
Megan	1	1	1	1	1	5	1	1		1		1
Alyssa				1	1	2	1	1		1		1
Heather	1[a]	1[a]	1[a]	1	1	5	1	1		1		1
Monica	1[b]				1	2	1	1		1		
Amy						0	1	1		1		
Professional pathway												
Achievers, *n*=7												
Brooke	1	1	1	1	1	5	1	1			1	1
Brenda	1	1	1	1	1	5	1	1			1	1
Lydia	1	1	1	1	1	5	1	1			1	1
Tracy	1	1	1	1	1	5	1	1			1	1
Erica	1[a]	1	1	1	1	5	1	1			1	1

Taylor	1a	1		1	1	5	1	1	1	1	1	1
Madison	1	1	1	1	1	4	1	1	1	1	1	1
Underachievers, n = 11												
Leah	1	1		1	1	4	1	1	1	1	1	1
Linda	1	1		1	1	4	1	1	1	1	1	1
Julie	1a	1	1	1	1	5	1	1	1	1	1	1
Lisa	1	1	1	1	1	5	1	1	1	1	1	1
Brianna	1	1	1	1	1	5	1	1	1	1	1	1
Morgan	1a	1	1	1	1	5	1	1	1	1	1	1
Natasha	1a	1	1	1	1	5	1	1	1	1	1	1
Mary	1	1	1	1	1	5	1	1	1	1	1	1
Emma	1	1	1	1	1	5	1	1	1	1	1	1
Becky	1	1	1	1	1	3	1	1	1	1	1	1
Olivia	1	1	1	1	1	5	1	1	1	1	1	1
Incomplete data, n = 6												
Angela	1a					1	1	1				
Eva						0	1					
Meredith						0	1					
Joanna						0	1					
Mollie	1a					1	1	1				
Rose						0	1					
RA	1					1	1					
Total, n = 53	42	37	36	41	46	202	47	53	16	13	18	46

Note: All women participated in the ethnography their first year.

a. These women were interviewed with their roommates.

b. The digital recording for the original interview of the two roommates together was lost although we reconstructed most of the content. We conducted a second interview with Karen the first year as she was deciding to leave MU.

APPENDIX **B**

Studying Social Class

In social mobility research, class of origin is traditionally operationalized using father's education, occupation, income, or some combination of the three.[1] More recently, scholars have argued for the merits of including indicators for mothers, particularly when studying women.[2] Our class groupings, discussed in Chapter 1, reference this legacy of work. They are based primarily on education and occupation measures for fathers and mothers and take into account family economic resources.

Yet we had far richer data than is typically available. We gleaned considerable information about social class background from our observations and interactions with the women. Our knowledge deepened when Laura interviewed their parents for her dissertation. Although not discussed in this book, these interviews provided a more nuanced understanding of parental class background. Most parental interviews took place in the family home or in another equally telling location. For instance, whereas Laura met one parent in his office overlooking Park Avenue in New York City, she met another at a rural truck stop with her young son.

The nature of our data allowed us to adopt a Bourdieusian approach to social class. We assumed that individuals from different social locations would start with different cultural tastes, knowledge about college, academic and professional skills, and social capacities. To the extent possible, we assessed women on all of these dimensions upon arrival at college. In most cases there was considerable harmony between traditional indicators of class and what Bourdieu refers to as *habitus*—taken-for-granted dispositions and ways of relating learned through the experiences and activities of everyday life.[3]

However, sometimes this was not the case. For example, Karen came from a family that, if we looked only at variables commonly used in stratification

263

research, was feasibly upper-middle class. Both parents were college-educated, and the family was, especially in their rural town, at the top of the economic ladder. At the same time, her parents had little knowledge of how a national university like MU worked: They had attended a small, noncompetitive, religious college ten minutes from the town in which they lived their whole lives. In addition, Karen's small-town upbringing left her at a disadvantage when navigating even a small city like Fairview, much less the competitive social scene on campus. Karen most closely resembled other middle-class (even lower-middle-class) students in our sample, in large part because of where she was from and with whom she had grown up. Culturally, she was middle class.

"Messy" Class

That we saw such complexities in the lived reality of study participants was largely a result of our sample. Unlike other qualitative researchers studying social class, we did not choose respondents on the basis of class background. For instance, Annette Lareau intentionally selected families that fit her criteria for poor, working class, and middle class.[4] Jenny Stuber interviewed students only from distinctively upper-middle-class and working-class families.[5] In contrast, by studying an entire residence hall floor, we encountered women from a full range of social class backgrounds. Many were not "ideal types," that is, they would not have cleanly fit into researcher-imposed classificatory criteria and would have likely been excluded on these grounds.

Our sample led us to realize just how messy social class really is. Divorce, remarriage, parental death, serious illness, job loss, and business failure shaped the resources available to some of the women we studied. Sometimes the event occurred so rapidly that a family's economic standing was recalibrated without leaving time to catch up culturally.[6] A few women were the product of cross-class marriages, in which their parents had disparate class backgrounds or occupational statuses;[7] others had parents who experienced mobility and were carrying a cultural imprint of their class roots despite their current economic status.[8] These situations created variability in the class culture to which women were exposed and made it harder to predict the social environment in which they would be most comfortable, even the type of financial support they would receive.

As Karen's case suggests, when class of origin was not clear-cut, we took into account the full range of class resources available to women in making our determination of their class location. For this reason we intentionally left some flexibility in our class categorization schema. For instance, in Table 1.2, parental education alone does not easily distinguish those from upper-, upper-middle- and middle-class backgrounds. In fact, the table is intended to illustrate the typical features of individuals in each cell—not to establish exclusive criteria for all women from a given class background. This approach is not as black and white as those used by other researchers. However, we see it as preferable to making consequential differences in class-based resources invisible.

We also decided to discuss class in two different ways. At times there were commonalities in the experiences of working-class, lower-middle-class, and middle-class women on the one hand versus upper-middle-class and upper-class women on the other. In these cases, we aggregated, referring to less privileged and more privileged students. However, fine-grained distinctions were necessary when heterogeneity in class resources could explain differences within these two groups. For instance, lower-middle-class strivers were far more likely to stay at MU than those from working-class backgrounds, and many upper-middle-class partiers were ill-fated wannabes rather than socialites.

A Note on the Upper Class

Most scholarship on the upper class pegs only 0.5% to 1% of the American population in this group, and the 2010 Current Population Survey identified 3.9% of families as having incomes over $200,000.[9] Yet the children of the affluent are overrepresented at four-year universities and, at MU, in the residence hall we studied. We are confident in classifying 19% of our sample as upper class, given that all of their fathers held positions that are among the highest status and most lucrative in the United States (for example, chief executive officer, chief financial officer). These women had access to infinite sums of money and extensive social networks. They grew up in wealthy suburbs of major cities and traveled internationally. All possessed the cultural capital that comes from intimate familiarity with such locales. That a heavy concentration of women like these landed on our floor suggests the extent to which schools like MU successfully cater to a segment of the upper class.

Those that we have talked with about our study find the strong presence of upper class women at MU surprising. Most seem to implicitly assume that the children of the wealthy attend only elite private colleges. And, indeed, upper class young people are overrepresented at those schools. But the upper class does not place all of their offspring in the most elite colleges. Assuming that they do obscures variation in talent and drive within the upper class and downplays upper class anti-intellectualism.[10] As Hannah shows, not all children of the rich are academically oriented. Some simply want to have fun. In an earlier era, less academic upper-class women might have attended finishing schools or not attended college at all. Today the expectation that all privileged young adults attend college means that this is no longer an option. Large state universities with elaborate, expensive, and exclusionary Greek systems provide a contemporary alternative for the socially oriented offspring of the economic elite.

Data Collection, Analysis, and Writing

Below we provide greater detail on the methods used in data collection and analysis and describe the collaborative nature of this project.

Access

Getting permission to observe in a university residence hall is not easy. In this case, the project was made possible by the endorsement of a highly placed administrator in Residence Life. This support was crucial in convincing other university leaders that the project should be allowed. We also had to obtain approval from the Institutional Review Board (IRB), which is designed to protect human subjects. The IRB, for instance, required that we fully disclose our faculty–instructor statuses to the students. The women knew we were researchers from the moment they moved onto the hall, as the IRB required us to post flyers explaining our presence on the floor. We even made an announcement at the first floor meeting.

The IRB stepped outside of its usual bounds in asking that the university's legal counsel review the study—presumably to ensure that the university was protected. This process added months onto IRB review and resulted in the creation of a 10,000-word document explaining our roles in the site and how we would respond to any eventuality. We were not permitted to observe any illegal or dangerous activity.

The IRB did not ask us to conceal the name of the university. We ultimately chose to use a pseudonym because this book is not specifically about MU and should not be read as such. We are confident that our women's stories would have been similar at other residential four-year institutions with a robust party pathway. MU is implicated but only as a part of the higher education sector that is increasingly mismatched with the needs of the student population.

Ethnographic Data Collection

The research team, including the authors, four graduate students (Sibyl Kleiner, Evelyn Perry, Brian Sweeney, and Amanda Tanner), and three undergraduates (Katie Watkins, Teresa Cummings, and Aimee Lipkis), spent a year observing and interacting with the women on the floor. The team occupied a regular room on the floor and observed on evenings and weekends throughout the academic year but did not live there full-time. During the first semester, at least one member of the research team was there three to four weekdays and evenings and one to two weekend afternoons and evenings per week. Second semester, Laura, who had developed the best rapport with the women, observed two weekday evenings and one weekend evening weekly.

Prior to field entry, the research team spent time learning the craft of field note writing. The style used by the team was heavily influenced by Bill Corsaro's ethnographic expertise, as Laura brought in insights from his graduate-level class.[1] We also consulted Robert Emerson, Rachel Fretz, and Linda Shaw's *Writing Ethnographic Fieldnotes*.[2] Over the year, we developed a note archive of around 2,000 pages of single-spaced electronic text.

Notes were divided into four subtypes. In basic field notes, we recorded details of our interactions and observations during a session. Personal notes about how researchers felt in the field proved priceless when reconstructing our emotional reactions to the space and the women. Methodological notes provided running commentary on the mechanics of the ethnography, including interactional techniques, good times to observe, and even our own self-presentation. The number and depth of theoretical notes increased with time in the field, as they often identified themes or patterns across multiple observations. Team members read the previous notes prior to their session and these became a vital and ever-evolving source of communication.

Team ethnography of this sort has some downsides. We managed to mitigate the sheer logistical nightmare with shared field notes and group meetings. Other pitfalls—for example, falling back on each other for company when in the field—took constant vigilance to avoid. We also learned that it was easy to overwhelm the floor with researchers and began to structure our interactions more carefully.

The benefits, however, were far more numerous. Our team was intentionally diverse, with members from a range of class backgrounds, a variety of personal styles, of different ages, and from different regions of the country. How women responded to different members of the research team told us a great deal about how they made sense of the world and how they assigned value and status. For example, several socialites granted Aimee—an undergraduate, out-of-state sorority member—considerable deference, while snubbing Elizabeth outright. Sudhir Venkatesh's article " 'Doin' the Hustle': Constructing the Ethnographer in the American Ghetto" helped us think through what our very different experiences revealed about the field site.[3]

In order to break down barriers with the women, especially those who were high status, we learned to associate with them on their terms. Closing doors, using the cell phone, and surfing on the computer signaled intent to shut others out. Watching TV, preparing for a party, and playing a popular interactive video game—*Dance, Dance, Revolution*—were group activities in which we were often welcome, as was eating (doing so alone was the kiss of death socially). Women were also eager to teach researchers how to engage in their favorite activities. For instance, in a hands-on lesson, Laura learned to "stick out my ass more and arch my back" in order to dance provocatively. These were the moments in which we truly felt like part of the social ecology of the floor.

Longitudinal Interviews

There are few in-depth longitudinal studies of the movement of students through the university. The few that exist have generally focused on students at elite schools, on minority students, or exclusively on academic concerns.[4] Two older studies track women through the university: the Bennington College Study, which was conducted in the late 1930s, and Dorothy Holland's and Margaret Eisenhart's research, conducted in the 1980s and reported on in *Educated in Romance: Women, Achievement and College Culture*.[5] Initially, the longitudinal design of our study was driven by pure curiosity. Once we started observing in the residence hall, we became interested in the lives of the women and wanted to know what was going to happen next. Over time we realized that longitudinal research of an in-depth qualitative nature has particular strengths.

First, as we developed a deeper understanding of student life, we grew more sophisticated in our questioning. By tracking over time, we were also able to see the long-term consequences of early events in college. A bad roommate, a lingering relationship, a failed class—events like these often set women on different trajectories than they might have otherwise followed and revealed to us the deep connections between the social, sexual, and academic aspects of students' lives. At the same time, the women changed a great deal during this period. They often tried on new selves, attempted different courses of action, and, in time, reinterpreted past events. At times we were forced to entirely reassess early analyses, leading us to be skeptical of arguments based on a single snapshot of students' college experiences.

We were committed to including everyone on the floor in our research, insofar as it was possible to enlist participation. Many interview and survey studies introduce bias by requiring people to actively volunteer for participation. This may select for those who are more identified with the institution. Starting with the ethnography enabled us to more persuasively solicit interviews and to schedule them to mesh with demands of students' lives. By working hard to include everyone—and learning a lot about the few who did not elect to be interviewed—we ended up with voices and experiences not often represented in research on college students.

We conducted interviews with forty-one of the fifty-three women on the residence hall floor during their first year, thirty-seven women the second year, thirty-six the third year, forty-one the fourth year, and forty-six the final year. A total of forty-eight women were interviewed, along with the first-year RA, resulting in 202 interviews. Of these forty-eight, two were not included in the pathways analyses in Chapters 5–8. These women had joined their roommates for an interview their first year, said little during that interview, and opted out every year after. As noted elsewhere, one additional woman, on whom we had rich ethnographic data, was included where possible. Table A.2 details the interviews collected for all years. The interviews were digitally recorded and fully transcribed.

Laura collected around 85% of the interviews. The high response rate was due to her high and consistent level of contact with the floor residents and the ties she formed with many of them over the course of their first year. Yearly interviews with Laura eventually became a ritual of sorts, and the women would mentally "save up" stories and information to convey at the next session. Some women even told us that they could not imagine college without having been part of our study.

Most interviews were collected in participants' residences while they were in college. All first interviews were face to face. Though most women interviewed alone, six roommate duos elected to be interviewed together the first year.[6] When women left the institution early, we continued to follow them. After the first wave of graduations, Laura flew around the country to interview many of them in their new cities (and sometimes hometowns). Some interviews during the final year were collected over the phone when travel was untenable. Interviewing by phone did not interfere with rapport as the relationships were already well established. A small grant from the Spencer Foundation enabled the longitudinal data collection by making it possible to travel for interviews, offer generous incentives, and pay for interview transcription.

We drafted detailed field notes on all interviews immediately after their completion. In these notes we described the woman's physical appearance, her place of residence, and our responses to the interviewee. Through these notes we began developing concepts and hypotheses. These summaries proved to be invaluable as we moved into data analysis. For example, as new researchers joined the project, they were able to rapidly become accustomed with the data by reading the interview notes in advance of diving into the transcripts.

The interviews ranged from forty-five minutes to two and a half hours and covered relationships with parents and family, parental financial assistance, employment, academic engagement and performance, partying, relationships, sexuality, and friendships. Although we followed a general interview schedule each year (available from the authors on request), the flow of a typical interview was highly informal. We had, after all, shared their first year of college with them, were acquainted with many of the same people, and knew a great deal about their lives.

Handling Homogeneity

Explaining variation is at the heart of the sociological enterprise. Thus, the homogeneity of our floor—particularly with respect to race and gender—was initially disappointing. We were concerned that it would limit our analysis, and of course it did. This project would have inevitably moved in a different direction had we been able to directly compare the experiences of white women with women of color, for example.

However, the homogeneity of the floor created a natural experiment of sorts by "controlling" for many of the likely sources of variation in college experiences and outcomes. Not only were the women demographically similar, but they started college in the same living situation, at the same time, attending the same institution. They differed on one major dimension—class background, which was associated with religion, state residency, and family structure. The homogeneity of our sample allowed us to train our gaze primarily on social class. Larger data sets may offer more cases, but they also tend to introduce heterogeneity (especially unobserved differences) that obscure patterns. When it comes to making causal inferences with observed data, data like ours is, in some ways, a gold standard.[7]

In addition, we quickly realized the potential to also study gender and race even with a sample of white women. The work of Amy Wilkins and Julie Bettie provided examples of how to consider race, class, and gender within a relatively homogenous sample.[8] Along with Leslie McCall, they have been particularly attuned to thinking about variation within gender. Until more recently, this type of approach was a trademark of masculinity scholars.[9] Most notably, Raewyn Connell's foundational concept of masculinities—in the plural—recognizes that power relations among men shape the performance of gender.[10] We build on these insights and focus primarily on the way that social class intersects with gender to create hierarchies among women; however, we also attend to the ways that race shaped the experience of all the women on the floor, for instance, interrogating the meaning of "blonde" in the sorority recruitment process.

Collaborative Analysis

Just as data collection was a team effort involving Elizabeth, Laura, and the rest of the research team, data analysis was also a collaborative process involving both the original researchers and individuals brought on board after data collection was complete. The data analysis for this project occurred over many years. Analysis started the moment we had our first interaction on the dorm floor, intensified through the various papers we drafted, and continued up through and beyond putting the final touches on this book.

In the early stages, Elizabeth, Laura, and the original research team used ATLAS.ti to organize and process the transcripts and notes. Early analysis focused on the specific topics that generated the first papers from the project. For example, the sexual assault paper coauthored with Brian Sweeney analyzed first-year interviews and the ethnographic field notes.[11] Laura's paper "Trading on Heterosexuality" developed from watching the show *The O.C.* with the women and relied on first-year interviews.[12] "Gendered Sexuality in Young Adulthood" was the first to use the longitudinal data (from years 1 through 4), and advanced arguments that would prove central to the book.[13] In general, the longitudinal character of the study allowed us to build and refine our theories in continual dialogue with the data. Interview schedules for each wave were revised in light of new findings and lines of inquiry.

At the University of Michigan, Elizabeth recruited five students to participate in the ongoing process of data analysis. Rachel Lipson, Jessica Baer, and Shari Brown were undergraduates still immersed in "college life." Two graduate students, Elizabeth Marie Armstrong (EMA) and J. Lotus Seeley, also collaborated with Elizabeth on the analysis of data. They took the lead on the analysis for Chapter 7 as they read all the relevant transcripts, coded the material in NVivo, drafted memos, met with Elizabeth frequently, and drafted text that was incorporated into the chapter.

These individuals brought new perspectives to bear on the data. Their involvement also served as a means to ascertain intercoder reliability. For instance, we arrived at the categorization of women for Chapter 7 only through many, many meetings, spreadsheets, discussions, drafts, and debates. When the new analyses corroborated previously developed theories, intercoder reliability was deemed high. Where the new analyses conflicted with the earlier ones, new iterations of reading and coding took place. This recursive process continued until Elizabeth, Laura, EMA, and Lotus reached consensus.

Presentation of Data

Given the multitude of potential data sources, we indicate the source of each piece in the text. We refer to data from field notes in parentheses after the quotation with "Field Notes" followed by the date of the note. We refer to interview quotations by indicating the pseudonym of the woman and the year of the interview. All arguments are based on the analysis of all interviews discussed in that chapter. To improve the flow of the book, we often profile just a few women at a time. However, the themes and arguments are based on analysis of all cases.

APPENDIX **D**

Ethical Considerations

This appendix focuses on ethical issues particular to a longitudinal ethnographic study located in a site where participants know each other.

Relationships and Reactivity

Qualitative researchers take different stances on the appropriate role of researchers in field sites. On the one hand, Michael Burawoy endorses full participation in the site. He generally takes a position as a worker in the places of employment he studies.[1] In contrast, Annette Lareau studiously avoids participating in the family lives of those she observes in order to minimize the potential for passing judgment.[2] We took a middle position. The Institutional Review Board required us to stay "in role" as faculty-instructors and thus potential mentors to these young women.

It felt natural to interact with them in such a capacity. Particularly in the first year of the study, we were struck by how starved the women were for interactions with older individuals.[3] Although most were in constant contact with their parents, they also looked for guidance from those with more life experience who would not judge them or sanction their behaviors. Laura often positioned herself as an older sister to the young women; Elizabeth found herself serving as a mentor or advisor to the smaller group of women with whom she formed ties.

Over the course of the study, we offered advice on which sociology courses to take and the graduate school application process, even writing recommendation letters. Laura assisted at least one woman with her financial aid forms, and Elizabeth attended a campus event with Alana. More intimately, Laura offered a private place for a woman to take a pregnancy test—away from the tight confines of her sorority house—and advised others about potential sexually transmitted infections. We helped Megan extricate herself from a violent marriage and supported Brianna's move out of our residence hall to one more supportive of her lesbian identity. At times, we suggested that women seek psychological counseling and provided the information needed to access these services.

Our relationships with the women likely had some influence on their trajectories. Overall, though, we were struck by how much intervention it takes to redirect someone's fate. For example, Elizabeth tried to assist Valerie in the graduate school application process, but no amount of advice could overcome the constraints of a degree from MU and minimal research experience. Similarly, Laura was often terribly worried about Carrie—the woman who went hungry sometimes. Laura tried to help Carrie navigate her financial aid situation but could not compensate for her parents' uneven funding and unwillingness to grant their daughter financial independence. Nor could Laura keep Brianna from spiraling out of control once she entered the party scene. We generally could not override the powerful influences of funds, family, peer culture, and the organizational structure of the university.

Self-Recognition and Confidentiality

From the moment we set foot on the floor, we have been deeply concerned about protecting both the feelings and the identities of our research subjects. In the articles we have written, this has been a simple matter: we chose to chop up women's narratives into such small chunks, focused on such specific issues, that identification of a data source—even by the women themselves—was unlikely. This book is a different matter, as it follows specific women all the way through college and beyond.

In the process of writing, we found ourselves acutely aware of an abiding dilemma in qualitative research. As Karen Kaiser described in a recent article on ethical issues: "Qualitative researchers face a conflict between conveying detailed, accurate accounts of the social world and protecting the identities of the individuals who participated in their research."[4] Researchers vary in how they deal with this dilemma. We strongly believe that details matter and that changing them, even in service of protecting the identities of participants, can easily "alter or destroy the original meaning of the data."[5] Thus, we only made changes that obscured details, such as the use of pseudonyms, referring to a region and not a woman's actual hometown, and leaving out particularly unique information. We did not change details.

It is likely that the women who read the book will recognize themselves, especially those we have profiled. Some may not like what they see. As Annette Lareau has described, this is often the cost of telling a full, rich story with ethnographic data.[6] Indeed, if we protected every research participant from representations that might be unflattering, our analysis of the social world would be thin. Particularly when analyzing elite social groups and the workings of power, it is critical to reveal, as faithfully as possible, how social life unfolds.

At the same time, we tried to weigh the inclusion of data that might cause discomfort against its contribution to arguments about general social processes, especially the reproduction of social inequality. If we felt the piece of information was gratuitous, if a woman specifically asked for it to be excluded, or if we had reason to believe that she was sensitive about a particular point, we did not include it. Laura also avoided using information extended to her as a friend, not as a researcher. For instance, she frequently went out to dinner with the Hannah/Blair group, with whom she had the closest ties. What transpired in her interactions with this group was not treated as data.

We found ourselves referring to the methodological reflections of a number of ethnographers as we mulled about these ethical issues. Particularly helpful to us was Shamus Khan's suggestion that qualitative researchers treat "informed consent . . . [as] a process, not a onetime event."[7] We did this both formally and informally. We both engaged in a formal process of obtaining consent before each interview and engaged in ongoing discussion with participants about the evolution of the book project. We tried to make sure they fully understood how the data was being used.

We thought about allowing participants to read the manuscript and respond to how we portrayed them. We ultimately decided against this for a number of reasons. We realized that we may not have been willing to make the changes they requested. We thought it likely that only some women would have been willing to read the text, leading some portrayals to be cleaned up while others were not. It also seemed somewhat self-serving to thrust the book on those who might not want or need to see how they are portrayed. Here we were influenced by the pain experienced by some of Annette Lareau's study participants when she provided them with a copy of *Unequal Childhoods: Class, Race and Family Life*.[8] Given Laura's now distant but continual contact with these women, we adopted a policy of providing the text when women asked. We continue to answer questions and provide clarifications on an as needed basis.

Rich qualitative research, particularly ethnographic research, also introduces the risk of violating internal confidentiality, where participants recognize others in the research.[9] Here, too, we balance contributions to knowledge against the possibility that the women may learn private things about each other that they did not know. We also took into consideration how women would react to learning what others thought or to knowing that others might discover something about them.

Many of our decisions on ethical issues took into account the transitional nature of the community in study. The floor as a social world dissolved the moment the women moved out at the end of the first year. Although they had once cared about what others on the floor thought, most remain in close contact with only a few floormates. After college, most women reflected back on the time period as a finite, now-past period of their lives. Events that were mortifying at the time have since faded in intensity. With distance, many have, like Whitney, gained the ability to be reflexive about their own behaviors. Privileged women, in particular, also had access to a life stage discourse—of growing up and finding themselves during college—that helped to explain away less than admirable behaviors. Our decisions may have been very different had we been studying families, more permanent residential communities, or adults—populations and settings where the relationships are more stable.[10]

Notes

Preface

1. We refer to the university that we studied by the pseudonym Midwest University (MU) and to the town as Fairview.
2. See the Appendixes for more details on the methods. Graduate student members of the team included Sibyl Kleiner, Evelyn Perry, Brian Sweeney, and Amanda Tanner. Undergraduate members included Teresa Cummings, Aimee Lipkis, and Katie Watkins.
3. This comes in contrast to "studying down," or investigating a more vulnerable population—what we initially thought we were doing given that we were older and had more status within the university. See Morrill (1995, appendix A).
4. Hamilton and Armstrong (2009).

Introduction

1. See Table A.1 of Appendix A for a list of study participants by pseudonym.
2. We refer to participants as women, although they called each other "girls." Fifty-one of the women were freshmen. Two were sophomores. A resident assistant and a senior who graduated at the end of the first semester also lived on the floor.
3. One woman on the floor was of Latina heritage but identified as white. Another was born outside of the United States. Two identified as lesbian.
4. See Appendix C for details on the annotation of data sources. Y1, Y2, and so forth denote the year of the study an interview was conducted. Quotes from field notes are indicated with the date of the observation.
5. Hacker and Dreifus (2010).
6. Goldin and Katz (2008); Hout (2012).
7. For Bureau of Labor Statistics data on income and employment, see http://www.bls.gov/emp/ep_chart_001.htm; Hout (2012).

8. Blau and Duncan (1967); Coleman (1988); Jencks, Smith, Acland, Bane, Cohen, Gintis, Heyns, and Michelson (1972); Sewell and Hauser (1976); Lucas (2001); Cabrea, Burkum, and La Nasa (2003); Goldrick-Rab (2006); Roksa, Grodsky, Arum, and Gamoran (2007).

9. Karen (1991, 2002); Mullen, Goyette, and Soares (2003); Buchman and DiPrete (2006); Gerber and Cheung (2008); Brand and Xie (2010); Carnevale and Strohl (2010); Carneiro, Heckman, and Vytlacil (2011).

10. Bills (2003); Gerber and Cheung (2008).

11. Gerber and Cheung (2008).

12. A few works that bridge these literatures include Holland and Eisenhart (1990); Mullen (2010); Arum and Roksa (2011); Stuber (2011). James Coleman's *The Adolescent Society: The Social Life of the Teenager and Its Impact on Education* (1961), though about high school, is an early and influential example of research that links adolescent peer culture with stratification processes.

13. Willis (1977); Lamont (1992, 2000); MacLeod (1995); McDonough (1997); Schwalbe, Godwin, Holden, Schrock, Thompson, and Wolkomir (2000); Lareau (2003); Young (2004); Stuber (2006, 2009); Lacy (2007); Harding (2010); Rivera (2011); Streib (2011).

14. Burawoy (2009).

15. For a review, see Stevens, Armstrong, and Arum (2008). Also see Moffat (1989), Holland and Eisenhart (1990); Aries and Seider (2005); Nathan (2005); Goodwin (2006); Rosenbaum, Deil-Amen, and Person (2006); Aries (2008); Grigsby (2009); Mullen (2010); Stuber (2011); Binder and Wood (2012). Recent research on how members of minority groups move through college also contributes to this body of research. See Massey, Charles, Lundy, and Fischer (2003); Torres and Charles (2004); Massey and Fischer (2006); Charles, Fischer, Mooney, and Massey (2009). Interest in the experiental core of college life represents a revival of early sociological interest in college cultures; see Waller (1937); Scott (1965); Clark and Trow (1966); Becker, Geer, and Hughes (1968); Horowitz (1987).

16. Arum and Roksa (2011).

17. Skrentny (1996); Karabel (2005); Stevens (2007) Lamont (2009); Davies and Mehta (2012); Binder and Wood (2012); Gross (2013). We are influenced by scholarship in the field of higher education; see Boyer and Carnegie Foundation for the Advancement of Teaching (1987); Tinto (1987); Tierney (1992); Astin (1993); Kuh (1993); Matthews (1997); Hurtado and Carter (1997); Bok, Bowen, and Shulman (1998); Light (2001); Shulman and Bowen (2001); Bowen, Kurzweil, Tobin, and Pichler (2005); Pascarella and Terenzini (2005); Bok (2006). We also pull from research on the hidden curriculum in education— see Bowles and Gintis (1976) and Giroux and Purpel (1983); and institutional research on loose coupling—see Weick (1976) and Meyer and Rowan (1977).

18. Zweigenhaft (1993); Massey, Charles, Lundy, and Fischer (2003); Zweigenhaft and Domhoff (2003); Douthat (2005); Karabel (2005); Soares (2007); Stevens (2007); Aries (2008); Espenshade and Radford (2009).

19. But see Brint and Karabel (1989); Rosenbaum (2001); Deil-Amen (2011).
20. Brint (2012).
21. National Center for Education Statistics (2012).
22. Horowitz (1987); Brint (2012).
23. Despite the salience of these institutions, we know comparatively little about how students experience them. Exceptions include Moffatt (1989); Mullen (2010); and Stuber (2011).
24. Kerr (2001); Brint (2002, 239). Clark and Trow similarly describe the "state university campus" as a place "that appears as many things to many men" (1966, 39).
25. In her study of high school valedictorians, Radford (2013) shows that low- and middle-socioeconomic status (SES) valedictorians were about twice as likely as their similarly high-achieving, high-SES counterparts to enroll in four-year public colleges not considered "most selective." Also see Turley (2009).
26. In addition to Armstrong and Hamilton, the research team included Sibyl Kleiner, Evelyn Perry, Brian Sweeney, Amanda Tanner, Teresa Cummings, Aimee Lipkis, and Katie Watkins.
27. See Table A.2 for interviews collected by year. The table also indicates which women are included in which parts of the analyses. We only included women in the pathway analyses for whom we had adequate data. All were interviewed at least once, with one exception: we also chose to include one working class woman who was never interviewed because of the depth of ethnographic data on her situation and the theoretical importance of her story.
28. We are influenced by the reflexive approaches of Michael Burawoy and other ethnographers. Following this approach, we extend out in order to place our field site in context. Particularity—of the historical moment, type of school, and type of residence hall—matters; see Burawoy (2009).
29. Another example is *Educated in Romance: Women, Achievement and College Culture*, by Dorothy C. Holland and Margaret A. Eisenhart (1990). As the book is based on data collected in the early 1980s, it is time for an update.
30. We consulted unigo.com and collegeconfidential.com.
31. The term is not specific to Midwest University. See the Huffington Post's 2011 list of the "10 Biggest Party Dorms" in the nation, http://www.huffingtonpost .com/2011/09/26/10-biggest-party-dorms-do_n_980876.html.
32. Williams (2010).
33. Bae, Choy, Geddes, Sable, and Snyder (2000); Buchmann and DiPrete (2006); Sax and Harper (2007); Conger and Long (2010).
34. Powell and Steelman (1995).
35. Jacobs (1996); Armstrong, Hamilton, and Sweeney (2006); England and Li (2006); Charles and Bradley (2009).
36. Individuals are rarely self-aware as they pursue class-based agendas. At times, though, the largely implicit agendas associated with class projects become explicit (e.g., when a young woman rejects a potential boyfriend on

the grounds that he is not sufficiently "ambitious") or actively collective (e.g., when affluent students coordinate sorority rush in a way that effectively eliminates less affluent students from joining).

37. On the historical relationship between higher education and the American upper class, see Baltzell (1958); Clark and Trow (1966); Story (1980); Hall (1982); Horowitz (1987); Karabel (2005). Over the past fifty years, a number of scholars have developed typologies of college students. Early analysts, like Clark and Trow (1966) and Horowitz (1987), were attuned to the ways in which student orientations are shaped by the aggregation of individual class experiences and intersect with the organizational characteristics of the school.

38. Clark and Trow (1966) described wealthy students seeking social and extracurricular experiences as "collegiate" students. They indicated that this type of student should decline over time as universities become large, bureaucratic, student-processing machines. However, they failed to predict the extent to which tuition would provide a valuable cash stream on which universities would depend. More recently, Mary Grigsby (2009) documented the presence of collegiate students on today's college campuses.

39. Horowitz (1987); Karabel (2005).

40. Karabel (2005, 20). Original source: Bragdon (1967, 272).

41. Collins (1979) refers to the increasing expectations for higher levels of educational certification as "credential inflation."

42. Scholars of masculinity refer to this as "hegemonic masculinity." See Connell (1995) and Kimmel (2008). For more on privileged forms of femininity, see McCall (1992); Bettie (2003); Hamilton (2007). On the role of education in constituting selves, see Meyer and Rowan (1977); Tobin, Wu, and Davidson (1989); Stevens (2007); Gaztambide-Fernández (2009); Khan (2011). On culture and the constitution of selves more generally, see Bourdieu (1984); Swidler (1986, 2001); Lamont (1992).

43. Richard Arum, Josipa Roksa, and Michelle Budig (2008) demonstrate that, at least in the past, a sizable proportion of college graduates married or cohabitated with someone who attended a college with identical institutional characteristics.

44. Trillin (1994).

45. Attewell and Lavin (2007) show that these investments improve not only the lives of the generation who make them but those of their children as well.

46. All typologies of college students refer to this group. Clark and Trow (1966) called them "vocational" on the basis of their pragmatic focus on obtaining a job right out of college. Horowitz (1987) labeled them as "outsiders" given their distant relationship to "college life." Grigsby's (2009) "credentialists," whose primary interest is in obtaining a diploma, fit here, too.

47. Horowitz (1987); Karabel (2005).

48. See López (2002) for more on less privileged women's optimism that education—specifically in gendered fields—will provide mobility.
49. England (2010).
50. See Regnerus (2007) for more on the potential economic benefits of early marriage.
51. Musick, Brand, and Davis (2012) argue that less privileged students face a "marriage market mismatch" in which college attendance actually reduces their chances of marrying. College attending women from working- and lower-middle-class backgrounds, in particular, may have a difficult time finding similarly educated mates, as their male counterparts are less likely to follow them to college (Lewin 2006).
52. Musick, Brand, and Davis (2012).
53. Cookson and Persell (1985); Brooks (2001); Gaztambide-Fernández (2009); Atlas (2011); Khan (2011).
54. Atlas (2011). This orientation is not well described in existing typologies of college students because of its relative historical novelty. It is absent from Clark and Trow's (1966) four-part typology. In Horowitz (1987), these students make an appearance as "new outsiders," but her discussion lacks the insight with which she describes the other groups. Both Moffatt (1989) and Grigsby (2009), who examine college life in the 1980s and the early twenty-first century, respectively, describe the emergence of students focused on professional career development.
55. Leonhardt (2005).
56. Zelizer (1985); Hays (1996); Duncan and Murnane (2011).
57. Schneider and Stevenson (1999).
58. Kennedy (2009).
59. Meek, Goedegebuure, Kivinen, and Rinne (1996); Charles and Bradley (2002).
60. Mclcar (2002); Rojas (2007); Charles and Bradley (2009).
61. Arnett (2004); Rosenfeld (2007); Settersten and Ray (2010).
62. This is a difficult task given the legal status of college students. The passage of the Family Educational Rights and Privacy Act in 1974 prevents universities from conveying information about students' grades, misconduct, or health issues to parents.
63. Bae et al. (2000); Buchmann and DiPrete (2006); Sax and Harper (2007); Bureau of Labor Statistics (2010); Conger and Long (2010).
64. Wilkie (1991).
65. In 1970, the median age of marriage for women was 20.8; by 2005, it had increased to 25.3. Women's median age at first childbirth also increased, from 22.1 in 1970 to 24.6 in 2000.
66. Levey (2012).
67. For an interview with Donna Lisker, director of the Women's Center at Duke University, see Duke's Women's Initiative Web site at http://web.duke.edu /womens_initiative/undergrad.htm.
68. Hamilton and Armstrong (2009). See Cahn and Carbone (2010).

69. We are indebted here to the insights of K–12 educational ethnographers who have demonstrated that academic tracking in middle and high school tends to correspond closely with social cliques and popularity. For examples, see Coleman (1961); Eckert (1989); Eder, Evans, and Parker (1995); Bettie (2003); Pascoe (2007).

70. A number of higher education scholars have observed this dynamic, referring to it as a "mutual nonaggression pact," "disengagement compact," "tacit agreement," or a "truce" (Sperber 2000; Kuh 2003; Arum and Roksa 2011).

71. Kahlenberg (2010a).

72. Sperber (2000).

73. The share of funds colleges spend on recreation relative to instruction has been rising over the last decade (Dillon 2010). A recent report by economists Philip Babcock and Mindy Marks (2010) finds that since 1961, there has been a dramatic and consistent decline of student study hours.

74. Turk (2004); DeSantis (2007); McGrath (2008).

75. See Hamilton and Armstrong (2009) and England, Shafer, and Fogarty (2007) for more on hooking up. Previously, as Willard Waller suggested in his classic 1937 article "The Mating and Dating Complex," universities were the site for a competitive system of dating.

76. Reiss (1965); Scott (1965); Kalmijn (1991); Mare (1991). Research in this area died out in the mid-1970s, likely because the emergence of feminism made the investigation of the marital consequences of college unfashionable. Also, as the age of marriage increased, researchers assumed a decline in the likelihood of individuals meeting marriage partners in college. More recently, research has started to return to class sorting in the marital patterns of the college educated (see Musick et al. 2012).

77. Brint (2002, 232).

78. Charles et al. (2009) rank college classes according to the ease of obtaining a high GPA. Arum and Roksa (2011) compare Collegiate Learning Assessment (CLA) scores across majors. The CLA is a test designed to assess general skills—like critical thinking, analytical reasoning, and problem solving—that universities claim to build.

79. McPherson and Schapiro (1998); Paulsen and St. John (2002).

80. Alon and Tienda (2007); Carnevale and Strohl (2010).

81. Niu and Tienda (2010).

82. Attewell, Lavin, Thurston, and Levey (2006); Bahr (2008); Strayhorn (2011).

83. Stuber (2011).

84. Engle and Tinto (2008).

85. Tinto (1987).

86. Stevens (2007). In her discussion of cultural capital, Annette Lareau (2003) similarly argues that treating economic or cultural advantage as distinct from "merit" does not make sense.

87. After controlling for family background, SAT scores account for about 3% of variation in students' grades (Rothstein 2004).

88. Buchmann, Condron, and Roscigno (2010). See also Lemann (1999).

89. Coburn (2006, 11) argues, "The challenge for us in higher education is not whether to involve parents. The challenge is to figure out how to enlist these already involved parents in our mutual goal of helping students become engaged learners, competent and creative problem solvers, and responsible and effective citizens—in essence, helping students grow up." Coburn also mentions a new professional organization that has formed—Administrators Promoting Parental Involvement.

90. Winston (1999, 17).

91. For recent discussions of the ways in which the search for revenue is shaping American universities, see Slaughter and Leslie (1997) and Tuchman (2009).

92. Douglass (2007, 7, 8).

93. Winston (1999, 16), citing Estelle (1990). See also Espeland and Sauder (2007); Stevens (2007).

94. Karabel (2005); Stevens (2007).

95. Stevens (2007, 203).

96. Stevens (2007).

97. Bowen, Kurzwell and Tobin (2005); Kerr (2001).

98. On the concept of "typical student," see Stevens (2007).

99. The role of the university in crystallizing regional economic and political elites has largely been overlooked, as most research and popular discussion about privilege, exclusion, and the reproduction of class advantage in American higher education has focused on elite private schools—particularly Harvard, Yale, and Princeton.

100. W. Hamilton (2006).

101. Bound, Hershbein, and Long (2009).

102. Hallinan (1994); Gamoran (2010).

103. For exceptions, see England and Li (2006); Charles and Bradley (2009); Chambliss and Takacs (forthcoming).

104. Moffatt (1989); Arum et al. (2008); Grigsby (2009); Brint (personal correspondence, 2012).

105. We have reduced the complexity of women's movement through college. Many students had forays onto the party pathway, which had consequences for how successful they were on their primary pathway.

106. We borrow the term "wannabe" from Peter Adler and Patricia Adler (1998). They use it to refer to the strata of preadolescents just outside the top cliques who are included enough to motivate continual efforts at belonging but excluded enough to mark them as outsiders.

107. Richard D. Kahlenberg (2010b) also refers to low-income college students as "strivers."

1. The Women

1. Sax, Hurtado, Lindholm, Astin, Korn, and Mahoney (2005).

2. National Center for Education Statistics (2012). The Education Longitudinal Study of 2002 has been tracking the postsecondary experience of the

2003–2004 high school graduating class. The most recent data collection was in 2006.

3. National Center for Education Statistics (2012).
4. Buchmann (2009).
5. Buchmann and DiPrete (2006).
6. Lewin (2006).
7. Williams (2010).
8. Kingsbury (2007).
9. Jencks and Phillips (1998); Bennett and Xie (2003).
10. National Center for Education Statistics (2012).
11. Stevens (2007).
12. Lewin (2011a).
13. National Center for Education Statistics (2012).
14. Ibid. See Radford (2013) for more on how social class shapes where academically talented students land.
15. Marklein (2006).
16. See Steinberg (2011); Lewin (2011b).
17. In Appendix B we discuss the challenges of measuring class and defining the American upper class.
18. We report here on the forty-seven of the fifty-three women on the floor on whom we have complete data. We have class background data on the other six women. Inclusion of these women changes the class distribution of the women only slightly. See Appendix A for class categorization of all the women, including those not included in the core data set.
19. The discussion of Amy includes data from field notes collected by several researchers across several days: 9/6/2004, 9/9/2004, 9/14/2004, and 9/22/2004.
20. Stuber (2011).
21. On college as an assumption among privileged youth, see Grodsky and Riegle-Crumb (2010).
22. We include Chelsea here although she is classified as middle class. We struggled to classify her class position. We did not classify her as upper-middle class because of a divorce, which reduced family resources.
23. On the principle of homophily, see McPherson, Smith-Lovin, and Cook (2001).
24. Carr and Kefalas (2009).
25. Brian Sweeney was a graduate student and a member of the research team who conducted a few year one interviews.

2. The Party Pathway

1. Sperber (2000).
2. This practice may have changed. We suggested to the university administration that this practice had the potential to contribute to sexual assault by restricting women's freedom to return home safely.

3. Ray and Rosow (2009).

4. See Armstrong, Hamilton, and Sweeney (2006).

5. The source of this quote is not provided in order to avoid identifying the individual or the institution.

6. When official rush events begin has varied over the years. During our ethnography, women's rush began relatively early—in October.

7. This may be one reason why the tradition of MU Talent was recently ended after seventy-eight years.

8. Big Man on Campus is only one Greek philanthropic social event. Over time the more established of these events get folded into the social calendar at MU.

9. Coser (1967); Kanter (1972).

10. Demands varied depending on the ranking of the house. Higher-ranked houses could demand more of their members and expect compliance. The lowest ranked houses, which sometimes struggled to recruit and retain members, typically asked less.

11. Greek philanthropic events were often also social occasions. For example, one such event was a dance marathon that raised money for charity.

12. Pascarella and National Center on Postsecondary Teaching, Learning, and Assessment (1992); Kuh, Gonyea, and Palmer (2001); Clemons, McKelfresh, and Banning (2005).

13. Upper-division students quickly move out into sororities, fraternities, or off-campus housing. This is not discouraged as the university could not house all undergraduates on campus should they want to stay.

14. Ray and Rosow (2009).

15. Percentages are calculated from the forty-five women who did not drop out before declaring a major and from whom we have at least one interview.

16. Arum and Roksa (2011).

17. Jacobs (1996).

3. Rush and the Party Scene

1. This quote came from http://www.greekchat.com/.

2. A *New York Times* piece on women's preparations for sorority rush suggests that MU runs a fairly standard recruitment process. In the article, Sunday Tollefson, author of *Rush Right: Reveal Your Best You during Sorority Recruitment*, describes the process: "It's like speed dating meets interviewing meets beauty pageant meets upscale academic summer camp, complete with a counselor" (Moore 2012). We read *Pledged* by journalist Alexandra Robbins (2004) in the midst of the research and found it exaggerated but insightful.

3. Our knowledge of rankings is based on a list provided by a Greek research team member. It resonated with women's perceptions. At MU, sorority reputations were loosely linked to the built environment. Sorority chapters

housed in impressive buildings and those close to campus tended to be more prestigious.
4. DeSantis (2007); McGrath (2008).
5. Champman (2007).
6. Marklein (2007).
7. LGBT sororities and fraternities exist nationally and, in recent years, at MU. These groups provide new—albeit marginalized—models of Greek membership. See Yeung, Stombler, and Wharton (2006).
8. Bettie (2003).
9. For more on the Online College Social Life survey, see Armstrong, England, and Fogarty (2012). See also Bogle (2008).
10. Today's college hookup scene is similar to the competitive but nonsexual dating on college campuses in the first half of the twentieth century. See Waller (1937).
11. Holland and Eisenhart (1990).
12. For more on same-sex erotic behavior in the party scene, see Hamilton (2007).
13. Hamilton and Armstrong (2009).
14. For more on sexual assault and victim blaming among peers, see Armstrong, Hamilton, and Sweeney (2006).

4. The Floor

1. This chapter primarily relies on ethnographic data including all fifty-three women on the floor. See Table A.1 in Appendix A for information on floor isolates.
2. Two of these cliques were densely connected internally and overlapped heavily. The third, more loosely connected clique was composed of out-of-state Jewish women. With a few key exceptions (for example, Hannah and Tara), Jewish women did not experience the same sense of integration on the floor as other affluent women. This was likely a result of the religiously biased status system discussed in Chapter 3. However, all had at least a few friends on the floor and were not isolated on campus at large, as their connections—particularly with other women like themselves—ran deep.
3. Hamilton (2007).
4. Mary was also one of the two sophomores on the floor and thus had more opportunities to investigate other residential communities.
5. Milner (2004, 31).
6. An article by David Snow, Cherylon Robinson, and Patricia L. McCall (1991) on how women avoid interaction with men in singles bars helped us understand the techniques socially ambitious women used to avoid interaction with low-status floormates.
7. Milner (2004, 31).
8. Summers-Effler (2002); Collins (1990, 2004).

9. This is a significant difference at the .05 level, for a one-tailed test. Here we include only women for whom we have class trajectory information. See Table A.1 of Appendix A.

10. Tinto (1987); Kuh, Kinzie, Schuh, and Whitt (2005).

11. Coleman (1988). On college social networks, see Martin (2009).

12. Brint and Cantwell (2012).

13. This insight goes back to Emile Durkheim's *Suicide: A Study in Sociology* (1951). But also see Thoits (1983); Jackson (1992).

14. There are strong parallels here to wannabes, as discussed in Chapter 5.

15. These, and other similar organizations, are often explicitly open to students of all classes, racial backgrounds, and sexual orientations. Many include both men and women. However, they were not included in Greek rush at MU and, particularly in 2004, were marginalized and thus invisible to most students. See Yeung, Stombler, and Wharton (2006).

5. Socialites, Wannabes, and Fit with the Party Pathway

1. Thirty-four percent of women in the pathway analysis sample were socialites (or wannabes), as compared to 38% of the women on the floor. It was challenging to enlist socialites in interviews, as they were oriented to the opinions of peers rather than adults.

2. These women, wannabes in particular, switched majors frequently. Here we categorize them according to their final major. The one exception to the election of easy majors was Abby, who majored in psychology. However, as we will show, for Abby—who was quite bright—psychology was not challenging.

3. Women offered up numerous stories of bad freshman advisors. Freshman advisors at big state schools like MU are confronted by students who look alike—being mostly white—but vary in terms of class background, academic ability, and orientation to college. Without full information or the training to extract this information, they cannot provide the kind of tailored help students need. In this case, it is likely the advisor accurately read Alicia's career ambitions but, without knowledge of her academic abilities or her social orientation, ended up offering poor advice.

6. Strivers, Creaming, and the Blocked Mobility Pathway

1. In this chapter we address the experiences of thirteen out of fifteen working-class or lower-middle-class women included in the study. The other two women received substantial parental help, despite their parents' limited means—allowing them to avoid working during the school year. Their experiences are thus more similar to those of more privileged students and are described in the next chapter.

2. Twenty-eight percent of women in the pathway analysis sample were strivers, as compared to 26% of women on the floor. Strivers needed help

navigating the university, and in some cases turned to members of the research team for advice and support. As more than half of this group left the university before graduation, the challenge was in tracking them.

3. MU offers four programs designed for minority and less privileged students. The least selective—which offers no tuition assistance—is also the largest, admitting 200 students a year. The smallest admits only twenty a year. We estimated that 20%–25% of students at MU are first-generation attendees or from working-class backgrounds. This suggests that conservatively more than a thousand students in each class are "at risk" on entry, not including high-income students with academic deficits, students of color, or international students with weak English-language skills. In contrast, in 2010 the University of Michigan Comprehensive Studies Program enrolled 2,421 students (Kirby, Parkinson, and Mitropoulos-Rundus 2011).

4. Also see Deil-Amen and Rosenbaum (2002).

5. Tom Wolfe captures this dynamic in his novel about college life, *I Am Charlotte Simmons* (2004), in which wealthy Erica is described as giving poor Charlotte "a wide, flat, dead smile," running "her eyes over Charlotte's plaid bathrobe, pajamas, and slippers . . . slippers, pajamas, and bathrobe. That done, she turned her attention to [wealthy] Beverly and never looked at Charlotte again" (132).

6. See Hamilton (2007).

7. See Hamilton and Armstrong (2009) for more discussion of class differences in approaches to sexuality and relationships.

8. Below we discuss the fates of six of these women. Amy left MU so abruptly that we were unable to maintain contact with her.

9. See Goldrick-Rab (2006) for more on the transfers and stop-outs that often characterize less privileged students' movement through higher education.

10. Our assumption was also consistent with research showing that, on average, college students fare better when they attend the most selective institution possible. See Bowen, Chingos, and McPherson (2009). We return to this issue in Chapter 8.

7. Achievers, Underachievers, and the Professional Pathway

This chapter is coauthored with Elizabeth Marie Armstrong and J. Lotus Seeley.

1. This group was slightly overrepresented in our pathway analysis sample, in part because they tended to be more interested in the research project and in the researchers. Thirty-five percent of women on the floor fell in this group.

2. Stuber (2011).

3. Research suggests that involuntary celibates (most of whom are unhappily so) arrive at this status in large part because they missed normative sexual transitions with their peers (see Donnelly, Burgess, Anderson, Davis, and Dillard 2001). At some point, it becomes difficult to catch up when others

have moved on to other stages of sexual and romantic development. Linda and Mary appeared to be at risk for such an experience.

4. The business school boasts that 90% of its students accept jobs or confirm plans for graduate school within three months of graduation.
5. In this sense, she was better off than the few out-of-state wannabes who tried this rescue tactic with undergraduate debt or less privileged women who might have aspired to do the same.

8. College Pathways and Post-College Prospects

1. Laura interviewed the parents of the women as part of her dissertation, *Strategies for Success: Parental Funding, College Achievement, and the Transition to Adulthood* (Hamilton 2010).
2. This chapter discusses forty-six of the original fifty-three women on the floor and includes all but one of the core forty-seven women discussed in Chapters 5–7. We lost track of Amy, a working-class woman, along the way.
3. In a report on the postgraduate transitions of the *Academically Adrift* cohort, Richard Arum and colleagues report on debt and living at home with parents in their consideration of the financial circumstances of this cohort. The substantial debt burden of current graduates and how it is informed by class background suggests that future research on mobility in the United States will need to take this into account (Arum, Cho, Kim, and Roksa 2012).
4. Although socialites like Naomi and Tara were from families classified as upper-middle class, this was largely a consequence of the barest level of financial constraint in their lives. Parental interviews revealed that they were prepared to fully support their children, seemingly infinitely, if need be.
5. From middle-class origins, Whitney's $40,000 salary combined with her loans and the cost of living in a big city put upper-middle-class security just out of reach.
6. Bailey and Dynarski (2011). Steelman and Powell (1989) and Hamilton (2013) identify parental financial investments in higher education as an important mechanism driving class disparities in college completion.
7. Musick, Brand, and Davis (2012).
8. The quality of the credential is, however, important. Anthony Carnevale, Jeff Strohl, and Michelle Melton (2011) demonstrate a strong relationship between college major and earnings. Richard J. Murnane, John Willett, and Frank Levy (1995) demonstrate a relationship between college grades and earnings. Arum and coauthors find a relationship between scores on the Collegiate Learning Assessment and avoiding unemployment following college graduation (Arum et al. 2012).
9. This is a characteristic of the American system of "contest mobility." See Turner (1960).
10. Bowen, Chingos, and McPherson (2009).

11. Alexandria Walton Radford (2013) shows that the most talented less privileged students land at lower-prestige schools than their equally qualified affluent peers.

12. Maria Charles and Karen Bradley (2009) discuss the ways in which the majors that universities offer allow students to develop gendered identities. We expand this focus and argue that, together, the academic and social infrastructure of the university can reinforce this process for some students.

13. McCall (1992).

14. See http://urbanlegends.about.com/od/sex/a/gold_digger.htm.

15. Sweeney and Cancian (2004).

16. Schwartz (2010).

17. Gerson (2010); Graf and Schwartz (2011).

18. See Musick et al. (2012) for more on the "marital market mismatch" faced by less privileged students. As the gender composition of college campuses increasingly skews female, women from disadvantaged backgrounds will be especially affected.

19. Brand and Xie (2010).

20. For more on social capital in the family as necessary for the transmittal of parental advantages, see Coleman (1988).

21. Swidler (2001). Also see Arnett (2004).

22. Daniel Chambliss and Chris Takacs discuss the powerful influence an excellent instructor can have on a college student in their forthcoming book.

23. The paper she referred to was Donna Eder's (1985) wonderfully insightful analysis of the cyclical nature of popularity among middle school girls.

24. Hout (1988); Torche (2011).

25. Notably, Torche (2011) finds a U-shaped pattern of the association between class origin and destination, in which a strong link between the two returns among advanced degree holders.

26. See Gaztambide-Fernández (2009); Stuber (2011).

27. Chambliss and Takacs (forthcoming).

28. Allen, Epps, and Haniff (1991); Feagin, Vera, and Imani (1996).

29. Hout (1988); Torche (2011).

30. Torche (2011, 790).

31. Charles and Bradley (2002); Schofer and Meyer (2005).

32. Settersten and Ray (2010); Duncan and Murnane (2011).

33. Reardon (2011).

34. Beller (2009).

35. Torche (2011).

36. Others have written about how academic settings force less privileged students to leave behind their class identities in order to succeed. See Granfield (1991).

37. On the economic benefits of early marriage, see Regnerus (2007).

38. Carr and Kefalas (2009).

9. Politics and Pathways

1. Arenson (2002). Schools that have eliminated fraternities and sororities include Bowdoin College, Colby College, Alfred University, and Williams College (Gumprecht 2006).
2. Lyon (2011).
3. For more on these organizations, see Yeung, Stombler, and Wharton (2006); Ray and Rosow (2009).
4. Hurtado, Milem, Clayton-Pedersen, and Allen (1999).
5. Arum and Roksa (2011).
6. Sperber (2000).
7. See Lifschitz, Sauder, and Stevens (2012).
8. Rosenbaum, Deil-Amen, and Person (2006).
9. Freeland (2011); Khan (2011).
10. Turner (1960).
11. Kahlenberg (2010a).
12. Clark and Trow (1966); Horowitz (1987, 108, 111); Reyes and Rich (2003).
13. In *Campus Life*, Helen Horowitz (1987) chronicles the generally unsuccessful efforts of college leaders to encroach on "college life."
14. Kerr (2001) dates this period from 1940 to 1990.
15. Kerr (2001).
16. Gumprecht (2006, 243).
17. Horowitz (1987); Moffatt (1989, 50).
18. Newfield (2008) situates this decline of political and economic support for higher education in a series of culture wars, during which attacks against the university have been a linchpin of conservative efforts to gain political control.
19. Kerr (2001); College Board (2007a, 2007b); Fain (2009).
20. Rizzo and Ehrenberg (2004); Fain (2009); Zernike (2009); Desrochers, Lenihan, and Wellman (2010).
21. For details on the reasoning of the leadership, see Fain (2009).
22. Hemelt and Marcotte (2011); Newfield and Lye (2011).
23. Desrochers et al. (2010).
24. Dillon (2010).
25. Jencks and Riesman (1968); Boyer (1990); Bok (1992); Astin (1993); Massy and Zemsky (1994); Astin and Chang (1995); Massy and Wilger (1995); Milem, Berger, and Dey (2000); Kerr (2001); Arum and Roksa (2011). See Cole (2009) for a defense of the research mission of the American university.
26. Higher education author Murray Sperber has written an autobiographical essay and "apology" concerning his own contribution to the "metastasizing" of "the research imperative" (2005, 137).
27. Fairweather (2005).
28. Del Boca, Darkes, Greenbaum, and Goldman (2004); Wood, Sher, and Rutledge (2007); Olsen (2010); Skidmore and Murphy (2011).

29. Stripling (2011).
30. Ibid.
31. Ehrenberg (2006).
32. Brint (2012).
33. Delbanco (2012).
34. Ehrenberg (2006).
35. Brint (2012).
36. Duncan and Murnane (2011); Peck (2011); Brint (2012).
37. Levine and Cureton (1998). See also the rest of the edited collection *Declining by Degrees* (Hersh and Merrow 2005).
38. Deil-Amen (2011).
39. Hoover and Keller (2011).
40. See Brint (2012), who asks: "Can public universities continue to provide mediocre instructional environments for so many undergraduates and still retain their high levels of enrollment? . . . It is an expensive proposition to send one's child to 'public' schools with steadily increasing tuitions for the sake of four years of friendships, hooking up, and tailgating."
41. Hoover and Keller (2011).
42. Kamenetz (2010); Christensen and Eyring (2011); Walsh (2011); Wildavsky, Kelly, and Carey (2011). See the papers from the American Enterprise Institute's "Stretching the Higher Education Dollar" compilation for a sense of how innovators are rethinking higher education (Kelly and Carey 2012).
43. Hendrick, Hightower, and Gregory (2006).
44. Mullin (2010).
45. Baumol and Bowen (1966).
46. Levine and Cureton (1998); Levine (2005, 158).
47. Brint (2012).
48. Bowen, Chingos, Lack, and Nygren (2012).
49. Thille (2010).
50. Stevens and Pea (2012).
51. Gregorian (2005, 88).
52. Duderstadt (1999). See also Drucker (1998).
53. Hebel, Stripling, and Wilson (2012).
54. Stripling (2012).
55. For a defense of college, see Delbanco (2012).
56. See Rivlin-Nadler (2012) for an interview with Andrew Delbanco, author of *Can College Be Saved?*
57. Carr and Kefalas (2009).
58. Rivlin-Nadler (2012).
59. Wood (2011).

Appendix B. Studying Social Class

J. Lotus Seeley wrote the first draft of this appendix.

1. Hout (2012).
2. Beller (2009).
3. Bourdieu (1973, 1984, 1998); Lamont and Lareau (1988). For accessibility we avoid the concepts of capital, habitus, and field. Our use of the term "resources" throughout the book might be read as standing in for capital.
4. Lareau (2003).
5. Stuber (2011).
6. Little consensus exists as to whether particular family forms are the origins or outcomes of class status. We found that changes to family structure sometimes disrupted the intergenerational transmission of advantage. For example, in several cases previously upper-middle-class families experienced contentious divorces or business failures at the same time as their child transitioned to college. These families tended to provide less economic support and attend less closely to their child's college experience, contributing to some cases of likely downward mobility.
7. Streib (2012).
8. Roksa and Potter (2011).
9. Domhoff (1967, 7); DeNavas-Walt, Proctor, and Smith (2011). See also Baltzell (1964); Domhoff (1983); Ostrander (1984).
10. Karabel (2005).

Appendix C. Data Collection, Analysis, and Writing

1. Corsaro (2004).
2. Emerson, Fretz, and Shaw (1995).
3. Venkatesh (2002).
4. Bok, Bowen, and Shulman (1998); Massey, Charles, Lundy, and Fischer (2003); Charles, Fischer, Mooney, Massey (2009); Arum and Roksa (2011). Also see research coming out of the National Study of Student Learning and the Wabash National Study of Liberal Arts Education.
5. Holland and Eisenhart (1990). For more on the Bennington College Study see Newcomb (1943).
6. One roommate pair (Heather and Stacey) was interviewed together for three years.
7. P. Rosenbaum (2005).
8. Bettie (2003); Wilkins (2008).
9. McCall (2005).
10. Connell (1987). Also see Connell (1995).
11. Armstrong, Hamilton, and Sweeney (2006).
12. Hamilton (2007).
13. Hamilton and Armstrong (2009).

Appendix D. Ethical Considerations

1. Burawoy (1979).
2. Lareau (2003).
3. Other scholars mention this; see Eckert (1989); Clydesdale (2007).
4. Kaiser (2009, 1632).
5. Kaiser (2009, 1636).
6. Lareau (2011).
7. Khan (2011, 202). Also see Kaiser (2009).
8. See Chapter 14 of the second edition of *Unequal Childhoods* for Lareau's discussion of the responses of study participants to their portrayal (Lareau 2011).
9. Tolich (2004).
10. Guenther (2009); Piper and Sikes (2010).

References

Adler, Patricia A. and Peter Adler. 1998. *Peer Power: Preadolescent Culture and Identity*. New Brunswick, NJ: Rutgers University Press.

Allen, Walter R., Edgar G. Epps, and Nesha Z. Haniff. 1991. *College in Black and White: African American Students in Predominantly White and in Historically Black Public Universities*. Albany: SUNY Press.

Alon, Sigal, and Marta Tienda. 2007. "Diversity, Opportunity, and the Shifting Meritocracy in Higher Education." *American Sociological Review* 72(4):487–511.

Arenson, Karen W. 2002. "University Announces Ban on Fraternities and Sororities." *New York Times.* May 22: http://www.nytimes.com/2002/05/22 /nyregion/university-announces-ban-on-fraternities-and-sororities.html ?pagewanted=all&src=pm.

Aries, Elizabeth. 2008. *Race and Class Matters at an Elite College*. Philadelphia, PA: Temple University Press.

Aries, Elizabeth, and Maynard Seider. 2005. "The Interactive Relationship between Class Identity and the College Experience: The Case of Lower Income Students." *Qualitative Sociology* 28(4):419–443.

Armstrong, Elizabeth A., Paula England, and Alison C. K. Fogarty. 2012. "Accounting for Women's Orgasm and Sexual Enjoyment in College Hookups and Relationships." *American Sociological Review* 77(3):435–462.

Armstrong, Elizabeth A., Laura Hamilton, and Brian Sweeney. 2006. "Sexual Assault on Campus: A Multilevel, Integrative Approach to Party Rape." *Social Problems* 53(4):483–499.

Arnett, Jeffrey J. 2004. *Emerging Adulthood: The Winding Road from the Late Teens through the Twenties*. New York: Oxford University Press.

Arum, Richard, Esther Cho, Jeannie Kim, and Josipa Roksa. 2012. *Documenting Uncertain Times: Post-Graduate Transitions of the* Academically Adrift *Cohort*. New York: Social Science Research Council. http://highered.ssrc.org/wp-content /uploads/2012/01/Documenting-Uncertain-Times-2012.pdf.

Arum, Richard, and Josipa Roksa. 2011. *Academically Adrift: Limited Learning on College Campuses*. Chicago: University of Chicago Press.

Arum, Richard, Josipa Roksa, and Michelle J. Budig. 2008. "The Romance of College Attendance: Higher Education Stratification and Mate Selection." *Research in Social Stratification and Mobility* 26(2):107–121.

Astin, Alexander W. 1993. *What Matters in College? Four Critical Years Revisited.* 5th edition. San Francisco: Jossey-Bass.

Astin, Alexander W., and Mitchell J. Chang. 1995. "Colleges That Emphasize Research and Teaching: Can You Have Your Cake and Eat It Too?" *Change: The Magazine of Higher Learning* 27(5):45–50.

Atlas, James. 2011. "Super People." *New York Times.* October 2:1+.

Attewell, Paul A., and David E. Lavin. 2007. *Passing the Torch: Does Higher Education for the Disadvantaged Pay Off across the Generations?* New York: Russell Sage Foundation.

Attewell, Paul A., David E. Lavin, Domina Thurston, and Tania Levey. 2006. "New Evidence on College Remediation." *Journal of Higher Education* 77(5):886–924.

Babcock, Philip, and Mindy Marks. 2010. "Leisure College, USA: The Decline in Student Study Time." *Education Outlook.* Washington, DC: American Enterprise Institute for Public Policy Research. http://www.aei.org/files/2010/08/05/07 -EduO-Aug-2010-g-new.pdf.

Bae, Yupin, Susan Choy, Claire Geddes, Jennifer Sable, and Thomas Snyder. 2000. *Trends in Educational Equity of Girls and Women.* (NCES 2000–03). Washington, DC: National Center for Educational Statistics, Office of Educational Research and Improvement.

Bahr, Peter R. 2008. "Does Mathematics Remediation Work? A Comparative Analysis of Academic Attainment among Community College Students." *Research in Higher Education* 49(5):420–450.

Bailey, Martha J., and Susan M Dynarski. 2011. "Gains and Gaps: Changing Inequality in US College Entry and Completion." (17633). Washington, DC: National Bureau of Economic Research. http://www.nber.org/papers/w17633.

Baltzell, E. Digby. 1958. *Philadelphia Gentlemen: The Making of a National Upper Class.* Glencoe, IL: Free Press.

———. 1964. *The Protestant Establishment: Aristocracy and Caste in America.* New York: Random House.

Baumol, William J., and William G. Bowen. 1966. *Performing Arts, the Economic Dilemma: A Study of Problems Common to Theater, Opera, Music, and Dance.* New York: Twentieth Century Fund.

Becker, Howard S., Blanche Geer, and Everett C. Hughes. 1968. *Making the Grade: The Academic Side of College Life.* New Brunswick, NJ: Transaction Publishers.

Beller, Emily. 2009. "Bringing Intergenerational Social Mobility Research into the Twenty-First Century: Why Mothers Matter." *American Sociological Review* 74(4):507–528.

Bennett, Pamela R., and Yu Xie. 2003. "Revisiting Racial Differences in College Attendance: The Role of Historically Black Colleges and Universities." *American Sociological Review* 68(4):567–580.

Bettie, Julie. 2003. *Women without Class: Girls, Race, and Identity*. Berkeley: University of California Press.

Bills, David B. 2003. "Credentials, Signals, and Screens: Explaining the Relationship between Schooling and Job Assignment." *Review of Educational Research* 73(4):441–449.

Binder, Amy J., and Kate Wood. 2012. *Becoming Right: How Campuses Shape Young Conservatives*. Princeton, NJ: Princeton University Press.

Blau, Peter, and Otis D. Duncan. 1967. *The American Occupational Structure*. New York: Wiley.

Bogle, Kathleen. 2008. *Hooking Up: Sex, Dating, and Relationships on Campus*. New York: New York University Press.

Bok, Derek C. 1992. "Reclaiming the Public Trust." *Change: The Magazine of Higher Learning* 24(4):13–19.

———. 2006. *Our Underachieving Colleges: A Candid Look at How Much Students Learn and Why They Should Be Learning More*. Princeton, NJ: Princeton University Press.

Bok, Derek C., William G. Bowen, and James L. Shulman. 1998. *The Shape of the River: Long-Term Consequences of Considering Race in College and University Admissions*. Princeton, NJ: Princeton University Press.

Bound, John, Brad Hershbein, and Bridget Terry Long. 2009. "Playing the Admissions Game: Student Reactions to Increasing College Competition." *Journal of Economic Perspectives* 138(4):119–146.

Bourdieu, Pierre. 1973. "Cultural Reproduction and Social Reproduction." Pp. 77–112 in *Knowledge, Education, and Cultural Change*, edited by Richard K. Brown. London: Tavistock.

———. 1984. *Distinction: A Social Critique of the Judgement of Taste*. Cambridge, MA: Harvard University Press.

———. 1998. *State Nobility: Elite Schools in the Field of Power*. Cambridge, MA: Polity Press.

Bowen, William G., Matthew M. Chingos, Kelly A. Lack, and Thomas I. Nygren. 2012. "Interactive Learning Online at Public Universities: Evidence from Randomized Trials." New York: Ithaka S+R. http://www.sr.ithaka.org/research-publications/interactive-learning-online-public-universities-evidence-randomized-trials.

Bowen, William G., Matthew M. Chingos, and Michael S. McPherson. 2009. *Crossing the Finish Line: Completing College at America's Public Universities*. Princeton, NJ: Princeton University Press.

Bowen, William G., Martin A. Kurzweil, Eugene M. Tobin, and Susanne C. Pichler. 2005. *Equity and Excellence in American Higher Education*. Charlottesville: University of Virginia Press.

Bowles, Samuel, and Herbert Gintis. 1976. *Schooling in Capitalist America: Educational Reform and the Contradictions of Economic Life*. New York: Basic Books.

Boyer, Ernest L. 1990. *Scholarship Reconsidered: Priorities of the Professoriate*. Princeton, NJ: Carnegie Foundation for the Advancement of Teaching.

Boyer, Ernest L., and Carnegie Foundation for the Advancement of Teaching. 1987. *College: The Undergraduate Experience in America.* New York: Harper and Row.

Bragdon, Henry W. 1967. *Woodrow Wilson: The Academic Man.* Cambridge, MA: Belknap Press.

Brand, Jennie E., and Yu Xie. 2010. "Who Benefits Most from College? Evidence for Negative Selection in Heterogenous Economic Returns to Higher Education." *American Sociological Review* 75(2):273–302.

Brint, Steven. 2002. "The Rise of the 'Practical Arts.'" Pp. 231–259 in *The Future of the City of Intellect,* edited by Steven Brint. Stanford, CA: Stanford University Press.

———. 2012. "Beyond the Ivy Islands." Review of *College: What It Was, Is, and Should Be* by A. Delbanco. *Los Angeles Review of Books.* July 29: http://lareviewof books.org/article.php?id=799&fulltext=1.

Brint, Steven, and Allison M. Cantwell. 2012. "Portrait of the Disengaged." Unpublished manuscript. Center for Studies in Education. University of California, Berkeley.

Brint, Steven G., and Jerome Karabel. 1989. *The Diverted Dream: Community Colleges and the Promise of Educational Opportunity in America, 1900–1985.* New York: Oxford University Press.

Brooks, David. 2001. "The Organization Kid." *Atlantic Monthly.* April:40–54.

Buchmann, Claudia. 2009. "Gender Inequalities in the Transition to College." *Teachers College Record* 111(10):2320–2346.

Buchmann, Claudia, Dennis J. Condron, and Vincent J. Roscigno. 2010. "Shadow Education, American Style: Test Preparation, the SAT, and College Enrollment." *Social Forces* 89(2):435–461.

Buchmann, Claudia, and Thomas A. DiPrete. 2006. "The Growing Female Advantage in College Completion: The Role of Family Background and Academic Achievement." *American Sociological Review* 71(4):515–541.

Burawoy, Michael. 1979. *Manufacturing Consent: Changes in the Labor Process under Monopoly Capitalism.* Chicago: University of Chicago Press.

———. 2009. *The Extended Case Method: Four Countries, Four Decades, Four Great Transformations, and One Theoretical Tradition.* Berkeley: University of California Press.

Bureau of Labor Statistics. 2010. *Women in the Labor Force: A Data Book.* (1034). Department of Labor. Washington, DC: U.S. Government Printing Office.

Cabrea, Alberto, Kurt R. Burkum, and Steven M. La Nasa. 2003. "Pathways to a Four-Year Degree: Determinants of Degree Completion among Socioeconomically Disadvantaged Students." Paper presented at Association for the Study of Higher Education Conference, Portland, OR.

Cahn, Naomi R., and June Carbone. 2010. *Red Families v. Blue Families: Legal Polarization and the Creation of Culture.* New York: Oxford University Press.

Carneiro, Pedro, James J. Heckman, and Edward J. Vytlacil. 2011. "Estimating Marginal Returns to Education." *American Economic Review* 101(6):2754–2781.

Carnevale, Anthony P., and Jeff Strohl. 2010. "How Increasing College Access Is Increasing Inequality, and What to Do about It." Pp. 71–183 in *Rewarding Strivers: Helping Low-Income Students Succeed in College,* edited by Richard D. Kahlenberg. New York: Century Foundation Press.

Carnevale, Anthony P., Jeff Strohl, and Michelle Melton. 2011. "What's It Worth? The Economic Values of College Majors." Washington, DC: George Washington Center for Education and the Workforce. http://www9.georgetown.edu/grad/gppi/hpi/cew/pdfs/whatsitworth-complete.pdf.

Carr, Patrick J., and Maria J. Kefalas. 2009. *Hollowing Out the Middle: The Rural Brain Drain and What It Means for America.* Boston: Beacon Press.

Chambliss, Daniel F., and Christopher G. Takacs. Forthcoming. *How College Works.* Cambridge, MA: Harvard University Press.

Champman, Sandra. 2007. "DePauw Students Angry over Sorority Ousting." NBC-WTHR.com [Indianapolis]. http://www.wthr.com/global/story.asp?S=6144683.

Charles, Camille Z., Mary J. Fischer, Margarita A. Mooney, and Douglas S. Massey. 2009. *Taming the River: Negotiating the Academic, Financial, and Social Currents in Selective Colleges and Universities.* Princeton, NJ: Princeton University Press.

Charles, Maria, and Karen Bradley. 2002. "Equal but Separate? A Cross-National Study of Sex Segregation in Higher Education." *American Sociological Review* 67(4):573–599.

———. 2009. "Indulging Our Gendered Selves? Sex Segregation by Field of Study in 44 Countries." *American Journal of Sociology* 114(4):924–976.

Christensen, Clayton M., and Henry J. Eyring. 2011. *The Innovative University: Changing the DNA of Higher Education from the Inside Out.* San Francisco: Jossey-Bass.

Clark, Burton R., and Martin Trow. 1966. "The Organizational Context." Pp. 17–70 in *College Peer Groups: Problems and Prospects for Research,* edited by Theodore M. Newcombe and Everett K. Wilson. Chicago: Aldeline.

Clemons, Stephanie A., David McKelfresh, and James Banning. 2005. "Importance of Sense of Place and Sense of Self in Residence Hall Room Design: A Qualitative Study of First-Year Students." *Journal of the First-Year Experience & Students in Transition* 17(2):73–86.

Clydesdale, Timothy. 2007. *The First Year Out: Understanding American Teens after High School.* Chicago: University of Chicago Press.

Coburn, Karen Levin. 2006. "Organizing a Ground Crew for Today's Helicopter Parents." *About Campus* 11(3):9–16.

Cole, Jonathan R. 2009. *The Great American University: Its Rise to Preeminence, Its Indispensable National Role, and Why It Must Be Protected.* New York: Public Affairs.

Coleman, James S. 1961. *The Adolescent Society: The Social Life of the Teenager and Its Impact on Education.* New York: Free Press of Glencoe.

———. 1988. "Social Capital in the Creation of Human Capital." *American Journal of Sociology* 94(1):S95–S120.

College Board. 2007a. "Trends in Student Aid." *Trends in Higher Education.* http://
trends.collegeboard.org/downloads/archives/SA_2007.pdf.
———. 2007b. "Tuition and Fees over Time." *Trends in Higher Education.* http://
www.collegeboard.com/prod_downloads/about/news_info/trends/tuition_fees
.pdf.
Collins, Randall. 1979. *The Credential Society: An Historical Sociology of Education and
Stratification.* New York: Academic Press.
———. 1990. "Stratification, Emotional Energy, and the Transient Emotions."
Pp. 27–57 in *Research Agendas in the Sociology of Emotions,* edited by Theodore
D. Kemper. Albany: State University of New York Press.
———. 2004. *Interaction Ritual Chains.* Princeton, NJ: Princeton University Press.
Conger, Dylan, and Mark C. Long. 2010. "Why Are Men Falling Behind? Gender
Gaps in College Performance and Persistence." *Annals of the American Academy of
Political and Social Science* 627:184–214.
Connell, Raewyn. 1987. *Gender and Power: Society, the Person, and Sexual Politics.*
Stanford, CA: Stanford University Press.
———. 1995. *Masculinities.* Berkeley: University of California Press.
Cookson, Peter W., and Caroline H. Persell. 1985. *Preparing for Power: America's
Elite Boarding Schools.* New York: Basic Books.
Corsaro, William A. 2004. *The Sociology of Childhood.* Thousand Oaks, CA: Pine
Forge Press.
Coser, Lewis A. 1967. "Greedy Organizations." *European Journal of Sociology*
8(2):196–215.
Davies, Scott, and Jal Mehta. 2012. "The Deepening Interpenetration of Education
and Society." Paper presented at Education in a New Society Seminar, Rad-
cliffe Institute for Advanced Study, Harvard University, Cambridge, MA.
Deil-Amen, Regina. 2011. "The 'Traditional' College Student: A Smaller and
Smaller Minority and Its Implications for Diversity and Access Institutions."
Paper presented at Mapping Broad-Access Higher Education Conference,
Stanford University, Stanford, CA.
Deil-Amen, Regina, and James E. Rosenbaum. 2002. "The Unintended
Consequences of Stigma-Free Remediation." *Sociology of Education*
75(3):249–268.
Delbanco, Andrew. 2012. *College: What It Was, Is, and Should Be.* Princeton, NJ:
Princeton University Press.
Del Boca, Frances K., Jack Darkes, Paul E. Greenbaum, and Mark S. Goldman.
2004. "Up Close and Personal: Temporal Variability in the Drinking of
Individual College Students during Their First Year." *Journal of Consulting and
Clinical Psychology* 72(2):155–164.
DeNavas-Walt, Carmen, Bernadette D. Proctor, and Jessica C. Smith. 2011. *Income,
Poverty, and Health Insurance Coverage in the United States: 2010.* (P60–239).
Washington, DC: U.S. Census Bureau.
DeSantis, Alan D. 2007. *Inside Greek U: Fraternities, Sororities, and the Pursuit of
Pleasure, Power, and Prestige.* Lexington: University Press of Kentucky.

Desrochers, Donna M., Colleen M. Lenihan, and Jane V. Wellman. 2010. *Trends in College Spending: 1998–2008.* Washington, DC: Delta Coast Project. http://www .deltacostproject.org/resources/pdf/Trends-in-College-Spending-98-08.pdf.

Dillon, Sam. 2010. "Share of College Budgets for Recreation Is Rising." *New York Times.* July 10:A13+.

Domhoff, G. William. 1967. *Who Rules America?* Englewood Cliffs, NJ: Prentice-Hall.

———. 1983. *Who Rules America Now? A View for the '80s.* Englewood Cliffs, NJ: Prentice-Hall.

Donnelly, Denise, Elisabeth Burgess, Sally Anderson, Regina Davis, and Joy Dillard. 2001. "Involuntary Celibacy: A Life Course Analysis." *Journal of Sex Research* 38(2):159–169.

Douglass, John Aubrey. 2007. *The Conditions for Admission: Access, Equity, and the Social Contract of Public Universities.* Stanford, CA: Stanford University Press.

Douthat, Ross Gregory. 2005. *Privilege: Harvard and the Education of the Ruling Class.* New York: Hyperion.

Drucker, Peter F. 1998. "The Next Information Revolution." *Forbes ASAP.* August 24. http://www.forbes.com/asap/1998/0824/046.html.

Duderstadt, James J. 1999. "Can Colleges and Universities Survive the Information Age?" Paper presented at the American Philosophical Society Annual Meeting, Philadelphia, PA.

Duncan, Greg J., and Richard J. Murnane, eds. 2011. *Whither Opportunity? Rising Inequality, Schools, and Children's Life Chances.* New York: Russell Sage Foundation.

Durkheim, Émile. 1951. *Suicide, A Study in Sociology.* Glencoe, IL: Free Press.

Eckert, Penelope. 1989. *Jocks and Burnouts: Social Categories and Identity in the High School.* New York: Teachers College Press.

Eder, Donna. 1985. "The Cycle of Popularity: Interpersonal Relations among Female Adolescents." *Sociology of Education* 58(3):154–165.

Eder, Donna, Catherine Colleen Evans, and Stephen Parker. 1995. *School Talk: Gender and Adolescent Culture.* New Brunswick, NJ: Rutgers University Press.

Ehrenberg, Ronald. 2006. "The Perfect Storm and the Privatization of Public Higher Education." *Change: The Magazine of Higher Learning* 38(1):46–53.

Emerson, Robert M., Rachel I. Fretz, and Linda L. Shaw. 1995. *Writing Ethnographic Fieldnotes.* Chicago: University of Chicago Press.

England, Paula. 2010. "The Gender Revolution: Uneven and Stalled." *Gender & Society* 24(2):149–166.

England, Paula, and Su Li. 2006. "Desegregation Stalled: The Changing Gender Composition of College Majors, 1971–2002." *Gender & Society* 20(5):657–677.

England, Paula, Emily Fitzgibbons Shafer, and Alison C. K. Fogarty. 2007. "Hooking up and Forming Romantic Relationships on Today's College Campuses." Pp. 531–547 in *The Gendered Society Reader,* edited by Michael Kimmel. New York: Oxford University Press.

Engle, Jennifer, and Vincent Tinto. 2008. *Moving beyond Access: College Success for Low-Income, First-Generation Students.* Pell Institute for the Study of Opportunity in Higher Education. Washington, DC: Council for Opportunity in Education. http://faculty.soe.syr.edu/vtinto/Files/Moving%20Beyond%20Access.pdf.

Espeland, Wendy Nelson, and Michael Sauder. 2007. "Rankings and Reactivity: How Public Measures Recreate Social Worlds." *American Journal of Sociology* 113(1):1–40.

Espenshade, Thomas J., and Alexandria W. Radford. 2009. *No Longer Separate, Not Yet Equal: Race and Class in Elite College Admission and Campus Life.* Princeton, NJ: Princeton University Press.

Estelle, James. 1990. "Decision Processes and Priorities in Higher Education." Pp. 77–106 in *The Economics of American Universities: Management, Operation, and Environment,* edited by Stephen A. Hoenack and Eileen Collins. Buffalo: SUNY Press.

Fain, Paul. 2009. "Less for More." *New York Times.* November 1:20+.

Fairweather, James S. 2005. "Beyond the Rhetoric: Trends in the Relative Value of Teaching and Research in Faculty Salaries." *Journal of Higher Education* 76(4):401–422.

Feagin, Joe R., Hernan Vera, and Nikitah Imani. 1996. *The Agony of Education: Black Students at a White University.* New York: Routledge.

Freeland, Chrystia. 2011. "The Rise of the New Global Elite." *Atlantic Monthly.* January/February:44–55.

Gamoran, Adam. 2010. "Tracking and Inequality: New Directions for Research and Practice." Pp. 213–228 in *The Routledge International Handbook of the Sociology of Education,* edited by Michael W. Apple, Stephen J. Ball, and Luis Armando Gandin. London: Routledge.

Gaztambide-Fernández, Rubén A. 2009. *The Best of the Best: Becoming Elite at an American Boarding School.* Cambridge, MA: Harvard University Press.

Gerber, Theodore P., and Sin Yi Cheung. 2008. "Horizontal Stratification in Postsecondary Education: Forms, Explanations, and Implications." *Annual Review of Sociology* 34:299–318.

Gerson, Kathleen. 2010. *The Unfinished Revolution: How a New Generation Is Reshaping Family, Work, and Gender in America.* New York: Oxford University Press.

Giroux, Henry A., and David E. Purpel. 1983. *The Hidden Curriculum and Moral Education: Deception or Discovery?* Berkeley: McCutchan Publishing.

Goldin, Claudia, and Lawrence F. Katz. 2008. *The Race between Education and Technology.* Cambridge, MA: Belknap Press.

Goldrick-Rab, Sara. 2006. "Following Their Every Move: An Investigation of Social-Class Differences in College Pathways." *Sociology of Education* 79(1):61–79.

Goodwin, Latty Lee. 2006. *Graduating Class: Disadvantaged Students Crossing the Bridge of Higher Education.* Albany: SUNY Press.

Graf, Nikki, and Christine Schwartz. 2011. "The Uneven Pace of Change in Heterosexual Romantic Relationships." *Gender & Society* 25(1):101–107.

Granfield, Robert. 1991. "Making It by Faking It: Working-Class Students in an Elite Academic Environment." *Journal of Contemporary Ethnography* 20(3):331–351.

Gregorian, Vartan. 2005. "Six Challenges to the American University." Pp. 77–96 in *Declining by Degrees: Higher Education at Risk,* edited by Richard H. Hersh and John Merrow. New York: Palgrave Macmillan.

Grigsby, Mary. 2009. *College Life through the Eyes of Students.* Albany: SUNY Press.

Grodsky, Eric, and Catherine Riegle-Crumb. 2010. "Those Who Choose and Those Who Don't: Social Background and College Orientation." *Annals of the American Academy of Political and Social Science* 627:14–35.

Gross, Neil. 2013. *Why Are Professors Liberal and Why Do Conservatives Care?* Cambridge, MA: Harvard University Press.

Guenther, Katja M. 2009. "The Politics of Names: Rethinking the Methodological and Ethical Significance of Naming People, Organizations, and Places." *Qualitative Research* 9(4):411–421.

Gumprecht, Blake. 2006. "Fraternity Row, the Student Ghetto, and the Faculty Enclave: Characteristic Residential Districts in the American College Town." *Journal of Urban History* 32(2):231–273.

Hacker, Andrew, and Claudia Dreifus. 2010. *Higher Education? How Colleges Are Wasting Our Money and Failing Our Kids—And What We Can Do about It.* New York: Times Books.

Hall, Peter D. 1982. *The Organization of American Culture, 1700–1900: Private Institutions, Elites, and the Origins of American Nationality.* New York: New York University Press.

Hallinan, Maureen T. 1994. "Tracking: From Theory to Practice." *Sociology of Education* 67(2):79–84.

Hamilton, Laura. 2007. "Trading on Heterosexuality: College Women's Gender Strategies and Homophobia." *Gender & Society* 21(2):145–172.

———. 2010. *Strategies for Success: Parental Funding, College Achievement, and the Transition to Adulthood.* Unpublished PhD dissertation. Department of Sociology. Indiana University, Bloomington.

———. 2013. "More Is More or More Is Less? Parental Financial Investments during College." Forthcoming at *American Sociological Review.*

Hamilton, Laura, and Elizabeth A. Armstrong. 2009. "Gendered Sexuality in Young Adulthood: Double Binds and Flawed Options." *Gender & Society* 23(5):589–616.

Hamilton, William L. 2006. "At Ole Miss, the Tailgaters Never Lose." *New York Times.* September 29:F1+.

Harding, David J. 2010. *Living the Drama: Community, Conflict, and Culture among Inner-City Boys.* Chicago: University of Chicago Press.

Hays, Sharon. 1996. *The Cultural Contradictions of Motherhood.* New Haven, CT: Yale University Press.

Hebel, Sara, Jack Stripling, and Robin Wilson. 2012. "University of Virginia Board Votes to Reinstate Sullivan." *Chronicle of Higher Education.* June 26: http://chronicle.com/article/U-of-Virginia-Board-Votes-to/132603/.

Hemelt, Steven W., and Dave E. Marcotte. 2011. "The Impact of Tuition Increases on Enrollment at Public Colleges and Universities." *Educational Evaluation and Policy Analysis* 33(4):435–457.

Hendrick, Ruth Zimmer, William H. Hightower, and Dennis E. Gregory. 2006. "State Funding Limitations and Community College Open Door Policy: Conflicting Priorities?" *Community College Journal of Research and Practice* 30(8):627–640.

Hersh, Richard H., and John Merrow, eds. 2005. *Declining by Degrees: Higher Education at Risk*. New York: Palgrave Macmillan.

Holland, Dorothy C., and Margaret A. Eisenhart. 1990. *Educated in Romance: Women, Achievement, and College Culture*. Chicago: University of Chicago Press.

Hoover, Eric, and Josh Keller. 2011. "The Cross-Country Recruitment Rush." *Chronicle of Higher Education*. October 30: http://chronicle.com/article/The-Cross -Country-Recruitment/129577/.

Horowitz, Helen L. 1987. *Campus Life: Undergraduate Cultures from the End of the Eighteenth Century to the Present*. New York: Knopf.

Hout, Michael. 1988. "More Universalism, Less Structural Mobility: The American Occupational Structure in the 1980s." *American Journal of Sociology* 93(6):1358–1400.

———. 2012. "Social and Economic Returns to College Education in the United States." *Annual Review of Sociology* 38:379–400.

Hurtado, Sylvia, and Deborah F. Carter. 1997. "Effects of College Transition and Perceptions of the Campus Racial Climate on Latino College Students' Sense of Belonging." *Sociology of Education* 70(4):324–345.

Hurtado, Sylvia, Jeffrey Milem, Alma Clayton-Pedersen, and Walter Allen. 1999. *Enacting Diverse Learning Environments: Improving the Climate for Racial/Ethnic Diversity in Higher Education*. Washington, DC: Graduate School of Education and Human Development, George Washington University.

Jackson, Pamela B. 1992. "Specifying the Buffering Hypothesis: Support, Strain, and Depression." *Social Psychology Quarterly* 55(4):363–378.

Jacobs, Jerry A. 1996. "Gender Inequality and Higher Education." *Annual Review of Sociology* 22:153–185.

Jencks, Christopher, and Meredith Phillips, eds. 1998. *The Black-White Test Score Gap*. Washington, DC: Brookings Institution Press.

Jencks, Christopher, and David Riesman. 1968. *The Academic Revolution*. Garden City, NY: Doubleday.

Jencks, Christopher, Marshall Smith, Henry Acland, Mary Jo Bane, David Cohen, Herbert Gintis, Barbara Heynes, and Stephanie Michelson. 1972. *Inequality: A Reassessment of the Effect of Family and Schooling in America*. New York: Basic Books.

Kahlenberg, Richard D., ed. 2010a. *Affirmative Action for the Rich: Legacy Preferences in College Admissions*. New York: Century Foundation Press.

Kahlenberg, Richard D. 2010b. *Rewarding Strivers: Helping Low-Income Students Succeed in College*. New York: Century Foundation Press.

Kaiser, Karen. 2009. "Protecting Respondent Confidentiality in Qualitative Research." *Qualitative Health Research* 19(11):1632–1641.

Kalmijn, Matthijs. 1991. "Status Homogamy in the United States." *American Journal of Sociology* 97(2):496–523.

Kamenetz, Anya. 2010. *DIY U: Edupunks, Edupreneurs, and the Coming Transformation of Higher Education*. White River Junction, VT: Chelsea Green.

Kanter, Rosabeth Moss. 1972. *Commitment and Community: Communes and Utopias in Sociological Perspective*. Cambridge, MA: Harvard University Press.

Karabel, Jerome. 2005. *The Chosen: The Hidden History of Admission and Exclusion at Harvard, Yale, and Princeton.* New York: Houghton Mifflin.

Karen, David. 1991. "The Politics of Class, Race, and Gender: Access to Higher Education in the United States, 1960–1986." *American Journal of Education* 99(2):208–237.

———. 2002. "Changes in Access to Higher Education in the United States, 1980–1992." *Sociology of Education* 75(3):191–210.

Kelly, Andrew P., and Kevin Carey. 2012. "Stretching the Higher Education Dollar." Washington, DC: American Enterprise Institute. http://www.aei.org /article/education/higher-education/costs/stretching-the-higher-education -dollar-papers/.

Kennedy, Kirsten. 2009. "The Politics and Policies of Parental Involvement." *About Campus* 14(4):16–25.

Kerr, Clark. 2001. *The Uses of the University.* 5th edition. Cambridge, MA: Harvard University Press.

Khan, Shamus R. 2011. *Privilege: The Making of an Adolescent Elite at St. Paul's School.* Princeton, NJ: Princeton University Press.

Kimmel, Michael. 2008. *Guyland: The Perilous World Where Boys Become Men.* New York: HarperCollins.

Kingsbury, Alex. 2007. "Many Colleges Reject Women at Higher Rates Than for Men." *U.S. News & World Report Online.* June 17: http://www.usnews.com /usnews/edu/articles/070617/25gender.htm.

Kirby, Maple, Laura Parkinson, and Anastasia Mitropoulos-Rundus. 2011. "Diminishing Inequalities: The University of Michigan's Comprehensive Studies Program." Unpublished paper for OS495: The Organization of College Life. Organizational Studies. University of Michigan, Ann Arbor.

Kuh, George D. 1993. "In Their Own Words: What Students Learn Outside the Classroom." *American Educational Research Journal* 30(2):277–304.

———. 2003. "What We're Learning about Student Engagement from NSSE: Benchmarks for Effective Educational Practices." *Change* 35(2):24–32.

Kuh, George D., Robert M. Gonyea, and Megan Palmer. 2001. "The Disengaged Commuter Student: Fact or Fiction?" *Commuter Perspectives* 27(1):2–5.

Kuh, George D., Jillian Kinzie, John H. Schuh, and Elizabeth J. Whitt. 2005. *Student Success in College: Creating Conditions That Matter.* San Francisco: Jossey-Bass.

Lacy, Karyn R. 2007. *Blue-Chip Black: Race, Class, and Status in the New Black Middle Class.* Berkeley: University of California Press.

Lamont, Michèle. 1992. *Money, Morals, and Manners: The Culture of the French and the American Upper-Middle Class.* Chicago: University of Chicago Press.

———. 2000. *The Dignity of Working Men: Morality and the Boundaries of Race, Class, and Immigration.* Cambridge, MA: Harvard University Press.

———. 2009. *How Professors Think: Inside the Curious World of Academic Judgment.* Cambridge, MA: Harvard University Press.

Lamont, Michèle, and Annette Lareau. 1988. "Cultural Capital: Allusions, Gaps, and Glissandos in Recent Theoretical Developments." *Sociological Theory* 6(2):153–168.

Lareau, Annette. 2003. *Unequal Childhoods: Class, Race, and Family Life.* Berkeley: University of California Press.

———. 2011. *Unequal Childhoods: Class, Race, and Family Life.* 2nd edition. Berkeley: University of California Press.

Lemann, Nicholas. 1999. *The Big Test: The Secret History of the American Meritocracy.* New York: Farrar, Straus and Giroux.

Leonhardt, David. 2005. "The College Dropout Boom." *New York Times.* May 24:A1+.

Levey, Hilary. 2012. "Graceful Girls, Aggressive Girls, and Pink Girls: Femininity and Children's Afterschool Activities." Unpublished manuscript.

Levine, Arthur. 2005. "Worlds Apart: Disconnects between Students and Their Schools." Pp. 155–167 in *Declining by Degrees: Higher Education at Risk,* edited by Richard H. Hersh and John Merrow. New York: Palgrave Macmillan.

Levine, Arthur, and Jeanette S. Cureton. 1998. *When Hope and Fear Collide: A Portrait of Today's College Student.* San Francisco: Jossey-Bass.

Lewin, Tamar. 2006. "A More Nuanced Look at Men, Women and College." *New York Times.* July 12:B8+.

———. 2011a. "Michigan Rule on Admission to University Is Overturned." *New York Times.* July 2:A10+.

———. 2011b. "Universities Seeking Out Students of Means." *New York Times.* September 21:A21.

Lifschitz, Arik, Michael Sauder, and Mitchell Stevens. 2012. "Football: Field Ordering and Status Marking in U.S. Higher Education." Unpublished manuscript.

Light, Richard J. 2001. *Making the Most of College: Students Speak Their Minds.* Cambridge, MA: Harvard University Press.

López, Nancy. 2002. *Hopeful Girls, Troubled Boys: Race and Gender Disparity in Urban Education.* New York: Routledge.

Lucas, Samuel R. 2001. "Effectively Maintained Inequality: Education Transitions, Track Mobility, and Social Background Effects." *American Journal of Sociology* 106(6):1642–1690.

Lyon, Sarah. 2011. "Rumors about Fraternities Increase." *Colby Echo* [Waterville, ME]. http://www.thecolbyecho.com/news/rumors-about-fraternities-increase.

MacLeod, Jay. 1995. *Ain't No Makin' It: Leveled Aspirations in a Low-Income Neighborhood.* Boulder, CO: Westview Press.

Mare, Robert D. 1991. "Five Decades of Educational Assortative Mating." *American Sociological Review* 56(1):15–32.

Marklein, Mary Beth. 2006. "Are Out-of-State Students Crowding Out In-Staters?" *USA Today.* August 31: http://www.usatoday.com/news/education/2006-08-30-state-universities-cover_x.htm.

———. 2007. "Ousted Sorority Sues DePauw University." *USA Today.* April 3: http://www.usatoday.com/news/education/2007-03-28-sorority_N.htm.

Martin, Nathan D. 2009. "Social Capital, Academic Achievement, and Postgraduation Plans at an Elite, Private University." *Sociological Perspectives* 52(2):185–210.

Massey, Douglas S., Camille Z. Charles, Garvey Lundy, and Mary J. Fischer. 2003. *The Source of the River: The Social Origins of Freshmen at America's Selective Colleges and Universities*. Princeton, NJ: Princeton University Press.

Massey, Douglas S., and Mary J. Fischer. 2006. "The Effect of Childhood Segregation on Minority Academic Performance at Selective Colleges." *Ethnic and Racial Studies* 29(1):1–26.

Massy, William F., and Andrea K. Wilger. 1995. "Improving Productivity: What Faculty Think about It—And Its Effect on Quality." *Change: The Magazine of Higher Learning* 27(4):10–20.

Massy, William F., and Robert Zemsky. 1994. "Faculty Discretionary Time: Departments and the 'Academic Ratchet.'" *Journal of Higher Education* 65(1):1–22.

Matthews, Anne. 1997. *Bright College Years: Inside the American Campus Today*. New York: Simon and Schuster.

McCall, Leslie. 1992. "Does Gender Fit? Bourdieu, Feminism, and Conceptions of Social Order." *Theory and Society* 21(6):837–867.

———. 2005. "The Complexity of Intersectionality." *Signs* 30(3):1771–1800.

McDonough, Patricia M. 1997. *Choosing Colleges: How Social Class and Schools Structure Opportunity*. Albany: SUNY Press.

McGrath, Charles. 2008. "On Double Secret Probation." *New York Times*. January 6:35+.

McPherson, Michael S., and Morton O. Schapiro. 1998. *The Student Aid Game: Meeting Need and Rewarding Talent in American Higher Education*. Princeton, NJ: Princeton University Press.

McPherson, Miller, Lynn Smith-Lovin, and James M. Cook. 2001. "Birds of a Feather. Homophily in Social Networks." *Annual Review of Sociology* 27:415–444.

Meek, V. Lynn, Leo Goedegebuure, Osmo Kivinen, and Risto Rinne, eds. 1996. *The Mockers and Mocked: Comparative Perspectives on Differentiation, Convergence, and Diversity in Higher Education*. New York: IAU Press.

Melear, Kerry B. 2002. "From *In Loco Parentis* to Consumerism: A Legal Analysis of the Contractual Relationship between Institution and Student." *Journal of Student Affairs Research and Practice* 40(4):124–148.

Meyer, John W., and Brian Rowan. 1977. "Institutionalized Organizations: Formal Structure as Myth and Ceremony." *American Journal of Sociology* 83(2):340–363.

Milem, Jeffrey F., Joseph B. Berger, and Eric L. Dey. 2000. "Faculty Time Allocation: A Study of Change over Twenty Years." *Journal of Higher Education* 71(4):454–475.

Milner, Murray, Jr. 2004. *Freaks, Geeks, and Cool Kids: American Teenagers, Schools, and the Culture of Consumption*. New York: Routledge.

Moffatt, Michael. 1989. *Coming of Age in New Jersey: College and American Culture*. New Brunswick, NJ: Rutgers University Press.

Moore, Abigail Sullivan. 2012. "Pledge Prep." *New York Times.* July 22:ED28+.

Morrill, Calvin. 1995. *The Executive Way: Conflict Management in Corporations.* Chicago: University of Chicago Press.

Mullen, Ann L. 2010. *Degrees of Inequality: Culture, Class, and Gender in American Higher Education.* Baltimore, MD: Johns Hopkins University Press.

Mullen, Ann L., Kimberly A. Goyette, and Joseph A. Soares. 2003. "Who Goes to Graduate School? Social and Academic Correlates of Educational Continuation after College." *Sociology of Education* 76(2):143–169.

Mullin, Christopher M. 2010. "Rebalancing the Mission: The Community College Completion Challenge." (2010–02PBL). Washington, DC: American Association of Community Colleges. http://www.aacc.nche.edu/Publications/Briefs/Documents/rebalancing_06152010.pdf.

Murnane, Richard J., John B. Willett, and Frank Levy. 1995. "The Growing Importance of Cognitive Skills in Wage Determination." *Review of Economics and Statistics* 77(2):251–266.

Musick, Kelly, Jennie Brand, and Dwight Davis. 2012. "Variation in the Relationship between Education and Marriage: Mismatch in the Marriage Market?" *Journal of Marriage and Family* 74(1):53–69.

Nathan, Rebekah. 2005. *My Freshman Year: What a Professor Learned by Becoming a Student.* Ithaca, NY: Cornell University Press.

National Center for Education Statistics. 2012. *Educational Longitudinal Study of 2002 (ELS:2002).* Institute of Education Sciences. Washington, DC: U.S. Department of Education. http://nces.ed.gov/surveys/els2002/index.asp.

Newcomb, Theodore. 1943. *Personality and Social Change: Attitude Formation in a Student Community.* New York: Dryden.

Newfield, Christopher. 2008. *Unmasking the Public University: The Forty-Year Assault on the Middle Class.* Cambridge: Harvard University Press.

Newfield, Christopher, and Colleen Lye. 2011. "The Struggle for Public Education in California: Introduction." *South Atlantic Quarterly* 110(2):529–538.

Niu, Sunny Xinchun, and Marta Tienda. 2010. "The Impact of the Texas Top Ten Percent Law on College Enrollment: A Regression Discontinuity Approach." *Journal of Policy Analysis and Management* 29(1):84–110.

Olsen, Morgan. 2010. "Friday Classes Mean Fewer Thursday ER Visits, Study Contends." *Daily Iowan* [Iowa City, IA]. March 30: http://www.dailyiowan.com/2010/03/30/Metro/16407.html.

Ostrander, Susan A. 1984. *Women of the Upper Class.* Philadelphia, PA: Temple University Press.

Pascarella, Ernest, and the National Center on Postsecondary Teaching, Learning, and Assessment. 1992. *Cognitive Impacts of Living on Campus versus Commuting to College.* Washington, DC: Distributed by ERIC Clearinghouse.

Pascarella, Ernest T., and Patrick T. Terenzini. 2005. *How College Affects Students: A Third Decade of Research.* San Francisco: Jossey-Bass.

Pascoe, C. J. 2007. *Dude, You're a Fag: Masculinity and Sexuality in High School.* Berkeley: University of California Press.

Paulsen, Michael B., and Edward P. St. John. 2002. "Social Class and College Costs: Examining the Financial Nexus between College Choice and Persistence." *Journal of Higher Education* 73(2):189–236.

Peck, Don. 2011. "Can the Middle Class Be Saved?" *Atlantic Monthly.* September:60–79.

Piper, Heather, and Pat Sikes. 2010. "All Teachers Are Vulnerable but Especially Gay Teachers: Using Composite Fictions to Protect Research Participants in Pupil-Teacher Sex-Related Research." *Qualitative Inquiry* 16(7):566–574.

Powell, Brian, and Lala Carr Steelman. 1995. "Feeling the Pinch: Child Spacing and Constraints on Parental Economic Investments in Children." *Social Forces* 73(4):1465–1486.

Radford, Alexandria W. 2013. *Trajectories of the Talented: How Social Class Shapes Where Top Students Go to College.* Chicago: University of Chicago Press.

Ray, Rashawn, and Jason A. Rosow. 2009. "Getting off and Getting Intimate: How Normative Institutional Arrangements Structure Black and White Fraternity Men's Approaches toward Women." *Men and Masculinities* 12(5):523–546.

Reardon, Sean F. 2011. "The Widening Academic Achievement Gap between the Rich and the Poor: New Evidence and Possible Explanations." Pp. 91–116 in *Whither Opportunity? Rising Inequality, Schools, and Children's Life Chances,* edited by Greg J. Duncan and Richard J. Murnane. New York: Russell Sage Foundation.

Regnerus, Mark. 2007. *Forbidden Fruit: Sex and Religion in the Lives of American Teenagers.* New York: Oxford University Press.

Reiss, Ira L. 1965. "Social Class and Campus Dating." *Social Problems* 13(2):193–205.

Reyes, Guillermo de los, and Paul Rich. 2003. "Housing Students: Fraternities and Residential Colleges." *Annals of the American Academy of Political and Social Science* 585:118–123.

Rivera, Lauren A. 2011. "Ivies, Extracurriculars, and Exclusion: Elite Employers Use of Educational Credentials." *Research in Social Stratification and Mobility* 29(1):71–90.

Rivlin-Nadler, Max. 2012. "Can College Be Saved?" (Interview with Andrew Delbanco). *Salon.* April 1: http://www.salon.com/2012/04/01/can_college_be_saved/.

Rizzo, Michael, and Ronald G. Ehrenberg. 2004. "Resident and Nonresident Tuition and Enrollment at Flagship State Universities." Pp. 303–353 in *College Choices: The Economics of Where to Go, When to Go, and How to Pay for It,* edited by Caroline M. Hoxby. Chicago: University of Chicago Press.

Robbins, Alexandra. 2004. *Pledged: The Secret Life of Sororities.* New York: Hyperion.

Rojas, Fabio. 2007. *From Black Power to Black Studies: How a Radical Social Movement Became an Academic Discipline.* Baltimore, MD: Johns Hopkins University Press.

Roksa, Josipa, Eric Grodsky, Richard Arum, and Adam Gamoran. 2007. "United States: Changes in Higher Education and Stratification." Pp. 165–191 in *Stratification in Higher Education: A Comparative Study,* edited by Yossi Shavit, Richard Arum, and Adam Gamoran. Stanford, CA: Stanford University Press.

Roksa, Josipa, and Daniel Potter. 2011. "Parenting and Academic Achievement." *Sociology of Education* 84(4):299–321.

Rosenbaum, James E. 2001. *Beyond College for All: Career Paths for the Forgotten Half.* New York: Russell Sage Foundation.

Rosenbaum, James E., Regina Deil-Amen, and Ann E. Person. 2006. *After Admission: From College Access to College Success.* New York: Russell Sage Foundation.

Rosenbaum, Paul R. 2005. "Heterogeneity and Causality: Unit Heterogeneity and Design Sensitivity in Observational Studies." *American Statistician* 59(2):147–152.

Rosenfeld, Michael J. 2007. *The Age of Independence: Interracial Unions, Same-Sex Unions, and the Changing American Family.* Cambridge, MA: Harvard University Press.

Rothstein, Jesse M. 2004. "College Performance Predictions and the SAT." *Journal of Econometrics* 121(1–2):297–317.

Sax, Linda, and Casandra E. Harper. 2007. "Origins of the Gender Gap: Pre-College and College Differences between Men and Women." *Research in Higher Education* 48(6):669–694.

Sax, Linda, Sylvia Hurtado, Jennifer A. Lindholm, Alexander W. Astin, William S. Korn, and Kathryn M. Mahoney. 2005. *The American Freshman: National Norms for Fall 2004.* Los Angeles: UCLA, Graduate School of Education and Information Studies. http://heri.ucla.edu/PDFs/pubs/TFS/Norms/Monographs/TheAmericanFreshman2004.pdf.

Schneider, Barbara, and David Stevenson. 1999. *The Ambitious Generation: America's Teenagers, Motivated but Directionless.* New Haven, CT: Yale University Press.

Schofer, Evan, and John W. Meyer. 2005. "The Worldwide Expansion of Higher Education in the Twentieth Century." *American Sociological Review* 70(6):898–920.

Schwalbe, Michael, Sandra Godwin, Daphne Holden, Douglas Schrock, Shealy Thompson, and Michele Wolkomir. 2000. "Generic Processes in the Reproduction of Inequality: An Interactionist Analysis." *Social Forces* 79(2):419–452.

Schwartz, Christine R. 2010. "Earnings Inequality and the Changing Association between Spouses' Earnings." *American Journal of Sociology* 115(5):1524–1557.

Scott, John Finley. 1965. "The American College Sorority: Its Role in Class and Ethnic Endogamy." *American Sociological Review* 30(4):514–527.

Settersten, Richard, and Barbara E. Ray. 2010. *Not Quite Adults: Why 20-Somethings Are Choosing a Slower Path to Adulthood, and Why It's Good for Everyone.* New York: Bantam.

Sewell, William, and Robert Hauser. 1976. "Causes and Consequences of Higher Education: Models of Status Attainment Process." Pp. 9–28 in *Schooling and Achievement in American Society,* edited by William Sewell, Robert Hauser, and David L. Featherman. New York: Academic Press.

Shulman, James L., and William G. Bowen. 2001. *The Game of Life: College Sports and Educational Values.* Princeton, NJ: Princeton University Press.

Skidmore, Jessica, and James G. Murphy. 2011. "The Effect of Drink Price and Next-Day Responsibilities on College Student Drinking: A Behavioral Economic Analysis." *Psychology of Addictive Behaviors* 25(1):57–68.

Skrentny, John David. 1996. *The Ironies of Affirmative Action: Politics, Culture, and Justice in America.* Chicago: University of Chicago Press.

Slaughter, Sheila, and Larry L. Leslie. 1997. *Academic Capitalism: Politics, Policies, and the Entrepreneurial University.* Baltimore, MD: Johns Hopkins University Press.

Snow, David A., Cherylon Robinson, and Patricia L. McCall. 1991. "'Cooling Out' Men in Singles Bars and Nightclubs: Observations on the Interpersonal Survival Strategies of Women in Public Places." *Journal of Contemporary Ethnography* 19(4):423–449.

Soares, Joseph A. 2007. *The Power of Privilege: Yale and America's Elite Colleges.* Stanford, CA: Stanford University Press.

Sperber, Murray A. 2000. *Beer and Circus: How Big-Time College Sports Is Crippling Undergraduate Education.* New York: Henry Holt.

———. 2005. "How Undergraduate Education Became College Lite—And a Personal Apology." Pp. 131–144 in *Declining by Degrees: Higher Education at Risk*, edited by Richard H. Hersh and John Merrow. New York: Palgrave Macmillan.

Steelman, Lala Carr, and Brian Powell. 1989. "Acquiring Capital for College: The Constraints of Family Configuration." *American Sociological Review* 54(5):844–855.

Stevens, Mitchell L. 2007. *Creating a Class: College Admissions and the Education of Elites.* Cambridge, MA: Harvard University Press.

Stevens, Mitchell L., Elizabeth A. Armstrong, and Richard Arum. 2008. "Sieve, Incubator, Temple, Hub: Empirical and Theoretical Advances in the Sociology of Higher Education." *Annual Review of Sociology* 34:127–151.

Stevens, Mitchell, and Roy Pea. 2012. "Education's Digital Future: Proposal for Stanford GSE Forum 2012–2013." Unpublished manuscript. Stanford University.

Story, Ronald. 1980. *The Forging of an Aristocracy: Harvard and the Boston Upper Class, 1800–1870.* Middletown, CT: Wesleyan University Press.

Strayhorn, Terell L. 2011. "Bridging the Pipeline: Increasing Underrepresented Students' Preparation for College through a Summer Bridge Program." *American Behavioral Scientist* 55(2):142–159.

Streib, Jessi. 2011. "Class Reproduction by Four Year Olds." *Qualitative Sociology* 34(2):337–352.

———. 2012. *Intimate Experiences with Inequality: Cross-Class Marriages and Class Reproduction.* Unpublished PhD dissertation. Department of Sociology. University of Michigan, Ann Arbor.

Stripling, Jack. 2011. "Flagships Just Want to Be Alone." *Chronicle of Higher Education.* March 13: http://chronicle.com/article/Flagships-Just-Want-to-Be /126696/.

———. 2012. "Departing President Defends Her 'Incremental' Approach to Change at University of Virginia." *Chronicle of Higher Education.* June 18: http:// chronicle.com/article/Sullivan-Defends-Her/132379/.

Stuber, Jenny M. 2006. "Talk of Class: The Discursive Repertoires of White Working- and Upper-Middle-Class College Students." *Journal of Contemporary Ethnography* 35(3):285–318.

———. 2009. "Class, Culture, and Participation in the Collegiate Extra-Curriculum." *Sociological Forum* 24(4):877–900.

———. 2011. *Inside the College Gates: How Class and Culture Matter in Higher Education.* Lanham, MD: Lexington Books.

Summers-Effler, Erika. 2002. "The Micro Potential for Social Change: Emotion, Consciousness, and Social Movement Formation." *Sociological Theory* 20(1):41–60.

Sweeney, Megan M., and Maria Cancian. 2004. "The Changing Importance of White Women's Economic Prospects for Assortative Mating." *Journal of Marriage and Family* 66(4):1015–1028.

Swidler, Ann. 1986. "Culture in Action: Symbols and Strategies." *American Sociological Review* 51(2):273–286.

———. 2001. *Talk of Love: How Culture Matters.* Chicago: University of Chicago Press.

Thille, Candace. 2010. "Quality Control Isn't the Problem—It's Knowing whether Students Are Learning." *Chronicle of Higher Education.* August 29: http://chronicle.com/article/Quality-Control-Isnt-the/124198/.

Thoits, Peggy A. 1983. "Multiple Identities and Psychological Well-Being: A Reformulation and Test of the Social Isolation Hypothesis." *American Sociological Review* 48(2):174–187.

Tierney, William G. 1992. "An Anthropological Analysis of Student Participation in College." *Journal of Higher Education* 63(6):603–618.

Tinto, Vincent. 1987. *Leaving College: Rethinking the Causes and Cures of Student Attrition.* Chicago: University of Chicago Press.

Tobin, Joseph J., David Y. H. Wu, and Dana H. Davidson. 1989. *Preschool in Three Cultures: Japan, China, and the United States.* New Haven, CT: Yale University Press.

Tolich, Martin. 2004. "Internal Confidentiality: When Confidentiality Assurances Fail Relational Informants." *Qualitative Sociology* 27(1):101–106.

Torche, Florencia. 2011. "Is a College Degree Still the Great Equalizer? Intergenerational Mobility across Levels of Schooling in the United States." *American Journal of Sociology* 117(3):763–807.

Torres, Kimberly C., and Camille Z. Charles. 2004. "Metastereotypes and the Black-White Divide: A Qualitative View of Race on an Elite College Campus." *Du Bois Review: Social Science Research on Race* 1(1):115–149.

Trillin, Calvin. 1994. "Messages from My Father." *New Yorker.* June 20:56–72.

Tuchman, Gaye. 2009. *Wannabe U: Inside the Corporate University.* Chicago: University of Chicago Press.

Turk, Diana B. 2004. *Bound by a Mighty Vow: Sisterhood and Women's Fraternities, 1870–1920.* New York: New York University Press.

Turley, Ruth N. Lopez. 2009. "College Proximity: Mapping Access to Opportunity." *Sociology of Education* 82(2):126–146.

Turner, Ralph H. 1960. "Sponsored and Contest Mobility and the School System." *American Sociological Review* 25(5):855–867.

Venkatesh, Sudhir. 2002. "'Doin' the Hustle': Constructing the Ethnographer in the American Ghetto." *Ethnography* 3:91–111.

Waller, Willard. 1937. "The Rating and Dating Complex." *American Sociological Review* 2(5):727–734.

Walsh, Taylor. 2011. *Unlocking the Gates: How and Why Leading Universities Are Opening up Access to Their Courses.* Princeton, NJ: Princeton University Press.

Walton, Alexandria. 2013. *Trajectories of the Talented: How Social Class Shapes Where the Top Students Go to College.* Chicago: University of Chicago Press.

Weick, Karl E. 1976. "Educational Organizations as Loosely Coupled Systems." *Administrative Science Quarterly* 21(1):1 19.

Wildavsky, Ben, Andrew P. Kelly, and Kevin Carey, eds. 2011. *Reinventing Higher Education: The Promise of Innovation.* Cambridge, MA: Harvard Education Press.

Wilkie, Jane Riblett. 1991. "The Decline in Men's Labor Force Participation and Income and the Changing Structure of Family Economic Support." *Journal of Marriage and the Family* 53(1):111–122.

Wilkins, Amy C. 2008. *Wannabes, Goths, and Christians: The Boundaries of Sex, Style, and Status.* Chicago: University of Chicago Press.

Williams, Alex. 2010. "The New Math on Campus." *New York Times.* February 7:1+.

Willis, Paul E. 1977. *Learning to Labor: How Working Class Kids Get Working Class Jobs.* New York: Columbia University Press.

Winston, Gordon C. 1999. "Subsidies, Hierarchy, and Peers: The Awkward Economics of Higher Education." *Journal of Economic Perspectives* 13(1):13–36.

Wolfe, Tom. 2004. *I Am Charlotte Simmons.* New York: Farrar, Straus and Giroux.

Wood, Peter W. 2011. "The Higher Education Bubble." *Society* 48:208–212.

Wood, Phillip K., Kenneth J. Sher, and Patricia C. Rutledge. 2007. "College Student Alcohol Consumption, Day of the Week, and Class Schedule." *Alcoholism: Clinical and Experimental Research* 31(7):1195–1207.

Yeung, King-To, Mindy Stombler, and Renee Wharton. 2006. "Making Men in Gay Fraternities: Resisting and Reproducing Multiple Dimensions of Hegemonic Masculinity." *Gender & Society* 20(1):5–31.

Young, Alford A., Jr. 2004. *The Minds of Marginalized Black Men: Making Sense of Mobility, Opportunity, and Future Life Chances.* Princeton, NJ: Princeton University Press.

Zelizer, Viviana A. Rotman. 1985. *Pricing the Priceless Child: The Changing Social Value of Children.* New York: Basic Books.

Zernike, Kate. 2009. "Paying in Full as the Ticket into Colleges." *New York Times.* March 31:A1+.

Zweigenhaft, Richard L. 1993. "Prep School and Public School Graduates of Harvard: A Longitudinal Study of the Accumulation of Social and Cultural Capital." *Journal of Higher Education* 64(2):211–225.

Zweigenhaft, Richard L., and G. William Domhoff. 2003. *Blacks in the White Elite: Will the Progress Continue?* Lanham, MD: Rowman & Littlefield.

Acknowledgments

Our greatest debt is to the young women who shared their college experiences with us. They arrived at college to find researchers on their dorm floor. Although initially a bit puzzled by our presence, they gradually let us into their worlds. We became acquainted with them at a fraught moment in their lives: they had just moved away from home into very close quarters with total strangers. They patiently participated in interview after interview over a period of five years. This book could not exist without their generosity, openness, and trust.

It is difficult to get permission to study schools. Access to the dorm required not only the approval of the Institutional Review Board but a sponsor in Residence Life. This individual—whom unfortunately we cannot name due to confidentiality—granted us a room in a residence hall on campus for the academic year. We are deeply appreciative of this sponsorship. We thank the many other individuals at Midwest University whose assistance made this project possible.

The Spencer Foundation provided critical support at both beginning and ending stages of data collection. A National Academy of Education/Spencer Foundation Postdoctoral Fellowship provided Elizabeth the time to launch the project, while a Spencer Foundation Small Grant provided funds for interview transcription, Laura's travel to all parts of the country for post-graduation interviews, and participant incentives. We appreciate both the financial support and the early vote of confidence in the project.

Of course, we thank the team who assisted in the collection of ethnographic and interview data. Sibyl Kleiner, Evie Perry, Brian Sweeney, and Amanda Tanner were graduate students at the time, and Teresa Cummings, Aimee Lipkis, and Katie Watkins undergraduates. Their participation ensured that we connected with virtually all of the women on the floor, and they offered valuable insight into the social dynamics of this world. A veritable army of students

317

served as transcriptionists on the projects. Thanks to Pam Jackson for paying student transcriptionists from her research funds when we had no other funding for the project. Thanks also to Absolute Marketing and Research for doing an absolutely fantastic—and very rapid—job of transcription.

A Spring/Summer Research Grant from the Rackham Graduate School and the Vice President for Research at the University of Michigan enabled Elizabeth to hire J. Lotus Seeley and Elizabeth Marie Armstrong (EMA), who provided stellar research assistantship in the analysis and writing stage of the project. Lotus and EMA conducted the analysis and prepared much of the initial draft of Chapter 7. They read and coded the nearly 80 transcripts that provide the empirical basis for that chapter. They drafted many data analysis memos and met with Elizabeth frequently over a period of 18 months to arrive at the argument of that chapter. We found this chapter to be one of the most difficult to draft. Without EMA and Lotus's assistance, we would likely still be trying to work our way through this interview material. EMA also conducted network analysis that ultimately did not make it into the book. Lotus prepared the first draft of Appendix B, and worked closely with us in preparing the manuscript for publication—formatting the endnotes, compiling the reference list, completing references, and preparing the index. Sarah Gram did the initial work of compiling the references. Organizational Studies undergraduates Jessica Baer, Shari Brown, and Rachel Lipson also assisted with data analysis.

Elizabeth and Laura both owe deep debts to the Department of Sociology at Indiana University. Although our positions in the department differed— Elizabeth was an assistant professor while Laura was a graduate student—we share an appreciation for the mentoring that we received there.

Elizabeth and Laura both benefited in immeasurable ways from the steadfast support of Brian Powell, who has touched every aspect of both of our intellectual work over the past decade and has become a treasured friend. Indeed, Brian is often the first person Laura calls about matters academic, personal, or a little of both. (Before unlimited cell minutes, she found this out the hard way.) He has the uncanny ability to know, even from a great distance, when a little push or a little kindness is needed. This book bears his stamp, as from early on he urged us to never overstate and always carefully contextualize our claims. He was also the first person that we shared the jacket design with, and will likely celebrate its publication with nearly as much genuine excitement as we do.

Elizabeth is also deeply appreciative of the mentorship she received at Indiana University from Clem Brooks, Donna Eder, Tom Gieryn, Bernice Pescosolido, Rob Robinson, Scott Long, Pamela Walters, and Marty Weinberg, as well as the friendship and intellectual collegiality of Art Alderson, Tim Bartley, Tim Hallett, Ho-fung Hung, Ethan Michelson, Fabio Rojas, Brian Steensland, Quincy Stewart, Melissa Wilde, and Leah VanWey. A critical conversation with Tom Gieryn over Thanksgiving in 2011 helped with the framing of the book. It is possible that it was through many intellectually engaging lunches with Clem Brooks over the years in Bloomington that Elizabeth became a stratification scholar. He was present at both the origins and the completion of the project—talking about project ideas in 2003 and offering comments on the manuscript, which provoked a complete rewrite of the Introduction. Other Bloomington colleagues and friends whose conversation contributed to the book include Jim Capshew and Ilana Gershon.

Laura was early in her career at the start of the project. She might have left graduate school had Donna Eder not encouraged her to stay and pursue her interests in gender and qualitative research. Much later, Donna's comments on "The Floor" chapter crystallized the arguments of that chapter at the last moment and saved it from being cut from the book. Robert Robinson and Nancy Davis have been Laura's steadfast cheerleaders, watching her grow over the past fifteen years and helping her through several major transitions. Pamela Walters nudged her further into the sociology of education, and Eliza Pavalko has remained a source of intellectual and personal support. We are both indebted to Bill Corsaro, who trained Laura in ethnographic methods. His approach deeply informed the project. Louise Brown, then the Assistant Director of the Karl F. Schuessler Institute for Social Research, played a critical role in managing the financial side of the project and worked closely with Laura as she arranged travel around the country.

While at Indiana University, we participated in synergetic discussions of college life with what we referred to as the Collegiate Cultures group. Thanks to Janice McCabe, Sandi Nenga, Evie Perry, Jenny Stuber, and Brian Sweeney for their enthusiasm and creativity, as well as their companionship. Jenny Stuber's dissertation, which became the book *Inside the College Gates: How Class and Culture Matter in Higher Education*, provided us with insights that profoundly shaped our thinking. Rashawn Ray, Jason Rosow, and Shelley Nelson also helped to further this discussion. The work of Brian Sweeney and Rashawn Ray also provided us with vital insight into the college experiences of men.

Elizabeth thanks the Radcliffe Institute at Harvard University for the opportunity to spend a generative year at the Radcliffe Institute of Advanced Study in 2007–2008. The time allowed us to develop the broad contours of the book. Elizabeth thanks Judy Vichniac for her stewardship of the fellowship program and the staff of the Institute for making the year a collegial and productive one. Presenting the research to her colleagues at the Radcliffe Institute—a number of whom had limited experience with big Midwestern research universities—taught us to assume less and explain more. It was during this year that Elizabeth began a conversation with Elizabeth Knoll, our editor at Harvard University Press, which has continued over meals and drinks in the intervening years. (Thanks to Mitchell Stevens for this introduction.) Michèle Lamont extended a gracious invitation to the Culture Workshop at Harvard University. The incisive comments of workshop participants informed us for years as we drafted the manuscript. We thank Chris Bail, Lydia Bean, Neil Gross, Jason Kaufman, Michèle Lamont, Jal Mehta, and Lauren Rivera.

Midway through this project Elizabeth moved to the University of Michigan, lured by the promise of a rich new set of interdisciplinary discussions. Thanks to Howard Kimeldorf and Al Young for their efforts to create a stimulating and productive intellectual environment and to Mike Bastedo, Sarah Burgard, Steve Garcia, David Harding, Michael Heaney, Victoria Johnson, Howard Kimeldorf, Karin Martin, Johanna Masse, Greggor Mattson, Mark Mizruchi, and Jason Owen-Smith for engaging conversations. During a visit at Michigan, Laura had a critical conversation with Yu Xie about the value of qualitative data for uncovering and understanding unobserved heterogeneity that proved central to the book. Thanks to Jen Eshelman for everything she does to make the Michigan sociology department run and for her assistance and advice on matters of all sorts. Two senior seminars in Organizational Studies read the manuscript in full. A group project conducted by Maple Kirby, Laura Parkinson, and Anastasia Mitropoulous-Rundus on the Comprehensive Studies Program at the University of Michigan provided useful insights.

After completing her graduate work at Indiana University, Laura accepted a position at the University of California–Merced. Her colleagues—Paul Almeida, Irenee Beattie, Kyle Dodson, Tanya Golash-Boza, Nella VanDyke, and founding sociology faculty member Simón Weffer—offered unwavering support and valuable input during the writing of the book. She also received institutional support, particularly during the summers, which facilitated the end stages of producing the manuscript.

We are grateful to be embedded in a network of generous and intellectually astute colleagues. Those who commented on parts or all of the draft manuscript include Richard Arum, Steven Brint, Clem Brooks, Sarah Burgard, Bill Corsaro, Donna Eder, Paula England, Tim Hallett, Brian Powell, Jamie Small, Mitchell Stevens, Jessi Streib, Jenny Stuber, Chris Takacs, Geoff Wodtke, and the participants in the University of Michigan's workshops on Economic Sociology and Inequality.

Conversations with colleagues across the country have shaped this project. We thank Amy Binder, Dan Chambliss, Randy Collins, Scott Davies, Regina

Deil-Amen, Nina Eliasoph, Neil Fligstein, Adam I. Green, Heather Haveman, Mike Hout, Jerry Jacobs, Maria Kefalas, Annette Lareau, Paul Lichterman, John Levi Martin, Woody Powell, Josipa Roksa, Jim Rosenbaum, Mike Sauder, Amy Schalet, Rich Settersten, Ann Swidler, Florencia Torche, Natasha Warikoo, and Amy Wilkins. Thanks to Dan Chambliss for the opportunity to participate in and present at the Ninth Annual Mellon Foundation Assessment Conference at Hamilton College. Thanks to Dan Clawson for an invitation to present a plenary session on this research at the Eastern Sociological Society meetings in 2012.

We see this book as one small contribution to ongoing efforts to incorporate insights from organizational, cultural, and political sociology into the sociology of education. We are grateful to be part of this discussion—particularly the working group "Education in a New Society" organized by Jal Mehta, Scott Davies, and Michèle Lamont. This group, which convened in Cambridge as part of a Radcliffe Institute Seminar, provided a sounding board for the arguments of the book.

From our first conversation with Elizabeth Knoll, our editor at Harvard University Press, it was evident that she got what we were trying to do. She intuitively understood the connections between social life and inequality, and pushed us to describe the nuances of the social world ever more carefully. She has steered the development of the manuscript through careful comments on draft chapters and her selection of insightful reviewers. We particularly appreciate her patience as the initial deadline for producing the manuscript came and went. She remained convinced—or at least she persuaded us that she did—that the final product would be worth the additional time and effort. Thanks to Joy Deng, Editorial Assistant, and others at Harvard University Press for their work on this book. Thanks to Eric Mulder, who designed the book jacket, which we loved on sight; to Julie Palmer-Hoffman for her careful copyediting of the manuscript; and to Judi Hoffman for proofreading the book.

Elizabeth appreciates the support of her friends and family. This project provided insight into what parents do to get their children through college and launched into the world. She (belatedly) thanks her parents for these efforts. She thanks Floy Stryker for her companionship and housing over two book writing summers. During the course of this project Elizabeth's son Aaron has matured from a small child into a young man with whom she can converse about the arguments of the book. Although Aaron did not speed the progress of the book, he served as a constant reminder of why quality higher education matters. Over the decade that this project gestated, her Bloomington friends queried her about its status at book group meetings, while preparing Thanksgiving dinners, on the beach in Saugatuck, on back porches over wine, and even on the slopes of Mount Washington as we hiked from hut to hut in the

White Mountains. Thanks to Melissa Carter, Laddie Derenchuk, Mary Favret, David Goodrum, John Hamilton, Dawn Johnsen, Andrew Miller, Jeff Palmer, Sean Stryker, Moira Wedekind, and Mimi Zolan. A special thanks to Mimi Zolan for directing us to Calvin Trillin's *New Yorker* essay: We wish that higher education were a more reliable glass escalator to success today.

Elizabeth offers her final thanks to her dear friend and colleague Mitchell Stevens. His role in shaping this project—and her life—is difficult to convey. He provided comments on the book proposal and the final manuscript. Elizabeth enjoyed working with Mitchell and Richard Arum on a conference on higher education at NYU. The discussions to plan the event, the conference itself, and the work on the *Annual Review of Sociology* essay profoundly influenced this book. Mitchell and Elizabeth spent many hours on the phone and in person talking through the arguments of the book. His invitation to present work in progress at SCANCOR at Stanford yielded helpful comments and reactions. These working sessions were always interspersed with personal conversation about life, love, and career. Mitchell has also taken Laura under his wing, and invited her to participate in the Mapping Broad-Access Higher Education Conference at Stanford. This experience highlighted the needs and interests of the majority of today's college students. Mitchell's wit, wisdom, and loyalty are priceless.

For Laura, the data collection and writing of this book have corresponded with perhaps the busiest ten years of her life. During this time she got married, gave birth to her daughters Lane and Sage, obtained her PhD, and moved across the country to work at the University of California–Merced. Laura engaged her husband and colleague Kyle Dodson—willingly or not—in conversations about this book while they cooked dinner, changed never-ending diapers, attacked mountains of laundry, and generally corralled their zoo of two children and three pets. Kyle's insights have deeply shaped the project. He is the reason that Laura remained sane throughout major life transitions and is her partner in life. Laura's eldest daughter, Lane, also played a special part in this book: As a newborn, she accompanied Laura (and Kyle) around the country to conduct the post-college interviews. Many of the women met her and several still follow her as she grows. Laura also wishes to thank her mother and father, Melody and Edward Hamilton, and her sister and brother, Ellen Johnson and Eddie Hamilton, for their love and support over the years. Even though academia is a strange and different world for them, they have cheered her on every step of the way.

Index